To Bobbie
Hope you enjoy

It Was All Just Rock-'n'-Roll II

A RETURN TO THE CENTER
OF THE RADIO & CONCERT UNIVERSE

By Pat O'Day
with JIM OJALA

Ballard Publishing, Inc.

Comments and suggestions from readers are welcome.
You may write to Pat O'Day in care of:

Ballard Publishing, Inc.
Post Office Box 17330
Seattle, Washington 98127 USA
(206) 726-2123

Visit us at www.pat-oday.com & www.ballardpublishing.net

Printed by
St. Joseph Print Group
1165 Kenaston Street / P.O. Box 9809, Stn. T
Ottawa, Ontario, Canada K1G 6S1

Design & Typesetting: Jim Ojala
Featuring the photography of Jini Dellaccio
Cover photo/page 1 photo by Peter Riches
Copyright © 2002 by Experience Music Project

Library of Congress
Cataloging-in Publication Data applied for
ISBN 0-9706264-8-7

It Was All Just Rock 'n' Roll II:
A Return to the Center of the Radio & Concert Universe
November 2003
Second Edition, revised

Contents

Pat O'Day, Hall-of-Famer

In 1998, a plaque featuring Pat O'Day and bearing the above picture was added to the permanent disc jockey exhibit at the *Rock and Roll Hall of Fame and Museum* in Cleveland, Ohio. At the party celebrating the occasion, O'Day was joined by a bevy of other legendary broadcasters being similarly honored: Porky ("The Daddio of the Raddio") Chedwick, Bruce ("Cousin Brucie") Morrow, Arnie ("Woo Woo") Ginsberg and Dick ("The Screamer") Biondi among them. Even Dick Clark of *American Bandstand* fame dropped by to say hello. O'Day eschewed choosing a gimmicky nickname. It would have gone against his grain—and against the time-honored Northwest tradition of being cool.

Preface

OR YEARS, COUNTLESS FRIENDS have insisted my story is special and *must* be told. A busy life kept me from acting until recently, when an unexpected e-mail from a stranger provided the needed push. Jim Ojala, who previously produced two lavish books featuring Seattle-area icons Stan Pocock and Josef Scaylea, essentially told me, "Pat, you're next!" and that was it. It *would* be wrong not to write this book—wrong not to tell the story of radio during its most exciting years, wrong not to chronicle the development of the rock-'n'-roll business at its most explosive stage and wrong not to share a magical adventure which has been the stuff of dreams. And so, here is the serendipitous tale of how a Nebraska-born preacher's kid grew up in Bremerton, Washington dreaming of someday becoming a radio announcer, and how that dream came true beyond his wildest expectations.

Ask anyone who knows me. Lifelong, I have lacked the good sense to listen to other people's advice, to accept the conventional wisdom that certain things can't be done. This basic flaw in my personality helped catapult me into a life which defies belief—except that it really happened. Many of its details were reported in the media, sometimes heralded, occasionally denounced. I was often the center of controversy, envied by some, reviled by others, listened to by many. Now that I have added it all up on paper—and discretely subtracted a few episodes—it seems unreal even to me. Still, everything told here is true.

We are all a product of the elements we enjoyed through birth and of the elements impacting us after birth—nature *and* nurture. It's not always easy to realize the full potential this notion implies, and falling short does not make one bad. Sometimes, as we pursue our dreams, we escape the realm of the possible. We gamble on dreams we have no right to assume will come true. We take risks that defy logic and common sense. The chance of failure always looms large. Yet, some of us are genetically wired to behave this way. We feel compelled to try the untried and test the unknown. We turn sullen and become dangerous to ourselves when not confronting a new challenge or chasing some quixotic end.

This compulsion substantially impacts all aspects of our being. Our behavior may discomfort many, but go forward we must. Like Satchel Paige, we dare not look back for fear that something will be gaining on us—worst of all, reality. We have been reminded, over and over, all of our lives, that we must be realistic. Of course, that is the last thing we want to hear. Reality brings death to dreams. Its foundation is accepted, conventional, practical norms. Some of us would rather be dead than be forced to stop chasing our dreams. These character traits make us a challenge to live and work with, and unabashedly so. Hopefully, in my case, they make for a good book. Good or otherwise, books need facts, and here are a few to get mine started.

A 1921 disaster deep in the earth beneath Boone, Iowa had a defining impact on my life. My grandfather, John Berg, was a Swedish immigrant who worked as a carpenter in a coal mine there, installing timbers in new tunnels after blasting. One summer day, a sudden cave-in trapped him beneath tons of rock and black anthracite. My father, a 21-year-old apprentice, was working nearby on the same vein and rushed to the site to help dig him out. Weeping, he carried my grandfather's lifeless body down the tunnel, into the elevator and up to the surface. Laying his father down, he ran, deep in grief, to the family home a mile away to break the news. That same day, seeking greater meaning for his own life, he determined to leave the mines and become a minister. He did not leave soon enough. Mixed in with the coal dust he inhaled daily since graduation from high school were all-too-common tuberculosis spores. When he left the mines, he carried with him those deadly pathogens. That fall, he entered a theological seminary in St. Paul, Minnesota; three years later, he was ordained the Reverend Paul E. Berg.

After eight years of ministering to churches in small towns in Iowa and Nebraska, he met my mother, Wilma, the daughter of a fellow country preacher in Nebraska. They married in 1932, and I arrived in 1934, in Norfolk, Nebraska. The family next stopped in the state capital, Lincoln, where my father founded the Depression-era equivalent of one of today's mega-churches. With the outbreak of World War II, he accepted an offer to shepherd a congregation in Tacoma, Washington. In 1948, after lying dormant in his lungs for over 25 years, the tuberculosis bacteria suddenly sprang back to life, just as suddenly taking his. Two years later, a new type of penicillin appeared as a cure for tuberculosis, too late to save my father.

I don't overstate when I say my family's coal mine tragedy set forces in motion that determined my destiny. So much of me stems from my childhood within the church. As a broadcaster, I unconsciously emulated my father's speech patterns, or sermon patterns if you will. And I remain deeply indebted to the many ministers and countless sermons I was forced to endure, often under protest, during my formative years. They showed me the ultimate power of the spoken word. I hope this book wields some of that same power.

I believe it is the ability to persuade through verbal communication that truly moves mountains. Consider the lasting impact of the words of Dr. Martin Luther King—an evangelist of the highest order—and you will realize that no Bill Gates software or Ted Turner satellite feed can equal the power of spoken words, carefully selected and dramatically delivered.

As a youth, at every opportunity I accompanied my father to a Tacoma radio station, KMO, to watch him deliver his daily program (religious, naturally). At KMO, I decided my life's direction—broadcasting. I never thought of entering the ministry, leaving that mission for others to fulfill. Instead, I sought my future elsewhere, in another calling. As for rock-'n'-roll, the subject of most of this book, it just happened to come along at the same time I was making my entry into radio. Call it fate. Dame Fortune. Good timing. Kismet. Blind luck. Divine providence. Whatever. I like to think that rock-'n'-roll and I have made good companions.

—Pat O'Day
Friday Harbor, Washington
September 2002

NO.	TITLE	ARTIST	No. Last Week		NO.	TITLE	ARTIST	No. Last Week
1.	JUDY'S TURN TO CRY	Leslie Gore	2		31.	Hello Muddah-Hello Fadduh	Allen Sherman	Debut
2.	SO MUCH IN LOVE	Tymes	1		32.	Wipe Out	Surfaris	32
3.	MY BLOCK	Four Pennies	3		33.	I Wonder	Brenda Lee	33
4.	CANDY GIRL	Four Seasons	4		34.	Dina	Dore Alpert	DJ Pick
5.	SATURDAY SUNSHINE	Burt Bacharach	17		35.	Hey Girl	Freddie Scott	Debut
6.	DEVIL IN DISGUISE	Elvis Presley	6		36.	Detroit City	Bobby Bare	24
7.	JUST ONE LOOK	Doris Troy	7		37.	True Love Never Runs Smooth	Gene Pitney	37
8.	ROCKING IN THE CRADLE	Dee Dee Sharp	8		38.	Blue on Blue	Bobby Vinton	38
9.	BLOWING IN THE WIND	Peter Paul & Mary	9		39.	If I Had A Hammer	Trini Lopez	44
10.	GREEN GREEN	Christy Minstrels	14		40.	Please Don't Talk To The Lifeguard-Diane Ray		Debut
11.	Tie Me Kangaroo Down Sport	Rolf Harris	6		41.	More	Vic Dana	Debut
12.	Scarlet O'Hara	Lawrence Welk	12		42.	The 12th Rose	Browns	23
13.	Surf City	Jan & Dean	13		43.	Daughter	Blenders	35
14.	Fingertips	Stevie Wonder	10		44.	The Dreamer	Neil Sedaka	47
15.	Abilene	George Hamilton IV	11		45.	You Can Never Stop My Loving You-J. Tillitson		Debut
16.	Easier Said Than Done	Essex	16		46.	It Hurts To Be Sixteen	Barbara Chandler	49
17.	How Many Teardrops	Lou Christie	25		47.	My Boyfriend's Back	Angels	DJ Pick
18.	Danke Shoen	Wayne Newton	32		48.	Martian Hop	Ran-Dells	45
19.	Hopeless	Andy Williams	22		49.	Lucky Lips	Cliff Richards	Debut
20.	I Want To Stay Here	Steve & Edie	21		50.	Tips Of My Fingers	Roy Clark	30
21.	From Me To You	Beatles	29					
22.	Ring of Fire	Johnny Cash	28					
23.	When A Boy Falls In Love	Mel Carter	23					
24.	Surfer Girl	Beach Boys	34					
25.	Wait Till My Bobby Gets Home	Darlene Love	33					
26.	Little Dancing Doll	Shelby Flint	37					
27.	Lonely Surfer	Jack Nitzsche	Debut					
28.	At The Shore	Johnny Caswell	36					
29.	Not Me	Orlons	19					
30.	Birthday Party	The Pixies Three	30					

KJR PICK ALBUM OF THE WEEK:
"THIS IS RAY STEVENS" MERCURY label

Channel 95

This KJR survey from July 29, 1963 has special interest. At number 21, 10 spots behind Rolf Donner's *Tie Me Kangaroo Down, Sport*, sits *From Me to You* by a then-obscure (in the U.S.) British group from Liverpool calling themselves by a most unlikely name, *The Beatles*. "The what!?" O'Day remembers thinking when he first heard it. The record has climbed eight spots from the previous week. Some say that Murray the K, the acclaimed "fifth Beatle," was the first deejay to play a Beatles record in the U.S — in September 1963. Not true. KJR and other stations played them earlier.

Introduction to the Second Edition

BLAME IT ALL ON KJR-AM Sports Radio and the Seattle Super-Sonics. In late January 2002, I was driving along Western Avenue approaching Pike Place Market trying to catch the start of a Sonics game being played somewhere back east. It was too early for Kevin Calabro to be calling the game, and instead I was greeted by the sound of KJR's Dave Grosby and Mike Gastineau carrying on about this and that, most of their banter unrelated to basketball—or to any sport, for that matter. Suddenly, one of them (The Groz) exclaimed, "Hey, I saw Pat O'Day yesterday!"

"Oh, really?" responded the other (The Gasman). "What's Pat doing these days? He sure has a lot of great stories to tell!"

The two proceeded to exchange Pat O'Day stories, second-hand but colorful nonetheless. At that moment, the proverbial light bulb went on in my head. I operate a small publishing company and have turned out several books involving Seattle/Pacific Northwest "legends." Having just completed a family history for a client, I was wondering what project to tackle next. Pat O'Day! What could possibly be better than his story?

As a baby-boomer who moved to Seattle in 1962, I came of age listening to the voices of Pat O'Day and Dick Curtis and Lan Roberts and Larry Lujack and all the other insane personalities that once manned the mikes at KJR. Together, their on-air antics and choice of music helped define my teenage years; the dances O'Day staged at the Spanish Castle and Lake Hills Roller Rink gave me my first taste of night life; and the "Pat O'Day and Dick Curtis Present..." concerts on the revolving stage in the Seattle Center Coliseum provided me with a trove of memories of great bands and fabulous music. My first thought upon hearing Groz and Gas talk about Pat O'Day was, This man needs to be in a book. My second worried thought was, What if he's already written one? I didn't think he had, but I wanted to be sure.

That evening, I searched the internet 'til well past midnight, devouring every morsel of information I could find about Pat O'Day. The meatiest piece was posted on Walt Crowley's historylink.org web site (a cornucopia of Northwest history, by the way). Written by Peter Blecha and titled "Pat O'Day — Godfather of Northwest Rock?" that essay, while helpful and informative, served only to pique my appetite for more information, not sate it. I went to bed hungry, unfulfilled. The next evening, I resumed my search and 'round about two in the morning came upon a web site informing visitors that Pat O'Day was selling real estate in the San Juan Islands and offering an e-mail address for anyone interested in contacting him.

"What the heck!" I said to myself and proceeded to write a letter to Pat that forever affected both of our lives. Under the subject heading "Greetings from a stranger" I introduced myself and my work and suggested that, were Pat willing, I would like to talk with him about doing a book. The very next morning, he e-mailed back a resounding "Yes!"

A few days later we met face to face for the first time at the Highliner Pub just west of the Ballard Bridge at Fishermen's Terminal. After four hours of trading tales — all of them no doubt true — with a simple handshake Pat and I embarked on an eight-month, hell-bent-for-leather race to write, edit and publish his memoir in time for the 2002 Fall/holiday season. We began exchanging e-mails — as many as 10 a day — laying out plans for the book, and by March Pat was churning out stories at a prodigious rate. The writing/editing, re-writing/re-editing consumed countless hours of both of our time. (I have in my files over 40 re-writes of one particular chapter.) Along the way, I tried to keep track of how many e-mails we had shared; somewhere around 400, I stopped counting.

In late Spring, we decided to seek additional resources to help us meet our October 1 target date for going to press. When a legitimate offer finally materialized, the book had already been printed and copies were on their way to

Seattle. We had managed without assistance, and I turned down the offer and plunged forward with the distribution, marketing and sale of the book.

Vital support came from other sources. Dick Curtis, Pat's long-time friend and one-time business partner, generously ageed to critique the stories as they were being written. His enthusiasm and sage advice provided badly-needed encouragement at several crucial junctures. On another front, an acquaintance of Pat's from Peru made a pivotal suggestion regarding the organization of the stories, breaking up a mental log jam and clearing the way for completing the book. Pat's e-mail to me that day read, "Thank you, Peruuuuuu!!" Other individuals, too—family and friends of Pat's, family and friends of mine—played their parts. My personal thanks go out especially to Mischelle Day and Josef Scaylea and Otto Lang, enthusiastic and stalwart supporters from day one.

A key impetus to completing the book came from the good folks at Experience Music Project. In June, we met with Jim Fricke and his staff at EMP's Third Avenue offices. Pat has a history of working together with EMP, and they readily offered support to our venture, promising to co-host a book-release party in November and pledging their full resources to assure its success. At that moment, I knew we were going to make it—not, however, without additional months of intense effort, neglected duties and missed sleep.

Thanks to EMP, we tracked down Jini Dellaccio, considered by some America's premier photographer of rock-'n'-roll in the '60s. During Pat's halcyon days as a concert promoter, he gave Jini unlimited access to his Seattle shows, allowing her to photograph performances by local groups like The Wailers and The Sonics and by national and international acts like The Beach Boys, The Rolling Stones and The Who. "If we can find Jini," Pat insisted, "she'll have some great pictures for the book." He was right. Jim Fricke provided an Arizona phone number, calls were made and, on September 11, 2002, we met at Jini's home in Gold Canyon and spent most of the day poring over thousands of images, selecting ones for the book. Pat returned to Seattle that evening, while I stayed on for four more days scanning negatives. Jim Valley, Merrilee Rush and Buck Ormsby all call Jini "an angel." They couldn't be more right.

The scope and impact of Jini's work precipitated a series of difficult decisions about the book's structure and content. Those took us well beyond our original plans and necessitated much additional work at the exact moment when final deadlines were approaching. The text was completely reformatted, the pages re-sized and the layout scheme significantly altered and compressed.

Mere days before St. Joseph Print Group in Ottawa was slated to run the job, other decisions were made dramatically affecting the outcome. We had no room left, yet a host of important stories remained homeless. So we opted for another 32-page signature. When that proved too little, we tacked on 16 more pages, and that, too, was not enough. In the final hours, with presses running, stories were still being trimmed or dropped altogether until, at last, neither space nor time remained. To steal a line from a departed friend, "What a way to run a railroad!" We broke nearly every rule there is in publishing, yet somehow survived. My strongest memory is of the moment when I raced out to the press room and shouted, "Stop the presses!" I had signed off on a signature that was missing half of one story. Thankfully, that mistake I caught.

Certain critics have had a field day pointing out errors in the first edition I didn't catch—some spelling, some grammar, some punctuation, some typo, some factual, some imaginary. To them, and to all readers of that book, I offer here my *mea culpa*—in fact, my 1,001 *mea culpas*. For, when I later combed through the text cover to cover looking for mistakes, I marked that many and more for correction, a staggering number, almost three per page. Many of them involved formatting and were artifacts from changes made in mid-September to the organization and contents of the book. Others were tweaks only a picky editor (which I can be, given time to properly do the job) would ever notice. Far too many, however, were of the sort that a good proof reader ought to have caught, the kind that have no place in a published work. The fact that even one such mistake made it into the first edition will forever haunt me; knowing that *hundreds* made it in gave me headaches and heartaches for months. All bets are off on how many goofs will make it into this new edition. I don't want to think about it just yet. Fewer than 1,000, I hope. Start counting.

We could have limited mistakes by hacking huge chunks of flesh from the body of the story or by delaying printing a month. Instead, with fingers crossed, we gambled readers would welcome more stories over fewer flubs. We guessed right, if success is judged by sales figures and demand. Another measure? The first edition's suggested retail price was $34.95. Today (October 21, 2003), the book is selling used on Amazon for a low of $142.50 and a high of $189.50. One curmudgeonly reviewer admonished readers to wait for copies to appear at garage sales before buying one. He was wrong. Nevertheless, should you ever happen upon a first edition of *It Was All Just Rock 'n' Roll* at a neighbor's yard sale, I suggest you thank your lucky star and buy it.

Anyone who has ever put together a business plan knows that the numbers included in one's projections rarely translate exactly into the numbers one encounters in reality. In the case of Pat's book, I was off target by many miles. A supply of books I thought would last six months barely lasted six weeks. Had I printed twice as many copies, those would have disappeared, too.

The public had its first peek at the book in late October at Northwest Book-fest. The *Post-Intelligencer*'s Bill Virgin published our first review the next week, creating an immediate spike in demand. By mid-November, we were exactly on target with my sales projections, and I was feeling quite proud of myself. Then entered Experience Music Project, and history of sorts was made.

The week before Thanksgiving, we held a book-release party in the Sky Church at EMP. Pat's good friend, Steve "Fly Like an Eagle" Miller, donated his performance to help our cause and headlined the show. Merrilee Rush opened the program and was joined on stage by members of The Kingsmen and The Fabulous Wailers for a no-holds-barred rendition of *Louie Louie*. The shaking, rattling and rolling of Steve and Merrilee and everyone else that evening must have released a host of Serendips, for good things followed in rapid succession for the book. For a few days, we ranked in the Top 10 on Amazon, and stayed in their Top 100 for a considerable time after that—not bad for a regional title. By the end of the first week of December, all copies were gone from our warehouse; in the following weeks, we had to turn down urgent requests for thousands more. My prognostic gifts proved inadequate to the task. I had underestimated market demand by at least half. I could not have been more wrong.

How to explain such success? It starts with Pat's great stories, of course. But it also involves the people who devoured the book—mostly baby boomers who grew up in the Northwest. My take after talking with hundreds of fans over the past year is they felt they were reading their own life stories while reading Pat's. A generation's preternatural attachment to music and radio and dance could not be more graphically illustrated than by the performance of his book.

Less than two weeks later, the joy of that evening at EMP was tempered by unexpected tragedy. One morning in early December, I found waiting on my answering machine a tearful message from Merrilee Rush: "Jim, call me! Seattle's music community has just suffered a terrible loss!" *Who can it be?* I asked myself, my heart and mind racing as I called her back. Her answer was one of several I feared—Rich Dangel, lead guitarist for "the Boys from Tacoma," The Fabulous Wailers. At EMP, Rich had joined the throng on stage for *Louie Louie* despite complaining he didn't feel well. Two Mondays later, he gathered together with band members, family and friends to celebrate his sixtieth birthday. The next morning, he was gone.

Few passings could devastate a community more than Rich's did Seattle's music family. By common acclaim, he was the archetypal Northwest guitarist, the spiritual forebear of all who followed, from Bob Bogle and Nokie Edwards and Don Wilson of The Ventures through Jimi Hendrix and Larry Coryell and beyond. His most famous contribution to rock history is the guitar arrangement of *Louie Louie*, including the song's thumping bridge. B. B. King said this of Rich Dangel: "Rich's place as the founding father of the Northwest guitar sound will last forever." Yet Rich's contributions as a mentor and friend and colleague transcended all else he did. So say those who knew him best.

In February 2003, at Seattle's Moore Theatre, Rich's friends and musical heirs gathered. The Fabulous Wailers, The Kingsmen, The Ventures, Gail Harris, Merrilee Rush, Little Bill Engelhart and Larry Coryell were part of the stellar lineup that night. Together, they transformed a memorial concert into the joyous celebration of a life well lived by a man much loved. To close the show, everyone returned to the stage for a stunning ensemble performance of *Louie Louie*, with Larry Coryell performing Rich's bridge. Afterward, an usher barely out of her teens offered her verdict: "That was the greatest concert I've ever seen!" Why? "These guys are the originals!"

Her words describe perfectly the music Pat O'Day promoted and played, music that has achieved hallmark status well beyond the confines of the Northwest. Pat told much of that story in the first edition of his memoir. Here he adds new wrinkles to his tale while sprucing up the original stories. In all, 2,000-plus textual changes have been made, some minor, many major, and 20 pages of new stories added. (Special thanks to Alec Palao for his relentless work weeding out errors.) In short, this revised second edition is really a second first edition, if there is such a thing. It surely is the edition Pat and I wanted to appear first. Is it better than its predecessor? You must decide. At least, it's done.

Many worthy stories related to the regional music scene remain untold, so don't be surprised should books from The Fabulous Wailers, The Kingsmen and other Northwest music types someday appear in local bookstores. Helen of Troy's face reportedly launched a thousand ships; Pat O'Day's memoir has already launched many thousands of recalled memories and just might help launch another book or two or three. As the KJR jocks of yesteryear once said, Stay tuned! [Jim Ojala]

1 – Spanish Castle Magic
Jimi Hendrix, 1969

IT WAS A TYPICAL FRIDAY NIGHT at my sanctuary for Seattle-Tacoma teens, the Spanish Castle, a place where the young flocked to dance to the Northwest's unique brand of rock-'n'-roll. The parade of local talent performing on the Castle's stage was long and impressive. At least once a month, it was the Wailers from Tacoma singing rock's original interpretation of *Louie Louie*. Sometimes, it was another Tacoma band my radio station uncovered, the Ventures, performing their number-one hit *Walk—Don't Run*. Other talents from the Northwest included a young Larry Coryell with his group the Dynamics and 15-year-old Merrilee Rush with her band. Later, Paul Revere & the Raiders, the Kingsmen and the Sonics joined the list. Listening to the heavy sounds of the Wailers, and later the Sonics, area teenagers unknowingly witnessed the birth of grunge. On some special nights, this pioneering hideaway hosted national talents like Conway Twitty, Gene Vincent, brothers Johnny and Dorsey Burnette, Jan & Dean and Roy Orbison. On more than a few occasions, Jerry Lee Lewis with his pumping piano allowed the teenage audience to gather around the stage—so close they could touch him—as he belted out his endless string of hits.

In the late '50s and early '60s, the Castle served as the hallowed temple for a new kind of secular religion, the worship of a fresh, dynamic art form called rock-'n'-roll. Rock's roots sprang from pure American genes, fusing together musical elements from the mountains of Tennessee and the black churches of the South. It combined drums, pianos, electric organs, saxophones and occasional brass instruments while exploring the limitless potential of Les Paul's recent breakthroughs with the electric guitar. Inventive vocal arrangements, vibrant new singing styles, dazzling delivery and innovative lyrics—all were vital elements of rock. And every weekend you could see this new social phenomenon taking its first brave steps at the Castle.

Did I realize the deep significance of what I was helping spawn? Of course not! None of us did. Not the musicians, not the teenagers, not even the Dick Clarks of our world foresaw how over a 50 year period our widely-criticized rock-'n'-roll would change the world.

On this one particular evening in 1961, I was standing to the side of the Castle stage listening to the band when a skinny young man touched my arm and said, "Mr. O'Day, can I talk to you for a minute?" His striking facial features spoke of a distinctive heritage, and his penetrating eyes told me his subject matter to him was deadly serious. I was the hot new disc jockey in Seattle and owed my success to listening to what young people had to say. So I listened.

We walked to a small room directly behind the stage where it was relatively quiet, and I asked, "What's on your mind, my friend?"

He had an idea. Back then, the amplifiers bands used were not the strong, reliable powerhouses we are accustomed to seeing today. Generally made by Gibson, Fender or Sun, they contained numerous tubes and primitive circuitry which overheated, overloaded and blew out with irritating regularity. Because sound systems in those years were so inadequate, those amplifiers were over driven in order to fill ballrooms and auditoriums with sound. Local rock musicians were mostly poor, and few of them could afford to carry extra amplifiers with them.

Lacking backups, when an amp expired we wound the metallic portion of a chewing gum wrapper around the fuse to bypass the built-in safeguards. If the amp blew out again, it signified serious internal damage and meant that both the amp and the guitar player were finished for the evening. Knowing this, the young man made a simple offer: He said he always carried his high-wattage Gibson amp in his car and proposed that, should one of the band's amps blow, we could use his amp with the understanding that he could then play his guitar on stage along with the group. "I'll stay in the background," he promised me. "And don't worry," he added, "I know every note of every song these guys do."

His idea was pretty straight-ahead. I looked at him, saw his sincerity and readily agreed.

For the next several weeks, he reappeared at the Castle on Friday nights, listening to the bands and awaiting his chance. It came one evening, in the middle of a performance by Tiny Tony and the Statics, when one of their amps blew. This time a gum wrapper failed to fix the problem. When I looked for him, the young man was already on his way to his car!

Returning a few moments later, he quickly set up his amp. Once plugged in, he spent the rest of the evening on stage backing up the Statics.

In the following months, the young man often returned to the Castle, always polite, ever patient, but I don't recall there being another opportunity for him to play. Sometime later, he stopped showing up, and soon the incident was filed away in the furthest recesses of my memory, where it reposed undisturbed until fate intervened.

Are You Experienced?

Jimi Hendrix, 1967

NEARLY 40 YEARS LATER, MICROPHONE IN HAND, I stood on a temporary stage in the shadow of Seattle's Space Needle emceeing ground-breaking ceremonies for Paul Allen's dream museum, Experience Music Project. An extravagant rock-'n'-roll Taj Mahal, EMP was designed by world-renowned architect Frank Geary to celebrate American music, with a powerful emphasis on the music and writing of Jimi Hendrix. As I looked around me, trying to grasp the enormity of Allen's vision, my mind flashed back to 1970 and a procession of Jimi's fans following his hearse to an open grave at a cemetery in the city of Renton, six miles south of Seattle. A few days before, we received a phone call from London with the shocking news that Jimi Hendrix was dead. A tragic sequence of events marked by callous negligence had stopped his magnificent heart. It was so bizarre. Not nearly the drug user some people make him out to be, Jimi proved fatally vulnerable to the influence of careless friends and died in the apartment of a young German women for reasons which were wholly avoidable. Upon his death, many people financially enriched by their involvement in Jimi's brief career showed almost total indifference. Their lack of class only heightened the sense of tragedy.

Three days after Jimi's death, we learned that his body remained unclaimed at the London mortuary. His father, Al Hendrix, called our office, frustrated by the total failure by Jimi's record company and British management to offer assistance. At Concerts West, we told Al we would take care of everything, not to worry, and sent our Tom Hulett to London, where he claimed the body and brought Jimi back to Seattle on his final trip home. We purchased a grave site selected by the family and covered all expenses, including the funeral. We did not think twice about the cost and were pleased to be able to help. But we were deeply disturbed by what we saw transpiring elsewhere. Jimi Hendrix was dead, and most of the people who raked in millions off him were slinking away like rats from a spotlight.

The lawyer for one American company that should have been front-and-center gave some feeble excuse about heavy drug implications and concerns about the company's image. Another company said they couldn't help due to royalty misunderstandings. We called them only because we thought they would want to participate. It was sickening, but we said nothing to Al—or to anyone else for that matter—not wanting to cause a distraction out of love and respect for Jimi. A flood of expressions of sympathy from thousands of Jimi's fans all over the world gave the family much needed comfort.

There on Paul Allen's stage, I could finally laugh within at the insignificance of those small-minded twerps with their petty, self-serving agendas, laugh at the so-called "personal managers" who had financially raped Jimi for years before deserting him at the end. Who would create monuments for them? At best, their families.

My mind ricocheted back to a night in 1968. I sat beside Jimi in a dressing room beneath the stands in Moody Pavilion on the campus of Southern Methodist University in Dallas, Texas. My firm, Concerts West, had evolved from modest beginnings into a rock-'n'-roll concert heavyweight, with Jimi Hendrix our prize client. More importantly, he was my friend.

Awaiting the start of the show, Jimi said something he often said to me: "Pat, can you believe this is happening?"

It truly was unbelievable, his meteoric rise. After departing the Army, Jimi was discovered playing in a Greenwich Village nightclub by Chas Chandler of the Animals and relocated to England, where he teamed with bass guitarist Mitch Mitchell and drummer Noel Redding to form the Jimi Hendrix Experience. On the London club scene, Jimi's musical depth and unsurpassed mastery of the guitar were revealed to the world. He released his first album in America on Reprise Records in 1967 and created a sensation with a series of spectacular performances, like his legendary appearance that year at the Monterey Pop Festival. Almost overnight, Jimi Hendrix conquered the American music scene, bringing with him musical thoughts and impressions from another universe. Through his instrument and voice, he awakened in us feelings we never knew we possessed. Jimi was amazed and humbled by his early success, and his statement, "Pat, can you believe this is happening?" was typical of the genuine humility, surprise and gratitude he felt over his good fortune.

That night at SMU, our conversation went further than usual, when Jimi said, "Pat, I don't think you remember when we first met!"

"You mean in New York?" I answered, thinking about my initial talk with Jimi after he chose us to represent him in his concert appearances. A gentleman about to join our staff—Ron Terry, then Jimi's agent at Creative Management in New York—first approached him with the idea. When Ron mentioned my name and assured Jimi I was indeed *the* Pat O'Day from KJR in Seattle, Jimi quickly agreed, telling Ron something like, "Two Seattle guys working together can't go wrong!"

"No, Pat," Jimi corrected me, "not New York. I mean, do you remember when you gave me that shot, I loaned you my amp and you let me play on stage at the Spanish Castle?"

I remembered now! The skinny kid who played backup to Tiny Tony at the Castle back in 1961? That was Jimi Hendrix!

"That was my first time on a real stage, and you made it happen, and when I heard your name from Ron, I figured, That's it! I'm going with Pat!"

It was my turn to feel humble.

Jimi wrote a song, *Spanish Castle Magic*, which he dedicated to that evening in 1961. The lyrics read in part:

It's very far away,
It takes about half a day
To get there, if we travel by my a.....dragonfly

No, it's not in Spain,
But all the same,
You know,
It's a groovy name
And the wind's just right.

Hang on, My Darling,
Hang on if you want to go
You know it's a really groovy place
And it's just a little bit of Spanish Castle Magic....

Purple Haze
Jimi Hendrix, 1967

JIMI AND I SHARED OTHER SIMILAR CONVERSATIONS, and he always began them the same way: "Man, are you ready? I mean, Pat, here we are sitting in Oakland [or Los Angeles or Birmingham or somewhere else] with another sellout! I mean, who ever thought growing up in Seattle that we could pull this off? Is this really happening?" And he would smile ironically. One time, he said it while we were lying in the sun on the roof of the old Beverly Rodeo the night after a sellout at the Los Angeles Forum. And there was a time in Houston. Whenever Jimi began a conversation like this, I knew he was leading up to something. I never knew, and Jimi never said, *why* he became pensive like this just before going on stage, but he always did.

After several pauses in our dressing room conversation in Houston, he told me he was getting huge heat to part company from Concerts West. He said the Black Panthers were pressuring him constantly to dump us and let them handle his personal appearances.

"They're calling me a stupid Uncle Tom and saying that I'm just working for the man," he said. "They say I'm being disloyal to blacks, black causes, that I'm just a m— f—ing traitor! That's what Bobby Seals said, that's what Cleaver told me on the phone this afternoon."

"Man, what do I say to them?" Jimi asked me. "I want things to keep on just as they are, but what in the hell do I tell them?"

My God! I thought to myself, *How can I be honest with my friend?*

My conflict of interest on this one was bigger than Texas. We had an absolute gold mine with Jimi as our client, and he was asking me as a friend what he should do with his concert future and, just as importantly, how he should handle a sensitive racial issue. Then came a bolt of irrefutable logic from I know not where in my brain. Jimi later called it "f—g genius." I told him,

Jimi, they've got it all wrong and they know it! That's totally unfair to you. You're no Uncle Tom. How can you be? Let's examine this thing. Everyone in this building is either paying to see you or working for you. For example, here I sit beside you, and yes, I'm your friend, but all you have to say to me is, "Pat, thank you, you're fired!" and I'm gone, we're gone, Concerts West is gone. We all work *for you*. You have total power over us. Sure, we have a contract, but you know you can cancel it tonight if you want. Every single worker in this building is working for you. Every cop, every technician, every usher, me, my partners. We all serve at your pleasure, Jimi. Wasn't Uncle Tom a slave? You, Jimi Hendrix, you are the king, the owner, the total boss of this traveling domain. You have all the power, you are the man, and they have the balls to call you an Uncle Tom? Don't let them jerk you around like that. If you want to work with them, that's a different matter. But if you want things to stay just as they are, tell them to chase someone else and knock off the Uncle Tom crap!

Jimi burst out laughing, something totally out of character when he was in one of his pensive pre-show moods. "Pat, man," he exclaimed, "you're absolutely right! You're totally right! I'm not an Uncle Tom. All of this is mine! Thank you, man! I'm gonna call them tonight. You're right! God, they were really getting to me with that shit!"

Third Stone From the Sun
Jimi Hendrix, 1967

SEATTLE WAS THE CITY WHERE JIMI HENDRIX GREW UP, the city he left to join the Army after being expelled from high school. Acquaintances there heard of his rocket ride to stardom and wondered about their friend who had achieved so much fame in so little time. Most puzzling was the fact that Jimi was a black artist enjoying an almost totally white response. The previous June, his now-legendary burning of his guitar to close his set at the Monterey Pop Festival propelled him to the forefront of the counterculture music scene. Even so, in February 1968 black music circles and Jimi's fellow black artists had barely acknowledged his existence—yet.

Jimi returned to his hometown hoping to make a statement, and he did exactly that in three memorable ways. First, he sold out every seat in the Seattle Center Arena and on concert night wove a spell over the packed house, taking listeners to lands beyond their imagination. Head tilted back, one leg thrust slightly in front of the other, Jimi made Seattle understand he had opened a new frontier—forging a relationship between man and guitar that achieved the supernatural, traveling through distant galaxies of expression and chordal communication. That night, I told Pat McDonald of the *Seattle Times* "If God ever wants a replacement for Gabriel and his horn, He should consider Jimi and his guitar!"

The second part of Jimi's statement was the stuff of great story-telling. The concert business in general is not known for its sober, predictable after-show parties, and this was true in spades the night Jimi Hendrix returned in triumph to his home town. Following their Arena show, Noel, Mitch and Jimi limo'd back to Seattle's staid old Olympic Hotel (today the Fairmont Olympic). There, in their suites on a middle floor of the tall structure, it was party time. Old friends, new friends, groupies and some family members joined Jimi to celebrate a performance that had been truly spectacular, even by his stratospheric standards.

The refreshments served were typical of what one saw on such occasions: ample amounts of liquor, an abundance of joints and a plentiful supply of various other contraband. Before long, everyone was having a grand time. Jimi wasn't a significant user of drugs—although he would do a joint before and after shows—but he did like a good cocktail or six. Still on a natural high from his concert, he didn't need artificial stimulants for his spirit to soar. He deserves full credit for the incredible pageant he produced at the Olympic that night.

With a big convention in town, the hotel was full and the downstairs bar/showroom packed. Closing time at 2:00 A.M. sent hundreds of guests streaming to the elevators for the ride up to their rooms. Seeing this inspired Jimi, whose creative juices were overflowing. He outlined his impromptu production and, moments later, Jimi, Noel, Mitch and three young ladies of the groupie persuasion stood, side-by-side, stark naked, directly in front of the bank of elevators across from the party suite.

Draw this mental picture: The three members of the Experience were skinny as rails, and all sported *naturals*, the official hairdo of rock stars in the late '60s. Jimi's dark body and black Afro (sticking straight out eight inches or more in all directions) contrasted nicely with the snow-white bodies, legs like streams of milk and curly red bushels of hair of Noel and Mitch. The sight of this trio of unclad musicians alone was enough to stop a train. Add to that lineup the three nubile ladies with their own abundance of remarkable features and, I submit, you had a vision to challenge Mount Rushmore, the Leaning Tower of Pisa and the Northern Lights for breathtaking scenic splendor.

This was 1968, a time when television and radio were devoid of four-letter words. Nudity in the media in any form was limited to the pages of *Playboy* and back-alley girlie magazines. America remained for the most part a society constrained by Victorian mores, and the substantially down-scaled sensitivities we see today had yet to be accepted as part of our national or Pacific Northwest culture. Was America, was Seattle, ready for someone like Jimi Hendrix?

Jimi plotted the scenes perfectly. By pressing the up button, soon a packed elevator car stopped at their floor, opened its doors and revealed to the conventioneers within a scene to jar the most dormant of senses: six expressionless faces and a panorama of skin and hair defying belief. After a moment, the doors automatically closed, and the elevator resumed its rise to the top. Continuing the performance, Jimi pressed the up button again and again, and pair after pair of elevator doors slid open to new sets of astonished eyes. That was only the beginning, and Jimi predicted exactly what happened next.

Once the cars reached the top, they began to descend, and this time no button-pressing was needed. Every down elevator stopped again at the Hendrix floor and opened its doors, revealing the same guests from the ride up. They were returning to confirm the impossible, to convince themselves that what they thought they saw but couldn't believe they saw really was what they saw.

Jimi was reconnoitering the surreal, the sort of experiment one might expect from an artist who had entitled his debut album *Are You Experienced?* That night, at that moment, he was as happy as anyone on earth could be. He was back in Seattle and held the town in the palm of his hand. Magic was everywhere. The scene the next morning played out not nearly as well.

A week before his homecoming concert, Jimi called me to say he would like to go back to his old high school from which he had been expelled. He wanted to play his music in an assembly for his former community: the predominantly black students at Garfield High School who likely would not be attending his concert. Jimi thought that the morning after the Arena show, the road crew could bring a sufficient portion of his equipment to the school on the way to the airport, set it up and tear it down with time to spare for making their flight.

Pat O'Day & Jimi Hendrix at Garfield High School, Seattle
with principal Frank Fidler watching in the background —1968

After promising Jimi to do everything I could, I telephoned Frank Fidler, then principal at Garfield, and broached the idea with him. I pointed out that Jimi had achieved a level of musical success equal to or surpassing that of another famous Garfield graduate, Quincy Jones. I added that whereas the student body was mostly unfamiliar with Jimi's music, they all certainly had heard about his sudden rise to stardom. Perhaps he could serve as an example of courage and the willingness to stretch the limits of one's abilities. Frank said he would call me back.

Frank Fidler was the best-known principal in Seattle. A totally dedicated man—and my friend—he earned an impeccable reputation coaching high school sports and was doing an equally outstanding job as principal at Garfield, then considered Seattle's toughest school. I would work to make Jimi comfortable with whatever decision Fidler reached. Frank called me back that same day, explained there were rules governing how many assemblies a school could have in a year and said they had already used up their quota.

"We do have one option," he went on to say. "It's within my authority to call a special pep assembly if the right situation presents itself. Next Friday we're scheduled to play Franklin, and we're both fighting for the championship. Maybe we can do something with that."

Frank phoned again and said it was a "go." We agreed to make the event 50 percent pep rally and 50 percent Jimi. That was my kind of thinking, and I thanked Frank profusely on behalf of Jimi and me.

Unfortunately, when making our plans we failed to factor in the possibility of a post-concert party and its likely aftereffects. The carnage I encountered when I returned to the Olympic at 8:00 A.M. the next morning to wake everyone up and get them ready for the show-and-tell at Garfield should not have surprised me, given the dimensions of the previous evening's celebration. In their post-concert exuberance, those recently-healthy young people had consumed record quantities of every intoxicant on hand, and their bodies and minds had deteriorated substantially as a result. Jimi was uncertain where he was, and Noel and Mitch were comatose. The only roadie I could rouse stated that he had no idea where they left the truck with their equipment the night before and that, for that matter, he didn't much care. I immediately concluded there was no way this package of performers could entertain a high school student body in three hours. Worse still, there was good reason to doubt they would be able to walk any time in the foreseeable future.

I finally woke up Jimi, and we hurriedly conferred. Neither of us wanted to let Frank Fidler down, and there was also Jimi's sincere desire to appear in person at his alma mater. I came up with an emergency plan:

> Jimi, why don't we say that the equipment has been accidentally taken to the airport and put on the plane? I'll introduce you to the students and talk about your success. After that, you'll come out and say a few words, and the audience can ask questions about your career. That way, you can talk to them about your tours, about Monterey, you know, and they'll leave the assembly totally aware of your accomplishments.

Jimi agreed, and we launched Plan B.

Following the cheerleader-and-pep-band portion of the assembly, I was introduced. After I told of Jimi's recent rise to world fame, he emerged from behind the gym's grandstands to thunderous applause. Sidling up to the microphone Hendrix-style wearing jeans, a cowboy hat and lots of beads, Jimi grabbed the mike and mumbled, "Hey, glad to see you're still doing the purple and white thing. [The school's colors were purple and white.] Purple and white, fight, fight!"

A long, uncomfortable pause followed. Standing to the rear of the microphones beside Frank Fidler, I sensed that Jimi was lost. Jimi Hendrix, who could mesmerize thousands with his guitar and his poignant conversations between songs, Jimi Hendrix, who showed no fear when stepping before crowds of strangers numbering in the tens of thousands, was petrified appearing in front of a few hundred non-demanding youngsters from his old school! His epic hangover was partly responsible for the brainlock he was suffering, but there was something deeper and more personal involved: Jimi was scared to death! Before the audience could sense this calamity-in-the-making, I rushed up to one of the microphones and said "Standing before you today is a man who may soon surpass the Beatles in popularity!"

This brought loud applause, for the all-white Beatles enjoyed less-than-unanimous approval among Garfield's predominantly minority students. Young black girls didn't paste pictures of Paul McCartney on their bedroom walls. They preferred Diana Ross, Aretha, Tammi Terrell and Smokey Robinson.

I continued: "Jimi would like to answer your questions. You can ask him anything that is on your mind. This is your opportunity to hear firsthand how someone went from Garfield to the very top of the world's music business."

We had connected a long cord to one of the microphones to reach as close as possible to any questioners. Jimi answered one question, then came a lengthy pause. Finally, one of the cheerleaders, wanting to encourage participation, went to the mike and asked, "Mr. Hendrix, how do you write a song?"

Jimi thought for a long moment, then answered:

> I'm now going to say good-bye to all of you. This has been cool! As I go out the back door of the gym and get in my limousine, the assembly will be over and I will remember that they always ring the bell. I will hear that bell ringing in my head and as I ride to the airport I will be able to write a song about today.

With that, Jimi turned, looked at me and walked out the door. I grabbed the mike and said, "Let's send him on his way with a big thank you!" The students responded with some enthusiasm, the bell rang and Jimi headed not to the airport, but to the Olympic Hotel for some additional, badly-needed sleep.

History of sorts was in the books. Jimi had made his triumphant—although peculiar—return to Garfield High School. I can't remember whether Garfield beat Franklin that night, but I *do* remember Frank Fidler looking at me as if to say, "Pat, you owe me one!"

Years later, Patrick McDonald retold the story of this occasion in the *Seattle Times*, and I was pleased to see that his recollections mostly matched mine.

That afternoon, I received a call at the station from another Garfield cheerleader. She thanked me for bringing Jimi to their school and wondered whether there was any way to get an autograph. She said she could tell Jimi didn't want to be there. She thought the whole thing was the school's idea and restated how nice it was for Jimi to do it. This supported two old bromides: "Perception is everything" and "All's well that ends well."

Star Spangled Banner
Francis Scott Key, 1814 / Jimi Hendrix, 1969

AT CONCERTS WEST, WE PIONEERED A NEW APPROACH to the concert industry. Until the late '60s, the talent agencies contracted to represent a given act. They then sold tour dates to promoters on a city-by-city basis. This gave the Hollywood and New York agencies power to pressure local promoters into handling the agencies' other performers whose shows were less likely to produce a profit. Under this system, new acts or artists or groups could go on the road and make their money as they pioneered their concert careers, while local promoters covered any financial shortfalls. Naturally, the big agencies took their cuts off the top, regardless. We resented this arrangement.

There was a larger issue to consider. Until the late '60s, requirements for performers remained basically the same everywhere. Existing sound systems at auditoriums were used "as-is," and local promoters handled shows however they pleased. They used their own advertising plans to sell tickets, booked acts into hotels of their choice and rarely provided security because, for the most part, it wasn't needed. Specifications for lighting and staging were simple: whatever an auditorium had to offer sufficed. As a result of this haphazard approach, conditions varied wildly from town to town and venue to venue.

We successfully sold performers on the idea that Concerts West could handle all of their appearances, bypassing the influence of the talent agencies, whom we would still pay. The acts became ours to promote nationally, and Jimi Hendrix was one of the first major performers we signed. From 1968 on, we handled nearly all of his concerts in the States, with one notable exception: his appearance at Woodstock in August 1969. Speaking of which, I always found it amusing that his now-treasured rendition of *The Star Spangled Banner*, delivered live at Woodstock, was so dramatically misunderstood for so long. If you've never heard it, you've missed a tear-jerking treat.

By playing our national anthem on stage, Jimi created an essential dichotomy. Woodstock was the Mt. Everest of the counterculture movement, closely associated with antiwar protests and dissent. People sometimes forget, there were other performers like Three Dog Night on stage who delivered old-fashioned love songs. Jimi's music was misinterpreted by people seeking support for their anti-everything points of view. Unawares, they mistakenly assumed that Jimi's startling, electric, powerful rendition of the National Anthem was a put-down of the United States. Like with so many other things, they got that all wrong!

If you listen to that recording today with an open mind, you will instantly recognize it as a breakthrough in musical and emotional expression. This wonderful man felt that performing *The Star Spangled Banner* at that huge gathering was entirely appropriate and played it the way he thought his magic guitar wanted it played. In 1969, Jimi was not all that long out of the Army; at Woodstock, he wasn't protesting anything—rather, he was playing his national anthem the best way he knew how. Anyone who greeted Jimi's rendition of the song as supportive of their hatred of America was dead wrong.

Frankly, Jimi should be remembered as someone who was apolitical. Try as they may, those who attempted to enlist his persona and energy in one political cause or another were simply out of luck. His depth of understanding exceeded theirs and he just wouldn't play their game. The following tale probably tells the story best.

We were in Birmingham, Alabama in 1968. Portions of that state had yet to experience an awakening where racial matters were concerned. One significantly-unyielding portion of the populice appeared to be the Birmingham Police Department. Concerts West had Jimi performing in the city's auditorium. He was, as was usually the case, playing to a totally white audience. Jimi arrived at the stage door prior to the show and entered with his companion at the time, a very attractive young lady, Caucasian, blonde, about five-foot-two, and in her young twenties. She had her arm around Jimi's waiste, and he had his arm around hers. A Birmingham police officer, stationed at the backstage door, went nuts. Screaming racial epithets, he lunged at Jimi, who jumped backwards. The officer then un-holstered his weapon, screaming "By God, this is wrong! Get your f-----g hands off that girl!"

Another officer, standing nearby, as well as our staff, intervened and pulled the enraged cop back from brink of disaster. But it didn't end there. A hurried meeting of all the officers on duty was held, and, en masse, they walked off the job in protest. All because Jimi had shown the temerity to walk in the door of a Birmingham city building with his hands on a white woman. Jimi went to his dressing room, and I followed him, thinking I would need to soothe a frightened, humiliated young man. To my surprise, Jimi wasn't the least bit ruffled.

I said, "God, Jimi, I'm so sorry!"

He replied, "Hey, fifty years ago, things down here were really bad. Fifty years from now, it won't make a damn bit of difference!"

Right there, with his few words, you gain great insight into Jimi's intellect, comprehension, understanding, and grasp of life's big picture. He refused to bother himself with the trivial, knee-jerk activism that was so prevalent in his world.

All Along the Watchtower
Bob Dylan, 1967 / Jimi Hendrix, 1968

ABOUT FIVE YEARS AGO, MY WIFE STEPHANIE AND I were sitting at home one Sunday night casually watching *60 Minutes*. They were airing an investigative report on the continued strength of the Mafia in the New York area since the imprisonment of the don of organized crime, John Gotti. Suddenly I exclaimed, "There he is, Steph! It's that guy I told you about! That's Phil Basile!"

They were showing photos of purported Mafia kingpins still operating in New York, and there on the screen in my living room was Phil. The reporter explained how this Phil Basile was the feared boss of organized crime on Long Island, where he allegedly controlled nightclubs, prostitution and other rackets. I had told Stephanie about a run-in I'd had with Phil years before and now, here he was! The reporter said that Basile was considered a powerful, dangerous figure. I knew Phil Basile all too well, and here's the story of our relationship:

I was at my desk at KJR in April 1969 when it all started with a call to me, early in the week, from my business partner, Terry Bassett. According to Terry, a meeting was going to be held in Oakland on the Monday morning following Jimi's Sunday night show at the Oakland Coliseum. Phil Basile had requested the meeting to inform us that we would be well-advised to turn Jimi's work east of the Mississippi over to him and his associates. "He told me we could have big problems," Terry revealed—not only with the unions at the auditoriums throughout the East, but also with police, ticket agencies and a long list of others. Basile's forecast for our future, should we not comply with his demands, was on the dark side of grim. However, if we went along with his request, Phil promised we would have nothing to fear when we operated in the New York area.

Terry said it sounded like a threat to him, adding "What are we gonna do? This guy is Mafia and he's not kidding!"

Some background on Phil Basile. He was a longtime friend of Ron Terry from their growing-up days in Brooklyn. Phil operated a night club on Long Island and managed the group Vanilla Fudge. Judging from my brief times spent with Phil, I really liked him. Recently, I had become aware of his possible ties to a New York crime family, and a record business friend told me Phil was "a made man," by which I assumed he meant, a member of the Cosa Nostra. *Mafia*!

In 1968, I merged my companies Pat O'Day & Associates and Concerts West with Lester Smith's and Danny Kaye's radio stations. Shortly thereafter, my friend Ron Terry left Creative Management, joined our staff and opened an office for us in the Big Apple. Ron thought there may be occasions when we could do things better under a separate name, and *Concerts East* seemed to make sense as a name for our East Coast operations. Ron brought in a likeable gentleman named Red Ruffino to help with details, and somehow Phil Basile came along as part of the package. (I never knew exactly how this came about; in the end, it didn't much matter.) Ruffino was hard-working and joined us with expectations of a bright future. This was a loose relationship, very different from how we usually operated, but we were growing so fast, it vaguely made sense at the time. Also, our decision to allow the creation of the name *Concerts East* was made before we totally understood the giant we were already creating with Concerts West. Once we knew that, Concerts East looked like a dumb idea.

Back to the issue at hand. Shortly after my conversation with Terry Bassett, Tom Hulett called (Tom later become a partner; at this point, he was still an employee rapidly developing skills in the business). Tom said "This is critical! It's a serious threat! They called me and threatened me, too! Pat, you simply have to be at the meeting!"

Tom didn't have to tell me. Of course I was going to be there! Here was my company, expanding our dream of handling acts on a national and maybe international level. Jimi's tours were the showpiece of what we could do. It was not the profit from Jimi's tours that was most important. In fact, we were *overspending* on Jimi to prove to the industry what we could do and how successful such an arrangement could be. Jimi was one of the keys to our future. To my way of thinking, to let someone horn in, no matter the threat, was out of the question. While that was a strong, noble position to take, the problem remained: How to thwart Basile without starting a war.

Hulett, always impatient, thought I should call Phil immediately. I told him "No way! We've got to come up with a game plan first."

I decided to erase from my heart any fondness I felt for Phil Basile. Suddenly, he was a mortal enemy and, it appeared, a powerful one at that. Are you kidding? Pat O'Day, deejay-turned-radio-manager-turned-promoter, up against a Mafia figure from New York? How in the hell had it come to this? Seattle kids are ill-prepared to deal with such situations, and I was no exception.

Hulett's words of comfort were: "Jesus, we can't afford to lose half of Jimi, but let's not get ourselves shot!" Wow! What insight!

That Saturday night show was a big one for Jimi, his first appearance at the Fabulous Forum in Inglewood. The Forum was the almost-brand-new home of the Lakers and had attained the stature of Madison Square Garden as a concert venue. Jimi headlined a show which had as its opening act a new Columbia Records group, produced by Jimmy Guercio, calling themselves *Chicago Transit Authority*. (Shortly thereafter, they shortened it to *Chicago* when Mayor Daly threatened to sue them over the rights to their original name.) They featured a brilliant young lead singer named Peter Cetera, incredible musicians and a big, fat sound coming from a combination of horns and guitars. Jimi liked them and, although the group wasn't yet much of a ticket seller, there was something special about having this new and fast-rising act on the same bill.

On Friday morning, I caught an early flight out of Sea-Tac to LA and, later that day, joined Jimi, Terry Bassett and Ron Terry on lounges next to the pool on the roof of the Beverly Rodeo Hyatt. I probed Jimi, trying to determine whether there was something going on between him and Phil Basile that I wasn't aware of. Terry Bassett looked concerned. He was building his life around Concerts West, and we were the co-founders of this rapidly-growing company. Successfully resolving this crisis was critical to both of our futures. Ron Terry, as head of our New York office, was caught between his relationships with us and Basile and correctly said, "Guys, I can't have a horse in this race!"

Jimi claimed to know nothing of Phil's threatened intrusion, and it soon became evident this was nothing more than a heavy-handed Basile power play, pure and simple. The problem was, Phil appeared to have the forces to back it.

Saturday night, Jimi brought down the Forum roof with another powerful show. [There ain't nuthin' like a night in Tinsel Town to open up one's adrenal glands!] The last-minute calls for backstage passes and special treatment told the story of how far Jimi had come in a very short time. So many movie stars were crowded together backstage, it was like Oscars night. After Jimi was introduced, he walked from his dressing room to the stage. Along the way, a sea of oh-so-familiar faces parted to let him through. As he climbed the steps, Jimi flashed the damnedest grin. He had arrived. Oh, had he arrived!

The next night the scene switched to Oakland and another sellout. That show was a great one for people-watching. In the late '60s, the Bay Area was the world capital of the bizarre. You didn't need to bring your own pot to that show—all you had to do to get stoned was take a deep breath. This was pure heaven for the band. The flower children were there to worship a new deity. Chicago Transit Authority again opened the show and drew two encores. That's saying something for an opening act. Jimi didn't mind what others may have interpreted as being upstaged by the kids from Chicago. They were that good—they were sensational—and Jimi knew it. Still, he wasn't bothered at all. He knew the house was still his, that San Francisco loved him. They had since Monterey.

The concert lasted past midnight, bringing me ever closer to our fateful meeting the next day. It was scheduled for noon in Terry Bassett's room at the Oakland Edgewater, by the airport. An idea had been forming in my mind for several days and was almost complete. It was to be a gamble, a big gamble. And for it to work, I couldn't risk sharing it with my partners beforehand. I was going to attempt a world-class bluff and pray I could pull it off! It wasn't as though I had a multitude of attractive options to choose from. The sold-out shows and the excitement of our successes in LA and the Bay Area inspired me. We were operating in the center of the known entertainment universe, we seemingly had arrived and I sensed our company was approaching greatness. Our fate was up to me, for better or worse. I was ready for the summit.

Luck Be a Lady Tonight
Frank Sinatra, 1954
Frank Sinatra purchased radio stations kjr in Seattle, kxl in Portland and knew in Spokane in 1958. To do so, he formed a partnership between Essex Productions (one of his companies) and the great entertainer, Danny Kaye. Lester Smith, about whom a great deal more is said elsewhere in this book, was the previous owner, along with two California associates, Link Deller and Les Malloy. Les Smith agreed to stay on as chief executive of the stations, and that was the situation when I started working at kjr in late 1959.

If Sinatra was excited by his radio properties, I failed to see any indication of it. His disassociation from the stations was never more evident than in 1962 during the Seattle World's Fair. One day, Les Smith was informed that The Man himself, Frank Sinatra, was coming to Seattle for the Fair and would make the radio station his headquarters. It was suggested that any sprucing needed should be done quickly.

Sprucing up was indeed needed. We were still operating out of the station's original transmitter building on the West Waterway in Seattle's industrial port section off Elliot Bay. To call KJR's offices *spartan* would have been kind, but it hadn't made any difference to date. Radio doesn't need impressive offices. After all, you can't hear an office. With the Chairman of the Board on his way, the feeling among the station's hierarchy changed to "Wow, let's loosen the purse strings and make this place nice!"

Frederick & Nelson was Seattle's big, upscale department store at the time, and they prided themselves in their interior design department. Accordingly, they were given the job of remodeling, and an expensive, unique transformation took place. Over the course of a few days, old walls were moved, expensive imported Philippine mahogany paneling put up, tasteful wall paper hung, new light fixtures mounted, expensive carpeting laid, fancy brass door knobs installed and fine furniture brought in. Nothing was left to chance, nothing was too good or expensive for Frank's visit.

What happened when Sinatra's private plane landed in Seattle was relayed to me afterwards by Jim Price, an executive at Reprise, Frank's record company, who was invited along. The plane rolled to a stop at the general aviation facility at Boeing Field on a typically chilly, inclement Northwest spring day. Frank stepped out of the plane and spied a wet tarmac. The wind was blowing, and it was raining, raining hard; the water was *pouring* down! Frank descended one or two steps, glowered at the sky and shivered angrily as raindrops kept falling on his head. He stopped, hesitated for maybe 10 seconds, then turned around and re-boarded the plane. As he entered the cabin, he snarled at the pilot, "Let's get the hell out of here!"

Frank Sinatra's visit to Seattle and his radio station was over, and that was as close as he ever came to stepping inside KJR's offices and studio. Those Philippine mahogany walls stood for years as a mute testament to the grand Sinatra visit that never quite took place.

Rain-soaked legends and spiffed-up offices aside, I was facing my meeting with Phil Basile, and the plan I had developed called for me to play my Sinatra card. Although Frank had sold his shares in the broadcast company to Danny Kaye and Lester Smith some time before, I figured Phil wouldn't know, if he even was aware in the first place that Frank once owned the station. My play would be a gamble, and gambling is defined as an activity with prize, chance and consideration. The move I was about to make involved all three elements in abundance, with a heavier-than-normal dose of chance. I would have to live with that, come what may. After all, my Sinatra card was the only one I had to play.

Fire
Jimi Hendrix, 1967

TERRY BASSETT BOOKED A SUITE AT THE OAKLAND EDGEWATER and ordered up juice, coffee and rolls for the gathering. I made it a point to enter the room a few minutes late to avoid any conversation before the summit meeting actually began. Six anxious men filled the room once I arrived: Terry Bassett, Ron Terry, Tom Hulett, Phil Basile, Red Ruffino and me. Tom fidgeted nervously, while Terry, juice in hand, typically sat off in a corner, a good spot from which to watch everyone else. Red and Ron were perched side-by-side on the edge of a bed, and Phil stood in front of the window.

I stationed myself nearby the refreshment cart and said, "Well, Phil, I've heard sketchy reports about your suggestions, if we can call them that. I'd like to just listen for a while and have you tell me what this whole thing is about."

I was nervous, but dared not let it show. A better way to describe my feelings that day would be *downright scared*. Before leaving Seattle, I had placed inquiring phone calls to several more business friends in New York and was told by all that this guy I truly liked, Phil Basile, was Mafia-attached and that he was "not someone to mess with." Well, I was about to mess with Mr. Basile *real good*, and the pit of my stomach was telling me it would rather be elsewhere at this moment.

Turning my way, Phil began. He went on about how he was a peaceful kind of guy and how he was really a friend of Concerts West and of all of us as individuals. He pointed out, however, that it made sense to him that Concerts East—he and Red—handle all Hendrix dates east of the Mississippi. We would call these *Concerts East* dates, and they would be all his. It was clear he already considered Concerts East his private property. The benefit he offered to us in exchange for this gift of gifts—awarding him Hendrix in most of the nation's biggest cities—was his protection from a host of problems he assured us we would otherwise face. Problems with the unions, problems with the ticket agencies, problems with the police, problems with people who just plain didn't like us, every one of whom, he indicated, was in a position to make our lives a living hell. He said he was well aware of our growth pattern, with other big acts opening dialogs with us daily. The protection package he proposed would allow us to conduct our other tours in his territory without concern. He made it clear that, were he not granted his request for Jimi in the East, unhappy consequences were likely to result. (Although this closely approximates the words Phil used to explain his position, it's not an exact, word-for-word rendering. His actual words and sentences were jumbled and vague, with ominous, sinister overtones, and I find them hard to precisely recreate after all these years.)

Phil concluded, and there followed a long, tense pause as I walked about the room, appearing to be deep in thought. In fact, it didn't take much thought to see the big picture. If we gave Jimi Hendrix and Concerts East as a package to Basile, we could kiss the entire East Coast good-bye. The concert-world grapevine would quickly have him as the eastern power, and Concerts West's image as a national power would be forever fractured. We dared not let that happen. We could live without the name *Concerts East*, but we had to have Jimi *en toto*. I was preparing myself, knowing I had one shot and one shot only with which to win a war. I allowed the pause to grow uncomfortably long, and finally walked over to Phil, stood directly in front of him and began. I will attempt to quote exactly my speech of that day. In my mind, it has remained frozen and pure. I commenced:

Phil, Red, I have always liked you both. Phil, I respect what you have accomplished in the business. You're a good friend of Ron's, and I consider you my friend. I have, however, been totally wrong about one thing. I believed that you had taken the time to get to really know us, and that you respected us. I thought that someone in your position would be smart enough to figure out who it was they were dealing with. Then, I got the phone calls this week from Terry and Tom, and I couldn't believe my ears. I wanted to be here today because I just couldn't come to grips with what they thought you were saying. I just couldn't believe that you would try and lay this kind of shit on us.

I elevated my voice from a conversational tone to a higher volume and pitch. I got right up in Phil's face and said,

> Phil, don't you know who you're dealing with? Don't you know who you're fucking with? Don't you know whom I've worked for the past eight years? Do you think I'm some dumb shit from Seattle who somehow just stumbled into this whole operation? You're standing here, threatening our operation, thinking you've got a hammer to bang out a piece of us for yourself. Either you don't know who we are, or you're crazy. Which is it?

My adrenal glands were pumping, I was on a roll, my confidence level was building, and I was starting to believe my own stuff! Basile looked puzzled as I pressed the attack.

> Phil, you could have made a couple of phone calls, a couple of simple phone calls. You would have found out that *Frank Sinatra* bought KJR 10 years ago. KJR is now half of Concerts West. You know I am the general manager of KJR! Now, Phil, can you tie those two things together? Phil, are you standing there telling us that you're so big, so powerful, you can muscle a Sinatra operation? Is that what you're telling me, Phil? Phil, may I tell Frank that?

Phil suddenly looked frightened, and with good reason. Frank Sinatra had accumulated great power over the years. Everyone suspected the source of that power, but no one knew for sure. Nonetheless, it was there. Senate Committees hoping to figure it out questioned him about his rumored Mafia ties. Some thought his connection was Sam Giancana, the feared Don of Chicago (which was most likely). Others associated him with the hierarchy of the New York crime families. Whatever his arsenal of relationships was, it added up to power, mysterious, awesome power which commanded respect and fear. Frank, in fact, had sold his portion of the broadcast company a couple of years earlier to Danny Kaye and Lester Smith. Frank wanted out because he needed cash to hold together his Cal Neva Lodge Casino which suffered a "pulled" license when Frank hosted Sam Giancana as a guest.

Giancana and his girlfriend, Dorothy Maguire of the famous singing Maguire Sisters, got into a fist fight outside their unit at the Cal Neva. The press arrived and took pictures, and Giancana's supposedly secret getaway to Frank's place became very public. Having known crime figures stay at your hotel/casino was taboo with Nevada's Gaming Commission, which promptly suspended Sinatra's license. At the same time, Frank's radio partner, Danny Kaye, was worried about holding onto their FCC license with a partner who was being called before Senate committees probing possible gangster connections. As a result, Danny turned to Lester Smith, who was running the stations for the partnership, and together they bought Frank out.

My big gamble here, my all-or-maybe-nothing bet, was that Phil Basile didn't know that Sinatra had once owned the station. Or, if he did, that he didn't know that Frank had since sold out. I continued my verbal assault on Phil, further increasing my volume and feigning great anger. That same morning, before the mirror in my room, I practiced an eye twitch I noticed in some movie which gave the appearance of someone about to lose control. I now employed that twitch. "Phil!" I screamed, "What in the hell are you doing to yourself? What in the hell are you doing threatening my people?"

Tom Hulett looked ashen, Terry Bassett surprised and pleased. Ron Terry was wearing his tinted think glasses, so I couldn't read his reaction (I suspected he had it all figured out). I had worked myself into a full-blown rage. This was an Oscar-caliber performance, and I wasn't finished.

After standing face-to-face with Phil for several moments, letting my words and their impact sink in, I continued:

> Phil, I thought about this all the way down here. I hardly slept last night trying to figure out what to do about this big problem you've created. This is so unbelievable to me that you would try something like this! This is so unbelievable that you would think you could pull this kind of shit on us! Well, I've decided what to do. I haven't told Terry and Tom yet, so this is going to be news to them. I've talked to everyone else about this, and they all agree with me. [I didn't identify who *everyone else* was; there *was no* everyone else!] I like you, Phil, but after this, after this dumb move, after this shit, I don't feel that we can be associated with you any longer. We can't afford to be around someone who would try a move like this.
>
> So, here is where we are, and here is where we're going to stay. First of all, forget about Jimi! Now, to show our friendship, and to prevent anything like this from ever happening again, we've decided to let you and Red take the name Concerts East. It's all yours, you've put time and

effort into it, so take it. But now listen, and listen good! Never, *ever* will you indicate, in any way, that you are associated with us. We are now competitors. We may do a date or two with you, but only, and I mean *only*, if it makes sense to us. We're no longer connected with you in any way. And now, last but not least, listen to me very carefully! If Concerts West, or any of our people, ever, *ever* have a bad experience around New York, around the East, we're going to assume it's your doing. I'm talking about the unions, the whole long ugly list you gave us. If anything goes wrong for us, and you know what I mean, I'm picking up the phone and calling Frank. Do you understand me, Phil? If all goes well, all is forgiven. But never, ever mess with us again. *Never!!!*

Phil babbled his response. He kept saying, over and over again, "I'm sorry, man, I'm really sorry! I just didn't know! I'm really sorry! I'm so sorry!"

He was still repeating himself when I shook his hand, turned to Bassett and Hulett and said, "See you in Seattle!" and stomped out the door, muttering for all to hear, "I can't believe this happened, it's so damned stupid!"

I was halfway back to Seattle on Hughes Airwest before I returned to near normal. I never aspired to be an actor, but I knew that, though scared to death, I had just put on the show of my life. And it appeared I had pulled it off! Time was to prove I had. My eternal thanks to the late Frank Sinatra, not only for his subsequent decision to use Concerts West for all his touring appearances, but also for the totally unauthorized use of his name and great power!

I recently learned that Phil Basile died a couple years ago. I *did* like him, despite his associations, and hope that he passed on from natural causes.

The Wind Cries Mary
Jimi Hendrix, 1967

JIMI'S DEATH IN LONDON IN SEPTEMBER 1970 WAS A SHOCK. He was still a young man, he was in great health and he didn't appear to me to be using drugs to the point of danger. I could understand what happened to Jim Morrison of the Doors in Paris a year later. I could understand how Mama Cass, whose health was mediocre, succumbed to a drug-driven heart attack in 1974. The death of Elvis in 1977 was no great puzzle, either, given his family's history of heart problems, his excessive weight and his appetite for drugs which a whole pharmacy couldn't satisfy. But Jimi's death was different. After the fact, I was told that his little girlfriend living with him in London knew how to probe his vulnerabilities and could keep him in a mess for extended periods of time when she had the chance. That night in her London flat was apparently one of those chances.

Tragic is the level of greed, disingenuousness and cruelty permeating the world of rock-'n'-roll, and it was no different with Jimi's death. In some ways, it was worse! Where were Jimi's co-managers after he died? Where was the damn record company that profited so richly from his great genius and his constant promotion of his music on the road? Publicly, they all responded to the press with expressions of grief. But privately, in person, at the real level, where were they?

The world should know that one young man in Seattle cared a great deal. His name is Paul Allen, co-founder with Bill Gates of Microsoft. I don't know exactly when the dreaming began or where the idea first formed, but somehow a vision of commemorating Jimi and his music took shape. Allen, an accomplished guitar player in his own right, saw that Seattle had given birth to a musician who, in his own way, was truly a Mozart or a Beethoven. It was such a thrill for me to act as emcee at the official ground breaking of the gorgeous, expansive building that brought his dream to life. The ceremony wasn't in some remote spot or out-of-the-way park. Paul Allen wanted the best for his tribute to Jimi and to music. He wanted the electric spirit of Jimi to live on in music and structure forever. The new museum was built directly under Seattle's most visible symbol, the Space Needle. Today, the two great signatures stand side by side: the Space Needle, built as the symbol of the 1962 Seattle World's Fair, and Experience Music Project, built nearly four decades later in part to preserve and celebrate Jimi's creativity. The Needle is fortunate to have such good company as Jimi Hendrix.

It was also a thrill for me personally when Paul's staff, while preparing the exhibits for EMP, asked me to contribute my knowledge of the history of Northwest rock-'n'-roll. They also asked me to do some narration for the Northwest Passage section of the museum, which I proudly did.

Another thrill was to discover, when EMP opened, that they have my picture with a story about me displayed in that same section. To be included, even in a small way, in the "House of Jimi"—frankly, I don't feel worthy.

Paul Allen was never personally acquainted with Jimi Hendrix, and I hope to sit down with him sometime and tell him all I know about this most wonderful man. Allen's affection for Jimi Hendrix and his architectural tribute to him are surpassed only by the depth, compassion and genius of Jimi himself.

Hear My Train A Comin'

Jimi Hendrix, 1970

MY PERSONAL FRIENDSHIP AND PROFESSIONAL RELATIONSHIP with Jimi Hendrix changed my life. When we first met at the Spanish Castle in 1961, Jimi's career in music was still in the future, and mine in radio was just beginning to take off. On one of those nights, I unknowingly gave Jimi one of his first opportunities to perform before a live audience. Seven years later, Jimi was master of the musical universe, and I was founder of a national concert concern and general manager of Seattle's AM radio powerhouse, KJR. And somehow, we were reunited. Returning a kindness shown years before, Jimi chose my company, Concerts West, to represent him on his tours. His decision to go with us, and his loyalty to us in the years that followed, played a major role in our success. Without Jimi, we may well have succeeded; with Jimi, our success was swift and stunned the industry. Looking back, none of it was inevitable. Without Jimi, life certainly could have gone differently for me.

A GOLD RECORD SYMBOLIZES SUCCESS in the music world, with over one million copies sold. When the Tacoma group The Ventures went gold with *Walk—Don't Run*, their record company thanked Pat O'Day for his support by presenting him with the plaque pictured here. In 1960, he attended the song's original recording session and carried a tape back with him to the station. Prior to the record's release anywhere else, Pat started playing it on KJR every hour just before the news break. Today, he's credited with the radio discovery of one of the world's greatest instrumental groups. In Japan, the Ventures have outsold the Beatles, and guitarists Don Wilson, Bob Bogle, and Nokie Edwards were the first three foreigners elected to Japan's prestigious Academy of Music.

2 – What a Wonderful World

Louis Armstrong, 1968

S OME WRITERS WOULD HAVE YOU BELIEVE that my company single-handedly invented the rock-'n'-roll dance and concert business in the Pacific Northwest. Not true, not even close! We were innovators with a fresh new approach, yes. But the urge to present dances and concerts probably dates from sometime back when our cave-dwelling ancestors were still gathering around campfires at night to celebrate the arrival of spring or the felling of a woolly mammoth. More recently, in gold rush days, long before the transcontinental railroads were completed, legions of performers traveled by ship from the East Coast around Cape Horn to play in far-off California. Later, William "Buffalo Bill" Cody traversed the land with his Wild West Show, dragging along an Indian chief or two and herds of livestock for impact and authenticity. The traveling entertainment business grew as transportation infrastructure improved, and the railroads helped by offering large discounts and entire railcars to the barnstorming troupes. By the 1900s, performing companies incessantly crisscrossed the country, bringing their shows to theaters, ballrooms, fairgrounds, bars and clubs on the coasts and in every corner of the hinterlands.

Touring musicians were always part of this industry, and their travels and experiences, generally by train or bus, particularly from the 1920s on, would make a good book. The big bands, from Paul Whiteman to Guy Lombardo, to Glenn Miller, to Benny Goodman as we moved forward in years, were practically full-time residents of the road. Just about every other musical group of distinction at that time joined them in their wandering ways—Les Brown and his Band of Renown, Les Baxter, Billy Vaughn, Stan Kenton, Tommy and Jimmy Dorsey, Artie Shaw, Gene Krupa, Les Elgart, Bing and Bob Crosby, a guy named Lawrence Welk from Yangton, South Dakota, and Louis Armstrong and his All Stars from New Orleans, to name a few.

Ain't Misbehavin'
Louis Armstrong & His All Stars, 1947

SPEAKING OF LOUIS ARMSTRONG, an aside if I may. A performance by Armstrong and his All Stars on one of their Midwest tours impacted my life forever. In the summer of 1949, I was 14 years old, my father had just died and my mother, my brothers and I were living for a few months in Boone, Iowa, my father's home town. Just south, in Des Moines, my Uncle Elmer managed the Hoyt Sherman Auditorium. One magical night, Louis Armstrong and his band came to town to play. I was staying with my uncle and aunt in their apartment in the Auditorium building. Already a big Louis Armstrong fan, I was half crazy with excitement. How vividly I remember their arrival in the back parking lot. Satchmo and the band materialized from out of the ether in a makeshift trailer house—a long silver vehicle, something like an Airstream trailer on steroids, pulled by a truck. When no one was looking, I peeked inside and saw makeshift bunks and a table. Amazing! This was the traveling headquarters, the sanctum sanctorum, of the great Louis Armstrong! The accommodations were primitive by most standards, but not by mine. In my youth, I didn't understand that the black members of the band needed to bring their own beds with them because hotels in many towns across America denied them lodging. To me, this trailer symbolized romance, not economic necessity or racism. This was big, mysterious, adult entertainment stuff—not kid stuff—and I was mesmerized. At once, I hatched a secret plot to watch that night's performance, not daring to ask my uncle for permission.

My scheme centered around a basement passageway running beneath the auditorium from the furnace room to the other side with a door opening into the sunken orchestra pit. That evening, after dinner, as the first bars of the band's opening number filtered upstairs, I crept from the apartment, sneaked down to the furnace room, slipped along the dark passageway and pried open the orchestra pit door a sliver. The door sat on the side of the pit away from the stage. Peering up through the crack, I saw before me, not 20 feet away, trumpet in one hand, handkerchief in the other, one of my true idols—the Satchmo. And on stage with him, that great band. To the left I spotted Trummy Young with his trombone. Farther back where I could hear but not see him, the immortal Cozy Cole was laying down the beat on his drums. Satchmo was singing *Ain't Misbehavin'* — and *misbehavin'* was exactly what I was doing. At that moment, a young man felt he had died and gone to heaven. In some important ways, he has never returned to earth.

Fifteen years later, I sat at the Polynesian Restaurant on the Seattle waterfront having lunch with the man himself. He was passing through town promoting his *Hello Dolly* release. The day before, the representative from Kapp Records had called and asked whether I would like to have lunch with Louis. "Are you kidding?" I answered. "Yes, of course I would. I'd be thrilled!"

Over lunch, I told Satchmo my story about that young man watching him from a darkened orchestra pit in Iowa. He laughed as only Louis Armstrong could laugh. Having shared that happy moment from my childhood with him, I further confessed that our brief encounter that night in Des Moines possibly influenced my life, that I considered it one root cause of my all-consuming drive to stage live musical shows myself. Louis held as how that was probably true in that he, too, decided at an early age (six), while living in the Colored Waifs Home in New Orleans, what he would do with his life—play the brass cornet. The whole world should have met Louis Armstrong, "the Ambassador of Jazz," in person. His infectious laugh, his kindness, his unselfishness would have changed history. His song *What a Wonderful World* typifies the spirit of this great man.

That's All Right Mama
Elvis Presley, 1954

THE BIG BANDS TRAVELED CONSTANTLY from place to place, usually playing in local ballrooms. Most burgs in America larger than Two Dot, Montana had at least one, either within their precincts (often in a hotel) or at a stand-alone facility somewhere nearby (like at a lake or riverside resort). Those facilities generally sported a bar, booths or tables for the customers and a large hardwood dance floor. In cities and villages large and small, people gathered to dance, look and listen as famous musicians whose sounds they knew from records and radio performed in person.

Back then, royalties from record sales could not provide enough income to meet the needs of sometimes over a dozen musicians and their families. Traveling thousands of miles performing hundreds of shows a year was therefore essential for a band to survive and stay together. There were regional variations on this theme. In the South and Southeast, country musicians did much the same thing, playing mostly in bars and small halls. The Great Depression of the '30s constrained this life-style, then World War II reinvigorated it and brought it to its swan-song zenith. Individuals and families flocked to the coasts to fill tens of thousands of defense manufacturing jobs. Servicemen and women, many of them away from home for the first time, went looking for entertainment and companionship, and ballrooms filled the bill.

Local bands developed to plug performance gaps between visits by nationally-recognized stars. They rarely offered original material, relying instead on sheet music from the five-and-ten-cent store to play hit songs and old-time favorites. As best they could, they replicated the signature sounds of the famous. By the late 40s and early '50s, with the war over and television revolutionizing how Americans spent their leisure time, tastes and life-styles changed, and the ballroom era waned. People were staying home, glued to their newfangled TV sets, watching Tommy Dorsey and Lawrence Welk, Milton Berle and Captain Video, and no longer going to boogie at their local dance halls. Ragged around the edges and turning a bit musty, these relics from a bygone era staggered on for a while, fending off the onslaught of television, trying to lure new customers and looking for something to replace the long-departed national acts. In the late '50s and early '60s, the ballroom phenomenon finally passed into history.

Vaudevillians rarely hit the highway or rails after World War II. As live theater, their product slipped below the American consciousness save for a handful of acts (Jack Benny, Burns and Allen, the Marx Brothers and some others) that successfully made the transition to the tube. A few performers—Louis Armstrong among them—could still fill theaters on the road, but their numbers were dwindling, and they were no longer the major force they once had been in the entertainment industry. Many performers abandoned the road altogether for the convenience of television, which gobbled up live entertainers at an ever-increasing rate to fill its programs. There was no prerecording of shows in those early TV days, as equipment had yet to evolve that could accommodate that process. Television contracts in the early '50s brought performers to New York and Los Angeles, near the network television studios, and kept them there year 'round. That left little time for touring.

About the only musical promotion then happening that resembled what we did later was "Jazz at the Philharmonic," the creation of LA promoter Norman Granz. Granz recruited major names from the music world and put them out on tour from city to city, working with local promoters. Some early rock-'n'-roll packages were assembled, featuring several acts and playing in smaller venues like theaters. Major concerts remained an extreme rarity until the rise of Tupelo, Mississippi's favorite son, Elvis Presley. His vaulting onto the live concert scene in 1956, following an unbroken string of giant hit records, opened my eyes to the vast potential of this entertainment medium. I say *potential* because for years, only Elvis could sell 15,000 tickets a night, and only one of him existed. No one held second place. There *was* no second place. The public was not yet accustomed to the rock-'n'-roll concert business, and Elvis remained a phenomenon without precedent or equal.

Elvis flourished under the guidance of Colonel Tom Parker, who acquired his management rights from Bob Neal in late 1955. Parker also managed country singer/songwriter Hank Snow, and they had a booking agency together. Snow helped Elvis land a spot on the Grand Ole Opry in 1954 and encouraged him in his early career. Elvis provided the raw material from which Parker, an old carnival man, built an entertainment empire the likes of which the industry had never seen. One after another, Elvis's records reached the top of the nation's music charts as a new development — Top 40 radio stations — played them hourly as part of their "current hits only" play lists.

Parker made a fateful leap in January 1956 when he brought Elvis to network television for the first of six appearances on the CBS program, *Stage Show* produced by Jackie Gleason and hosted by Jimmy and Tommy Dorsey (what a contrast between old and new!). That same year, Parker also booked Elvis on *The Milton Berle Show*. Real television history unfolded on September 9, 1956 when Elvis performed for the first time on *The Ed Sullivan Show* on CBS. Sullivan's one-hour variety show, airing Sunday evenings at 8:00 P.M., was TV's top-rated program by a wide margin. Every week, Americans *en masse* sat down before their sets to consume whatever fare Sullivan offered. Before Elvis, rock-'n'-rollers rarely appeared on his show, in part because their music was still so new. When Parker came knocking, he offered such a spectacular new attraction, Sullivan could no longer say no to him.

Elvis's unrestrained sensuality during his first Sullivan appearance — his famous bumping, grinding and hip-swivelling — shocked many Americans' sensibilities. In the following weeks, newspapers everywhere carried stories expressing pious outrage. People condemned Presley's moves as lewd and lascivious, as suggestive of heathen-like behavior. They saw the very soul of young America at risk. The canny Sullivan, after weeks of front-page stories, faced with community leaders demanding restraint on the network's part, finally agreed to have his cameramen show Elvis only from the waist up in January 1957.

Here was this handsome 19-year-old kid from a small town in Mississippi moving his body to music the way anyone would respond to a great rhythm and beat if they let go of their inhibitions. Yet, his moves disturbed most adult Americans, who couldn't cope with this raw challenge to accepted behavior. Similar cries were heard everywhere: "Ballroom dancing was never like this!" / "The world as we know it is coming to an end!" / "Good Lord, what are we going to do?" / "This wickedness has got to stop!"

The inevitable result of all this ruckus was a huge audience for Sullivan's shows in October 1956 and January 1957 featuring Elvis, with ratings unequaled for another eight years, until the Beatles' first *major* American TV appearance, also on *The Ed Sullivan Show* (they had appeared on *The Jack Paar Show* earlier). The ploy of shooting Elvis from the waist up during his third Sullivan appearance only added to the excitement, further enhancing the singer's image. His upper body projected its own fair share of sexuality and inspired viewers to fantasize about what was going on *below* his belt. People were forced to imagine for themselves the possibilities of what they could not see. After listening to the screams of the teenage girls in the audience, many concluded that Elvis performed naked from the waist down.

How the human imagination loves to fill in blanks. Given the chance, we conjure up mental pictures far more graphic and shocking than any reality we have been denied seeing. We somehow feel compelled to complete in our minds what is incomplete in our eyes. That September night, left to draw its own conclusions, America's collective imagination produced the wildest, most vivid and provocative images possible. For baby boomers, the experience was exhilarating, for their parents, unsettling. For Elvis, it resulted in unrivaled stardom from that night forward. His stature has remained unsurpassed, and only the Beatles have approached the magnitude of his brilliance.

In the afterglow of Elvis's appearances on *The Ed Sullivan Show*, Parker put his protégé on the road, staging sold-out concerts across America. Backed by the Jordanaires, wearing a sparkling gold suit and arriving at shows in big long Cadillacs, Elvis ushered in a new era in the concert business. In Seattle, he performed outdoors at Sick's Stadium, the city's minor league baseball park. I was there, having driven that morning over the Cascade Mountains from Yakima in eastern Washington, where I was an aspiring young deejay working my way up radio's ladder. Like everyone else in attendance that night, I was overwhelmed. Not so much by his songs, though I knew all of them by heart. Nor by his dancing or singing, great though they were. But rather by the grand theater, by the spectacle of it all. In my mind, I silently saluted Colonel Parker: *Sir, you are a genius*! This was a presidential address, a professional wrestling match, a Billy Graham revival, a heavyweight championship fight and a World Series game—everything exciting a person could imagine—all wrapped up in one package. Years passed before anyone duplicated Presley's and Parker's feat, before America's youth developed a taste for the electric energy a giant concert can generate, before auditoriums were built that could accommodate large crowds and before adequate sound systems were developed capable of making such shows a valid musical experience.

Elvis and the Beatles did not have to be heard. The excitement of seeing them in person was enough to satisfy concert audiences. In both cases, the deafening screams—mostly the shrill voices of young girls—were so loud, the music itself was obliterated. It didn't matter, for the crowds already knew every note, every beat, every word by heart.

The music world had to wait nearly a decade before young people enjoyed the discretionary income necessary to afford tickets priced high enough to make such events economically feasible. Elvis and the Beatles were exceptions to the prevailing rule. Much work remained, many seeds needed to be planted and nurtured and great patience had to be exercised for the embryonic concert business to grow and mature. Its successful evolution was never guaranteed. Seeing Elvis perform live for the first time, I felt a magical genie lived in that rock-'n'-roll bottle, and I intended to set it free.

These feelings that filled me with such fervor came not only from rock-'n'-roll. The son of a fundamentalist minister, I grew up around church services, camp meetings and tent revivals. Twice I attended Billy Graham crusades in outdoor stadiums with 50,000 others and was spellbound by the thousand-voice choir, the emotional upswelling and the galvanizing sermon. I noticed that the electricity charging the atmosphere at such gatherings arose from more than just the message being delivered. With Graham, it rapidly gained strength as the size of his audience grew, and the same math applied with Elvis. The pulsating force did more than match the audience in growth; it squared itself, it expanded exponentially. The larger the crowd, the deeper are the emotions, the greater the spiritual experience. Vast crowds can bring tears when matched with powerful music and oratory—most especially with music. When the music packs the right emotional punch, this combination delivers a highly personal experience, one with a narcotic-like effect, one that's sometimes euphoric, other times exhausting, and always genuine and meaningful. Rather than dangerous, emotional trips like these are a vital part of life, something which individuals should be encouraged to embrace and not be denied. Sounding like a shrink, I believe that such emotional experiences serve as a natural release. They can soothe anger, lessen frustration, soften disappointment and cure disillusionment—all of which life offers in generous quantities. As well, they help us develop a sense of community and inclusion— a potent elixir. Mostly, these experiences are satisfying and innocent.

I carried this attitude with me as I progressed through my life in radio and pursued my objectives as a promoter of dances and concerts. From my earliest days in the entertainment business, I believed concerts would someday become a staple in American life, and it happened. Although today I attend such events not nearly as often as I once did, I have seen my projections come true. The wonderful staging, lighting, sound systems, music and choreography surrounding the 2002 Winter Olympics in Salt Lake City reassured me that we continue to climb that grand mountain with ever-better production values and new turns of imagination. U-2's Bono singing at the 2002 Super Bowl with the names of the victims of the 9-11 attacks scrolled in laser lights was another deeply-moving emotional experience. It was only surpassed by the previous bowl, when Ray Charles sang *America The Beautiful*. For me, the feelings were even more intense because I remember how it all began.

At work at KUTI-AM *Yakima, Washington* —1957

Paul's Platter Party, KVAS-AM *Astoria, Oregon* —1956

Above: The Kingsmen with Pat O'Day & the Jolly Green Giant
Left to right: Mike Mitchell, Barry Curtis, Lynn Easton, J. G. Giant,
Pat O'Day, Dick Peterson, Norm Sundholm —1964

Above: The Fabulous Wailers with a friend
Left to right: Rich Dangel, Kent Morrill, Mike Burk,
Ron Gardner, Buck Ormsby —1966

3 – At the Hop

Danny & the Juniors, 1957

ASTORIA, OREGON, SEPTEMBER 3, 1956. The place, the date I began my first full-time radio job after finishing college and broadcasting school. As Paul Berg, I was the afternoon deejay at KVAS, a tiny 250-watt station in a beautiful, serene town on the Pacific Ocean at the mouth of the mighty Columbia River. The area's other claim to fame was nearby Fort Clatsop, where explorers Meriwether Lewis and William Clark, along with their Indian guide Sacajawea, spent the winter of 1805-06. Winters in Astoria are heavenly if you are fond of wind and heavy rain. Storms moving into the Northwest from the Pacific Ocean tend to make this town their port of entry. If you read the journals of Lewis and Clark, they confirm that without modern structures, heat, lights, et cetera, a winter in Astoria is the soggy equivalent of hell. In 1956-57, I was too excited and energized by my new life in radio to let the area's less-than-perfect weather distract me.

Earlier that summer, Merle Kimball, head of my school's broadcast department, told me about an opening in Astoria, and I drove down in mid-August for an audition and interview. Nervously entering the studio with some commercial copy and a ream of news wire stories, I sat down at a microphone while the station's owner, general manager and program director went to the control room to listen. I looked at this audition as the defining moment in my young life. Radio was my dream from early grade school on, and the focus of my education. *Do I have what it takes to make a career in radio?* In broadcasting school, I worked part time as an engineer at KTAC in Tacoma. Now I was auditioning for an actual on-air job. Suddenly, this was no longer KVAS in lil' ol' Astoria, Oregon. To me, at that moment, this was NBC in New York, the big time. Again I wondered, *Will they like what I do?*

I delivered the most powerful newscast I knew how, including commercials, drawing inspiration from all those stirring sermons I listened to in my youth. Sitting alone in the silent glass cage afterward, I watched through the studio window the all-powerful triumvirate deciding my fate—thumbs up or thumbs down. *I could have done better!* I kept thinking. *Why didn't I do better?*

In surprisingly few minutes, they joined me, and the owner said, "That was very, very good! We will pay you $250 per month. You will do morning news and be the host of our afternoon program. Can you start in two weeks?"

"Yes!"

Soon after arriving in Astoria, I developed a sizeable teenage following in the region. The station's management allowed me to try new music options, and I relied heavily on this emerging style called rock-'n'-roll for my radio show. I got a bright idea from a television show I once saw and developed a weekly evening program I could take on the road. With the enthusiastic sponsorship of a local dairy, I called the show *Paul's Platter Party*. (*Platter* was the affectionate name the industry gave the new, small 45 RPM records that contained the hits of that time and of the next 20 years.) The Platter Party traveled to a different middle school or high school every Wednesday night. An amazingly high percentage of the student bodies filled the gyms as live on air I played several new record releases. A pre-selected panel of students then commented on the songs and voted. The audience joined in the act, bestowing or withholding their acclamation. The question was always: Is this record a hit or a miss? Local teens loved these shows, and my Platter Parties quickly established me in that all-important demographic group.

As a member of the National Guard, I noted that the town armory, with its central location and large floor area, was well-suited for hosting teenage dances. My radio show provided the perfect vehicle for promoting such events, and I easily convinced myself that it was a natural step for me to launch a new side career as a dance promoter. I can't remember the name of the band I recruited for my maiden dance, only that they performed for part of the night, and that I played records for the balance of the evening. The dance drew a good crowd of local teens and made a little money.

Before I could schedule a second dance in Astoria, I accepted an offer from a station in Kelso/Longview, Washington and moved up in the world. I say "up" because Kelso/Longview sat upriver from Astoria, was considerably larger than Astoria and was a significant step closer to Seattle. Seattle, that big city to the north where I hoped to ultimately land. In Kelso/Longview, my dance business truly began.

That'll Be the Day
Buddy Holly & the Crickets, 1957

KELSO/LONGVIEW. LIKE IN ASTORIA, a convenient National Guard Armory beckoned me. As part of my military commitment, I transferred to the local guard unit and found them happy to rent their facilities to me on Saturday nights. They enjoyed hiring out their barren hall, as the funds went to the Guard Recreation Association. I was now morning deejay (and play-by-play sports announcer) at radio station KLOG. Influenced by my impassioned pleas, KLOG turned to more of a rock-'n'-roll format and enjoyed a new position as number one with the young adults and teens of the area, which made the station perfect for my dance commercials.

I had a dance location, I had a radio station, I had the right audience, but I didn't have a band. Scouring the Columbia River Basin as far upriver as Portland, Oregon, I found a promising new group calling themselves Vinnie and the Rhythmaires. Vinnie Dumane was the lead guitar player and singer and had put together a neat little band, playing some original material but mostly covers of the year's newest rock-'n'-roll hits. Appearing at the Armory every Saturday night, they instantly became local stars.

Suddenly, I was making nearly $100 a week with my dance business, a substantial windfall when you consider that in 1957, a new Chevy Bel Air convertible cost $3,000, a nice house in town $5,000. The radio station paid me $350 a month. It seems shockingly low by today's standards, but it was a fair sum at that time in a market that size. My earnings from my dance business approached my earnings as a deejay, and I paid a like amount each month to the radio station for the dance commercials I purchased.

More important than earning money, I spent time on stage entertaining audiences during intermissions and the equipment failures so common then. This gave me a chance to test my routines on real people. It's one thing to be the class clown in high school; it's quite another to stand in front of a crowd of teens you've never met personally and try to capture their attention, make them laugh and gain new radio friends.

A Whale of a Tale
Kirk Douglas, 1954

MY TIME IN KELSO WAS ENJOYABLE AND REWARDING, and included one remarkable episode which proved once more the power of radio. Orson Wells scared the entire country on Halloween night in 1938 with tales of Martians invading Earth in his infamous broadcast of *War of the Worlds*; I frightened a few Kelso/Longview citizens in the Spring of 1957 with my tale of a man-eating whale invading the Cowlitz River. It was sort of a '50s-era radio version of Stephen Spielberg's *Jaws*!

Intuition told me that to become a well-known radio figure, I needed to self-promote. They didn't teach that in broadcast school, but somehow I knew it. So, when I read in the paper that attendance was plummeting at the annual Cowlitz River Festival (a local celebration of Spring, fishing or something), I concocted a self-promoting scheme to solve the problem. The very next morning on my show, I announced to my listeners that there was evidence of a man-eating whale in the river dividing the towns of Kelso and Longview. I supported my claim by citing rumors that a woman had disappeared off the back of her houseboat. Her departure, I explained, went unreported because she had been living with her son-in-law who was glad to see her gone. I proclaimed her absence a deep dark mystery, and went on to report other strange events, like numerous footprints leading down to the river's edge with no tracks leading back. It all added up to the likelihood that a carnivorous whale had made its way upriver from the Pacific Ocean and was roaming local waters in search of prey.

Reaction was swift. Normally considered a reliable source of information, radio for years had confined the preposterous to its adventure programs. Breaking the rules, I reported the whale's visit as factual and temporarily landed in trouble. Calls flooded local newspapers and police departments. That evening's edition of the *Longview Daily News* devoted much space to the issue, describing the town's new morning radio star in unflattering terms, including *irresponsible* and *callous*. But forces had been set in motion. Soon, TV news crews from Portland drove up to our little towns to cover the story. Facing television cameras and klieg lights, I bared my plan: I stated to reporters my

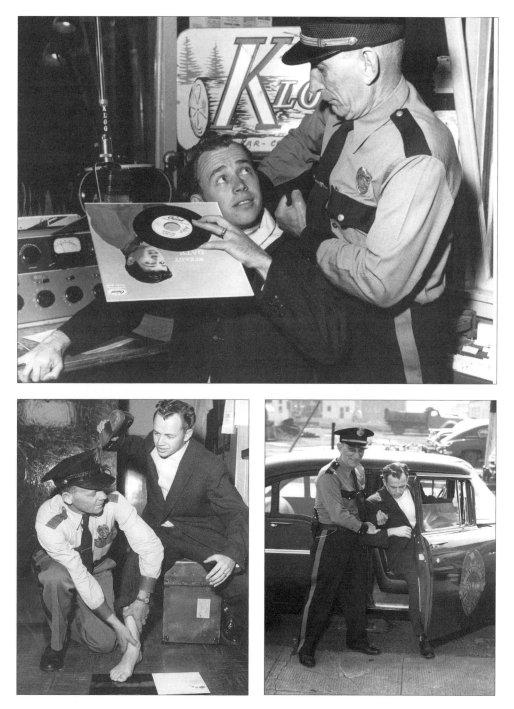

Crime doesn't pay, unless it's harassing make-believe whales

deep concern for the upcoming Cowlitz River Festival. With a man-eating whale swimming around the river, people were likely to stay away in droves, and I felt something must be done about it.

The Chamber of Commerce immediately caught on. After a brief meeting with me, they hurried to the local city councils, trumpeting the widespread attention my whale of a tale had already brought to the River Festival. They requested an ordinance to protect the whale from injury and capture. That afternoon, a joint vote of the Kelso/Longview city councils brought forth a new regulation prescribing stiff penalties for anyone caught disturbing or harming the whale.

Those Portland television reporters returned two days later when I was arrested while on the air doing my show and charged with harassing the whale. The police claimed that my tracks had been found in mud along the river bank. With cameras rolling, they footprinted me as evidence and marched me off to jail, where I remained for an hour until the Chamber of Commerce bailed me out. At a hastily-scheduled hearing, a judge accepted my explanation that I was only feeding the whale. At the same time, he declared that, having attracted so much attention to the whale's presence, I had a special obligation to protect it and ordered me to water-ski up and down the river during festival ceremonies to ensure that no harm befell our prize mammal. Now in full retreat, the *Daily News* ran the story of my arrest along with a picture. Instantly, I was locally famous, and the town's River Festival was rejuvenated thanks to radio and the television and other news coverage my scam had created.

All I Have to Do Is Dream

The Everly Brothers, 1958

BEFORE 1957 WAS OVER, opportunity knocked again, this time in the form of a radio station in Yakima in eastern Washington. They offered me their afternoon drive slot and a program directorship as well. There was no way I could turn them down. The money wasn't that much better—only $450 a month—but my priority at this juncture was not increasing my income so much as furthering my radio career. With a touch of sadness I gave my notice at the station and gifted my dance business to my friends in the National Guard. I advised them how best to run the operation and introduced them to another local deejay who could do their commercials. Later, I was delighted to learn that the Kelso/Longview Guard Recreation Program fund grew to considerable size thanks to revenue from the dances and became the envy of guard units across the state. Good for them!

Soon after arriving in Yakima and starting my new job at KUTI, I learned the station was changing hands. A hero from my high school days, Seattle radio legend Wally Nelskog, decided to sell KUTI to one Harrison Roddick, an industrialist from Chicago who found business in the Windy City too stressful. Roddick took two steps to cure himself: first, he bought a radio station in Yakima and second, he moved out west to operate it. He proved capable of only step one!

Cutie (which was what the station called itself) was the area's top station with a strong signal at 980 on the AM dial. Business flourished. Not long after Roddick's arrival—the Monday after Thanksgiving 1957, to be exact—he called me into his office for a most unhappy meeting. He revealed that he recently joined the Yakima Country Club and was experiencing great humiliation at the hands of his peers. He asked, "Are we playing songs by some outfits called the Bobbettes and the Del-Vikings and by someone named Fats Domino?"

One look at the top songs of 1957 will give you a clue as to my answer, which was not well-received.

"Well, not anymore," Roddick continued. "They make jokes at the country club about the music you play on my radio station, and I won't tolerate it!" He then asked me to follow him out to his car, where he opened the trunk, looked at me and said, "We are no longer Cutie. I will not be part of any station people call *Cutie*! From this day on we will be *Kay-You-Tee-Eye*. We will say it that way. We are going to grow up! I'm not going to be the laughing stock of the country club one more day!"

"And here is our new Kay-You-Tee-Eye music," he went on, pointing to cardboard boxes in the trunk overflowing with new record albums still in their wrappers. "Please take it inside and get it on the air immediately."

I began to look through the several hundred record albums as he proudly announced, "I went to Seattle and picked them out myself!"

I couldn't believe it. Much of the collection was from music's Dark Ages. There was some more recent stuff: Broadway show albums, a record or two by someone named Carmen Cavallero, others from Glenn Miller, Artie Shaw, Liberace and Mel Torme, and the sound track from *American in Paris*, to mention a few. I dutifully transported the music into the library, then headed straight to Roddick's office. Sitting down, I tried to be diplomatic, and was. I tried to be logical, and was. I tried to be persuasive, and failed! I told Roddick I was his supporter. I said, "You've just paid a great deal of money for this radio station, and the high price you paid was based on this station's success and profitable posture. Right?"

He agreed with that part of my speech. I expanded my point.

> Harrison, this station's revenues are due to our large audience and who they are. We're number one in this town with an audience of young people, young families, young singles, and they're a volatile group of consumers which our advertisers want to reach. Be it Sears, Coca-Cola, Budweiser, Ford, the drive-in restaurants or the movie houses, they all pay you the big money they do to reach our audience. The music I select from national surveys to play on the air is the music of that audience. Without it, they will leave the station quicker than it took you to drive back from Seattle!

I can still hear Harrison's next words: "Well, young man, it's obvious you don't agree with what I'm doing. You're fired!"

I generally like it when someone comes directly to the point, but not this time. I could have kicked myself in the teeth. Our second child, Garry, was due in 60 days, and our first, Jerry, was not yet one. I had recently gone to the expense of moving across the state and now, by opening my big mouth and thinking I was so damned smart, I got myself canned. I couldn't have felt any lower had I tried. It was nearly Christmas, I had been in the broadcast business for slightly over a year, a radio station had just fired me and I had done it to myself. Yet, I knew I had acted in Roddick's best interests. I told him the truth.

Harrison Roddick, stuffy Chicago socialite, was resisting change, a perfect example of the reluctance of many people within the broadcast industry in 1957 to face up to the dramatic shift in music tastes the country was experiencing. Whether from stubbornness or blindness or both, Roddick ignored the truth and did it his way, going broke within two years. Meanwhile, I got lucky.

Frosty Fowler, veteran announcer, afternoon deejay and program director at KLOQ across town, was hired by radio station KING to come to Seattle starting February first. Upon learning of my sudden availability, his station immediately contacted me and offered to make me Frosty's replacement.

My answer was affirmative, but KLOQ was such a small station, they couldn't afford to pay me anything until I assumed my on-air duties. Knowing this, I hastened to Sears, responding to their ad in the newspaper for Christmas help, and spent the next month selling overalls, socks, underwear and work coats (great Christmas gifts in farm country). After New Years, I went on the street for my new station selling advertising time until Fowler left. Working on commission only, I made 1,000 badly-needed dollars in January, which KLOQ was happy to pay me. Everything turned out well, the timing and circumstances were good. Once I was back on air, my new station gave me total freedom, and we quickly assumed the rock-'n'-roll lead in the community.

Having survived a near catastrophe at Cutie, I found an obstacle in the path of my dance promotion business. Six months earlier, a promoter from Oregon named Pat Mason had focused his sights on the Yakima market and set up his own teen dance operation. He had the Yakima National Guard Armory tied up, and I decided to adopt the policy of "If you can't beat 'em, join 'em" and learn as much as I could. Mason was tuned in to the new trends in the business and was booking dates for national recording acts that had begun touring the country. We became friends, and soon I found myself recording and voicing his radio spots for all the stations in the area. In return, Pat made me emcee of his dances, and I was content for the moment.

I started to make up for lost income from live dances by making frequent appearances at junior high and high school sock hops. (That's what they called rock-'n'-roll dances held in school gyms, where the coaches understandably wanted the floors protected, and shoes were forbidden; kids danced in their socks; thus, a new buzz word was coined, *sock hop*.) I went out of the box and developed a beefed-up sound system with heavy wood cabinets capable of handling cranked-up volume and enhancing the bass. My equipment included two turntables for playing records. In addition to my stacks of 45s, I brought along some 33⅓ albums as well and put on a show along with the music, employing all kinds of gimmicks to keep shy teens involved and dancing. Rock-'n'-roll dancing was new to many of them, and what few patterned steps they knew they had learned mostly by watching Dick Clark's *American Bandstand* on ABC. The old ballroom style of dancing was passé. As Danny and the Juniors sang, "Rock and roll is here to stay!" At every sock hop, a few self-conscious teens were reluctant to jump in, but it never took too long to get them dancing along with everyone else. Many teenagers just improvised.

40-TOP-TUNES
from
KLOQ-RADIO 1390 ON DIAL

Compiled from information secured from Yakima's Juke Boxes,
Record and Sheet Music Sales, and KLOQ's Dee Jays.

TOP 40 TUNES FOR WEEK ENDING JUNE 8TH.

Is	Was		
1	30	RUMBLE	LINK WRAY
2	1	PURPLE PEOPLE EATER	SHEB WOOLEY
3	2	OH, LONESOME ME	DON GIBSON
4	7	HIGH SCHOOL CONFIDENTIAL	JERRY LEE LEWIS
5	4	ALL THE TIME	JOHNNY MATHIS
6	11	GUESS THINGS JUST HAPPEN THAT WAY	JOHNNY CASH
7	5	BIG MAN	4 PREPS
8	13	ENDLESS SLEEP	J. WITHERSPOON
9	3	WE BELONG TOGETHER	ROBERT & JOHNNY
10	9	I CAN'T STOP LOVING YOU	DON GIBSON
11	6	ALL I HAVE TO DO IS DREAM	EVERLYS
12	40	FOR YOUR LOVE	ED TOWNSEND
13	10	DRIFTING & DREAMING	RUSS HAMILTON
14	8	SECRETLY	JIMMIE RODGERS
15	21	I LOVE YOU SO	CHANTELS
16	23	WHEN THE BOYS TALK ABOUT THE GIRLS	VALERIE CARR
17	12	HANG UP MY ROCK & ROLL SHOES	CHUCK WILLIS
18	16	JOHNNY B. GOOD	CHUCK BERRY
19	18	RAVE ON	BUDDY HOLLY
30	14	EL RANCHO ROCK	CHAMPS
21	28	SATURDAY NITE DANCE	TERESA BREWER
22	29	JOSHUA & FLIP	LAURIE LONDON
23	19	ZORRO & FLIP	CHORDETTES
24	34	DING DONG	McGUIRES
25		TRUE FINE MAMA	LITTLE RICHARD
26	15	DO YOU WANNA DANCE	BOBBY FREEMAN
27		SINGING HILLS	BILLY VAUGHN
28	20	CRAZY LOVE	PAUL ANKA
29		POOR LITTLE FOOL	RICKY'S LP
30	24	FLIP FLOP AND BOP	FLOYD CRAMER
31	17	LOOKING BACK	NAT COLE
32		MOONLIGHT BAY	DRIFTERS
33	32	THIS HAPPY FEELING	DEBBIE
34	38	BLUE HAWAII	FRANK CHACKSFIELD
35	39	DREAM	BETTY JOHNSON
36	33	WEAR MY RING AROUND YOUR NECK	ELVIS
37	22	JENNIE LEE	JAN & ARNIE
38	26	HOW WILL I KNOW MY LOVE	ANNETTE
39	25	DANCE ONLY WITH ME	PERRY COMO
40		LITTLE ROCKIN' DEACON	PLAS JOHNSON

KLOQ PICKS of   DAN K. - LONELY BOY, KENNY LOREN
  the WEEK: PAUL B. - REBEL ROUSER, DUANE EDDY
                 JER K. - WHAT'S SO BAD ABOUT IT, SARAH VAUGHN

HOT BISCUITS - NEW PLATTERS; NEW PATTI PAGE, BOTH SIDES
LOTS MORE MUSIC ON KLOQ — 1390
★ ALBUM OF THE WEEK . . . S'AWFUL NICE, RAY CONNIFF!

Top 40 list from Pat O'Day's Yakima days

Working with Pat Mason, I made some interesting acquaintances. He brought national groups to the Northwest and played them in Portland as well as in small cities in Oregon and Washington. He avoided Seattle and cautioned me "That town will eat you alive!" I chose to ignore his warning. [Such views are relative. Pat was from Seaside, Oregon, another small village on the Pacific coast, and Seattle made him uncomfortable, as teen dances had not yet been introduced there.] Through Pat, I met Bill Haley and His Comets, Jerry Lee Lewis, Gene Vincent and the Blue Caps, Fats Domino, Lloyd Price, Phil and Don Everly and Eddie Cochran, a veritable *Who's Who* of rock-'n'-roll pioneers. (Eddie later died in an auto accident while riding with Gene Vincent in a chauffeured car outside of London; Gene was seriously injured but survived. Eddie had the big hits *Summertime Blues* and *C'mon Everybody*.)

As I became more comfortable working with such stars, I started to probe them for stories and reports of the performance business in other parts of the country. Again and again, they spoke of how this or that promoter stiffed them. By *stiffed* they meant being told by the promoter beforehand "Okay guys, you go on stage and I will pay you as soon as the show is over" and learning afterwards that he was one of those business sorts whose *modus operandi* was to "scoot with the loot." Other horror stories included showing up for a date, only to discover the promoter forgot or had not bothered to set up a sound system, forcing the performers to beg the crowd to come closer to the stage so they could at least shout the vocals to them. Or arriving in town and learning that their appearance had been poorly promoted or that no tickets had been sold. Sometimes they'd show up at the auditorium and find it locked and dark and the promoter nowhere in sight. Bounced checks, lousy (literally and figuratively) hotel accommodations or none at all, promised meals never served, stages not set up, pianos missing or out of tune—the list of the indignities they suffered went on and on. Life on the road for these pioneering rockers was all too often a frightening ordeal, consistent only in its inconsistency. The performers felt pain and disappointment. I saw opportunity.

One evening, while unwinding after a dance, I asked Fats Domino the Big Question: "Fats, if a promoter came to you and said, 'Here's my checkbook. Here are my finances. Can I handle all your shows, everywhere, every night? And I promise I'll make everything perfect for you.' What would you say?"

Fats rolled his eyes (I loved this guy), looked at me and said, "'Yes, sir!' That's what I'd say. But there ain't no such promoter."

Yes! Yes! Yes! I thought to myself, *There's a real opportunity here!*

Gotta Travel On
Billy Grammer, 1959

MY BROADCASTING CAREER CAME FIRST and, in just over a year, I was on the road again following my radio dreams. Uncertain whether I was ready yet for the big time, I wasn't sending out applications or audition tapes as has forever been the custom among ambitious jocks. Therefore, I was surprised when a call came in for me one day from radio station KAYO in Seattle. Their sales manager was driving across the state listening to the radio and happened upon one of my broadcasts. Intrigued, he asked someone to tape my show. After listening to the tape, they decided to offer me a job sight unseen. Here was my chance to return to my home country, to work as a morning newsman and afternoon disc jockey in the Big City. They flew me to Seattle to explain the benefits, but they could have saved their money. My answer would have been an immediate and emphatic *Yes!* with or without the plane ride.

Arriving back in Seattle in January 1959 was thrilling. In the aftermath of World War II, there was an oversupply of deejay types on the market, and most big radio jobs were held by men much older than I. Bucking the odds, there I was, where I had always dreamed of being: on air in Seattle, with my career advancing at a pace well beyond my most fervent prayers.

Born Paul Berg, I proudly shared that name with my father and used it throughout my early years in radio. In time, I sensed that something was wrong, that an important element was missing. My name lacked recall power, a fact I noticed in the three small markets where I helped bring radio stations to the top. Despite personal appearances, station promotions and other efforts to establish a high profile, I failed to achieve the sort of name recognition I felt I should. Maybe my name didn't match the devil-may-care radio style I embraced. Maybe my name was hard to remember. Maybe…Who knows? For whatever reason or reasons, the name Paul Berg wasn't working to my satisfaction. The Seattle station hired me not for my name, but for what they heard on the air. I decided the time was right to change identities. During a conversation with Ted Bell, the veteran program director at KAYO, we kicked around some ideas and soon determined I liked the idea of being a *Pat*. For some reason, I felt more like a *Pat* than a *Paul*. Then we tossed around several Irish last names, which made sense because I'm part Irish. Which one of us suggested *O'Day* first I don't recall, but I do remember liking it the first time I uttered it: "O'Day! Pat O'Day! That's it! That's me!" Contrary to what some people have written, I didn't take my name from O'Dea, the Catholic high school in Seattle. Also, I preferred not to spell my new last name the same way the former University of Wisconsin football placekicker, Pat O'Dea, spelled his. (At that time, he held the NCAA distance record for field goals.) One morning, Ted Bell and I decided on *Pat O'Day*. It was as simple as that.

Back on my home turf at last, I realized I was forgetting one of my youthful fantasies. Growing up, I had dreamed countless times I would make it big, that someday my thousands of former schoolmates and friends would tune in their radios and find their old buddy Paul Berg holding forth on the dial. Starting in junior high school, I told everyone who would listen that I was going to be a radio announcer *in Seattle*. The side of me ruled by my healthy ego said, "You need to show them that Paul Berg has made it!" The side of me that kept my priorities straight told me, "You can't be Paul Berg any longer. You're Pat O'Day now. If you work hard enough, stay dedicated and continue to improve, all your old friends will figure out it's you."

So it was that on January 15, 1959, the newly-christened Pat O'Day spoke for the first time into a microphone over the airwaves of Seattle. The next few months were filled with all sorts of personal appearances. Within weeks, I found myself in great demand for high school and community events. The station encouraged this by plastering my mug on numerous billboards around the area. Salary-wise, I was still lagging behind. A monthly paycheck for $650 didn't go very far living in Seattle with a wife and two little O'Days, Jerry and Garry, to support. Additional income had to be found, and pronto. I had this vision which wouldn't stop running across my mental screen in an infinite loop: dances, lots of dances, dances with major stars, dances across the state, dances with the local rock bands then beginning to proliferate, dances with Pat O'Day at the mike, dances, dances, dances. It was driving me.

Tall Cool One
The Wailers, 1959

THUS, I WAS ON HIGH ALERT WHEN TWO MEMBERS of a rock-'n'-roll band from Tacoma—a group calling themselves *The Wailers*—walked into the station one day to talk about a hit record they had recently released. *Tall Cool One* was already a Top-10 hit nationally and had landed them a spot on Dick Clark's *American Bandstand*. Lead singer/keyboardist Kent Morrill and guitarist (at the time) John Greek introduced themselves, and we sat down to get acquainted. They spoke about their need to find work, and I commented about the apparent lack of teen dances and dance halls in the Seattle area. They mentioned one possible venue I should consider, an ornate old ballroom, the Spanish Castle, a former roadhouse from the '20s and '30s on Highway 99 midway between Seattle and Tacoma. It was owned for years by the Knudsen and Morrill (no relation to Kent) families and now was busy only on Saturday nights when they turned on the lights so a traditional big band-type group, the Gordon Greene Orchestra, could play their grand old swing music. Six nights a week the place sat dark, and even Greene's crowds were rapidly diminishing. The Castle faced an uncertain future and needed a boost.

There in the lobby, Morrill, Greek and I struck a deal. They knew of a car club wanting to do a fund-raiser. I suggested we stage a dance together at the Spanish Castle and make it a benefit, which would get us free airtime on the radio. I could oversee the dance, we could use the Wailers' music and my voice for the public service announcements and I could coax local stations to play them. The band would receive their cut off the top, the ballroom a guaranteed rental fee plus a percentage of the take and the car club the balance of the proceeds. This setup offered a perfect opportunity to test the potential of the Seattle market for my dances without risking my meager personal resources.

The evening proved a giant success. Over 1,000 fans went home happy, the car club was all smiles and the Wailers were thrilled. Before I left the Spanish Castle that night, Wes Morrill and I sat down and hammered out what proved to be a historic long-term deal. I would take over Friday nights at the Castle and underwrite many of the costs, including artists, sound systems, security and advertising. The Castle would receive 25 percent of the gross ticket sales and keep all proceeds from concession sales. They would pay all parking lot and cleanup costs, some of the security expenses and the insurance. Seventy-five percent of the gross ticket sales would go to me to cover the costs I underwrote. Anything left over after I paid my bills would be my profit.

Monday morning I began contacting rock bands in the area, including a Seattle group called the Frantics who had just signed a deal with local Dolton

Records, which released their material nationally through Liberty Records. Auditioning the newer bands, some of which were already appearing at high school dances, I began to fill our schedule. The Wailers, by far the most important act in the region, agreed to play the Castle at least once a month. Within three weeks, the place was exploding with energy from sold-out shows on Friday nights. I began advertising these affairs as *Pat O'Day Dances* and sharpened my focus. It was plain to see — the new kid in town had a tiger by the tail.

It's Only Make Believe
Conway Twitty, 1958

NOVEMBER 26, 1959, THE DAY BEFORE THANKSGIVING, was an off night for a country and western tour being run through the area by a local promoter, Jack Roberts. One member of this tour was a young Conway Twitty, who enjoyed three crossover hits on MGM Records: *Mona Lisa*, *Lonely Blue Boy* and *It's Only Make Believe*. Roberts called me and wanted to know whether I would like to buy Twitty for the night. I answered in the affirmative, figuring I could double my normal ticket price, pay Twitty his fee and just maybe hit a home run. The next day I recorded some spots, booked the ads on several local radio stations and crossed my fingers. Come Wednesday night, a King County Sheriff and a district fire marshal made us cut off ticket sales after 2,200 teenagers had stuffed themselves into the Castle. That left a long line of disappointed fans standing in the cold wishing the place had a larger capacity and gave me an inkling of what might be. Twitty roused the crowd and filled my coffers with the greatest one-day take of my young life.

You never want to lose momentum, and you will if you stand still. To keep moving forward, I branched out immediately to the city of Bremerton on the Kitsap Peninsula, a 45-minute ferry ride from Seattle across Puget Sound. This was old home week for me. I graduated from Bremerton High School and Olympic College and knew practically everyone in town. Recreation Hall in the Sheridan Park Navy Housing Project had good capacity and a nice-sized stage. Used primarily for basketball, offering spaciousness and a hardwood floor, it was the perfect venue to add to my lineup. By Christmas 1959, Pat O'Day Dances featured two dances a week, one at the Spanish Castle on Fridays, the other at Sheridan Park Hall on Saturdays. Like the Castle, Sheridan Park earned a profit from the first night. Two of my mentors from college days came on board to help—Ken Chase, by then a teacher and coach at the high school, and Bob Miller, who coached me when I played basketball in the Bremerton City League. They were joined by Wes Henry, a Bremerton police officer who issued more traffic tickets to a teenage Paul Berg than either one of us could count. Ken, Bob and Wes comprised my Saturday night staff, and things couldn't possibly have gone better. So they didn't. All of a sudden, I found myself engulfed in the second major crisis of my radio career. It would not be the last.

Since my arrival at KAYO, the station had fought an all-out radio war with another Seattle station, KOL. Our enemy captured the Top 40 leadership in town in late 1957 and had defended it to the last man ever since. I went to work for KAYO to reinforce the staff and take part in a frontal assault on KOL's position. KAYO was owned at that time by a successful business woman, Jessica Longston. She had two other stations in the state in smaller markets which were running well, but the operation of her big one puzzled her. For years, KAYO veered first one way, then another and then another, and at present there were too many generals at headquarters trying to command the troops and plot strategy.

Soon the station's committee approach to waging war (it *was* war) brought disaster. In the Fall of 1959, Ted Bell, the longtime program director who helped me choose my name, retired. In November, a new PD arrived out of Stockton, California—Ray Golden. I am sure Ray was a wonderful person, you know the type: loving to his wife, kind to his mother and children and dog. He even had a college degree in communications, earned fair and square, no doubt. Still, you could have taken everything he knew about the new kind of radio sweeping the country, poured it all into a thimble and still had room for your thumb. With Golden as the station's new generalissimo, our reversal was instant.

He quickly imported two aging deejays who had worked in Seattle radio years before—Bob Salter and Dale Starkey. Both had been pioneers in the days when disc jockeys were still a new element in the radio business, a time when pace, energy and excitement were not factors. In fact, Salter was my hero when I was in school, and I respected and liked him. Years before, their laid-back style worked reasonably well. But make no mistake. In 1959, their approach to the radio art, when compared with a yawn, made the yawn appear more potent.

When asked what they wanted, one of them expressed a preference for the station's afternoon drive slot, presently occupied by me. He was granted his wish, and I was moved to middays. Even worse, Salter and Starkey were given complete freedom to select their own music. Forget about the day's hits, ignore the songs that were captivating America, they could play whatever music they wanted. This totally disrupted the station's flow and threw us off target. We were fighting, I thought, to win the hearts and minds of teens and young adults away from KOL. Overnight, our new target audience became all those young adults out there who didn't much care for rock-'n'-roll or Top 40 radio. Golden and Salter and Starkey were convinced that such an audience existed, but I knew of no group of any substance or size that matched that description.

At the all-staff meeting held the Monday after Thanksgiving 1959, I had just returned from a weekend in Yakima spent consulting for the station I departed from 10 months before. On Wednesday I had emceed my big Conway Twitty victory at the Spanish Castle. Somewhere between the Castle and Yakima, I developed a world-class case of laryngitis. The station manager was kind enough to state that my opinion was important and to inquire as to my thoughts on the new plan. I grabbed a pen, wrote my response on a piece of paper in big block letters and held it up for all to see: *A FATAL MISTAKE!* The manager was indulging me. The new plan was already in place, and my opinion wasn't needed. And now that it was known, it wasn't much appreciated. Yet, I was just trying to be honest, like I had been with Harrison Roddick at KUTI. To me, being the second-place rock-'n'-roll station in a market like Seattle offered higher ratings and greater revenue potential than going after some imaginary audience.

Though barely out of diapers and walking, rock-'n'-roll music, properly used, could propel a station to the top of the ratings battle in its broadcast area. Stations were doing it successfully all over the country. Two years before, KOL used rock music to take over the number one spot in Seattle, and KAYO could do it, too. Instead, I was surrounded that morning by people, led by Ray Golden, who wished it would all quietly go away and leave them in peace. None of them understood rock. They were frightened by it, and they were out of their comfort zones trying to work with it. The writing on the wall was plain to see, but I seemed to be the only one at the station able—or willing—to read it.

He'll Have to Go

Jim Reeves, 1960

ANOTHER DEVELOPMENT INFLUENCING KAYO'S DECISION was radio station KJR'S recent announcement that they were abandoning their futile attempt to succeed as an adult music station and were going to embrace instead this new rock-'n'-roll/Top 40 format many seemed to be succeeding with. This news caught my attention. I grew up listening to KJR. The station served as Seattle's NBC network affiliate during my youth and commandeered my time after school with programs like *Jack Armstrong, the All-American Boy, The Green Hornet* and other adventure serials. In the aftermath of the sea changes in the radio marketplace brought about by television, KJR shed its network ties and went independent. Like so many other stations that did the same, they struggled to find an identity that worked and made money.

In the mid-'50s, they took a stab at being a rock-'n'-roll station, with people like Bob Salter, Dick Stokke and Wally Nelskog, but gave up too soon. I loved the call letters K–J–R, and the station had a great signal at 950 on the AM dial. If KAYO meant to throw in the towel in its battle with KOL, I knew that behind a mike at KJR was where I had to be. KOL was winning the Seattle rock radio war by default. KAYO could have defeated them, but they were surrendering without a fight. I had already made my decision to leave KAYO when, out of the blue, a phone call came from the new program director at KJR, John Stone. My growing dance empire was about to be threatened.

At my interview, Stone delivered a speech which shocked me. He said,

> I love your work on the air, and we need you here, so I am willing to offer you a position. But I think you need me more than I need you. I hear KAYO is changing formats, and you will be dead in the water. I'll hire you for the six-to-nine evening slot, but if I do, I want you to make me a partner in your dance business. If you'll split your dances 50-50 with me, you can have the job.

I don't mean to imply that I invented the teen dance business in the Northwest or anywhere else. Teen dances were being held in ballrooms and Grange halls and armories all across the nation, so I wasn't alone. But the business was still in its embryonic stage, and I felt I was developing the proverbial better mousetrap. I envisioned a chain of venues hosting dances that delivered quality and consistency and showed respect for the young audience. Plus, I wanted to make sure that parents could feel confident their kids were spending their nights in a safe and secure environment. With some investment to back the development of local bands, and with national recording stars added to the mix, a new entertainment genre could be developed with Pat O'Day Dances taking the lead. I foresaw a business with real legs, one which would benefit my on-air career and the radio station where I worked.

I was now on the horns of a classic dilemma. This guy Stone was trying to sell me the new job I so badly wanted. I thought, *Why should I risk my family's welfare just to provide him with a stipend for employing me?* He came to Seattle as a veteran from WNOE in New Orleans, while I was still young in the business, and I wondered whether this was how things were done way down yonder in Louisiana. I decided quickly, focusing on my goal of making radio my life's work. I badly wanted to be a part of KJR's charge at success, and my present station was on a one-way trip to radio oblivion. I agreed to split my profits from the Spanish Castle with Stone, with the proviso that any new dances I opened elsewhere would remain my sole property. He instructed me to keep his involvement confidential, another part of doing business the New Orleans way, no doubt.

In mid-December I resigned from KAYO. For Christmas they sent a new television set to my home and pleaded with me not to leave, but the die was cast, and we went our separate ways. On New Years Day 1960, I went on the air at KJR for the first time. Little did I know it would be my home for the next 15 years.

Greg Gilbert, then a fledgling teenage photographer, today a shooter with The Seattle Times, *snapped this picture of Pat O'Day em-ceeing a DJ party at Olympia High School in* 1963.

4 – *Good Timin'*
Jimmy Jones, 1960

I OWE MUCH OF MY SUCCESS TO LUCK and good timing, and my timing for entering the dance business was perfect. Before, the East Coast and South were the seedbeds of rock-'n'-roll. Now, the West Coast was step-ping up, and new recording stars were emerging weekly. In Seattle, encouraged by the new teen dance halls and an opportunity to earn money playing the music they loved, a growing number of young bands were starting to come into their own. Bands you've heard of and some you've never heard of made vital contributions to the Northwest music scene and proved themselves viable ticket sellers. Little Bill and the Blue Notes from Tacoma, who had a hit with *I Love an Angel*. The Ventures, another Tacoma band, who reached number one nationally with *Walk —Don't Run*. The Dynamics (with lead guitar player Larry Coryell, who went on to national fame as a jazz guitarist). Tiny Tony and the Statics. The Dave Lewis Combo. The Frantics. Merrilee Rush (she of *Angel of the Morning* fame) and the Turnabouts. And a young group from Portland by way of Boise — Paul Revere and the Raiders with Mark Lindsay. All became regular acts at my dances.

Louie Louie
The Wailers, 1961 / The Kingsmen, 1963
STILL, IT WAS THOSE WAILERS AMONG LOCAL and regional bands that drew the biggest crowds. Their appeal was remarkably enhanced by the vocals of Gail Harris, who added so much vocally and visually. Only 13 years

old when she joined the group, she could easily have passed for a 21-year-old. Her extraordinary eye appeal high and low transfixed the teenage males in the crowd. Think of Jennifer Aniston from *Friends* and you have Gail Harris' face. Add to this stunning package one earth-shaking voice, strong, throaty, powerful, bluesy — a voice, like the rest of her, far beyond her years — and you have yourself one knockout package. In her post-Wailer years, Gail married a talented piano player, and the two of them formed a musical duo, working professionally for many years.

The Wailers cemented their position at the top of the heap when they released the debut single on their own label, Etiquette, the first rock-'n'-roll interpretation of rock's national anthem, *Louie Louie*. Their treatment of the Richard Berry song, featuring the voice of the late Rockin' Robin Roberts, went to number one on the Northwest music charts three times over a four-year period. Nowhere was the song played more often than on KJR. It knocked me out the first time I heard it, and I promoted it every chance I got. During my frequent conference calls with other program directors around the country, I touted *Louie Louie*, telling my cohorts they would have a giant hit on their hands if they played it for a week. "Why not beat the competition with this one?" I asked them. "Go ahead, be the first to give it a try!"

My pleading was to no avail. My friends around the country passed the song off as another one of my "O'Day Seattle oddities." They knew of my extensive dance circuit and the rising number of Northwest bands, and that's what they thought the Wailers were: just another Northwest band, nothing more. They all refused to give the Wailers' *Louie Louie* a shot. In their defense, at first listening the song *is* a bit weird, definitely atypical of the rock hits of that era. Another factor contributing to the Wailers' inability to get their *Louie Louie* off the ground was the eventual departure of Rockin' Robin from the group's revue. Robin left for college in California, only to be killed a few short years later in an automobile accident in the San Francisco area. Kent Morrill stepped in and proved he could perfectly replicate Robin's *Louie Louie* routine, but still he wasn't Rockin' Robin Roberts. Nonetheless, the Wailers were strong with Buck Ormsby, Mike Burk, Rich Dangel, Mark Marush and Kent.

In 1964, the Wailers added to their lineup the sax, keyboard and vocal genius of another young Tacoman, Ron Gardner. Ron was a brilliant musician and song writer, and I employed him many times to sing some of the radio commercials I was constantly producing. He also recorded a solo album at our studio in Seattle. In the 1992 holiday season, while selling Christmas trees to supplement his music income, Ron fell asleep inside the house trailer on the lot. The trailer caught fire, and Ron didn't escape in time. Yet another world-class rock-'n'-roll talent was lost.

On one of the occasions when *Louie Louie* rose to number one in the Seattle market, I took my plea directly to Bob Scaff and Don Blocker, who worked for Al Bennett at Liberty Records. I had nothing to gain but relief from my frustration. I *knew* the Wailers' *Louie Louie* would become a national hit were only someone outside of the Seattle-Portland-Spokane markets to give it a chance. Scaff talked to Bennett, and Bennett agreed to have Liberty distribute the band's second Etiquette pressing of *Louie Louie*. Later I realized he was only appeasing me to stay in my good graces. Bennett knew full well that KJR was one of the five most important radio stations in the country when it came to breaking a hit, and he wanted to keep me happy. Liberty (later Imperial/Liberty) put absolutely no effort behind the record. When I called a couple of stations back east, I was told they had not even received promo copies. With no one at Liberty making an effort to get it played, the Wailers' *Louie Louie* once again languished.

One year later, the bright owner of Seattle-based Jerden Records, Jerry Dennon, discovered that a Portland group, The Kingsmen, had just recorded *Louie Louie*. From listening to the Wailers' version on juke boxes and 45s, they were able to duplicate the song. Dennon signed the group and placed their recording with Scepter/Wand Records in New York. That helped created the impression that The Kingsmen were an East Coast group. Top 40 radio program directors sat up and took notice. Much to the frustration of the Wailers, it went on to become one of the biggest hits in rock-'n'-roll history. On December 2, 1963, the Kingsmen's rendition of *Louie Louie* reached number one on the national charts.

I write this with no intention of taking anything away from the Kingsmen. They were then, and remain today, one of the most entertaining and accomplished rock bands in history. These days they bill themselves as "America's Number One Party Band," and deservedly so. But for anyone who grew up in Seattle in the '60s, there will never be a substitute for the Wailers' original rendition of *Louie Louie*. The Kingsmen, always professional, always entertaining, have made hundreds upon hundreds of appearances over the years. They are dear friends. To the world at large, they personify *Louie Louie*. I congratulate them, and Jerry Dennon as well. They must concede one point, however: Much of Seattle still thinks that *Louie Louie* means the Wailers.

And how big is *Louie Louie* in Seattle? At Mariners baseball games at Safeco Field, *Louie Louie* is played right after *Take Me Out to the Ball Game* during the seventh-inning stretch. Go to any University of Washington Husky game and you will hear the band play the song several times at least. Like Paul Harvey says, "And now you know the rest of the story."

Be-bop-a-Lula
Gene Vincent, 1956

JANUARY 1960 FOUND ME EXPANDING my fledgling dance circuit to Tacoma in the south and Lynnwood in the north. Tacoma had an old dance hall, called the Crescent, unused since the departure of troops from Fort Lewis at the end of World War II. This facility operated nightly during the war and was now a little on the grungy side, though traces of its former grandeur remained. The teens never noticed either way, they were there for the music and dancing. Cobwebs in the rafters, cigarette burns on the floor and a broken window here and there didn't bother them one iota. Fifteen miles north of Seattle, Lynnwood's Rollaway Skating Rink became the fourth cornerstone of our growing dance chain. With four locations, I could finally afford to bring in big-name musicians, for now I could offer them four consecutive nights of work or, in some cases, two nights, two shows a night at two locations.

Later that same month, Gene Vincent called. Gene, with his group the Blue Caps, stormed to the top of the music charts in the late '50s with his Capitol Records hits *Be-bop-a-Lula, Dance to the Bop, Lotta Lovin'* and *Wear My Ring*. Taking advantage of his sudden fame, he joined Eddie Cochran for a tour of England. Their chauffeured car crashed outside of London, killing Cochran and seriously injuring Vincent, exacerbating leg problems stemming from a motorcycle accident in 1956. Gene recovered slowly and was crippled for life due to extensive leg injuries. He now lived in Portland, Oregon, flat broke and needing a break. His group left him, and he was hitting the bottle hard. He reminded me of our conversations three years earlier in Yakima and asked me to give him a chance to perform at one of my dances. "I don't want much," he said, "just a chance to work again and make a few bucks and cover my expenses." He hesitated, then added, "I have a problem, Pat. I don't have a band."

"That's not a problem, Gene," I answered. "I can find you a band," and the deal was done.

I no longer remember which band I recruited to back Gene. Whoever it was, I gave them a copy of his album and told them to memorize every lick. My message to them went: "Gene Vincent is coming back to Seattle, and, dammit, we're going to do this right!" We built up his return like it was the second coming of Christ. Gene had been out of the music picture for well over a year, and I thought this would work to our advantage. He couldn't walk without a cane, but his unique voice was undamaged. The commercials I produced for the occasion were the most emotional of my career, before or since. And they worked. Every ticket was sold, every facility jammed. We could have sold twice as many tickets. How Gene managed it, I still wonder. He could hardly walk, yet he threw himself into his songs with an intensity that transported his audiences. They loved listening and dancing to his songs and loudly acknowledged his bravery. Gene, in turn, was thrilled. After the final show, he was in tears as I paid him four times the previously-agreed-to amount.

He asked, "You saw it all, Pat. They loved me! Do you think I can make it back to the top?"

I gave him a hug and said, "Gene, I don't know why not!"

Sadly, he never did.

It's You Alone
The Wailers, 1966

EVERYTHING I TOUCHED IN THOSE MAGICAL DAYS seemed to turn to gold. Early in March, we grabbed a package of touring singers that included Johnny Burnette (*Dreamin'*), his brother Dorsey Burnette (*Tall Oak Tree*) and, fresh from an appearance on Dick Clark's show, Johnny Preston (*Running Bear*) and booked them for a string of shows, every one a sellout. My dances were big news, and their popularity grew and grew. By 1961, I had expanded eastward across Lake Washington to Bellevue's Lake Hills Roller Rink. In Burlington, Washington, well to the north, we contracted for the Roller Dome. And we were actively searching for suitable locations in Olympia, Everett and other Washington cities.

That year we brought in Jerry Lee Lewis, Roy Orbison, Bobby Vee, Dick & Dee Dee and a rising duo from Los Angeles, Jan & Dean. Even with all of that high-priced, high-profile talent, our biggest draw remained the Wailers. Supreme rulers of our Northwest dance circuit, they performed *Louie Louie* twice every dance, and the crowds always went nuts. The group helped secure their popularity by coming out with their second album, *The Fabulous Wailers at the*

Castle. The recording resulted from a joint brainstorm. The band and I decided it would be a good idea to record their music live at the scene. We wanted to capture the energy of one of their dance performances, an elusive quality impossible to duplicate in the studio. For the occasion, I cobbled together a hodgepodge of microphones, along with a 10-channel broadcast mixing board.

On a Friday night, in front of a packed house, the music was recorded. I served as engineer/mixer. Afterward, when I listened to the tape, I thought it sounded good but needed presence. The next week we took the tapes to a studio equipped with an equalizer (the same equipment nearly every radio station has today, but unique at that time). That equalizer was designed for motion picture sound tracks, and with it we were able to enrich the bass and crisp up the vocals. Still, something was missing. I solved the problem by positioning a set of good-quality speakers at the end of the hallway at the old Commercial Recorders studio at Fifth and Pike in Seattle. I placed a microphone at the opposite end of the hallway, and the echo effect proved just enough to establish a large auditorium sound.

The Fabulous Wailers at the Castle became a big seller for the group, and somehow George Harrison of the Beatles acquired a copy. In 1964, when he and his fellow Liverpudlians visited Seattle on their first American tour, George inquired about the Wailers and asked whether they were still together. He said that he listened to their Castle album so many times he nearly wore the grooves off, so impressed was he by their music. To my relief, he said nothing about how well the album was produced and engineered.

Many elements made up the dance phenomenon. At the dances themselves, everything was cool. That was the operative word, *cool*. I would send my deejays from the station to emcee the intermissions, which presented a great opportunity for them to see and be seen and to give away promotional copies of records. This was also their best chance to meet and talk with listeners and learn to understand them. Hopefully, this new-found wisdom would be reflected in their on-air performances and result in better entertainment. Such appearances by KJR jocks were at all costs to be devoid of false excitement. No shouting allowed. No hype. Be adult, be funny, be cool. And always remember, the real stars are the bands, not the deejays.

America in the early '60s was vastly different from America today. Parents still retained some semblance of control over their teenagers. Alcohol was forbidden around our dance venues, and security officers patrolled the parking lots checking for people drinking in cars. Persons so found were instructed to leave. If you smelled of alcohol or appeared inebriated, you were turned away at the door. If your behavior became an issue, you were ejected from the building, no questions asked. We refused admission to anyone 21 or over, likewise to anyone 14 or under. And, believe it or not, these rules worked. We were the toughest deal in town and the coolest deal in town, both at the same time.

Great Balls of Fire
Jerry Lee Lewis, 1957

MY DANCE BUSINESS KEPT ME IN CONSTANT CONTACT with some of the most important talents in the music business. Roy Orbison, in particular, stands out. He was a close friend, a gentlemen and a genuine, deep, lovable human being. Summers, he and his band worked for me up to 20 nights in a row at dances around the state. Like most bands then, Roy and his group traveled in station wagons pulling U-Haul trailers stuffed full with their equipment. The undeveloped state of the concert business allowed them to earn money this way and stay in touch with the public. Record royalties alone still couldn't pay everyone's bills. Work like this was essential for Roy and the others, and my Northwest dance circuit was the only place in the country where they could perform night after night, always within short driving distance, for one promoter. That crazy Yakima dream of mine was coming true.

While working with Roy Orbison was a joy, working with Jerry Lee Lewis presented challenges. In 1958, not long after *Great Balls of Fire* became a hit, Jerry Lee's career, at its very apex, crashed. In a London hotel, reporters inquired as to the identity of the young lady with him. She confessed to one scribe she was his wife (his third) and, under further questioning, revealed that she was also his second cousin, Myra, only 13 years old. While fine for the backwoods and bayous of Louisiana, the Brits declared, such tawdry goings-on had no place in the city of Buckingham Palace and Westminster Abbey. Nor, as it turned out, was the couple particularly welcome on the streets of middle-class America. The press back home seized this chance to attack the moral degradation they all knew permeated the world of rock-'n'-roll. Personally, I'm not able to judge whether God considers marriage to one's 13-year-old cousin a major deviation from His divine plan, but the American press corps assumed it was. Showing no mercy, the media barbecued, fricasseed and fried Lewis. TV appearances and concerts were canceled, and some radio stations refused to play his records.

I saw things differently. I knew Jerry Lee from my Yakima days and viewed him as a 24-year-old man-child whose bountiful musical talents thrust him into a world he was ill-prepared to handle. I once saw him walk into a room wearing only his jockey shorts for an interview with a female reporter from a Yakima newspaper. I witnessed firsthand how he turned to bourbon and more bourbon and more bourbon still for answers when confronted with too many pressures. His hits were remarkable pieces of music: *Whole Lotta Shakin' Goin' On, Great Balls of Fire, Breathless, High School Confidential* and the Hank Williams classic *You Win Again* were just a few of them. All were signal triumphs of a new type of musical revival sweeping the country, rock-'n'-roll. Jerry Lee played his "pumping piano" like no one before him had done. Amidst the controversy that followed his London debacle, it appeared that his accomplishments were all for naught.

Why can't we respect this young man for what he is? I thought. *He's one of the greatest rock-'n'-rollers ever born. Shouldn't that count for something?*

In the precincts Jerry Lee hailed from, I speculated, they probably considered his behavior normal or slightly abnormal at worst. His recent notoriety gave him the hint of a dangerous persona which I thought the Northwest would find attractive. Also, being able to watch him perform night after night looked like fun. Not that working with him was particularly easy. Suffice it to say, the escapades of Jerry Lee Lewis helped prepare me for all the insane rock star antics I encountered in the crazy years that followed.

My radio responsibilities prevented me from personally making it to all of Jerry Lee's performances, but whenever I did, invariably something memorable happened. Like the night when his band came out on stage ready to play, but no sign of Jerry Lee. Driving quickly to his hotel some five miles away, I went up to his room and found him sprawled across the bed with a half-empty bottle of Tennessee mash in his hand, watching TV. I told him his band was already on stage and that he should have started playing 15 minutes ago. Without a word, he climbed out of bed, pulled on his pants, gargled some mouthwash and walked out the door. In the car he finally spoke: "Now, Pat, don't you get pissed at me!" I wasn't. Another night, he shoved an expensive piano off a five-foot-high stage during rehearsal, claiming it was out of tune.

One special evening, this one in Bremerton, Washington, we had another sold-out house. Just as the opening act concluded, the fire marshal came up to me in a rage. "Pat, you know 1,000 is the limit, and you sold your thousandth ticket an hour ago. So why are you still selling tickets?"

I professed total innocence, explaining, "I personally closed the box office myself! I have the ticket roll right here in my brief case!"

The fire marshal dragged me to the stage, pulled back the curtain a crack and said, "Look at that floor! Now tell me, what's going on?"

I was shocked. This building, where I had staged dances for over a year, could comfortably hold a thousand dancers with room to spare. Before me, instead, I beheld a sea of bodies jammed together shoulder-to shoulder, uncomfortably tight. Again claiming innocence, I headed toward Jerry Lee's dressing room to fetch him and his band for the show. I promised the fire marshal that after that I would begin my search for the leak that was letting hundreds of extra fans into the building.

As I stepped out into the hallway, I was nearly knocked over by a swarm of young people racing past me toward the auditorium floor. Still more teens were emerging from Jerry Lee's dressing room, whereto I now hastened. Upon entering, it became obvious that someone had opened a second box office that night—none other than the evening's star performer. Noticing the large turn-away crowd, Jerry Lee had sent his assistant in search of a stepladder. He liberated one from the building's equipment room, and they lowered it through Jerry Lee's dressing room window to the ground below. The assistant then slipped out front to inform the disappointed throng about a back way in. As the fans clambered up the ladder and through the window, Jerry Lee greeted them with an outstretched hand. He was running his own private scalping business, collecting double what we charged at the front box office. If someone didn't have enough money, Jerry Lee instructed them to "just empty your pockets and give me what you have!" and waved them along. When Jerry Lee saw me, he showed no signs of embarrassment. I told him it was time to get his "Louisiana butt" on stage, adding something like "Thanks a lot!" as he walked by.

Jerry Lee turned and said, "Pat, these here good folks just want ol' Jerry Lee to have himself a new Cadillac. Now don't you go faulting them for that!"

Sometimes a moment like that is too precious to turn into an issue, and it's better to take a mental snapshot and file it away as a personal treasure. The memory of Jerry Lee's "back door banking" that night is worth a thousand times more to me today as a story I enjoy telling than all the money Jerry Lee pumped into his pocket through his dressing room window that night. No amount of aggravation could change the fact that I loved hiring the guy. Once he was on stage, pounding that piano, leaning into the microphone, singing those great hits, tearing his shirt off, throwing his curly blonde hair from side to side, all was forgiven.

The crowd danced their brains out that night, and wasn't that why we were all there? High volume, dangerously high energy and the best rock-'n'-roll in the world. Sheer excitement. Powerful emotions. Great fun. Endless surprises. Jerry Lee Lewis. Goodness gracious, great balls of fire!

Running Scared
Roy Orbison, 1961

A ROY ORBISON TOUR WAS THE EXACT OPPOSITE of one by Jerry Lee Lewis, except that the emotions were just as intense. A precious human being, Roy transmitted a unique spirit, a special love of life. His oft-broken heart sang along with his incredible voice and electric guitar. Girls danced to Roy's music with tears in their eyes. *Only the Lonely. Leah. Blue Angel. Crying. Running Scared. Blue Bayou. Pretty Woman.* He sang wonderfully on all of them. Roy always wore his trademark sunglasses on stage. One night over dinner he told me why: He thought his eyes were too close together. He feared that if he appeared without them, it would detract from his music. He must never have realized how powerful his music was, so clearly the product of a beautiful heart. No one would have cared how close together or how far apart his eyes were. In his humble way, he said "I think that wearing glasses is more considerate of my fans!" As God knows, every note Roy Orbison ever played, every song he ever sang, he delivered with thoughts of his fans foremost in his mind. Roy's writing, his singing, were so genuine, I often told people "The woman who ripped off his heart made him a millionaire".

One afternoon in 1989, Roy fell victim to a heart attack while flying one of his model airplanes. He long knew his heart was weak but, typical of him, he thought of his fans first and found it difficult to show proper concern for his own health. News of his death sent me into a deep funk. God just doesn't seem to send us enough people like Roy Orbison.

In the strangest of twists, following Roy's death a show was developed at the Imperial Hotel in Las Vegas called *Legends in Concert.* That show, which for years played to sold-out houses twice each evening, featured musicians who could imitate to the slightest inflection such departed stars as Elvis, Ricky Nelson, Patsy Cline and, yes, Roy Orbison.

One night I sat down to watch the show and was astonished. *That's not someone impersonating Roy,* I thought to myself. *That's Roy himself!* I knew, because I spent enough time with Roy to detect any significant difference. This man had the voice, the mannerisms, the movements, the sunglasses all down pat. He was so good, it turned out, the Orbison family brought him down to Texas every year to sing at their annual picnic honoring Roy's memory. This man playing Roy instantly brought tears to the eyes of the audience as he sang all those Orbison songs, just like Roy once did. Today, this musician has tired of the Vegas scene and no longer works at the Imperial. Now and then, he still performs a Roy Orbison tribute. Can you guess who that musician is? The same man who, along with his band, once shared the stage with Roy back in the early days at my ballrooms and dance halls—he is Kent Morrill, lead singer and keyboard player of the Northwest's favorite group, The Wailers.

Halfway to Paradise
Tony Orlando, 1961

I WISH TO RETURN TO A SUBJECT I touched upon earlier—how important it was to a Northwest teenager in the early '60s to be *cool*. Back then, what played on the East Coast, what played in the Midwest, sometimes—oftentimes—didn't play nearly so well on the West Coast, and especially up here in the top left-hand corner of the country, in the Pacific Northwest. Northwest audiences might greet performers with polite applause, but with screams, never. Not until the Beatles invaded the Seattle Coliseum in 1964 were screams heard at Northwest concerts, and that was in good part because the media alerted our local teenage girls well in advance that they *should* scream. Teenagers saw on television, read in newspapers, heard on radio how their counterparts in other cities screamed wildly at Beatles concerts, so that's what everyone did when the Fab Four first showed up on the shores of Puget Sound. The near-pandemonium at the Beatles' concert was an exception, however, not the rule. The Rule with a capital *R* in the Northwest had always been "Be cool!"

I mention this because the Be Cool Rule applied to performers on the stage as well as to listeners in the audience. Band members were expected to make their moves, show their dance steps—which all bands then had—and let their music do the rest. And they did. No dramatics, no hysterics, just general all-around coolness. Which brings me to one of the funniest incidents in all of my dance-promoting years, the night Tony Orlando visited the Spanish Castle.

Keep the description I just gave you in mind while you read the rest of this story. It will provide you with the proper mind-set for appreciating a moment when the Be Cool Rule was ignored with significant results.

One day in 1961, I received a phone call at KJR from a promotions man with Epic Records. "Hey Pat," he said, "I've got Tony Orlando coming through town on a record promo tour. He heard about your Spanish Castle dances all the way back in New York and wants to perform at one. How 'bout it? He'll sing his new song, and that's it. What do you say?"

The station was already playing the record in question, *Halfway to Paradise*, a Carole King song, and it was a great recording, so I figured *Why not?* I agreed immediately and set about taking care of the details. I enlisted the Wailers to serve as Orlando's backup band and provided them with a 45 RPM record of the song so they could listen to it, practice it and become comfortable playing behind him.

On another front, a second force was afoot which would help produce a totally unexpected outcome to Mr. Orlando's appearance. On several occasions at the Castle, I was approached by an awkward young man—short, chubby and lacking in the social graces. His voice was squeaky, and he might have been developmentally impaired. What he definitely was was insistent. His short visits with me on dance nights were always confined to discussing one subject and one subject only, his prowess as an acrobat. He had the ability—or so he claimed—to execute a running full somersault in midair and land on his feet. He was convinced that Spanish Castle crowds would love to witness this wondrous achievement performed live. Harboring doubts, I told him again and again—and quite clearly, I thought—that while his talent was wholly admirable, he would be well-advised to approach a local television program or talent show where people would truly appreciate him. I cautioned him not to anticipate performing his stunt at the Castle.

Segue to the Spanish Castle on Friday night, near the end of the evening, at an hour when all the area high school games were completed and the crowd was at its largest. Tony wanted maximum exposure, and I gave it to him. This is the same Tony Orlando who later gained fame with his group Dawn, his own TV show and a string of hit records, including *Tie a Yellow Ribbon 'Round the Old Oak Tree* and *Knock Three Times*. His first release, *Halfway to Paradise*, was a modest hit, reaching somewhere in the 30s on *Billboard*'s list. The song was a slow, mournful tale of unrequited love, not some Chuck Berry/Little

Richard/Jerry Lee Lewis all-hell-is-breaking-loose rocker. So it was with a deliberately low-key approach that I went on stage that evening and gave this new-but-possibly-rising star his introduction.

Enter Tony Orlando stage left, waving both arms in the air. Being from New York, Tony carried an East Coast set of expectations with him as he approached the microphone. S-o-p at theater rock shows in the Big Apple or Boston or Philadelphia in that era was to give a new talent like Orlando a spot late in the program after several accomplished stars had performed. That way, the audience would be warmed up by the time he appeared. He could then throw himself into his one or two songs with gusto, knowing that the crowd was already keyed up and expecting the max from him. *Cool* was not a term one would have applied to the teenage audiences Tony was used to. Not knowing the territory he had just entered, the 17-year-old Orlando failed to adjust to Northwest cool, as you are about to learn.

On cue, the Wailers began to play, and Orlando launched into his song.

"I want to be your lover," he began, somewhat sanely.

"But your friend is all I've stayed," he continued, showing the first signs of getting prematurely overemotional by reaching for his tie.

"I'm only halfway to paradise," he croaked, tearing off his cravat and tossing it into the audience.

"So near, yet so far away," he concluded the opening stanza, by this time reaching for the buttons on his shirt.

"I long for your lips to kiss my lips," we heard as the first button popped.

Then followed, "But just when I think they may" as the rest of the buttons, one-by-one, gave way.

"You lead me halfway to paradise," he warbled, dropping to his knees and thrusting his face only inches from the faces of the girls crowding the front of the stage.

Tony put himself into a trap from which escape was difficult. He was halfway to paradise and halfway through his song, and the girls weren't relating to it—far from it, they were laughing at him. At this point, he had the option of recognizing the futility of his approach and returning to his feet for the remainder of the song or digging himself a deeper hole. He chose the latter.

Literally tearing his shirt away, he reached the line, "It hurts me so to know your heart's a treasure."

As he continued "And that my heart is forbidden to touch," Tony started wiping away theatrical tears, which the crowd found equally funny.

A new problem now developed. The poor Wailers, standing behind Orlando, playing their instruments, were unprepared for his melodramatics and they, too, were laughing.

My eyes focused on Tony as he sang Carole's great line, "So put your sweet lips close to my lips," and I failed to notice until too late that, moving into position stage right, was my friend the acrobat. Apparently, his young showbiz yearnings noted the disaster unfolding on stage, and he sensed a vulnerability.

Tony, unaware that the worst was yet to come, was delivering the line "And tell me that's where they're gonna stay" when the acrobat made his move. Later, I could only speculate on what went wrong. Springing out of a three-point stance, the acrobat took several mighty strides and launched.

"Don't leave me halfway to paradise," was Tony's final plea of the evening. Our acrobat wasn't listening.

It's possible he miss-timed the run up. It's also possible his ability to success-fully complete an airborne running full somersault existed only in his mind. For whatever the reason, the acrobat completed but half of the required midair rotation and landed flat on his back with an enormous thud directly behind Orlando and across Tony's outstretched leg.

At this point, barely two minutes into the performance, total chaos engulfed the proceedings. Tony stopped singing and spun around on his knees to see what had happened behind him. A few feet away, the Wailers collapsed in hysterics. Drummer Mike Burk was laughing so hard, he fell off his stool and into his cymbals stand, and together they hit the floor with a mighty crash. Lead singer Kent Morrill was sprawled across the top of his piano, convulsed with uncontrollable laughter. Both the guitar and bass players were bent over their instruments, howling, while my acrobat friend was lying prone on the stage, wind knocked out of him, gasping for air. Roaring with laughter, amazed by the spectacle they just witnessed, the crowd abandoned any pretense of being cool and began shouting its approval.

Improvising, I ran up on the stage, helped the dazed acrobat to his feet, pulled him to one side of me and raised his hand in the air. Then I grabbed the arm of a terribly confused Tony Orlando, pulled him to his feet to the other side of me, raised his hand in the air as well and shouted into the microphone "Ladies and gentlemen, Tony Orlando and the acrobat! Now, let's have a brief intermission."

A minute later, the Epic Records representative was leading a spiritually shaken Orlando out the Castle's back door to their car. I didn't notice when the acrobat disappeared. Amidst the confusion, he slipped away into the night, dissolving into the shadows like a phantasm, ne'er to be seen again. Myself? I headed to the box office to settle the finances for the evening.

Speaking in financial terms, the "Orlando & the Acrobat" show? Priceless!

Tony never had a chance to deliver the final line of *Halfway to Paradise*: "Yeah, yeah, so near, yet so far away."

Left to right: Larry Lujack, Jan Berry, Pat O'Day & Dean Torrance

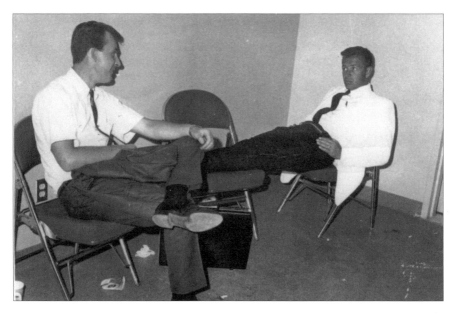

The Brain Trust: Dick Curtis & Pat O'Day backstage at a concert

5 – *Turn, Turn, Turn*

The Byrds, 1965

B Y THE EARLY '60S, people around the country recognized the uniqueness of the Northwest dance scene. During summers, we expanded to include midweek as well as weekend dances at each venue. The young between 15 and 21 had a seemingly unquenchable thirst for those dances, and we tried our best to meet that demand. In January 1961, I became the afternoon drive time disc jockey on KJR after John Stone, who hired me, was fired for some activities bordering on payola. Congress' payola investigations in 1959 and 1960 terrified radio station owners. Faced with strict new laws, no intelligent operation dared tolerate questionable activities. John Stone put together a concert, consisting of several recording acts, in late 1960. Afterward, it was alleged he made deals with record companies for free appearances by their acts. Added to this, there was grumbling among unpaid performers. The failure to pay them probably derived from the fact that there was *no money* to pay them with, for few people attended the concert in question, held in the old Seattle Memorial Auditorium. In short, the whole deal was a mess.

Amidst an internal investigation by KJR, I was summoned to the general manager's office for interrogation. The GM, a man named Galen Blackford, was feared by the air staff. He was gruff, intimidating, a heavy drinker, a person we all sought to avoid whenever possible. No sooner did I sit down than Blackford looked me square in the eyes and said, "Pat, there's a rumor

I'm hearing that you gave Stone 50 percent of your dance profits so he would hire you. Is that true?"

I had never uttered a single word about our secret deal to anyone other than my wife, and the tone of the question indicated I was in big trouble. In a few short months KJR had become my life, but I wasn't about to lie. Why should I? Stone's conduct was the station's problem, not mine, so I laid my cards on the table face up. I told Blackford that working at KJR was my life's dream, and at the time of my interview I was willing to do just about anything for an opportunity to be a part of its new direction and growth. I made it clear I never offered Stone a bribe to hire me. Indeed, he made the profit split a condition of my being hired.

Blackford listened carefully, giving no clue as to his own thoughts. Homer Pope, the station's operations manager, who had been with KJR for 35 years, also sat in on the meeting. He had a low tolerance for young rock-'n'-roll disc jockeys and he, too, wore a scowl on his face and said nothing. I stood up, excused myself and walked out of Blackford's office absolutely certain I faced imminent termination. How wrong I was.

Several tension-filled days later, KJR dismissed John Stone. Then came the shocker. They asked me to *temporarily* take the coveted three-to-six drive time slot. If they intended to off me, they were going about it in a strange way. Years later, Blackford and Pope told me they concluded after our interview that anyone who agreed to pay an amount equal to the salary being offered just to work at the station couldn't be all bad. It didn't hurt my case, either, that evidence was mounting I was fast becoming a major name in the Seattle radio market.

Walk Right In
Rooftop Singers, 1963
BY 1962, MY RADIO CAREER AND DANCE BUSINESS were in full bloom. I had been named the station's program director to go with my afternoon drive time job. Hiring, firing, news content, music selection, what to put on the air and what to keep off—basically these were all now matters for me to decide. I was only 28 years old, with three sons, and had built a large home on the shores of Lake Washington complete with dock, swimming pool, ski boat and all the artifacts of opulence one could envision. My annual salary at the radio station was a paltry $12,000, making a profitable, vibrant dance business essential if I

wanted to maintain or expand my present life-style. The problem was, I was working 18 hours a day, and days were still only 24 hours long. With my many responsibilities, and with no more time to give, expanding my outside activities any further was out of the question. Enter Dick Curtis.

Years before, Dick and I had attended broadcasting school together in Tacoma. Like me, he reached KJR after stops at three small-market stations, becoming the station's nighttime disc jockey in the summer of 1960. Improving rapidly, he took over my original spot at the station, the six-to-nine evening show. He was dedicated and cooperative and accepted criticism as a help, not a hindrance, and I was quite fond of him. When he approached me with a plan that looked like it would solve my problem, I quickly said *Yes*. Dick asked whether I would consider hiring him to help me with my dance business. His hours at KJR were from five in the evening until midnight because he worked in the newsroom for three hours after his show, as was customary then at the station. That left his daytime hours free, and he offered to devote them to the cause of Pat O'Day Dances. I made him a partner, beginning a relationship which continues even as I write this book, one which enabled our Northwest dance business to grow at a rapid rate and led directly to my initial efforts in the concert business.

With Curtis on board, we opened a modest office in an apartment house in West Seattle about a mile from the radio station. This allowed me to separate my various activities. Dick became indispensable scheduling bands, coordinating moves with a growing list of dance partners and dealing with our many landlords scattered around the state. We advanced well beyond the mom-and-pop stage in business, and ruling our dance domain became a serious, complicated endeavor. We were in constant negotiations with national acts. The all-important coordination of the local bands was by itself nearly a full-time job. Some of these groups were very young and badly needed coaching and occasional financial assistance.

One new group featured a superb keyboardist named Walt Wagner, who later in his career became one of the most admired pianists in the region, playing clubs, lounges and other places. In 1963, Walt and his band came to us seeking direction. I told them there was a need for a certain type of band, and they proved pliable and open to my advice. The concept called for adding an R&B flavor to the Northwest rock-'n'-roll sound. With some backup female singers and a Hammond B3 organ with Leslie speakers, they could pull it off. Young Walt's lack of the necessary funds held him back, and his parents could not see the wisdom of purchasing a Hammond. Stepping in, I accompanied Walt to the Sherman & Clay Music Store in downtown Seattle, negotiated a price, set up a time-payment plan and signed a personal guarantee. Walt and his new band—*The Good Guys*—had themselves a Hammond organ.

About that time, the matter of renegotiating the Wailers' performance fee came up. Lead vocalist and keyboard genius Kent Morrill, together with his mother, managed the band's affairs. The three of us met for lunch at Andy's Diner just south of downtown. Andy's, which somehow has survived all of Seattle's many changes over the past 40 years, consists of an interconnected cluster of vintage Union Pacific train cars parked side-by-side and end-to-end. It evokes an old-time railroad atmosphere and was a favorite hangout for Seattle's rock-'n'-roll radio people. Over lunch, Kent made his case: The Wailers had been working the past year for $250 a night, and this needed to be bumped up to $350. He cited as justification the increased cost of living and his planned purchase that week of a new Hammond B3 organ with Leslie speakers.

I allowed as how a cost-of-living allowance, coupled with a raise in recognition of their loyalty and always-satisfactory performances, was due them, no question. But an increase of 40 percent—that seemed excessive.

"Well," Kent replied, "It all has to do with the huge cost of the new organ."

It should be explained here that I greatly admired the Wailers, as individuals and as a group. We were pioneers together, jointly the engines that powered the growth of the region's dance scene. The amount of money we were quibbling over may seem small today, but understand we waged a constant battle to keep our dances affordable. We didn't want the price of admission to drive teenagers away. It only cost a buck-fifty to attend a movie in 1963, and we were determined to keep our admission prices commensurate. Look at the numbers. If we had 1,000 teens attend a dance—and not every event drew that number—and charged them $1.50 apiece, we grossed $1,500. Take $350 from that, and we would be left with just $1,150 to pay for rent, personnel, security, advertising and all the rest — not to mention a second band. Simple math behooved me to run a tight ship.

Kent maintained that a Hammond organ cost a lot of money, and that an increase of anything less than the amount he suggested would make it financially impossible to work for me. Our negotiations reached the critical point. His mom Lucille, an adorable woman with her son's best interests in mind, kept nodding her head in agreement. I decided to work things in reverse.

"Kent," I said, "You play for me about eight nights a month. Let's say we up your fee to $300 a night plus the cost of the organ. Does that seem fair?"

Kent and Mom acknowledged that it did, but returned again to the high cost of that organ. By good fortune, I still had my copy of the sales receipt and payment plan for Walt Wagner's Hammond in my wallet. I pulled it out, handed it across the table and said,

> Okay. Here's the monthly cost for a Hammond B3 with the Leslies. Let's see…160 dollars per month is what you can plan on for payments. Now, suppose I pick up the entire cost of your organ purchase. What you charge others you can put in your pocket. One-hundred sixty divided by eight dances a month comes out to $20 per dance. So let's set your new fee at $320 per night.

Faced with such overwhelming logic, and shocked by the evidence I carried, they caved in, and we quickly signed a new one-year agreement.

Dead Man's Curve
Jan & Dean, 1964

WE OPENED NEW DANCES AT A ROLLER RINK in Olympia, at Spanaway Lake south of Tacoma, at Parker's Ballroom up on Aurora, at the Cedars in Mount Vernon, and at the Roller Dome in Burlington, some 60 miles to the north. Summer saw us putting on as many as 20 events a week, and this required recruiting a great deal of talent, as we tried to include at least two bands at every dance. Our purchasing power when dealing with national acts was now substantial. They could come to the Northwest for two weeks of consecutive performances with minimal driving between venues. Roy Orbison, Bobby Vee (*Take Good Care of My Baby*), Jerry Lee Lewis, the Champs (*Tequila*), the T-Bones (*No Matter What the Shape*), Jan & Dean, Dick & Dee Dee (*Mountains High*), Leslie Gore (*You Don't Own Me*), the Cascades (*Rhythm of the Rain*), Johnny Tillotson (*Poetry in Motion*), Mel Carter (*Hold Me, Thrill Me*), and April & Nino (*Deep Purple*) were just some of the acts we brought to the area in the summer of 1963. I was especially thrilled to work again with Roy Orbison, whom I considered America's best rock vocalist. I wasn't alone in that opinion. Elvis Presley once called Roy "the greatest singer in the world," and far be it from me to argue with the King! I also enjoyed Bobby Vee, who never for a moment lost his North Dakota humility and friendliness. A side note: When Buddy Holly died in a plane crash outside Clear Lake, Iowa in February 1959 — I worked at radio station KAYO in Seattle "the day the music died" — the tour promoter hired Bobby Vee to finish out the balance of the concerts. Bobby's voice did remind one of Buddy, a fact some people criticized. Not me.

The best times of all I spent in the company of Jan & Dean. Jan Berry splashed onto the music scene in 1958 with *Jennie Lee*, a song about a stripper he performed with Arnie Ginsberg as the duo Jan & Arnie. I forget what happened to Arnie, but a year later Jan reunited with a pre-Arnie singing pal, Dean Torrence, to form Jan & Dean. Dean's voice will never be revered like, say, that of Pavarotti, or compared with other voices of great quality. But Dean had perfect pitch, an essential talent when it came to building tight harmonies with Jan. While not a Julliard graduate, he was blessed with boyish good looks, and the girls adored him. Jan, in contrast, handsome enough in his own right, was the musical genius of the pair. He was also dependable, reliable, friendly, cooperative and enjoyably human. Together, the two made a great music duo, and they recorded a string of Top-10 hits in the late '50s and early '60s — *Baby Talk* (their first number one hit) in 1959, *Heart and Soul* in 1960, *Linda* in 1962, *Surf City*, along with *Little Old Lady from Pasadena* and *Drag City* in 1963 and *Dead Man's Curve* in 1964. They were West Coast, surfin', rock-'n'-roll, up-tempo, upbeat singers who delighted in performing live. I'd hire them for several nights, and generally we'd make it to two dances an evening. At 10 P.M. they'd finish one performance, jump off the stage and into my car and rush to another location for a second show at 11 P.M. Loads of laughs filled those rides as I traded my radio stories for their music industry tales.

One evening, radio blaring, we drove from a dance in Bremerton to a dance in Tacoma. As we crossed the Narrows Bridge, the Ray Conniff Singers came on singing *Somewhere My Love* (actually, *Lara's Theme* from the movie *Doctor Zhivago*). Ray weathered the change to rock-'n'-roll and wanted nothing more to do with it, *ever*, save for covering an occasional rock ballad, sanitizing it and packaging it into one of his many compilation albums. From the back seat, Dean opined that the chord change that took place midway through the song was less than effective. Jan, riding beside me, turned to Dean and said, "Dean, I was talking to Ray just the other day, and he told me he really doesn't like anything you've ever done!" We all laughed for miles. The thought of Ray Conniff even listening to a Jan & Dean song broke us up.

It was a sad moment in April 1966 when I received a call from a friend in Los Angeles telling me that Jan Berry had been in a serious automobile accident. On his way home from a late night at the recording studio, he rammed his Corvette under the rear bumper of a semitrailer and was rushed to the hospital in a deep coma. To his credit, after a multi-year struggle, he regained his speech and ability to sing. Such accidents exact a long-term toll, and such was the case with Jan. He nearly made their giant hit, *Dead Man's Curve*, a personal reality. Jan & Dean eventually performed again, but nothing could equal the fame, fortune and fun of their early years. Like Jerry Lee Lewis did at the pinnacle of his fame, Jan crashed at the pinnacle of his — Jerry Lee at the side of his 13-year-old cousin/wife, Jan at the wheel of his speeding Vette. Nothing can diminish my love for Jan Berry and Dean Torrence. I treasure still every minute we spent together.

I Get Around
The Beach Boys, 1964

THE ONLY TIME WE EVER LOST MONEY during our five-year run at the Spanish Castle was the night we introduced the Beach Boys to the Northwest for the first time. Their father, Murry Wilson, called me on the phone regularly for months, begging for airplay for the Boys' early releases. *Surfin' Safari* was a fair-sized hit in the area, and I miscalculated how well the teenagers who attended our dances would relate to the group. I knew the tune wasn't your usual dancing song, but figured that everyone would realize the group played other music as well. *How can we miss?* I reasoned. We were offering as a gift for our customers an exciting new band from California with no increase in our price of admission. *How could I have been so wrong?*

I paid for the Boys' round trip airfare from Los Angeles and for their lodging expenses in town. And then there was the matter of their *pocket money*. Murry always told me, "Pat, we've got to give the Boys some pocket money," which meant upwards of a thousand dollars in cash each visit. It was far too much to pay them under the circumstances, but Murry had a standard answer: "You know, Pat, the Boys will always make it up to you." And they did make it up to me and my company, many times, over the years. To Murry Wilson's delight, in 1963 I booked the group into the Castle on a Friday night and into my downtown night club, Pat O'Day's Party Line, the following two nights.

The Beach Boys were regular performers at concerts organized by Pat O'Day, often in cooperation with Dick Curtis, throughout the '60s.

Pat O'Day & Dick Curtis Present
1966 NEW YEAR SPECTACULAR!

THE BEACH BOYS!

GARY LEWIS &
THE PLAYBOYS!
(first NW appearance!)
THE BEAU BRUMMELS!
THE YARDBIRDS!
THE VEJETABLES!
THE MOJO MEN!
"Freedom Child" ALEXYS

FRI. DEC. 31

HERE IN TACOMA!
UPS FIELD HOUSE 8 PM

The late Carl Wilson tuning his guitar backstage at the Coliseum

On the evening the Beach Boys debuted at the Castle, our good fortune deserted us. Fewer than 400 people attended, a small fraction of the crowd we usually attracted when big-name talent came to town (we drew nearly six times as many people for Conway Twitty). In fact, that was the smallest crowd during our entire operation of the building, before or after. I learned two hard, expensive lessons that night: (*a*) surfing music was enjoyable to listen to but not the easiest music to dance to and (*b*) our pre-show publicity campaign, along with the Boys' recent appearance on *American Bandstand*, unsold more than a few tickets. This was 1963, and all self-respecting bands in 1963 were nearly identical in appearance. They wore pegged slacks, shiny leather boots and matching sport coats and ties and styled their hair with the "Princeton look" (a short, feathered style with a hint of a duck-tail in the back). In contrast, I give you the Beach Boys: scraggly hair (bleached, of course), casual tan pants and Madras plaid shirts—totally uncool, really, according to Seattle's tastes, and probably according to most other cities' tastes at the time. This was a completely new Southern California surfer look, and teenage Seattleites weren't yet ready for it. Nor was our treasury. We lost a pile of dough that night. Attendance and take at my namesake club the next two nights were a little better, as we drew crowds that came more to listen than to dance. But the results were disappointing nonetheless. Our margins were slim, and our financial success depended on attracting sellout crowds. Mostly we succeeded; on these three nights we lost money while at the same time introducing the Seattle area to a group which will go down in history as one of the all-time great rock-'n'-roll acts. One-hundred years from now, I truly believe, the world will still be enjoying the music of the Beach Boys.

With their next two major hits, *Surfin' USA* and *Surfer Girl*, the Beach Boys exploded into America's consciousness, and by 1964 I was happy to pay them $10,000 a day. Murry Wilson continued to insist on calling that 10 grand *just pocket money for the Boys.*

(We're Gonna) Rock Around the Clock
Bill Haley & His Comets, 1955

PARENTS STILL EXERCISED SUBSTANTIAL CONTROL over their teenage progeny in the early and mid-'60s, and teens appreciated a predictable and secure environment. In 1955, the movie *Blackboard Jungle* introduced Bill Haley's *Rock Around the Clock* and depicted what was then a major societal concern, the rise of juvenile delinquency. The movie helped forge a link in the public's mind between rock-'n'-roll and teenage rebellion. Teenage drinking existed in 1963, of course, just as it always has, but was not yet a major problem. Beer was far more heavily advertised on radio and television than it is today, yet those ads didn't create appreciable demand among the young. The same went for cigarettes, whose commercials were an hourly radio staple. It was only in the rebellious days of the late '60s and early '70s that teenage drinking became a major problem.

That problem has intensified in recent years as more and more parents seemed to set mediocre examples, too many of them openly condoning teenage drinking. From what I have observed, these same parents often shirk family responsibilities and instead blame radio advertising, television programs, school systems and teachers for their children's mistakes. Some parents seem to want their children to explore the same excesses they explored themselves as teenagers in the '70s as though it will make them better people. Why they encourage their children to risk harming themselves is a mystery I cannot fathom. With apologies to all for expressing my opinions so bluntly, they have spent too much time transferring fault elsewhere and looking for others to take responsibility for their children's welfare and future. They reached maturity blaming the government, big business, other adults, their parents, everyone and everything in sight for every perceived ill society faced. In 2002, the same logic is often applied to parenting.

Getting back to our dances. Forever, music and dance have played a vital role in the mingling of the sexes, and it was no different on Friday nights at the Castle. Our dances were a place to see and be seen. Girls generally appeared in skirts or, less often, in dresses, as they were not yet given the option of wearing pants or jeans at school. Lots of the young men had on slacks, others jeans and denims. Never did you see a guy with just a T-shirt. As well, not often did you see someone dressed to the nines. You would stand out too much if you did. Mostly, the teens stayed within prescribed norms in attire and appearance, carefully modifying them as fashions changed. A few faddish or eccentric dressers always showed up, and their colorful garb added texture to the scene.

The movement of the crowd was choreographed by gender. Few ever sat down, even if booths were provided. The guys stood in groups or walked around checking out the girls. The girls clustered in groups waiting for the guys to come ask them to dance. An exception was when the musicians did something special, whereupon the girls (never the guys) flocked to the front of the stage. Most everyone was there to dance. Those who arrived as couples already had partners. The others paired off as the evening progressed, sometimes settling in, other times continuing to hunt or be hunted.

Our customers expected a suitable dance beat from the band, and the ritual's success depended in large part on the performers' ability to deliver the needed aural stimulation. A band's rhythm patterns needed to fit regional dance styles. When it came time to decide what moves to show on the dance floor, Northwest teens went their own way. The Twist? The Pony? The Watusi? Those were passing national fads and had little to do with the dancing seen at the Castle and our other venues. Around Seattle, the Twist and other such moves were embraced by adults more than by teens. Most of these dances were *American Bandstand*-oriented and never translated well onto local dance floors. Northwest dancing was innovative, involved and rarely had a name. Northwest kids in the '60s were simply "doing their own thing" which, incidentally, is a habit reflected in this region's adults today. Teens dancing at the Castle couldn't have cared less about national trends; they consistently did it their own way. One of the main points I try to make in this book is that, in the Northwest, things were and are different, and the way teens danced was no exception. Readers who were there know what I'm saying. Readers who weren't, try to envision Northwest teens in the early '60s dancing in ways similar to how teens in the '90s danced to grunge, and you'll be pretty close.

On the street, word spread quickly whether a band's music could be danced to or not. How a band appeared and delivered their message was important, too. They had to be cool. Northwest cool. Anything more, anything less, and the ritual would collapse upon itself. The box office determined which bands were invited back and which were left to fend for themselves. Not everyone agreed that the results were fair. Some bands didn't get a cool grade, or failed to draw crowds, even though their music, their beat, were comparable to those of other popular bands. That's just how it was. Our customers made those decisions for us. They voted with their dollars.

Overall, the Northwest dance scene was far from being monolithic; styles and tastes varied in some locales. In the affluent, rapidly growing suburbs of Bellevue and Redmond east of Lake Washington, a musical style some people point back to as a precursor of grunge could be heard. In Tacoma, similar bands were making inroads, bands with a harsh metallic edge to their arrangements. In the late '70s and early '80s, out on the Washington coast in the town of Aberdeen, a young Kurt Cobain listened to the records of the Wailers and the Sonics. These weren't cult bands, they were groups listened to and loved by teens throughout the Northwest. From Portland to Seattle to Spokane, in every city, town and village, these two groups became *our* Beatles. Cobain later recognized them as the foundation for his and Nirvana's rise to fame. It started with a sound initiated by the Wailers from Tacoma and emulated and expanded upon by the Sonics from Tacoma/Bremerton. If you listen to an early Sonics recording with the phenomenal Gerry Roslie singing, say, *The Witch* or *Psycho*, you will hear something that foreshadows grunge: a penetrating hard rock sound with vocals having one goal in mind—to mentally saw you in half.

Granny's Pad
The Viceroys, 1963

BY EARLY 1964, WE HAD ADDED THE KINGSMEN to our list of groups we knew would pack 'em in. They hailed from down the road in Portland, and the year before, their version of *Louie Louie* reached number one in the country. It was no wonder our clientele looked kindly upon them. Soon another group with Portland roots, Don and the Goodtimes, led by Don Gallucci and Don McKinney (who later worked for Concerts West), moved onto the favored list of Northwest bands. Epic Records signed them to a contract in 1967, and their hit, *I Could Be So Good to You*, enjoyed lots of radio play in the region. Another great group from that year still entertaining crowds today is the Viceroys. Totally rooted in Seattle, they pulled off a clever stunt which helped establish them in the area although, with their talent, they didn't need stunts to succeed.

The Viceroys featured Jim Valley, who later became Harpo with Paul Revere & the Raiders on their TV show on ABC. One and all, they were talented musicians. Their drummer, Fred Zuefeldt, was simply terrific, as was every member of that band. The stunt I am referring to involved a song they released in 1963, *Granny's Pad*. The *granny* in the song's title was Granny Peters, a product of my substantial imagination, a character I invented as part of my radio show. I still lapse into my Granny Peters voice now and then when the mood strikes. It was/is the voice of an 80-year-old woman who told the world she was my grandmother, a claim I always denied. Granny outlived six hus-

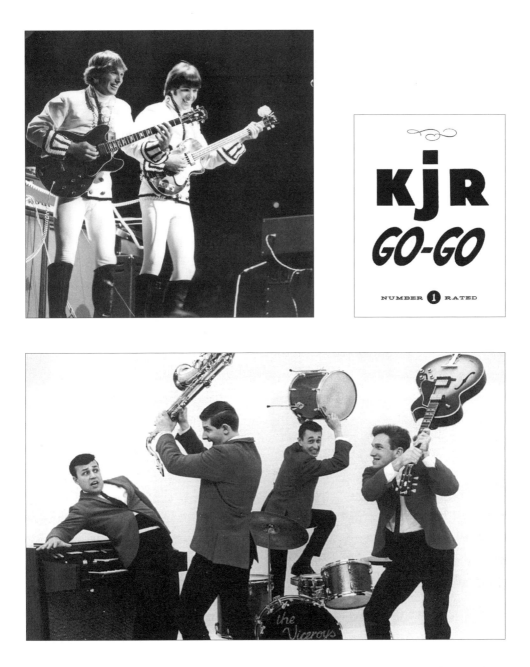

Northwest bands like Paul Revere & the Raiders (top, with Jim Valley on the left), and the Viceroys (bottom, with Valley on the right), believed in having fun.

bands, all of whom left her a great deal of money. She had a motto, "A Lear a year!" and proclaimed her fondness for jumping into her plane, which she always piloted herself, and flying off to Vegas or wherever the action happened to be that week. I often depicted her at the controls of her Learjet, martini in hand, as she made her final approach to Seattle's Boeing Field. She had a picture of a giant olive emblazoned right under the pilot's window and said it looked so good there, she had the whole fuselage painted pink. Granny made brief appearances almost daily on my show, where she never failed to relate another fascinating incident from her life and freely admitted to drinking a lot. I made occasional personal appearances at local events as Granny. The glasses, wig, cane and costume never fooled anyone. Without exception, all knew it was me, but that didn't matter. The thought of such a wild and wonderful 80-year-old woman was so enjoyable, they wanted to believe she truly existed.

Ironically, the competing rock radio station in town, KOL, first played *Granny's Pad*, not knowing the true story behind the name. At first, I declined to play the record, thinking the band's ploy too obvious. When KOL picked the song up, I took a wait-and-see attitude. Seattle audiences loved the song, and soon I had no choice but to add it to our play list. When the Viceroys finally 'fessed up that *Granny's Pad* was a salute to my fictional grandmother, KOL pulled the record off the air. Too late! By that time, the song was well on its way to becoming a big regional hit, eventually selling over 12,000 copies.

The Viceroys quickly joined the ranks of the region's hottest bands, and rate a spot on my list of the top five bands from that year. That list looks something like this: Number one? Still the Wailers. Number two, the Kingsmen. Then follow the Viceroys, the Sonics and Merrilee Rush and the Turnabouts. Merrilee, who started working for me when she was 14 years old, enjoyed a worldwide hit, *Angel of the Morning*, and it's deceiving. Merrilee is in fact as great a little rock-'n'-roller as ever belted out a tune. *Angel of the Morning* is a ballad delivered by an enormous voice. Dancing on stage with mike in hand, Merrilee can be a screamer of the first order when the song calls for it.

Another up-and-coming local group in 1964 called themselves the Bards. Signed to a contract by Capital Records in 1967, they hailed from across the Cascades in eastern Washington. Two other names remembered from those days are the City Zu and Sir Raleigh and the Coupons (with drummer Dewey Martin, who later helped form Buffalo Springfield). There were the Bumps, Tiny Tony and the Statics, the Dave Lewis Combo (who recorded for A&M

Records) and Nancy Claire (who went on to record for Warner Brothers). The Daily Flash. The Counts. George Washington and the Cherry Bombs. The Checkers. Ron Holden. The Liverpool Five. The Emergency Exit. I mean, we helped develop an army of local talent.

That same year we opened a new dance hall at Westport, not far from Aberdeen-Hoquiam on the Washington coast. We called it Pat O'Day's Dunes, and it was a stunning success. We built it on land we purchased overlooking the ocean. The Dunes was created for summertime-only use, three nights a week. About that same time, in the north end of Seattle on old Highway 99, we built an expansive dance club and named it *The Bummer*, which it proved to be anything but.

At this point, Dick Curtis and I reached the outer limits with our side business. He had a highly successful show at KJR, while I went on air daily from three until six. Plus, I wore the hats of program director and music director. We had no more time and not enough space to expand any further. Our dream of staging an annual teenage fair in Seattle had to be put on hold. We had started promoting regular concerts in the area and were now treading water, not swimming ahead, in that endeavor. Filled with new ideas we wanted to try, we had no practical way to implement even one of them. The parent company of KJR also owned radio station KNEW/KJRB in Spokane, and I was handed the job of overseeing their programing, adding further to my already substantial radio duties. That same year, the Beatles released yet another number one single, *Eight Days a Week*. Dick and I needed 18.

While expanding into eastern Washington the previous year, we often locked horns with an energetic young promoter from Wenatchee, Washington, Terry Bassett, who was growing a dance empire of his own. If I was born to do radio, if Bill Boeing was born to build airplanes, if Bill Gates was born to write software and grow rich, Terry Bassett was born to stage rock-'n'-roll events. To our good fortune, he approached Dick and me with the idea of merging his dance company with ours. He ran dances in places like Lake Chelan, Ephrata and Birch Bay, Washington, and the musicians who worked for him all praised the way he conducted his business. I liked Terry the moment I met him, and before the end of our first conversation, we struck a deal. To better handle our expanding company, we formed a new corporation, Pat O'Day *&* Associates with Dick, Terry and me as principals. We opened an office at 158 Thomas Street, adjacent to the former World's Fair grounds—now renamed the Seattle

Center—and four long stone's throws from the Space Needle. Signifying the fact that we had hit the big time, we hired a loyal and dedicated young woman named Linda Ott to take over as our secretary/receptionist. With fixed overhead and a growing staff, my once modest rock-'n'-roll business was no longer a hobby. Dick Curtis decided to leave his job at KJR and devote 100 percent of his time to building up our business. Our dances continued to be our bread and butter, and they dovetailed nicely with our move into the concert business. We brought national acts to town, featured them in concerts, and afterwards bicycled them—as we liked to call it—around our dance circuit.

This made for great commercials. They went something like this, with either Dick or me doing the voice and the group's music playing in the background: "You saw them at the Coliseum Saturday night, now see them up close, dance to all their great music. It's Bobby Vee and his band!" Or maybe, "It's that new sensation, Them, with their big hit *Gloria*. Yes, G–L–O–R–I–A, Glor–i–a at the Lake Hills Roller Rink Tuesday night, Wednesday night at Parker's Ballroom, Thursday in Olympia at the Rollaway Skating Rink and Friday night at the famous Spanish Castle." Or it might have been Jan & Dean, the Yardbirds with Jimmy Page (*For Your Love*), Sam the Sham & the Pharaohs (*Wooly Bully*), Tommy Roe (*Sheila*), the Lovin' Spoonful (*Daydream*), the Righteous Brothers (*You've Lost That Lovin' Feeling*), the Knickerbockers (*Lies*), Delaney & Bonnie (*Never Ending Song of Love*) or the Kinks (*Lola*). Always, we coupled the national act with a popular local band.

One great benefit of my enlarged staff was it enabled me to isolate myself from negotiations with the musical groups, both local and national. For years, I walked a precarious tightrope. The potential for conflict of interest was as big as Mt. Rainier and potentially every bit as explosive. I personally selected which music the area would hear on its dominant radio station and refused to share that challenge with anyone, as I saw every musical decision, big or small, as critical to the station's success. And, understandably, every group and individual my dance company employed to perform had at least one record they desperately wanted played on KJR. I always went overboard in negotiations—and believe me, when musicians were involved, there were *always* negotiations—explaining that the fee we were agreeing to constituted our entire agreement, and that nothing I said or did should ever be construed as a promise of future favors involving the radio station. Immaculate record keeping and lengthy memos-to-file were required for many of these conversations (C.Y.A.!), and such diligence later saved my radio life. With a professional staff at Pat O'Day & Associates, I relieved myself of many of these duties and the attendant exposure and anxiety.

Gone
Ferlin Husky, 1957

THAT MECCA OF NORTHWEST ROCK, THE SPANISH CASTLE, sat on one of the busiest, most dangerous stretches of pavement on the West Coast, Highway 99. Interstate 5, today running from Vancouver, Canada to Tijuana, Mexico, was still not completed, and north-south traffic between Seattle and Tacoma was all funneled down 99. For drivers, it was the only link, and it overflowed with high-speed traffic, resulting in an abysmal accident rate.

On a warm, beautiful Summer night in 1965, Jan & Dean were booked into the Spanish Castle, along with the Viceroys. That brought out a large crowd, and a long line of anxious fans queued up in front of the ticket office. At 8:45 that evening, the sun still shined brightly, for the Seattle area enjoys long summer days. As the line of ticket buyers crept slowly forward, a mother stopped her car on the opposite side of 99 and dropped off her daughter and two young friends. Why the trio didn't walk back a few feet to the Midway intersection, where a four-way stoplight and a brightly-painted crosswalk offered safe crossing, one can only speculate. Was it their youthful exuberance? Did they spy friends across the street? Were they anxious to join the line before all the tickets were sold? Linking hands, they darted out into the traffic. Three lanes across the four lane highway, they were struck by a large truck and died. In the face of such tragedy, we closed for the night. The next day, local news stories painted the Spanish Castle and our events there in the darkest of colors.

My sadness was deepened by the thought that commercials I produced drew those girls to their deaths. I realized that staging such events, and broadcasting on radio, set forces in motion which often went beyond one's ability to control. Yet, I felt so badly. Meetings with police officials absolved us of blame, and all agreed there was a crosswalk nearby the girls could have used. That did little to lessen the pain everyone felt. We mounted a campaign urging far greater caution from the teens, and the shows went on, but only briefly. A few weeks later, tragedy struck the Castle anew.

A young man who appeared to have been drinking was denied admission. Enraged, he squealed out of the parking lot and crashed head-on into an oncoming car. The collision claimed two more lives and, once again, the Spanish Castle became the center of a fire storm. In the press we took the brunt of the blame as reporters needed answers for what caused five deaths in less than a month. Factually, the two accidents were unrelated save that both involved the Castle, my dances and a dangerous, obsolete highway.

Reluctantly, we closed down our dances at the Castle. Public pressure to do so was intense, and attendance was shrinking. That special feeling vanished. You couldn't look out on Highway 99 without thinking about the recent mayhem. When word got out about the Castle closing, caller after caller phoned the station, begging me not to do it. They all told stories of how important the Castle was to them and the young people in south King County. We knew, however, that, were another death to occur, we would be held responsible and would have our own consciences to answer to.

There is a time and season for everything, and the time and season for the great Spanish Castle and my dances there came, shined brightly for a few precious years and left. Wrecking crews finally tore down the building to make way for a big Texaco station.

Occasionally, when driving on I-5 a few hundred yards to the east, I find myself taking the Midway exit, parking my car near the Old Highway 99 intersection and contemplating for a few moments those so happy/so sad days of the '60s. I think of all the brilliant young musicians who paraded across the Castle's stage. I remember the night a teenage Jimi Hendrix approached me asking to play in what turned out to be his first live on-stage performance. So many young talents went on from the Castle to international fame and fortune. Do I mist up? Hell, yes!

People sometimes approach me to tell how they met their husband or wife at one of my dances in that fabled building. I file their stories away in a special place in my mind where I store my Spanish Castle treasures, as well as eternal feelings for the parents and families of those innocent young girls who went dancing one summer night, never to dance again. If only the Spanish Castle magic Jimi wrote and sang about could have reached out and saved them.

6 – For What It's Worth

Buffalo Springfield, 1966

ESPITE THE UNEXPECTED LOSS of our flagship venue, our dance business enjoyed great momentum and continued to grow. By the end of 1965 we were in Washington's Tri-Cities (Richland-Pasco-Kennewick) and Olympia markets, we built a ballroom by the Pacific Ocean and a new dance club in Yakima. We sold out Lake Hills Roller Rink on the Bellevue/Redmond border two nights a week. Everything was turning platinum, and the prospects for Pat O'Day & Associates seemed secure. A sudden development showed me how life has its surprises. Just as we were reaching our peak, a powerful challenge to our very survival appeared without warning in the form of a Sherman Act federal antitrust suit.

My radio duties expanded again when KJR's parent company—Danny Kaye and Lester Smith—purchased a radio station in Cincinnati, Ohio, whereupon they named me national program director. This, despite the fact that at KJR I was already broadcasting a daily three-hour show, balancing the joint duties of program director and music director and playing an active role in the station's sales efforts. Selling time on rock-'n'-roll radio to advertisers and agencies required detailed schooling for both. We could move people young and old like radio had never done before, but needed to explain how best to use us as a sales platform. Several times a week, I found myself attending meetings, going to lunches or making phone calls pitching the power of our mighty station and the effectiveness of Top 40 radio. This was at a time when radio still struggled to effectively compete with television and newspapers for advertising dollars. Those were tough fights and, as often as not, they were fights we won. I was proud of KJR, and of the juggernaut we had become and derived great pleasure from contributing in this way to the station's bottom line success. (I will write more about this "juggernaut" later in this book.)

In the summer of 1967, wearing my national program director's hat, I traveled to Cincinnati to visit our new station, WUBE. On a stifling, muggy June evening I found myself sitting in a room on an upper floor of the city's Sheraton Gibson Hotel. I watched out my window as National Guard troops advanced through the streets on crowds of rioters. Even on better days, the Gibson would not have ranked as one of the crown jewels in the Sheraton chain; on this particular night, the surroundings had me asking myself that famous question from Larry Verne's *Mister Custer*—"What am I doin' here?" The power was out, the air conditioning was down and armed troops stood at the doors refusing to let anyone enter or leave.

The mid- and late-'60s were a time of great racial unrest in America. I was in Los Angeles in the summer of '65 when, on a hot Thursday afternoon, the Watts District went up in flames. In Cincinnati on this particular day, the Avondale district erupted in violent protest; elsewhere that summer, dozens of other American cities likewise exploded. This was not long after Stephen Stills of Buffalo Springfield wrote the jarring lyrics of *For What It's Worth*:

> There's somethin' happening here
> What it is ain't exactly clear
> There's a man with a gun over there
> Tellin' me I gotta beware
> I think it's time we stop
> Hey, what's that sound?
> Everybody look what's going down.

What went down in Cincinnati that night was cars were overturned and burned, stores were ransacked, bullets were fired and more. As I sat, window open, peering down from my ringside seat, a jingling sound told me that at least the phones were still operating. Lifting the receiver, I heard the voice of Dick Curtis calling from Seattle:

"Pat," he said, "I have some bad news. Are you sitting down?"

Without explaining the events transpiring before me on the banks of the Ohio River, I said "Give it to me!"

Dick proceeded to read to me the major front page story from that afternoon's *Seattle Times*.

The *Times* reported that two Seattle policemen, together with a local real estate executive, had filed charges against Pat O'Day, his company, Pat O'Day & Associates, and his employer, radio station KJR, accusing them of violating the Sherman Antitrust Act. They asserted we had unlawfully monopolized the teenage and rock-'n'-roll entertainment industry in the Northwest. The laundry list of charges included conspiracy to eliminate competition, coercion, restraint of trade, bribery and, to top it off, payola—a charge which by extension implicated KJR. The suit was for $300,000 the litigants claimed was due them, plus treble damages. The paper went on to exaggerate my grip on Northwest rock and allowed the plaintiffs to paint me as a crook. Newspapers in those years could rarely be accused of impartiality when covering the controversies surrounding rock-'n'-roll.

The fact that radio (their mortal enemy) and Pat O'Day were under attack had many Seattle scribes salivating. They took great delight in printing stories attacking the evils of rock-'n'-roll. I think that many in that generation of newspaper people saw rock radio's hold on the community's youths as a threat to their century-long domination of the media. That fear, coupled with their institutional distaste for this new music style I represented, moved *The Seattle Times* in particular to seize upon my travails. I fared better in *The Seattle Post-Intelligencer*, but then, I wrote a weekly column for that paper. The *P-I* reported the story fairly, showing no readily-identifiable enthusiasm for one side or the other.

Dick entertained me next with a tape recording of the afternoon news-cast on our competitor, radio station KOL. Ever since KJR surpassed them in 1960, KOL had tried everything possible to reestablish a foothold in the youth market, but our dominance was so great, they were still scraping by with an audience a fraction the size of ours. Imagine, therefore, the glee with which they devoted most of a five-minute newscast to trumpeting the news of my impending downfall. I later heard they considered this the break they were waiting for, and nothing could hold them back from exploiting it to the fullest. I understood the optimism the lawsuit somehow made them feel. Being soundly beaten year-after-year isn't fun.

Was I frightened? Strangely, no. Was I upset? Emphatically, yes! I knew at once where all of this came from. Several months before, these same three gentlemen decided to enter the teenage dance business on the east side of Lake Washington. One of the policemen involved once worked security for my dances. He convinced two of his friends that here was an opportunity for them to grab a juicy slice of the pie. Nothing wrong with that. America is the land of opportunity and free enterprise. Their fatal mistake was trying to jump into a fully-developed industry with no real understanding of the intricacies of the business. They targeted the lucrative Bellevue market and signed a long-term lease for space in a vacant bowling alley near Eastgate alongside I-90.

Spending a great deal of money remodeling the building, they turned it into something resembling a Las Vegas showroom with lots of booths and tables and a small dance floor. A beautiful place, but totally wrong for their intended purpose. The perfect facilities for teen dances in the '60s were roller rinks, armories and ballrooms. No one wanted to sit down. These were dancers who wanted to stand. We tried slick decors and found that our teenage audiences rejected them. By spending wantonly on worthless nonessentials, the dance king wannabes defeated themselves before the battle began.

I knew nothing of their plans until three months prior to the filing of charges against me. When I learned the details of their new venture, I was struck by their naïveté, in particular, by their total ignorance of how bands were hired, especially bands that could fill buildings with paying teenage customers. Bands in the area understandably wanted to make a living with their music and relied on other promoters' dances as well as ours for gainful employment. Some of these musicians were married with children, and many of them held second jobs. Only with proper scheduling could they work every viable night. That meant planning dance lineups months in advance. For the dances we held that summer, the bands were booked as far back as February.

Certain of their success, our neophyte promoters opened their club in April and tried to hire bands on short notice. Not surprisingly, they failed to find groups capable of attracting customers. After operating for a few weeks with a nearly empty house, they called me up and asked for a meeting. When we sat down a few days later, they complained they were stuck because we controlled all the musicians, and it wasn't fair. Dick Curtis, Terry Bassett and I explained to them how the dance business worked and pointed out the deficiencies of their building and the problems with their timing in hiring bands. We were open and frank, giving them a free hour of consultation—not the sort of thing a successful business normally gives to its competitors.

We spoke; they didn't listen. The meeting ended with them asking to talk with me in private. Once we were alone, they opened a briefcase and produced a cashier's check made out to me personally in the amount of $10,000—a year's salary to many people in those days. The money was all mine, they explained, if I immediately dumped Lake Hills Roller Rink and moved my Bellevue dances to their building, where they would make us 50-50 partners. I handed back the check and said, "Thank you, but I can't do that." I explained I had a handshake agreement with the Monta family, who pioneered the dance business with me east of Lake Washington and depended on income from the Roller Rink for their livelihood. My commitment to the Montas was binding, a matter of principle, and I wouldn't break it at any price. I advised them to keep their money, tear out the booths and fancy décor and start scheduling bands when they became available in the future. They retorted that the bands only wanted to work for me. I assured them that, if they gave the bands the proper environment and tenaciously competed for dates, they would eventually have the music they needed to succeed. I pointed out that it took us over six years to arrive at our present level of efficiency. "Be patient. You can make it!" was my message.

Strychnine
The Sonics, 1965

SOMETIME AFTER THE LAWSUIT BEGAN, it occurred to me that my accusers likely had already been planning legal action against me when they made their visit, and that the money they offered me was a clumsy attempt at entrapment. At the time, I hadn't a clue. The plaintiffs hired prominent Seattle attorney William L. Dwyer to argue their case. Dwyer, who passed away in 2002 at the age of 70—was appointed to the US District Court in Seattle by President Jimmy Carter in 1977. Still a practicing attorney back in 1967, he was a leading antitrust specialist well known for his liberal leanings. He no doubt saw me and my dance organization, and radio station KJR, as representatives of the Establishment, an odd notion considering that we made our living from rock-'n'-roll. Given our success at doing that, this courtroom battle represented in some people's minds a classic case of David versus Goliath. That notion no doubt appealed to Dwyer.

He reportedly took the case on a contingency basis, meaning if his clients won, he would be paid from the proceeds—likely one-third of whatever amount was awarded. If they lost, he would get nothing, and his firm would see red ink. Word on the street had it they were so certain of victory, they were carrying the expenses. Dwyer faced a costly long-term battle (and so did I). It would be a high-profile case, and he was staking some of his reputation on the outcome. Not a reckless gambler, Dwyer must have figured he had a super chance of winning.

Trapped in my Cincinnati hotel room, alone with my thoughts and thousands of miles from home, I had nothing better to do than contemplate what suddenly looked like an uncertain future. My squeaky-clean image back in Seattle was history. What concerned me most were the allegations of payola. Since the 1959-60 Alan Freed/Dick Clark scandals, if a broadcaster, program director, or deejay feared one thing more than low ratings or an angry station manager, it was being charged with payola. For the uninitiated, *payola* was the act of using broadcast time to advance one's personal business agenda. As long as any such advancement was purchased and paid for in the form of a commercial, everything was fine. To program a song in exchange for favors of any kind was illegal. Payola took various forms — cash payments (no receipt required), surreptitious gifts, sexual favors and other special considerations exceeding $25 in value. The classic scenario involved a record company bribing a deejay or music director to play a song by one of their acts. I knew what I had and had not done, and scratched my head trying to figure out what actions of mine they thought constituted payola. Still, with my deep—though appropriate—relations with the music industry, my possible exposure was significant. Trying to picture what was happening to me and why, my mind drew nothing but blanks. Finally, I concluded that innuendos can spread like LA County brush fires, even in rainy Seattle. And these flames were threatening my workplace *and* my home.

Over the years, I had struggled to operate in such a fashion that anyone who challenged the station's integrity or mine would do so in vain. We were about to find out how well I had accomplished that. This I knew for certain: Bill Dwyer was a formidable adversary in and out of court. What moves could I make to counter his talent and prestige and level the playing field? I needed help, legal help, the best I could find and afford. Where should I look?

Putting such thoughts aside for a moment, I phoned my wife in Seattle and told her to leave the television off that evening, or at least to avoid the news. She told me friends were already calling, and that she was puzzled as to why. I said I would be home the next evening and would explain everything to her and our sons then. Hoping to get to my children before someone else hit them with the news, I suggested that the boys stay home from school the next day to await my return. That confused them, I'm sure, but a day off from school was not something they would grieve over. Next, I called my dance office and told everyone at Pat O'Day & Associates to take a total "No comment!" posture.

Galen Blackford, KJR's GM, was next on my list to call. I liked Galen best in the morning before he began his day's drinking; I called him in the evening. That day's news had sent him to the bottle early, and an unhappy conversation followed. *My God!* I thought to myself. *If he's this hacked, what are Lester Smith and Danny Kaye thinking?*

The lawsuit carried potentially disastrous licensing implications. In the worst-case scenario, Smith and Kaye stood to lose millions. I wanna tell ya, when it comes to providing the ingredients for an interesting evening, you can't beat sitting in Cincinnati, trapped inside a steaming-hot hotel room, looking out your window at a race riot, no electricity, guns everywhere, bullets flying, your personal empire and reputation heading straight down the toilet! You just can't have much more fun in one evening than that! Returning to Seattle, I prepared to negotiate the rocky road before me.

On my air show, where I was known for my happy-go-lucky manner and avoidance of serious editorial commentary, I addressed my predicament my first afternoon back by saying, "Well, you may have read all about me in the paper or seen a story about me on the television last night. Don't worry, it's all just a big exciting new contest, and I'll have details, ah, after I've talked to my lawyer!" I laughed, and on we went.

Outside the control room, I began to search for a knowledgeable anti-trust attorney to represent me, while the station hired lawyers to investigate me. They had no other choice. Before responding to any charges, they had to determine for themselves independently whether the allegations being made against me were valid. They couldn't just take my word for it. To speed up the process, I opened my company's books, handed over my personal bank records and made sure my staff and dance partners were easily available for questioning. I made everything about my operations and dealings transparent. And why not? I had nothing to hide.

For 60 days, my staff and I underwent hours of intensive questioning, while the station's attorneys combed through every bank record and piece of correspondence associated with me. They included John Wallace of the firm Ogden and Murphy, along with Jim Murphy, who was chairman of the Washington State Association of Broadcasters and soon became a very close friend. Then Lester Smith, partner and CEO of the company, flew in from Portland and asked for a meeting. I had no idea about the outcome of his investigation and, though I thought I had nothing to fear, who knew how all those attorney/accountant types would interpret the evidence? The charges brought against me placed Danny Kaye's and Lester Smith's entire operation in jeopardy. What had they decided to do?

On the one hand, the easiest solution for them was to fire me and mount the best legal defense possible to protect themselves. On the other hand, the radio station I programmed and starred at was setting records with ratings as high as 33 percent of all radio listeners in the total region, including adults. In addition, Pat O'Day & Associates was the station's largest local advertiser. We were paying cold hard cash for all of our radio spots, and the total came to more than the salary the station paid me, a whole lot more. My dances and concerts added mightily to the station's success, I thought. We promoted KJR with signs and banners and always tried to involve the station's deejays. It was widely held that Pat O'Day, his concerts, dances and other activities were inseparable from radio station KJR. If that weren't enough, I always played the totally-loyal company man, helping with Kaye-Smith stations in Spokane, Cincinnati and, on occasion, Kansas City (although the KC station was country western, not my specialty). I was about to find just how much all of this counted for.

Les Smith, who never minced words, made it quick and painless. We sat down and he said simply,

> The lawyers all tell me you're clean. You're powerful, your people at Associates are sometimes a little pushy, but you're clean. We will defend the station. You hire your own attorneys to defend yourself and your company. It will probably take years, but let's go win this thing, and let's win it big!

I took a deep breath, thanked Les for his confidence and support and went out looking for legal counsel. The State of Washington had recently won a huge antitrust action against General Electric, a price-fixing case involving generators for the state's hydroelectric dams. Without admitting guilt, the defendants agreed to a multimillion dollar settlement. Lead attorney for Washington in the case was George Freeze. The state's Attorney General at the time, John J. O'Connell, was a friend of mine, and John confirmed that Freeze would be an excellent choice to defend me. Based on that recommendation, I hired George, and the countless hours needed to lay the legal groundwork for my defense began.

Our first major task involved scheduling depositions from the many witnesses. Both sides went before the judge and outlined their cases, explaining where they intended to go to gather evidence and what they expected to find. Evidenciary rules in an antitrust case are as wide as the Pacific Ocean, and into this vast expanse my opponents embarked on an exhaustive and expensive fishing expedition. Painfully, every dollar they spent I had to match, and every hour one of their people expended trolling for evidence, one of our people had to counter preparing a possible defense.

When Dwyer's team failed to find what they were looking for, they widened and deepened their search. They expected to uncover proof of wanton abuse of power, price fixing, bribery, intimidation, under-the-table payoffs and widespread efforts to restrain trade. Such evidence was missing. Where was it? They knew I had hidden it somewhere. Their clients assured them I had. Disgruntled rock bands were sure of it, too. Confident they would prevail, like a pack of Energizer legal bunnies, Dwyer's team kept going and going and going, and got nowhere. His law firm dug ever deeper into its pockets and began showing signs of desperation as their investigators ranged farther and farther afield. Musicians and agents in California were drawn into the proceedings. Personally, I spent 17 full days being deposed, and still my opponents weren't satisfied.

Amid this ordeal, the attorney I entrusted with my defense and future began to lose interest in my case. The signs were clear, but made no sense. I was paying him large sums of money every month, always on time, while he was sending underlings to the proceedings and not returning my calls. The answer came one night when a television newscast reported that at the time Attorney General John J. O'Connell hired attorney George Freeze on behalf of the state, the two of them made a deal agreeing to direct a percentage of Freeze's fees to a law firm still connected with O'Connell. Although O'Connell vigorously defended himself, arguing nothing in the law prohibited such an arrangement, the stench of payoff permeated the affair. Freeze worked on the state's case on a contingency basis, and his portion of the settlement totaled in the millions. Forget the finer points of the law, or the definition of the word "is." It smelled, and badly.

About that time, I started wondering *What else can go wrong?* We were already months into the battle, and it looked like the case would drag on for another year or two at least.

In a gentlemanly way, George told me that, given the distractions he faced, it was in my best interests for him to resign from my case. I felt for him. He was a brilliant young attorney who seized the opportunity when it came to try a truly big case. He probably felt that kickbacks to large law firms were how such business was done. While the applicable law at that time was gray at best, that did little to exonerate him in the court of public opinion. Coming off a huge victory, his good name was tarnished, a feeling I was becoming all too familiar with.

Wanting no further disruptions to my defense, and alarmed by Bill Dwyer's tenacity and the probe's vast scope, I needed to find the very best legal help money could buy, period. My antitrust Matlock soon appeared in the person of Paine Karr, senior partner in Karr, Tuttle, Koch and Campbell, one of the big law firms in town. Paine's reputation was second to none, his abilities unmatched. I explained my problems to Paine, and he agreed to take my case. My fate now rested in his hands.

The case's costs by this time were staggering. Had I not made a series of fortuitous real estate investments in previous years, I would never have been able to afford the legal bills I racked up. In early 1963, I moved into a new house in Newport Shores on the east side of Lake Washington, just south of Bellevue. The development consisted of a series of 150-foot wide canals dredged out of a peninsula, with home sites laid out along the canal banks. We built the third house in Newport Shores, and for several years we stood nearly alone. The concept was so new, other buyers were slow to follow suit.

Jim Clapp, the developer and a close friend, sank a fortune into an idea that was still ahead of its time and had to lower his prices dramatically to stimulate sales. A friend of mine worked for the real estate firm (John L. Scott) that had the listings on the lots. In order to maintain their relationship with the developer, they needed to meet certain annual sales quotas. Every December, as the New Year approached, they reached a point when they realized *We have to sell some lots fast!* Living in Newport Shores, I saw the development's future and, over a three-year period, purchased a series of waterfront properties at fire sale prices. By the time Bill Dwyer sued me in court, the value of those lots had skyrocketed, and by selling them off I was just able to pay my legal expenses. That wasn't why I originally bought them, but I had no choice. Today, those lots are worth millions; then, they allowed me to survive an unfair, unreasonable attack.

On the eve of the trial, Paine met me at his office, sat me down and said,

> Pat, here we are with a trial about to start, and I'm puzzled. What can Bill Dwyer possibly know that I don't? Pat, if you've laid all your cards on the table face up—and it appears you have—and there are no surprises out there you haven't told me about, he simply doesn't have a case, and that's not like him. We know that his firm has likely sunk $150,000 into this already, so financially, they're out on a limb. But they're showing no signs of quitting. I just don't get it!

I asked Paine, "What if Dwyer's bluffing?"

Paine answered that wasn't like him, but there was no denying his firm's huge investment. And it was going to cost them another $150,000 at least to make it through trial, which everyone expected would last a month-and-a-half. The cost to me to continue would likely equal that, and I didn't relish the thought of paying out that much more money. Under the Sherman Antitrust Act's provisions, I would have no recourse for recovering any of my legal costs, even if I prevailed.

You have heard or read about cases being settled on courthouse steps. Well, I saw it happen. As Paine and I walked up the stairs of the Federal Court House in Seattle on our way to listen to the judge's opening remarks and admonitions, we spotted Bill Dwyer climbing the steps ahead of us. Paine approached Bill and said, "You don't have it coming, but Pat will agree to thirty-five thousand, and we can all go home." Dwyer swung around and said, "One hundred thousand."

Paine responded, "Bill, you're just going to be embarrassed, and you know it. Thirty-five thousand, and not a penny more!"

Dwyer paused, stroked his chin, looked off into the distance and said, "Fifty-five thousand."

Paine looked at me, I nodded my head and he said to Dwyer, "Fifty-five thousand it is. Let's go home."

We both shook Dwyer's hand, and it was over, just like that, save for the paperwork. Les Smith and I signed the final settlement in March 1970. During this same period, I endured yet another shock to my system: an investigation by the Federal Communications Commission. That story's next.

7 — Kind of a Drag

The Buckinghams, 1966

WHILE I PREPARED MY DEFENSE against Dwyer and his clients, FCC investigators took increasing interest in my plight. The payola allegations stimulated their bloodhound instincts, and they sent a representative to Seattle to eavesdrop on the testimony and determine whether payola was among the many sins I surely had committed. Regardless of the outcome of my battle with Dwyer, the feds figured there was something still hidden that Dwyer couldn't find and they needed to expose. In a separate action, the FCC announced it was mounting its own investigation of Pat O'Day and KJR. Shortly thereafter, I was entertained by FBI investigators who grilled me mercilessly in their patented humorless way.

I resented neither the FBI nor the FCC. Both had their jobs to do, and feeling bitter about that fact would not have helped anyway. I wanted to be part of a clean broadcast industry, and if the spotlight needed to be focused on me, that was an unavoidable cost I had to accept. I fully respected the process. What I *did* resent were all the phony charges and knee-jerk reactions of the lawyers and plaintiffs that started the whole mess. They threw a large monkey wrench into the works of a clean, honest, responsible, previously smooth-running machine.

Over at 158 Thomas Street, by the Space Needle, the troops at Pat O'Day & Associates had a storm cloud hanging over their heads, but couldn't find an ark to put the animals in. We began to second-guess everything we did, wondering about legal implications. The FBI was commendably thorough, talking to every musician in town, my various dance partners, my banker, my neighbors, my mother and who knows whom else—perhaps our family dog? Once the FBI completed their preliminary investigation, the FCC notified us that they planned to conduct their own full-scale hearings in Seattle to complete the hunt. What a circus that was!

When the FBI turned over their findings to the FCC, the latter had been disappointed with the results. There were some bureaucrats in the other Washington who truly believed something was rotten in the state of Washington. I was told this several years later by Dick Rheil, a gentleman who at the time of my travails was working in the FCC's Complaints and Compliance division. Later he went into private practice and served as my DC counsel when I was buying radio stations. He told me that the FCC had been long overdue for an investigation of someone and decided to make me the lucky guy. In the late '50s, the payola scandal made big news nationally. Dick Clark from Philadelphia, Alan Freed from New York and many other figures in the radio and music industries were caught in the dragnet cast out by Congress and its investigators. Jobs were lost, careers were ruined or sidetracked and a few people went to jail.

One of the finer points of the law as it was then written that many people have overlooked is the fact that much of what we today condemn as payola was, in the late '50s, legal—if somewhat unethical—as long as you reported your play-for-pay income to the tax authorities. Anyone who went to jail probably cheated on their taxes. Just like with Al Capone, bad accounting, not more sinister crimes, did them in. In the wake of the Congressional hearings, new legislation was enacted and, *ex post facto*, the actions of all those errant deejays became criminal. Meanwhile, many East Coast deejays headed west before anyone could get too nosy regarding their behind-the-scenes dealings.

Among the central figures grilled by the investigating committee, Dick Clark was one of the few to escape virtually unscathed, although he was the one who hit the jackpot when it came to on-the-side payments. Findings from the widely-publicized hearings led many to proclaim louder than ever that rock-'n'-roll had corrupted the broadcast industry. They claimed it owed its success not to the quality of the music but rather to the clandestine payments handed over to all those shady deejays and crooked music directors. Their logic assumed that the youth of America were so gullible and stupid, they were incapable of making their own choices of music, blindly buying whatever records disc jockeys told them to buy, whether they liked the music or not. While all of this was, to put it kindly, muddled thinking at best, many in the music business held this new style of music sweeping the country in low esteem, especially older musicians and song writers, many of them big-name stars who couldn't or wouldn't adapt to change. In desperation, they hoped they were right, that we rock-'n'-rollers were every bit as corrupt as the payola scandal made us appear and that the grand old music of the past would rise again. History has shown the futility of their resistance. They wouldn't find contentment until years later when they narrowed their focus and concentrated their efforts on reaching the older generation that had grown up with them. The exhilaration of mass appeal was no longer theirs to enjoy.

Payola is the act of personally accepting money or favors or gifts in return for putting something on the public airwaves that isn't a paid-for commercial. Anything of value received in connection with a broadcast had to be recorded on the station's official program log which the station kept for six years. The FCC was investigating me for alleged violations of these rules, and the possible consequences weren't a pretty vision to contemplate. A variation of payola was plugola. *Plugola* refers to promoting a for-profit event or product in return for inducements.

In an attempt to reach the bottom of my misdeeds, the FCC held a lengthy round of hearings at the old Federal Office Building in Seattle, giving all comers with complaints against me a chance to step forward and air their accusations and grievances. Subpoenas went out to all of my business associates, to people working for me at Pat O'Day & Associates, to artists performing at my dances and concerts. The final list of witnesses was long, and when the FCC set aside a month to conduct their business. Allegedly, the hearings were held behind closed doors, with all witnesses sworn to secrecy. This, however, was the music business they were dealing with, and secrecy therein was and is unattainable. Who was feeding the print media with the rumors, innuendos and occasionally factual information they published, no one would say. My counsel and KJR's counsel, Gerard Borros of Washington, DC, was allowed to attend the hearings, and they provided me with daily reports of the progress which I compared with rumors on the street and occasional stories in the media. What would be my fate?

Fire
The Crazy World of Arthur Brown, 1968

CONSISTENT WITH THE WAY MY LUCK WAS GOING, another challenge to my sanity presented itself, this one from within my KJR family. For eight years, I toiled as a loyal, productive employee of the station. Afternoon drive deejay, program director, music director, national program director, biggest advertiser. Twice national Program Director of the Year, once national Radio Man of the Year. We absolutely owned the Seattle-area market, and KJR was considered one of the two or three greatest radio stations in the US. As a key member of the station's team, I had by general consensus been more than a little responsible for that success. Yet, I was constantly subjected to the unfair and occasionally abusive supervision of the station's general manager, Galen Blackford. Galen was a man I cared for a great deal; when he was sober, there were glimmers of camaraderie which I deeply enjoyed. Unfortunately, as my years at the station progressed, his moments of sobriety became more infrequent.

He liked to arrive at the station early, conclude business matters by 11:45 and leave for lunch just before noon. Three- or four-martini lunches were commonplace in the media and advertising business in those days. Some people could handle it, others could not. Galen was among those others, and everyone around him suffered badly as a result. In some people, excessive drink brings out their lighter side; in Galen Blackford, it brought out the dark and insecure. The hard-working Dr. Jekyl who left the station in late morning returned in late-afternoon as the angry, suspicious, dangerous Mr. Hyde, hungry for the blood of a deejay or two. I instructed my air staff to avoid him if at all possible during those afternoon hours. Around 4:30 he departed for home, and normality again prevailed. Knowing all this, I conducted my important business with Galen in the morning hours when the odds favored him being rational. Most times, he wouldn't remember or admit to any of his heated pronouncements made the previous afternoon. His behavior made separating fact from fiction nearly impossible.

That is the sort of Twilight Zone we worked in at Seattle's number one radio station through most of the '60s. I was always puzzled how Les Smith, head of the parent company, maintained his confidence in Galen, and assumed that because the station was so wildly successful, his excesses didn't matter. In part, I understood. Blackford possessed formidable business and sales skills. He was a Naval officer during World War II and later an executive with an outdoor advertising firm, before eventually arriving in radio. The lawsuit and investigation, brought on by me and involving his beloved station, pushed Blackford over the edge. My sympathies for one ravaged by alcohol were of little comfort to either of us. Countless times during this period, he informed me that Les Smith had little tolerance as far as I was concerned. He reminded me weekly that I had caused the company considerable grief, and that he alone stood between me and the cancellation of my contract with the station. Having had little personal contact with Les Smith, who lived in Portland where our home office was situated, I believed Blackford.

In August 1968, the steaming cauldron that was my station manager finally boiled over. The antitrust business was completed, and the FCC investigation was moving full speed ahead. Our GM was absent from the station for increasingly long periods, often for days at a time. Homer Pope, a precious individual who had been with the station since its infancy in the 20s and was now serving as office manager, became my close friend and almost my ally. I say *almost* because his loyalty to Blackford was total. Homer did everything in his power, at all costs, to protect and cover for Galen, and I understood that. Pope always provided a good reason to the home office for Blackford's absence, while I went through hell.

By now, Blackford was calling me at home at night, totally intoxicated. This is how our conversations typically went:

> Well, you've really done it this time! Now listen, you son-of-a-bitch, I'm tired of covering your ass. You probably think you're getting away with it, but I've been doing some checking around and I know exactly what's going on. Now, you had better tell it to me straight or I'm not protecting you from Les any longer. He hates your guts, and I'm the only friend you've got, but I have to know the truth, and I do, so you'd better come clean with me or your ass is out of here. Now, you be in my office at 8:00 A.M. tomorrow morning and I don't want to listen to any more of your fancy-sounding shit. I want you to come clean in writing, just lay it all out, everything, and I will try to save your job!

Those conversations were protracted and filled with redundancies, containing all of the above remarks and more. While I knew that Galen was always very drunk when he delivered these diatribes, I figured there had to be a morsel of truth in what he was saying. I felt myself standing on dangerous ground with nothing to confess. Although the morning meetings he called for never took place, I always reported to his office at the designated hour, ignoring the fact that he delivered the order while on a binge. Never once was Galen there to meet me. When he finally did arrive, he gave nary a hint of remembering the previous night's conversation.

My decision to resign from KJR was made at a time when I felt there was little else I could do. Blackford made my life at the station intolerable, while my concert business was taking giant strides forward. We had just opened an office in Dallas, and Terry Bassett recently left Seattle to run it. Our concert business was booming, our recently initiated teen fairs prospering. My entertainment company needed my full-time leadership. If the station was going to swing the axe anyway, I opted to leave on my own terms with my head still attached to my torso. It was time to say good-bye.

To leave was heartbreaking. The radio station was my real life, my outside business still a hobby in comparison. I loved radio. I loved being on radio. I loved radio station KJR-Seattle like an only child. Within its walls, my boyhood dreams came true, and I never wanted to wake up one day and find them gone. But it was time to do the unthinkable. One morning, after enduring another of Blackford's midnight specials, I sat down with tears in my eyes and composed a letter of resignation addressed to Lester Smith. Not once did I mention the deteriorated state of my relationship with Galen.

I stated that I felt it was time for me to move on, that my entertainment business was growing and clearly needed my supervision. I thanked Les for giving me the opportunity to work for him over the years and told him I would stand by the station and help in every way I could to absolve it from the charges of the FCC's inquisitors. I offered to stay on board long enough for the station to find a suitable replacement—if they wanted me to. Just 33 years old, I was ending a relationship and career that were the fulfillment of my life's dream. It was a miserable turn of events. I sent the original of the letter to our Portland headquarters by overnight courier and submitted a copy to Galen Blackford. True to form, KJR's station manager was, on yet another morning, missing in action.

The next evening, I was at home playing with my kids and trying to get the sad events I had just triggered off my mind when the phone rang. It was Les Smith. His message again was swift, painless and brief:

Pat, I got your letter and I'm ignoring it. I appreciate all of your concerns and the stress you're under. I've made reservations for you on the 7:00 A.M. United to LA. I'll meet you at the United Red Carpet room at the airport. Then we're driving over to Danny Kaye's house.

It was a shocked and thrilled young man who flew back to Seattle from Los Angeles the next afternoon, a shocked and thrilled young man just named the new general manager of KJR. It turned out that Les Smith was fully aware of the station's problems, but, with things going so well, chose to delay addressing the issue—until my letter arrived. My surprise resignation forced them to implement a plan which, unbeknownst to me, was already in the works. A second future-altering decision was made that exciting day. Lester Smith, Danny Kaye and Pat O'Day agreed to become full-fledged business partners. Les and the lawyers had audited my books more closely than an angry squad of IRS agents on a search-and-destroy mission. They must have liked what they found. Les and Danny asked me to take my entertainment company and merge it with their broadcast company. With unlimited capital now available, I would work to expand the entertainment division. In time, we would recruit a management team to run it, while I maintained my percentage ownership. The only thing making this arrangement less than perfect was knowing it meant bidding farewell to my listeners and abandoning my great passion, the afternoon Pat O'Day Program at KJR. In the brave new world we were about to enter, there would be no time left for live broadcasting by me.

I will always regret leaving that show so soon. The happiest moments of my life have been spent behind a microphone, introducing great music and trying to make listeners laugh or cry or do something. Even so, a chance to become the youngest general manager in Seattle radio history proved irresistible. As to Galen Blackford, Les and Danny gave him a generous retirement package which he enjoyed for a few short years before his health failed completely.

Jumpin' Jack Flash
The Rolling Stones, 1968

THE GOVERNMENT LOOSENED ITS PURSE STRINGS for the hearing, transforming Seattle into one big but not-so-happy (for me) rock-'n'-roll reunion. Most witnesses stayed at the five-star Olympic Hotel, a few blocks north from the building where the hearings were being held. On occasion,

Two views of the Rolling Stones in concert in the Seattle Center Coliseum, 1965

I stopped by to visit with old friends among those subpoenaed to appear, congregating evenings in the bar. Managers called to testify included people handling the Rolling Stones, the Beach Boys, the Mamas & the Papas, the Righteous Brothers and many other acts. Paul Revere and members of all the regional bands were summoned to town for interrogation. We never directly discussed the proceedings, but small clues dropped here and there indicated that the hearing examiner and the FCC attorneys were on a combination wild goose chase/snipe hunt. When it came time for me to testify, I occupied the witness stand for the better part of a week.

I almost—but not quite—sympathized with the government people, who had reached a dead end with no way out. They asked me the same questions repeatedly, slightly altering their wording each time in an obvious attempt to trip me up and extract incriminating or contradictory testimony. One lawyer asked me why I was playing the Rolling Stones' current record (*Jumpin' Jack Flash*—indisputably one of the greatest rock-'n'-roll songs of all time) as frequently as I was. Wasn't it because I was presenting them in concert at the Seattle Coliseum the next week? I provided evidence showing that KJR was actually playing the Stones' latest release no more often than any other rock station in the country. I asked them whether they thought I should deprive Rolling Stones fans of hearing the music of what was then the world's hottest group just because I happened to be bringing them to town. The Stones' airplay was totally appropriate.

My favorite memory of the hearings (there weren't many good ones to compete with it) was an exchange involving Merrilee Rush. The questioning reached the point where I was asked, "Isn't it true that Merrilee Rush gives you a new television set for Christmas every year?"

"No," I replied, "that's not true. But we do have a gift-giving tradition. Every year she gives me a bottle of Jack Daniels, and I give her a smoked turkey."

I couldn't help but overhear the questioning government attorney turn to a colleague and mumble, "That's the same damn thing she said!"

For his edification, I tried to explain to the hearing examiner at length why he was there. Over the years, in a fair and honest manner, we developed what was once a simple idea into an entertainment powerhouse. We were envied and feared and considered intimidating by some, which I attributed to our strength and professionalism. Also, for years I regularly made decisions which negatively impacted some musicians. To the point of harassment, record companies and bands approached me constantly with pleas to play their music. They all wanted airtime on KJR. Like it or not, that was essential for a record's ultimate success in the region, and there weren't enough minutes in the hour, or hours in the day, to give every record a shot. Inevitably, some lost out. By nature, the process was to several degrees subjective. Any decision to play one record as opposed to another was based on whether I thought it had hit potential. I pointed out to the examiner that it mattered not to me which record company or group enjoyed the resultant benefits. In the end, listeners and record buyers decided such questions. If a song drew support, I kept playing it; if a song rated a zero with our audience, I yanked it and tried another one. I wasn't in business to play the music I liked. I was in business to play the music KJR's listeners liked (although most times, I liked what they liked, a fortunate coincidence).

The same was true when it came to hiring bands for our entertainment company. If a band helped us sell tickets, we hired and rehired them; if a band didn't help us sell tickets, we hired them once or not at all. For economic reasons, and to keep our customers satisfied, we rarely could afford to give a band a second chance—unless they were the Beach Boys. These were basic business decisions, not always simple, but necessary. There was no mystery or black magic involved—and certainly no payola. I explained that was how my partners and I viewed it, while admitting openly that a sizeable number of bands over the years disagreed with me. For them, too, it was a question of economics, with bruised egos and lost dreams thrown in. They invested time, money and emotion into their recording efforts and were all convinced their musical output was the greatest thing since the Lord's Prayer. When they heard my refusals, they were disappointed, and understandably so. For some, disappointment morphed into frustration and anger and resentment. They wouldn't accept the fact that I didn't believe in the potential of their records. In some cases, they convinced a smaller station to give their records a try and exulted when they proved me wrong. When shown the error of my ways, like in the case of *Granny's Pad*, I reversed direction. I wanted my station to play the hits as much or more than any other station manager out there. That was all. Hits. More hits. Big hits. And some more hits after that.

Angel of the Morning
Merrilee Rush & the Turnabouts, 1968

ONE OF MY DETRACTORS DURING THESE TIMES was my longtime friend Neil Rush, then-husband of Merrilee. Backed by Neil's band, she recorded record after record after record, all of which I declined to play at KJR. Neil suspected an ulterior motive on my part. Maybe he thought I felt they charged me too much to play at one of my dances. Maybe this, maybe that, maybe some other thing. Whatever it was, it angered him. Then one day in 1968, after Merrilee went to Memphis and recorded for Amy Mala's Bell Records a number Chips Moman produced, Neil brought it to the station, no doubt fearing another *no* from me. I took the record into my office, listened, walked back out and said, "Neil, call Merrilee and tell her to turn on the radio. And Neil, get in your car and listen. We will play it every hour the rest of today and keep playing it!"

"Why?" Neil asked in shock. "After all this time, why?"

"Neil," I said, "because you've finally brought me a hit!"

Angel of the Morning certainly was that.

Under oath, I testified that rumors had circulated for years that some kind of fix was on over at KJR and Pat O'Day & Associates, and that nearly all of those rumors originated from among musicians and bands whose records I rejected. As I said this, I noticed the hearing examiner nodding his head in understanding. I was sure that many of those disgruntled musicians were called in to testify to the illegal barriers I allegedly threw across their roads to success. In every case, they failed to provide credible evidence to support their accusations.

How did it end? In dollars, my legal fees and settlement costs neared a quarter-of-a-million dollars, and those were 1968 dollars, when you could buy a nice four-bedroom home in Bellevue for $30,000. In the local media, the story ended like those famous last lines of that T.S. Eliot poem ["The Hollow Men"] we all had to read in high school, for reasons understood only by our English teachers: "This is the way the world ends / This is the way the world ends / This is the way the world ends / Not with a bang but a whimper." They jumped with excitement when my predicament first surfaced, followed my trial and hearings enthusiastically for a few weeks and, after that, grew bored and inattentive.

A slowdown at Pat O'Day & Associates cost me the services of my dear friend Dick Curtis (as it turned out, only for the time being). Dick faced heavy obligations and, until the slowdown, his compensation from the company was excellent. When that compensation fell below the critical point, he had no choice but to look elsewhere for work. I urged him to go back into radio full time and helped him land a deejay job at KOL, KJR's biggest competitor in the region's rock radio market, in the Fall of 1967. Go figure!

More than a year after the FCC's hearings in Seattle concluded, the results of several years of terror, suspicion, rumor, innuendo, frightening costs, self-doubts and valuable time squandered were totaled. The bottom line, delivered in a brief one-page letter from the Federal Communications Commission, read:

> After conducting one of the most exhaustive investigations we have initiated, we find absolutely no evidence of any wrongdoing on the part of radio station KJR or its manager, Pat O'Day. The station's license renewal, which has been on hold pending the outcome of the investigation, is hereby granted.

That was it. No apologies. No "Gosh, Pat, this shouldn't have happened!" Just a one-page letter, and it was over. I couldn't even laugh about it.

When The Saints Go Marching In

Louis Armstrong, 1933

I AM PROUD OF THE FACT THAT SEATTLE finally gained attention as a unique and vibrant rock-'n'-roll city. The lessons we learned we were able to transmit to other areas of the country with good results. Our dances spanned the state, and we developed teenage night clubs that were coming into their own. In downtown Seattle we formed a successful partnership with a club called the Trolley. I escaped my first club experience back in 1963 by the skin of my teeth. It was called the Pat O'Day Party Line and sat at 707 First Avenue, three blocks from where Safeco Field now stands. Like most bad ideas, it seemed like a good one at the time. Each table had a telephone and a brightly lit number overhead, and we stationed an operator in the balcony. You could pick up the phone, call the table of your choice and ask the person on the other end if they wanted to dance.

The club was well attended as long as we kept the cover charge low—lower than the number we budgeted before we opened. Our labor costs exceeded what we had anticipated and, due to the section of town we were in, the Police Department arbitrarily assigned us two officers. (The city held all the cards where teenagers were involved and made up the rules as they went along.) Also, we discovered that our customers never ordered the food that was available at high preparation cost and didn't drink as many soft drinks as forecast. Johnny Tillotson opened the club, and the Beach Boys played there, too. So did Roy Orbison, the Cascades and other national acts, all with little positive effect. Despite all of our efforts, the club continued to lose money with no sign of a turnaround. We had to do something, and quickly!

On a trip to New York, I visited a club enjoying great success employing a novel approach. I figured the same idea would work in Seattle. We closed the Party Line, applied for a beer-and-wine license, took out the phones and added a popcorn machine. Most importantly, I recruited the choir from Mt. Zion Baptist Church, an African-American church of great size and success. The talent, energy and musical opulence of its singers were unmatched. We leased that all-important Hammond B3 organ. Choir robes were another matter. The church, and rightfully so, would neither rent, loan, nor in any way allow their robes to be used in an establishment where alcoholic beverages were served. Instead, I made a donation to Seattle's Franklin High School, acquired their used choir robes, signed a contract with the singers and instrumentalist from Mt. Zion, and opened *The Sweet Chariot.*

On opening night, movie star Annette Funicello was my guest. On stage, she struggled to open the ceremonial bottle of champagne. When the cork finally popped, it shot to the ceiling, hit the center of a round aluminum air vent, bounced back down and banged off the top of the drummer's cymbals with a loud ring. The crowd cheered; it was a good omen.

The Chariot's music was no different than what echoed in the halls of Mt. Zion and most other Baptist churches on Sunday evenings: high energy spirituals. Customers were given tambourines and large containers of popcorn when they paid their admission and entered the club. The highlight of every evening was the performance of the Louis Armstrong classic, *When The Saints Go Marching In.* The music created such fervor, everyone joined in a joyous parade, snaking around the tables, marching through the club, playing their tambourines and singing loudly with the choir. It was spine-tingling fun.

Within two weeks, every night was a sellout, and on weekends lines of people waiting to get in wound around the block. Sixty days later, with queues continuing to stretch down First Avenue, someone approached us and offered to buy the club, and we accepted.

Good Golly, Miss Molly
Mitch Ryder & the Detroit Wheels, 1966

RETURNING TO 1968. We had four clubs we either owned or operated as partnerships. In Seattle, Spokane and Yakima we were staging annual teenage fairs. We called them *Teen Spectaculars*, and they were exactly that. In Seattle, we rented a large venue, the Seattle Center Coliseum (today called Key Arena and home of the Seattle SuperSonics), and filled the main floor with booths of every description and size, all with teen appeal: displays of new clothes, automobiles, electronic equipment, sports equipment, cosmetics. Every booth featured a game or activity of some sort. You could even shoot free throws and match your skills against SuperSonics players. Beneath the permanent seats, we set up four separate theaters and called them Clubs North, South, East and West. Untried local bands performed there continuously during the day, vying with each other for attention, while established bands from the area played in the evening.

In the arena itself, thousands of permanent seats stretched to the ceiling. On the main floor in front sat a large stage where at three in the afternoon and eight in the evening headline stars performed. Maybe it was the Beau Brummels (*Laugh, Laugh*) from San Francisco or the Fever Tree (*San Francisco Girls*) from Houston. Maybe Paul Revere & The Raiders, or Canned Heat (*Goin' Up the Country, Let's Work Together*) from LA. Or maybe one of those rocking groups from Detroit: a young Suzi Quatro and her all-girl band, The Pleasure Seekers (*What a Way to Die*) or Mitch Ryder & the Detroit Wheels (*Devil With a Blue Dress On*). What a choice teens had, and they only paid six dollars for admission. With low ticket prices like this, we depended on exhibitors' fees for a large portion of our income. The only way we could afford to bring in major acts was to shuffle them around our dance circuit for a few days before and after the fair.

Our teen spectaculars were so successful, I traveled to Japan with Tom Hulett to explore the possibility of staging an American-style teenage fair in Tokyo. The trip went well, and we established a relationship with the most powerful man in Japanese entertainment at the time, Tats Nakashima. We made tentative arrangements to rent Tokyo's Hirumi Dome in partnership with a Japanese newspaper and garnered enthusiastic support from the American Embassy. The US Trade Mission in Tokyo agreed to help underwrite the event. It would have been held, too, had not other sensitive issues been raised. It was about this time that Pat O'Day & Associates and Concerts West entered into a new partnership with Les Smith and Danny Kaye. Danny was known internationally for his tireless efforts on behalf of UNICEF helping the needy children of the world. He decided that holding a commercial for-profit event like one of our teen fairs in Japan might reflect badly on him in some people's minds, and I had to agree. It *would* have been unwise to do anything that might cause observers to question Danny's motives. As a result, we dropped our immediate plans to enter the Japanese market while maintaining our relationship with Tats, who proved enormously helpful in later years when we decided to develop our concert business overseas, especially in the Pacific Rim.

As if night clubs and teen fairs weren't enough, at about this time we became partners in the new Seattle franchise of the Continental Football League and started handling all of the team's promotions and advertising. Coincidentally, someone working for us, Tom Hulett, was starting quarterback on the team. (Hulett became a key player and a controversial element of our concert business in later years.) Tom was an all-state quarterback at Seattle's Garfield High School and went on to the University of Washington on a football scholarship. During his freshman year, he was caught up in an NCAA investigation into the team and alleged recruiting violations. He left school as a result of the scandal and enlisted in the Army, where he played football for a service team in West Germany. Upon discharge from the service, he went to work for Universal CIT, the flooring company for car dealers. They sent him to Salt Lake City, where he patrolled used car lots determining whether all the cars financed for the dealers were in fact there. Hulett was a friend of Dick Curtis, who met him through former Washington Husky all-American quarterback Bob Schloredt. We were looking for someone to sell booth space for our teen fairs, someone also qualified to handle related financial book work in the office. Hearing of the opening, Tom flew to Seattle and begged for the job, and we hired him.

Pat O'Day & Associates became agents and consultants for Seattle's CFL team, the Rangers. Some of our fellow investors thought that when Seattle was accepted into the NFL, the new team would have to pay the minor league team for territorial rights. Fanciful thinking that was. In the end, it never really mattered at all, because the Rangers ran out of money long before the NFL could supplant them. The team played in High School Memorial Stadium, not far from the Space Needle. Heavy promotion and public curiosity initially drew good crowds. Over the ensuing months, fans grasped the reality that the Rangers were just another band of minor league footballers dreaming of never-to-be-achieved big league greatness, and attendance dropped. One of our attorneys decided he wanted to buy our football team's shares, which we gave him in exchange for legal work.

All of this happened in 1968, a year when major social changes were being fought over from coast to coast. Martin Luther King was assassinated in April, Bobby Kennedy in June. Later that summer riots rocked the Democratic National Convention in Chicago. Subsequent trials produced the Chicago Seven. In Seattle, we had our share of turmoil, too. A growing counterculture obsessed over American involvement in Viet Nam. Their protests led the way, and in time many other Americans turned against the war.

The music was changing as well, in step with our country's mood. *Youth* is a transitory concept. By the long-applied standards of our dances (over 14/under 21), the teens who flocked to the Spanish Castle and the Sheridan Park Hall in 1959-60 were no longer youths in 1968. They were all in their twenties, some of them were still in college, most of them held steady jobs, many of them were married and the unmarried males were likely facing military service if they weren't already in. Our dances targeted the Northwest's youths, and by nature we were shooting at a moving target. In radio, we often spoke about being on-target or off-target with our listeners. We faced the same challenge with our dances. The teens in our targeted audience in 1968 had been 7-12 years old when we first opened at the Spanish Castle. With all of the changes going on around them, they were transforming into a different breed before our eyes. Partly in response, partly in anticipation, we were adapting as fast as we could. America was living the old Gypsy curse, "May you live in interesting times."

Not surprisingly, our dance business was impacted by all this. By 1968, rock-'n'-roll music that was danceable was considered frivolous by many teens, and it gave up most of the considerable ground it once held on the top-selling charts to songs of protest, songs of anger, songs attacking social injustice. Nonetheless, that year marked the zenith of our dance business. Every venue was jammed with teens as the final strains of the dance music played out.

By the end of the decade, current members of the teenage market we long had targeted could be seen sitting on dance hall floors listening to a new kind of music. Grass and other drugs were commonplace, and drinking was widespread. War, Big Business, the Establishment, government, the status quo— all were beginning to come under assault by the nation's young. This is not to say that dancing stopped entirely. There were still school dances and isolated functions. Even so, the booming industry we had championed for 10 years was in a free-fall. It all happened so quickly, we barely had time to kiss it good-bye.

Two outstanding young men who joined our company along the way decided they wanted to take a whack at it. Willie Leopold was brother-in-law of my partner, Terry Bassett, while Dan Fiala was a Seattle native who aspired to the entertainment business. From working closely with us, Willie and Dan knew of our desire to exit the dance world. When Pat O'Day & Associates/ Concerts West merged with Kaye-Smith Enterprises in late 1968, they saw their chance. They enlisted as a partner a local businessman named Mack Keith, and together the three of them bought our dance company lock, stock and barrel, taking for their name *Seattle Mercer*—what we had been calling our dance division for the past two years. They enjoyed modest success for a period of time, struggling constantly.

And so it ended. The name *Pat O'Day & Associates* went away, and we simply became *Concerts West*. Meanwhile, all those great years and talented musicians, all those thousands of nights and tens of thousands of teenagers having great, clean fun were fading into history. In the late '70s, a renewed interest in dancing emerged from a new wave of teenagers in the form of Disco. Any resemblance to the dancing days of the late '50s and '60s was slight. Disco moved the young into clubs, where they listened to overproduced, electronically-drummed, brainless urban music cranked out by the music industry like soda crackers. Disco's life-span was appropriately short, and few of its songs are fondly recalled.

Those Were the Days
Mary Hopkins, 1969
THE TRANSFORMATION OF PAT O'DAY & ASSOCIATES into Concerts West, followed by the successful resolution of the FCC investigation, brought a major era of my life to a close. The song I had been playing was over, and it was time to put a new record on the turntable. Thereafter, I turned my attention to Concerts West, and in a remarkably short period of time we became the largest concert company *in the world*. To think, it all began in Astoria, Oregon with "Paul's Platter Party" and a sock hop at the town's National Guard Armory.

Scene at a Teen Fair at Seattle Center in the late '60s

Whether the city was Detroit or Denver or Dover, teenagers across America were dancing in the '50s and '60s. In the Northwest, our teenagers were dancing, too, sharing a common experience which none have forgotten. Through serendipity and hard work, we developed the region's dance business into a new art form. Dancing was a vital part of what many of us remember as a wonderful age of innocence following World War II, an age never to be repeated. It is just not in the nature of today's rapidly changing world to look back. Dancing to the fresh new sounds of rock-'n'-roll helped make those post-war growing-up years carefree and special for many. I look back upon them with fondness. May these stories help preserve their memory.

8 – When I Was Young
Eric Burdon & The Animals, 1967

HILE STILL A CHILD, I FELL IN LOVE with radio and began telling everyone I was going to be a broadcaster when I grew up. I imagine that, like many a son, I looked to my father for inspiration. A minister with his own daily radio program, he often brought me to the station where I watched him perform and became hooked on the medium. The studios and their equipment were impressive, but more fascinating by far was what they produced—the music and messages coming out of a radio's speaker. As expected in the home of a fundamentalist preacher, my family's radio listening focused on news and religious programs. Discouraged were entertainment shows perceived as sinful or having too worldly a slant. I discretely listened to those over an old headset radio tucked away in my room.

One incident stands out. Only six years old, I sat on the floor in the front parlor of our home in Lincoln, Nebraska listening to an Omaha station on my parents' Trutone radio, a console model ordered from a Sears catalog. They were broadcasting live from the scene of a deadly fire at the Henshaw Hotel in downtown Omaha, and I was there. I watched with the reporter on that blocked-off street as fire fighters struggled with their hoses; I smelled with him the acrid smoke billowing from the building as ladders telescoped to the upper windows in a desperate attempt to save more lives. In body only, I remained seated on the living room floor in Lincoln; in spirit and mind, I stood sixty miles away in Omaha. Radio had transported me to the scene.

That same day, inflamed by my own fire within, I escaped to the solitude of the corn field next door, put a tin can to my ear to better catch the sound of my voice and delivered my own report on the fire. Throughout my childhood, I continued to act out such fantasies. Often I was Gabriel Heatter, renowned news commentator for the old Mutual Radio Network. Heatter's voice cracked and rattled and squeaked and would fail to pass muster on today's network news. Yet, despite its anomalies, that voice never stood as a barrier between his material and his audience. Dramatic and persuasive, when Heatter spoke his signature line, "There's good news tonight!" we believed him without question. His voice was so different, listeners never forgot it. Nor did we want to. When not pretending to be Gabriel Heatter, I sometimes portrayed his fellow Mutual newscaster, Glenn Hardy.

Evenings, I variously assumed the personas of Jack Benny, Bob Hope, Red Skelton, the Lone Ranger and Red Ryder. Johnny Carson, who grew up in my town of birth, Norfolk, Nebraska, took his principal inspiration from Benny, whose dry character and precise timing set him apart and made him radio's most popular figure through much of the '40s. At a time when comics were mostly chatterboxes, Benny delivered punch lines with a subtle, slow, deliberate, devastating style. His is yet another unique voice permanently inscribed in this fan's memory.

I considered Jack Benny's use of the pregnant pause his grandest comedic tool and in the mid-'60s explained its power to a talented young deejay working at KJR-Seattle, Larry Lujack. Shortly thereafter, Larry moved back east, eventually landing at station WLS-Chicago. The Jack Benny pause became a devastating tool in his hands as he climbed to the top of the broadcasting profession at Chicago's WCFL and WLS. That pause was also one of my favorite on-air ploys.

Bob Hope was Bob Hope and never my favorite. But, with his always topical humor and ability to self-promote, oh, did he have legs! He was a comic of the old school who skillfully adapted from generation to generation as tastes changed. Still, other than Hope's work ethic, little in his approach could be transposed to another performer.

Then, *The Lone Ranger*, pure theater of the mind. Strains of its stirring theme music, the *William Tell Overture*, played throughout, and producers wisely never tampered with it. At KJR, my incredibly talented morning deejay Lan Roberts and I often returned to those golden days of yesteryear with our own warped takeoff on the show. Listeners indicated they loved it, so with Lan as Tonto and me as the masked man, every so often we recorded a series of episodes and used them for weeks afterwards, leading listeners through a succession of increasingly outrageous adventures. In a typical episode we produced, with the *William Tell Overture* playing in the background, Tonto expressed deep concern over his partner's fixation on sheep. Insulted, the Lone Ranger responded, "Tonto, mind your own business! You're lucky just to have a job here on my show! You know, Tonto, it's not easy being the Lone Ranger, and I get very lonesome. Here, let me reach into my gun belt and give you one of my famous silver bullets." Tonto responded, "Never mind, Kimosabe, me Tonto already hav'em saddlebag full of your dumb silver bullets!" After a Jack Benny pause, a crestfallen Lone Ranger replied, "Oh!" We produced scores of such episodes, and listeners begged for more.

In my childhood, radio carried me daily to a dreamland where I played make-believe like it was real. I wrote several scripts for the *Green Hornet* and *Jack Armstrong, The All American Boy*, mailed them to the networks back east and eagerly listened in the following weeks, hoping my suggestions would be used. Who knows what the reactions were when those scripts arrived at the studios in New York. Did they immediately dismiss my scribbled, childlike scenarios? Probably. Did they even look at them? Probably not. It didn't matter. Out west, a naïve ten year old was so fascinated by this wonder called radio, he had to contribute in some way—and cling to the conviction that someone would notice.

In the parsonage we called home, where religious radio programs were a staple, I found similar (though not equal) fascination listening to gospel hours and sermons and noting how they were presented. Perched before the family radio, I could see the choir and pianist, the congregation, the pastor in the pulpit. The results linger on, for even now I can hear Rudy Atwood playing the piano on Charles Fuller's *Old Fashioned Revival Hour* from the Civic Auditorium in Long Beach, California, and the Reverend Walter Meier preaching on the *Lutheran Hour* from his church in St. Louis, Missouri. The contrasting styles, techniques and pacing radio ministries employed—all calculated to keep listeners spellbound and donations flowing—did not escape me. As a schoolboy, I sensed radio's potential if one could keep an audience emotionally involved. Gently nudged and provided the right clues, the mind can paint an entire canvas. Radio at its best supplies those nudges and clues.

Radio needs no pictures to work its magic—never has and never will. Thank goodness, too, for such would only do harm to a unique art form which compels listeners to connect the dots and fill in the blanks themselves. Using nothing more than sound, radio stimulates a different area of the brain than does television, transmitting layered images far richer than what sight alone can produce. Combine those self-developed pictures with emotional, high-impact audio and you can take control of a person's entire being. So total was *my* youthful radio experience, I looked neither to the left nor the right concerning my future; I stayed the course with the broadcast booth always my focus and ultimate destination. I was driven to follow my heart and ear and yearned to paint pictures myself in people's minds, fresh new images to make them laugh and cry, scenes to entertain, inform and thrill them.

Take Me Out to the Ball Game
Jack Norworth, 1909

BY AGE 12, I WAS LIVING IN TACOMA, WASHINGTON convinced I would end up as either a newsman or a sportscaster at a local radio station. Most entertainment programming then originated from network studios in Los Angeles and New York, locales too far away for me to imagine. In a rare fit of practicality, I set my sights instead on broadcasting in Seattle, 30 miles to the north. I visualized myself as Ted Bell, play-by-play man for University of Washington Husky football, or Leo Lassen, the stunningly popular voice of Seattle Rainiers Pacific Coast League baseball. Were Leo alive and looking for work today, program directors would dismiss him in an instant without a second thought. Their canned formulas make no allowance for a nonconforming original like Lassen with his twangy, nasal voice and staccato delivery. Throughout the '30s, '40s and '50s, in contrast, fans in the Pacific Northwest unanimously embraced the man and his unique style. During those years, Leo was unquestionably the most recognized name and voice in the Seattle area. His words shot from Northwest radios like bullets from machine guns, painting multihued and intensely exciting verbal pictures.

He loved to describe the varying shades of green of the outfield grass, the shifting blues of the daytime sky, the inky vastness of the heavens at night. Snow-capped Mt. Rainier commanded the southern horizon beyond Sick's Stadium, Seattle's picturesque minor league ballpark, and Lassen kept listeners abreast of its ever-changing moods. One afternoon, the giant mountain

Summer in Seattle: The Blue Angels, Seafair Hydroplane Races & Mt. Rainier

Pat O'Day, Bill Muncey & Mira Slovak at play on Mercer Island

reminded him of a vanilla ice cream cone. A few evenings later, he switched flavors and reported, "With the setting sun, Rainier is a strawberry ice cream cone sitting atop the center field wall, right behind Old Glory hanging limply on her pole." Turning from what locals call "the Mountain" to calling the ball game, he offered comments like, "As Barrett strolls slowly in from the bullpen, we listen to the murmur of a thousand conversations from the stands beneath us." Leo drew us through our radios to the ballpark and kept us glued to the seat beside him from first pitch to last. Leo Lassen, our Voice of Summer.

I have a confession to make — and what is a memoir without at least one confession? This August (2003), I broadcast Seattle's Seafair Unlimited Hydroplane Race for the thirty-seventh straight year. The Hydros are to Seattle what the Indy 500 is to Indianapolis and allow me to keep alive the style and spirit of Leo Lassen. I have never forgotten the standards for excitement and graphic description he instilled in me as a child. He remains my benchmark for excellence in sports announcing. I suspect the principal reason they keep asking me back every year to anchor the Seafair broadcast is because of the many pages I have stolen from the book of the late Leo Lassen.

In my teens, I impersonated other radio figures, like Clay Huntington, who broadcast high school games for the Tacoma stations. Mornings, I focused on being a news reporter, some days Dick Kepplinger, the Richfield Reporter on KIRO-AM Seattle, other days Lou Gillette, another Seattle radio news fixture. Returning to sports, I pretended to be Gordon McLendon, who recreated Major League baseball games from around the country in his Dallas, Texas studio for his Liberty Broadcasting Network. With Gordon describing the action, you could taste the hot dogs and smell the popcorn, and he wasn't even there.

Forgive my indecisiveness where these finer career points are concerned — you see, we're talking about a dreamy kid with multiple heroes and shifting loyalties who needed time to sort them out. Be assured, there was no indecision as to the industry I vowed to enter. It was radio, only radio, always radio. In the long run, in terms of vocation, my childish inflexibility proved a blessing. It drove me, in effect, to study for my future career many hours a day throughout my adolescence. Whenever I found myself near a radio, I dropped everything else as I inadvertently prepared for the day when I would sit behind a mike myself. No heroic or Protestant work ethic drove me. It was more like a fixation, or a compulsion, or a fanciful dream that refused to let my mind rest or turn elsewhere. When it came to schoolwork and classroom performance, that dream occasionally impeded my scholastic achievement. Despite my decent grades, teachers always insisted I could do much better.

I was too preoccupied with radio and current events like World War II to heed their admonitions, grabbing every opportunity out there for public speaking: school plays, choir, band, PA system announcements, sports, any and every chance to perform. Teachers cringed whenever I stepped forward to deliver an oral report, certain I planned to stray far from the assigned subject. They knew my only goals were to hold the spotlight for as long as I could and to somehow make the class laugh. Shameless, I rarely let them down. One of my reports, delivered in science class, won actual applause for arguing the advantages of coal-burning submarines. My instructor chose to ignore the reasonably solid evidence I marshalled. Rather, she confined her critique to my unwise choice of topics. Oh, well!

My compulsion to entertain produced a common theme which appeared frequently on my report cards: "Occasionally disruptive. / Class clown. / Show-off / Deportment needs improvement." (All true, most likely!) These comments elicited the expected frowns from my father and mother, which I considered a small price to pay for the inner joy I felt when successfully entertaining.

The three R's taught at school were no substitute for lessons delivered at home. With words and by example, my parents were my greatest teachers, although, at home like in school, I was not always the ideal student. August 2003, my mother turned 91; were my father still alive, he would be 103. Both belonged to what Tom Brokaw recently dubbed "the Greatest Generation." They were everything he wrote about and more: my father, the son of immigrant parents, my mother, the issue of sturdy Great Plains pioneer stock. Both reflected the courage and conviction, the kindness and selfless generosity of their parents, of another age. They lived through two world wars and the Great Depression, facing hardships in the present and making sacrifices for the future without complaint. Through it all, their bedrock faith in God never wavered, giving them the strength to carry on. With the patience of Job, they endured trials and disruptions many today would resent and blame on others. Tom Brokaw has it right, theirs was the greatest, the best generation.

At age 35, my mother suddenly found herself a widow with three young sons to raise. From that point on, she placed our welfare first, well ahead of her own. When marriage offers came, she rejected them, and the personal companionship and financial security they brought, for fear a new husband would drive a wedge between her and us. Pastors in the40s rarely had Social Security or insurance, and my father was no exception. His death left my family poor at the bank but rich in spirit, and Mom's Midwest pioneer fortitude saved the day. She simply said, "If we all work hard and are careful, we can make it," and we did. My kid brothers Dave and Dan both had paper routes at an early age, as did I, along with lawn mowing and multiple other odd jobs. In high school, I departed class at noon to work at a meat market, and later at a men's clothing store. Our sacrifices were nothing compared with our mother's, and I thank her every day for the superb, caring home environment she provided and for the work ethic she instilled. I reap the benefits even today.

On the other hand, my father's unexpected death when I was 14 left many blank pages in my lesson book. Ever since I could remember, he was consumed by his ministry, while I developed into something of a rebel by my early teens. Our relationship and communications needed more time and work to mature, but that was not to be. Honest introspection tells me we were similarly driven and way too much alike. His campaign to spread the good news of Jesus differed greatly from mine. Yet, I carry his genes and seem to have inherited his voice. And the memory lives on of the examples he set. These things, along with my mother's intolerance of anger and conflict, helped make me whatever it is I am.

Several months after my father's death in 1948, following a brief stay with relatives in Iowa, my mother moved the family from Tacoma to Bremerton where, along with my younger brothers, I entered strange schools and set about making new friends. By the time I graduated from Bremerton High School three years later, I had traded my newcomer status for a place in the school's Hall of Fame, voted in by my 1,000 fellow students for having the "Best Sense of Humor." From my point of view, that beat valedictorian! That fall, I continued my studies at Olympic College, also in Bremerton. Olympic had its own radio station, broadcasting only to the cafeteria, and spinning records while manning their mike added momentum to my radio quest. Last year, Olympic College named me to *their* Hall of Fame, the thirtieth person in the school's 60 -year history to be so honored. My acceptance speech at the induction gala included the observation that "academic achievement appears not to be paramount in the selection criteria!" All joking aside, I was stunned and deeply moved by the honor.

My next stop, Tacoma Vocational Institute, featured a respected broadcast department. I became student body president and sort of zoomed through the curriculum. After class, I worked part time as an engineer at radio station KTAC and, at night, washed and drove (mainly washed) transit buses. Within a year, Merle Kimball, director of the broadcast department, recommended me to a station looking for a deejay and newscaster. An interview arranged by Kimball landed me my first on-air radio job — in Astoria, Oregon beginning September 3, 1956.

Do You Believe in Magic?
Lovin' Spoonful, 1965

PROVING MY DOUBTERS WRONG AND MYSELF RIGHT , something I always relish, I landed in Seattle in 1959 and soon enjoyed a level of fame. It didn't just happen, though. I made sure everyone in town knew I was available for whatever function they had in mind. "Schedule it, and he will come!" Anything offering the promise of television or newspaper coverage immediately grabbed my attention. One time, in 1959, using tank-driving skills developed in the National Guard, I did dozer duty with two famous daredevils off the unlimited hydroplane racing circuit, Seattleites Bill Muncey and Mira Slovak. Together we spent a balmy summer day clearing land and grading slopes for a large new park on Mercer Island, which sits in the middle of Lake Washington halfway between Seattle and Bellevue. For the occasion, the local Euclid heavy equipment dealer loaned us some massive earth moving equipment they wished to have demonstrated. I took command of the double-dozer — a pair of Euclid bulls yoked together side by side — while the Muncey-Slovak team assumed control of the earth-movers. We scooped and scraped and piled and pushed like three kids playing in a giant sand box and were rewarded with extensive television news coverage that evening. Meanwhile, the citizens of Mercer Island had themselves a fine new park.

Later that year, I set a new Guinness world record by water-skiing non-stop around Lake Washington for four hours and fifty-two minutes. Next, I attempted to set a go-cart endurance world record at a local indoor facility and just missed breaking the old standard when exhaust fumes overcame me at the 23-hour mark. It took an ambulance ride to the hospital, emergency treatment and some much-needed oxygen to undo the effects of the noxious vapors I had accumulated in my lungs and body during that hell-bent-for-glory escapade.

When not flirting with carbon monoxide poisoning, I made time for a steady stream of public appearances of every kind imaginable—you name it: school assemblies, dances, parades, festivals, sporting events, carnivals, bar mitzvahs, fairs and more—all part of my goal of making no fewer than two public appearances every week. A busy schedule enabled me to quickly build an inverted pyramid of people who had personally met me or seen me. I tried to make each one of my appearances in some way special and freely lifted humorous material from comedians, joke books and wherever else I could find it. When introduced in public, I blended jokes and anecdotes with prepared topical material, and audiences responded. I believed then and remain convinced today that if you want to be perceived as a good entertainer on the air, you need to perform even better when seen in person. If you do that, you leave your live audience with the impression that, when broadcasting your show, you always have something more to offer.

I abhorred the thought of appearing in person and not making people laugh. In fact, I nearly vomited recently when teamed at a grand opening with a current Seattle deejay (or *air personality* as they prefer being called today). After I finished my schtick, this poor individual, seemingly clueless to the opportunity afforded with an audience of a thousand people on hand, came out on stage and said "Whaz happenin'?" not once but three times. And that was all, nothing more. With his prepared remarks thus exhausted, he concluded his performance by saying "Now, let's give it up for..." as he introduced the musical act headlining the event. I won't mention the *air personality*'s name or the occasion, but I *am* tempted to identify the program director who stupidly allowed his deejay to appear in public and personally destroy any positive image he had created through his on-air work.

He's a Rebel
The Crystals, 1962

BY EARLY 1962, I WAS PROGRAM DIRECTOR and afternoon drive-time deejay of KJR-Seattle, where we vanquished all foes and ruled Seattle's airwaves for 15 years. For nearly a year before, I served as program director in all but name and, with my busy schedule, couldn't afford the luxury of worrying about my lack of a formal title. By the time the station made my status official, the Seattle World's Fair was about to open, and I determined to take my new role seriously.

Stomach woes delayed my first official day on the job as KJR PD. For the past three years I had experienced constant, severe abdominal pains. Four different doctors came up with four different explanations for my discomfort, every one of them wrong. The day after the announcement of my promotion, I passed out in the bathroom while shaving and fell backwards into the bathtub. I had grown accustomed to severe cramps after my first cup of morning coffee, but this episode, and the nasty cut on my head it produced, were over the top. Belatedly, my doctors took drastic action. They called in Dr. Hilding Olson, a gifted Seattle surgeon, and he performed an exploratory lap operation. Basically, he sliced me wide open from top to bottom and poked around my innards looking for the cause of the problem. The trophy scar he left runs from my ribs down to the lower stomach area and could have been much smaller had I used good sense. Years before, I was confined to my bed for three days with what we all thought was a world-class case of stomach flu. The pain was intense, the recovery slow and my body badly weakened. Maybe I should have complained louder about my case of "flu," and I certainly should have mentioned the incident to Dr. Olson before he started carving. In both cases, I didn't

When I awoke after surgery, the surgeon stood beside my bed grinning. Only then did I learn I had lived for three years with a ruptured appendix, one of those one-in-a-thousand deals where someone narrowly escapes death thanks to the sudden response of his white corpuscles. Scar tissue from the break had grown onto several organs, and once the good doctor trimmed those adhesions and patched up a few rough spots, I was fine. In fact, other than maybe a cold, I haven't been sick a single day in the 40 years since! If cats have nine lives and I'm a cat, I used up one of mine that time. According to the odds, I should have died.

Seven days after my surgery, I boarded a plane bound for Los Angeles, tape recorder in hand, on my way to record several Southern California radio stations. Above all, I wanted to capture for study KFWB-AM in Hollywood, programmed by my friend, Chuck Blore. There was already evidence that my Seattle station was approaching greatness, but I was hungry to explore the frontiers of total dominance. What my tape recorder captured was, for me, vindication of the direction I dreamed of heading: Never-ending music and fun, not just the phony fun that stations try to tell you you're having, but genuine and constant hilarity. I wanted newscasts that would leave listeners breathless, and Blore's KFWB was approaching that threshold. My dedication became complete!

You've Really Got a Hold on Me
The Miracles, 1962

KJR'S SWITCH TO TOP 40 PROGRAMMING had been a long-running radio soap opera, with a succession of program directors parading through a revolving door beginning in 1959. The station had toyed with rock-'n'-roll in the mid-50s with some success, but had made an ill-fated vector to softer music. Then, in 1959, Lester Smith saw the light. To inaugurate the new Top 40 format, the company brought in Chris Lane from San Francisco's KYA-AM, part of the Bartell chain. Thirty days later, Lane got into a fracas with Galen Blackford, the station's mercurial general manager, and was sent packing. Next up was John Stone, of whom I wrote in an earlier chapter. He held the job for less than a year before stubbing his toe on regulations. Then, one of the true fathers of rock-'n'-roll radio, Bill Stewart, took the helm after Stone's fall from grace. Bill, who worked with legendary station owner Todd Storz from the earliest days of the rock movement, lasted just 10 days longer than Chris Lane, likewise losing a turf battle with Blackford. Miraculously, a talented on-air staff, aided by our great signal, weathered these storms and kept the station at number one in the market. After Stewart left, Lee Perkins, a Gordon McLendon graduate, was appointed interim PD, which stood until I formally took on those responsibilities in early 1962. Even though we already occupied the top spot in our market, I believed we could double our audience with broad targeting and mature rock-'n'-roll programming. To do so, we needed both teens and adults in our audience mix, and to be adult in our approach. So many radio stations who thought they were talking to teens were in fact *talking beneath* them. Teens can easily tell when someone is patronizing them, so don't! Teens are adults in their ability to understand humor and current events, so why not address them as such? I felt we must be exciting, even earth-shaking, with our news and perfect in our balance and selection of music. Above all, our entire air staff, news people included, needed to become household names in the region. Inside, I felt as good as I did about the course we were selecting because I saw Blore making it work to a degree in LA. He was also an alumnus from the Gordon McLendon chain of stations in Texas. McLendon's group developed a sound set of principals for radio entertainment, with outlets in Dallas, Houston and El Paso. Chuck graduated from the El Paso station and now worked for Crowell-Collier (better known for publishing encyclopedias) at KFWB.

Chuck had a stellar deejay lineup consisting of Elliot Field, Ted Quillan, Joe Yokam, B. Mitchell Reed, Bill Ballance, Bruce Hayes and Gary Owens to mention a few. Most of them were older, formerly straight announcers converted by Blore (after scattered howling and whining) into exciting, funny, fast-paced radio stars. Despite some strong personality conflicts, they perfectly meshed as a team with the overall format he carefully designed to include exciting newscasts, memorable station jingles and a distinctive tempo all its own from morning till night till morning again. When you passed a radio tuned in to KFWB, you didn't need to hear the call letters to identify the station. Chuck Blore and KFWB confirmed everything I believed about radio; now I wanted my station to do even better.

On the plane ride back to Seattle, I mulled over what needed to be done. I wanted KJR to become a station listeners found difficult turning off lest they miss something important. There weren't many stations like that out there then, and there are even fewer of them out there today, but in KFWB I had just listened to one and now knew it could be done.

Experience told me our current 12 percent share of the audience in our 20-station market was just a first step. While that made us number one among Seattle stations, it could be dramatically expanded. When I was paying my dues as deejay and PD at KLOQ in Yakima, Washington, we carried about 40 percent of the listening in town. Granted, there were only four radio stations but, of that 40 percent share, teens made up just a portion, and the adults we attracted could easily have switched to one of the other stations save for the mature excitement we offered. The success of KLOQ with a rock-'n'-roll/Top 40 format proved to me that an aspiring station could expand well beyond any perceived youth base. I saw similar proof at KLIF in Dallas, where the McLendon folks stretched the range of Top 40 radio's appeal with a spectacular air staff of talented deejays and newscasters. By the time my plane landed in Seattle, I concluded that now, with full control of KJR's programming in my hands, we could double our audience, even in sophisticated, culture-driven Seattle. Doing so would require increased effort, constant innovation and talent galore.

To deliver successful radio, you must start with a signal strong enough to enable listeners to enjoy your programing without interference. Once you know your signal can be heard, you must decide who your audience will be. If your aim is too narrow, competition can squeeze you out of success. If your aim is too wide, you will end up trying to be all things to all people, and failure at this is catastrophic. For optimal success, you must set an absolute, obtainable destination and, upon reaching it, expand outwards, never standing still and never turning your back on your critical mass.

Merle Kimball, my radio instructor in broadcasting school, once said "radio is a second-by-second business. It takes only a second of discontent and the dial can be turned, a listener lost." I coupled this admonition with a theory of my own, one that many deejays had to sit in staff meetings and endure listening to me repeat again and again. My theory contends that radio relationships are no different than human relationships, and that human relationships are bound by the laws of nature. We can look at a block of wood and say that there is nothing moving within that block of wood, that it's just what it appears to be: a lifeless, still block of wood. Wrong! Within that block of wood, electrons are revolving around nuclei at blinding speed. Molecules within that block of wood are in constant motion, turmoil prevails, and this truth applies to every object in the universe. Apply the same logic when considering the turmoil and movement constant to relationships. I contend that, at any given moment, relationships are coming closer together or moving further apart and are never standing still. If, as performers, we stay ever-cognizant of this truth, we must then strive every second to draw our audience, our listeners, closer to us. We must prepare, knowing they use radio for mood enhancement. Moment by moment, we must remind ourselves that on the other side of that microphone is a real human being, someone who has given us the opportunity to be their companion. Understanding that a listener is always coming closer or drifting away should compel a performer to communicate differently. No longer can he or she say "Well, it was just my usual show, nothing special" or "Some days I just coast, my listeners know me." Attitudes like these erode radio relationships.

At KJR, we labored to always be the best on a second-by-second basis. We tried to act on a fundamental truth that Billy Graham exemplifies in his preaching, a foundational skill that allows him, from a stage at one end of a football stadium, to convince an individual sitting 100 yards away in a crowd of 100,000 that he is personally aware of that man or woman and is talking directly to them. If it can be done in a football stadium with an echoing public address system and a sea of bodies separating the speaker from the listener, why not in a radio studio? It seemed reasonable to me. Our primary goal became to reach out and entertain every listener as an individual, leaving them convinced we cared about them personally. I never researched this or asked a consultant. I knew I was right.

These were the cumulative essentials I sought when recruiting talent. At a minimum, I looked for open minds, fertile soil for planting such thoughts. Demanding criteria brought staff turnover. One good/bad problem we faced was talent rarely desired to leave our station. While there were exceptions, like Lujack and Roberts, Jerry Kaye, Mike Phillips and Tom Murphy, who couldn't resist outstanding offers from other stations and bigger markets, all in all, our people badly wanted to stay on our team. This made the occasional terminations painful.

I was demanding and parted company with some good on-air talents, but the radio station I heard playing in my head required a certain level of performance: (a) Billy Graham's level of one-on-one communication skills to make people cry and (b) Jack Benny's ability to make people laugh with nothing more than a simple pause. Good wasn't good enough; great was good for starters. I broke the hearts of some dedicated and loyal radio performers in my search for excellence, but my intent was to create the best radio station on earth. I never used ratings to evaluate talent. If I waited for the ratings to come out, it would be too late to correct a mistake. I used my ears to determine the quality of an individual's performance and to judge their impact on our audience.

The same held true for the other important fixtures heard on the air at KJR. Fixtures like the station's jingles, news introductions, contest introductions, public service campaigns and more. Again, good wasn't good enough. I cite as an example the KJR jingles. After creating the song that went, "K-J-R Seattle, channel ninety-five," we tried to add fresh new wrinkles to it every year. We must have succeeded as today, on KJR 95.7 FM Seattle, they are still playing, several times an hour, that jingle I wrote in 1962.

To me, news introductions were a way of telling listeners what time it was and what station was playing by creating high impact, monumentally memorable words and sounds. *Justifiable pomposity* would be a good way to describe my approach when designing these elements. During the Seattle World's Fair, for example, I wanted something special. The station's parent firm at that time was called *Seattle, Portland & Spokane Radio*. So, at the top of each hour, following a grand, full orchestral rendition of the KJR song, I added the unique, thundering voice of Joe Long from KLIF in Dallas saying, "This is the flagship of the Seattle, Portland and Spokane Broadcasting Company, K-J-R Seattle!" It sounded like a message beamed straight down from heaven, and the rewards for our effort continue to roll in. Some 40 years later, people still come up to me and say, "This is the flagship, KJR Seattle!" If listeners can remember that 12-second recording 40 years later, that's good enough for me.

Monster Mash
Bobby "Boris" Pickett & the Crypt-Kickers, 1962

We worked hard to make the station's community involvement meaningful and remarkable. Examples included our efforts on behalf of the Children's Orthopedic Hospital and the Variety Club's Children's Charities. One day in 1963, while visiting with impresario Zollie Volchok and much-loved record distributor Lou Laventhal, both active in the Seattle chapter of Variety Clubs International, an idea struck me: It was leading up to Halloween, so why not create a haunted house? We'd make it a truly frightening place, promote it heavily on the radio, call it the *KJR Haunted House*, charge admission and give the money to Variety Club, who could pass it on to the hospital. While commonplace today, this concept was unique in 1963 and proved an instant success!

The Variety Club provided the needed actors and volunteer workers. For the idea to work, the haunted house had to seriously frighten anyone brave enough to venture inside. If we couldn't make visitors "wet their pants," they wouldn't tell their friends about their experience or bother to come back again the next year. I gleefully set about making detailed plans for a haunted house that would scare the bejesus out of Seattle.

A young Martin Selig, who later built Seattle's tallest skyscraper, had acquired many old houses on the outskirts of downtown by then and every year generously donated one of them for us to use. Each room contained a uniquely frightening scene imagineered by me. A personal favorite featured Grandma being tortured by her grandson. In a dark and dusty basement room, Grandma (a mannequin) sat strapped to her rocking chair, arms tied behind her. Powered by unseen cables, the chair rocked back and forth while

Grandma moaned and cried for help. Why? Maybe it was the catcher's-mask-like cage she wore over her face with the two rats inside. The rodents constantly nibbled at her face, which was smeared hourly with cheese. Meanwhile, her loony grandson sat cross-legged on the floor in front of her, rocking back and forth himself and saying repeatedly, "It's all right Grandma, it won't be long now!" Annually, we created eight or so equally-shocking rooms, and crowds lined up for blocks to get in as on the air we warned listeners that "only the strong can survive a trip through the KJR Haunted House." Every year we added something new, attendance increased and tens of thousands more dollars were turned over to the Children's Hospital. That Halloween promotion we initiated 40 years ago continues to this day.

A call one day from Fred Westberg of the Washington State Fruit Commission again triggered us to be our best. Through someone's mistake, several train cars loaded with apricots destined for international shipment sat idle on a siding in the freight yards and were about to go to waste. We concocted a simple solution. The station immediately went on the air with a dramatic report that the mighty 5,000-watt KJR rock-'n'-roll transmitter had contracted a disease, a strange electronic malady for which there was only one known cure if our great sound was to continue. The transmitter doctor had examined the patient and declared, "The KJR transmitter must be fed apricot pits, thousands and thousands of apricot pits, or else!" We offered cash prizes to listeners sending in the most apricot pits to keep us on the air. The impact was immediate: buyers in search of apricots flooded area stores, the unexpected spike in demand sent wholesalers scrambling for a new source of supply and, within two days, the wayward apricots found happy homes in the tummies of KJR listeners. The only problem was experienced by the US Postal Department, which battled jammed cancellation machinery poorly designed to handle thousands of packages of apricot pits.

Sweet Georgia Brown
Ben Bernie & His Orchestra, 1925

ONE OF OUR MOST EFFECTIVE PROMOTIONS EVER was a campaign to raise money for public school systems in the region, an on-going effort which spawned the KJR All Americans basketball team. To fully understand what this was all about, let's go back to the 1960's. Seattle was yet to have its NBA franchise, the Sonics. Further, the "slam dunk" was in its infancy. KJR enjoyed

The KJR All Americans in action: left, Tom Murphy shooting free throws, guided by Pat O'Day; top right: Pat O'Day driving for a lay-in; bottom right: team photo

unique supremacy and, thankfully, Les Smith, the chief exec of the our radio chain, let me do just about anything I wanted! So, an idea evolved into a promotion that is fondly remembered today. Not just by the participants but by thousands of high school students who, some 35 years later, still bring it up and fondly recall a visit to their school by our basketball team. The following was the premise.

Schools back then always needed additional funds, just as they do today. Our station's jocks always needed to make personal appearances, especially in the high schools of the Puget Sound region. Such appearances needed to be meaningful and entertaining. What could be better than jumping "out of the box" and presenting our deejays as entertaining and caring athletes and showmen? What could be better than putting our personalities on the floor in front of thousands of students in a brand new light? It seemed like — and turned out to be — a new and exciting promotion that worked year after year. The KJR All Americans played well-promoted basketball games against teams comprised of school faculty members. Any such faculty has its share of good athletes from its coaching staffs and also had its share of clumsy-but-much-loved teachers. Now, how do you take this cast and make it truly exciting, funny and memorable? How can you make this a show that will pack them in the stands your next visit and the next one after that for years to come?

The KJR All Americans added headliners to the team. Charlie Williams, who had been All-state at Stadium High in Tacoma and All-American second team at Seattle University, but was caught up in a point shaving scandal. He was later found innocent of the charges and went on to an all star career with the American Basketball League Pittsburgh Pipers, where he played alongside the legendary Connie Hawkins. Well, Charlie Williams played a full season for us while his case was being investigated. Other names, typical of the players the team added, included Steve Bramwell, All-American football player from the Washington Huskies. Steve Wilson, Bob Flowers and Levi Fisher, all former Husky basketball stars. Todd Hullin, Husky quarterback returned from being selected MVP of the annual Shrine Bowl game to play two seasons with the All Americans. Ernie Dunston, following his successful years with the Detroit Pistons. Willie Campbell, ex-University of Nebraska all-conference player who then spent two years with the Harlem Globetrotters. We're talking talent!

We arrived on the floor in striking, red white and blue uniforms. (All our players wore the number 95 front and back in keeping with the radio station's dial position) with our own PA system, announcer (Lan Roberts), officials, and a giant four-foot-high trophy. After pre-game warm-ups, where the All Americans mesmerized the crowd with astounding slam dunks and other impressive displays, the National Anthem was played. Then, Lan introduced the night with words as follows:

"Ladies and Gentleman, tonight, the KJR All Americans are pleased to accept the challenge of your school's faculty. The All Americans come into tonight's game with a lifetime record of 146 wins against only 7 losses. If tonight your faculty can defeat this powerful team, this magnificent trophy [which was then wheeled onto the floor] will become a permanent fixture in your school's trophy case." With that, the students would be on their feet, cheering on their faculty as they and the All Americans were introduced with great fanfare. Sometimes our roster would include music stars such as Bobby Vinton, Pat Boone and Dean Torrence of Jan & Dean. All performed for our team.

The game itself started with one athlete and the KJR deejays on the floor. In a pre-game agreement with the faculty, we asked them to go along with our stunts, and there were many. We in turn promised them that, with two minutes to play in the game, we would make sure the score was tied. The final two minutes would be "Let the best team win!" Those in attendance would witness everything from remarkable basketball to some of the funniest pranks. We stole several chapters from the Globetrotters' book of tricks along with introducing some of our own. For instance, at one point in the game, one of our players would yell at the officials "This is getting rougher than a football game," at which point the official would signal time out, go to the scorer's bench, grab the microphone and shout, "Well then, lets play football!" and a football would be thrown onto the floor. After a touchdown by each team, the basketball was re-introduced.

With two minutes left and the score tied, we'd call time out. The students and many parents would be on their feet screaming as a victory, the trophy, and great fame for their school seemed so near at hand. In the final seconds, our superior athletes always pulled it out of the fire, and we would leave the floor with a one- or two-point victory. The crowd, not knowing this was our regular routine, would leave the gymnasium believing their school had almost accomplished the near impossible—beating the KJR All Americans—and that's

KJR Super Car with Pat O'Day, pilot & Lan Roberts, navigator

what brought them back in a year or two later when our team returned to their school. On the air, we never gave the final scores. Only that the KJR All Americans had won again, thus protecting each school's and student's notion that their game had been unique and next time could be a victory!

We raised hundreds of thousand of dollars for high schools. We even played the coaching staff of the University of Washington at Hec Edmundson Pavilion before a big crowd. We later played the Harlem Clowns in a double-header with the Seattle SuperSonics, We traveled to Victoria, BC in a chartered DC-3, arranged by the school, they so badly wanted to play us. We were the most popular station in Victoria, despite the fact the city was in the territory of the great Vancouver deejay, Red Robinson. We played over 30 games a year and appeared before over 50,000 listeners. This fabulous feature continued until my departure from the station in 1974. It even survived the protest years when cheering about anything was "uncool!"

Drive My Car
The Beatles, 1965
SPEAKING OF PROMOTIONS THAT SMOKED, in the music business, you never knew what sort of strange and wondrous new thing was going to pop up next. Sometimes we found something, sometimes something found us. Ever vigilant, we tried to be ready for anything and everything and did our best to make the most out of every new opportunity that appeared. A classic example was the case of the legendary, short-lived, gone-but-not-forgotten KJR Super Car.

As usual, it started with a call to the station. Lan Roberts, our morning drive time star, picked up the phone early one day and found himself talking to James Brown. Not the *Papa's-Got-A-Brand-New-Bag* James Brown, but the Boeing engineer James Brown, who told an amazing tale. He had just designed a new type of apprehension vehicle for the Washington State Patrol. A prototype was nearing completion, but the advance payment he had anticipated receiving from the troopers was slow in coming. That left him hanging and looking for someone else to help promote his invention. His mention that the vehicle, which he called *The Enforcer,* would eventually be jet powered had Lan and me jumping in my car immediately after Lan's show ended. We headed south to the Skyway area of Renton, drove around until we found Mr. Brown's place and knocked on his door, eager to see for ourselves his curious brainchild.

What greeted us when we entered his shop is pictured on the preceeding page. I leave it to my readers to judge the market potential of this vehicle. Its creator proudly claimed that, when powered by a jet engine, it would be able to take off and fly over traffic jams with lift provided by its fenders. However, at this stage in its development, it was powered by an old Edsel automobile engine mounted in the rear on the truck frame Brown had used as the platform for building his car. The inventor foresaw installing machine guns in the nose, along with tear gas dispensers, as presumably the Enforcer could be used to swoop over rioters and quell public disturbances. Reality was the only element not factored into the design of this remarkable vehicle. The State Patrol's reluctance to provide funding was perfectly understandable.

Here was this astonishing car, ready to run, with its mad scientist creator begging us for promotional help. I looked at Lan, Lan looked at me. How could we refuse? We made only one promise to James Brown: We would give his car a great deal of exposure, on the air and on the streets of the city. He was thrilled that someone cared, and a written agreement was prepared on the spot.

The station's insurance agency, not nearly as thrilled as Brown by the Enforcer's prospects, reluctantly agreed to grant us coverage. With KJR hand painted in large letters on the sides, and Lan's name emblazoned on the starboard rear fender and mine on the port, the rechristened *Super Car* accelerated down Seattle-area streets enjoying momentary fame on the road to its ultimate fate.

Soon, our swift chariot began appearing at local beaches, parks, shopping centers and other locations, always heavily laden with prizes and one or two of our deejays to hand out the loot. By this time, the station had developed such a special relationship with its audience, we could communicate "tongue in cheek" fully confident that our listeners would be 100 percent aware of what was up and reading from the exact same page as us. We had the "hippest" listening family of any station before or since, and the Super Car saga proved it. On the air, we proclaimed it the coolest car under God's creation, we claimed it had a top speed of 300 mile per hour and we insisted it was probably worth millions of dollars. Was our public disappointed, then, when they actually saw the monstrosity? No, because they were already in on the game. They touched it lovingly, cooed over its sensuous design and exclaimed things like "It's so neat!" "It's simply beautiful!" "Far out!" and "Totally cool!"

Armed with a piece of early correspondence between the inventor and the State Patrol, we entered Super Car as a float in the Seafair Torchlight Parade, an annual summer spectacle where beautiful floats and colorful marching bands and carloads of celebrities and beauty queens proceed through the streets of downtown Seattle in front of half-a-million parade goers. We benefited from a temporary mental lapse on the part of the parade's directors, who were of a much older age cell than our audience and were unaware of the actualities of Super Car. They innocently accepted our "float's" entry, sight unseen.

Anticipating surprise on their part, we waited until everything was staged and ready to go before pulling our glorious entry into the parade line, whereupon the first of two explosions that evening occurred. After just one look, the parade director went ballistic. Using words like "the ugliest God-damned thing I've ever seen" and even worse, he ordered Super Car removed from the parade line.

I patiently explained that our entry form was in order, that we had paid the specified fee with coin of the realm, that I viewed the contract as legally binding and that we were ready to perform. Even more important, I pointed out that we had no fewer than 200,000 listeners lining the parade route anticipating the appearance of their beloved Super Car. If, at the last moment, we were forced to announce on the air that *their* Super Car had been kicked out of the parade by him—an announcement I pledged I would make were we not allowed to proceed—I simply could not be held responsible for what might happen along the parade route. I suggested that riotous behavior on the part of the distraught was one likely outcome. A hurried conference of parade officials was held, and they quickly agreed: Let Super Car roll!

The cheering crowd chanted "Super Car, Super Car" as KJR's prize vehicle crept along the three-mile route with waving deejays sitting astride the engine cowling. With a block to go, a second explosion came, and Super Car became a lighted torch. It really doesn't matter what went wrong; faulty wiring coupled with a leaking fuel line was the most likely culprit. By the time the fire engines arrived, it was too late. Flames burned out of control, and Super Car was no more!

Monday morning at the station, on Lan Roberts' show, a brief and touching memorial service was held, after which some ashes from our recently-departed friend were scattered out the control room window.

You Turn Me On (Turn On Song)
Ian Whitcomb & Bluesville, 1965

BY THE MID-'60S, KJR HAD BECOME SOMETHING more than just another radio station. It was a living, breathing, informative, enormously funny member of hundreds of thousands of Seattle-area families. That had been my dream on my return flight to Seattle from Los Angeles in 1962 following my surgery for that ruptured appendix. The ratings sheet shown on the opposite page details the extent to which that dream came true.

Jini Dellaccio

J INI DELLACCIO WAS THE FOREMOST PHOTOGRAPHER of the Northwest rock music scene in the '60s, pure and simple. Her innumerable images of local groups and international stars alike are unequaled. Pat O'Day gave her unlimited access to concerts and, on the side, Jini ran a business taking photographs for individual bands. The Sonics, The Fabulous Wailers, Don & The Goodtimes, The City Zu, the Emergency Exit, Merilee Rush & The Turnabouts —these groups and many more turned to Jini for their group portraits, their album covers, their promotional material.

Now retired and living in Gold Canyon, Arizona, Jini is working on the ultimate book of her photographs, which range in subject matter far beyond the rock-'n' roll music scene. Still, the musicians she shot remain special to her, and many of them she still considers close friends. Here we offer a sampling of her work, focusing on Northwest rock with a strong infusion of national acts that appeared in Seattle. The Rolling Stones, The Who, The Lovin' Spoonful, The Mamas & the Papas, The Beach Boys and Johnny Rivers are just a few of the world-famous acts whose pictures appear here. All of them performed in concerts put on by Pat O'Day in association with Dick Curtis. Tens of thousands of Northwest baby boomers attended the concerts and events pictured here. For them, these pages will be a trip down memory lane. For others, we hope they will provide some enjoyable browsing.

All of Jini Dellaccio's photographs reproduced in this book are available for purchase. To learn more via the worldwide web, you may write to Jini at: Jini Dellaccio, , Post Office Box 17330, Seattle, Washington 98107.

Mick Jagger (above), lead singer of The Rolling Stones, performed in the Seattle Center Coliseum in 1965. On the opposite page, at the far left, stands guitarist/singer Brian Jones. In June 1969 Jones suffered an untimely death, one of many in rock music's history.

The Rolling Stones performing at Seattle Center Coliseum, 1965

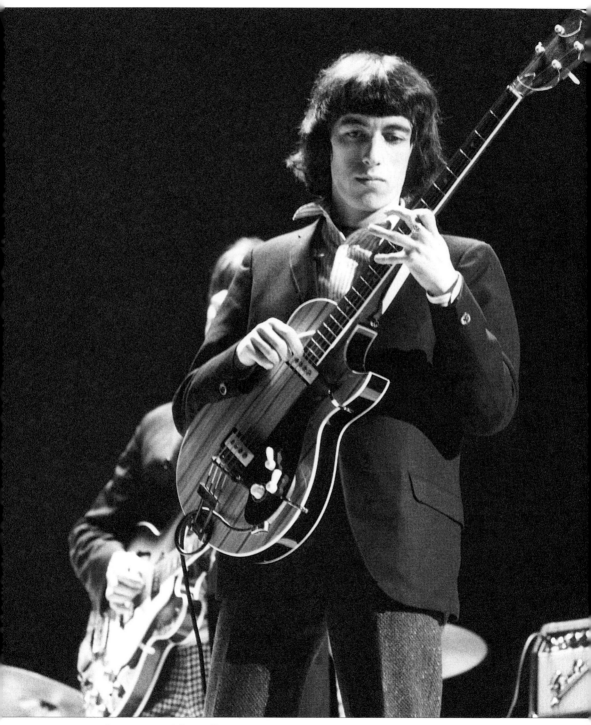

Bill Wyman of the Rolling Stones performing at Seattle Center Coliseum, 1965

Merrilee Rush & The Turnabouts, 1967

Paul Revere & The Raiders, hailing from Portland, Oregon by way of Boise.Idaho, rank as one of the all-time great Northwest bands. Pictured above is Paul Revere (on keyboard)

Opposite page: The Sonics; This page: The Lovin' Spoonful

Above: The Liverpool Five performing at Seattle Center Coliseum, 1966
Below: Ian Whitcomb performing at Seattle Center Coliseum, 1965, backed by Seattle's Counts

The Mamas & the Papas performed for the first time before a large concert audience at the Seattle Center Coliseum in 1966. Mama Cass was so nervous, she ran down the stairs of the revolving stage and threw up. Later, she blamed the moving stage for making her sick. In truth, it was nerves!

Two figures often seen together on stage in Seattle were Ian Whitcomb (above) and Pat O'Day (right). Whitcomb, later to become a disc jocky himself, scored his biggest hit with You Turn Me On in 1965.

Mama Cass Elliot (opposite page) threw up during this performance on the Seattle Center Coliseum's famous (infamous?) revolving stage.

Above: The Shangri-las; Below: Patty LaBelle & The Bluebelles

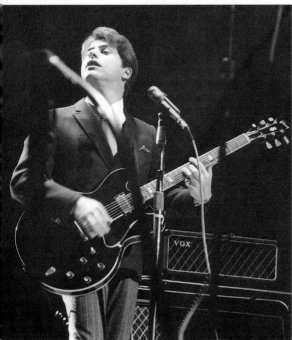

Johnny Rivers was one of the last two singers, along with Trini Lopez, who continued to wear a suit and tie while performing in live concerts. Pictured on the upper left are Lou Adler and Johnny Rivers conferring backstage at the Seattle Center Coliseum with Pat 'O'Day prior to a 1967 concert.

Ron Gardner performing with The Fabulous Wailers at the Seattle Center Coliseum in 1965.

The Fabulous Wailers from Tacoma hit number one on Northwest music charts three different times with their version of Louie Louie. Together with Pat O'Day, they pioneered the rock 'n' roll dance business in the Pacific Northwest. Their appearances at the Spanish Castle are legendary. Above, left to right: Rich Dangel, Buck Ormsby, Ron Gardner, Kent Morrill and Mike Burk.

Bottom right: Buck Ormsby, The Wailers' long-time bassist.

Peter Noone of Herman's Hermits

The Who performed in concert in Seattle in 1967 as opening act for Peter Noone and Herman's Hermits. Concerts West produced the concert and Pat O'Day emceed the festivities. Pictured: Top: Pete Townsend; Bottom Right: John Entwistle plays bass, Roger Daltrey sings lead and Keith Moon plays drums.

Roger Daltrey of the Who performing at the Seattle Center Coliseum

Mitch Ryder & His Detroit Wheels performed at one of Pat O'Day's TeenSpectaculars. The site was Seattle's High School memorial Stadium, within the shadow of the Space Needle, the base of which can be seen in the background of the picture on the lower right. When looking through files for images to include in this book, Jini Dellaccio rediscovered these pictures, which she thought she had lost over 30 years ago.

Dino, Desi & Billy performing at the Seattle Center Coliseum

Gary Lewis & the Playboys

Four scenes from concerts at the Seattle Center Coliseum

The Beau Brummels performing on the revolving stage at the Seattle Center Coliseum, with the faces of Larry "Superjock" Lujack & "World Famous" Tom Murphy festooned on its sides.

Jim Valley (left) frequently performed for Seattle audiences as a member of various Northwest groups. Fans of Jim when he was with Paul Revere & The Raiders (below) made their feelings known.

Pat (above) emceed hundreds of concerts coast to coast during his years as a disc jockey and concert promoter. In Seattle, his shows on stage at the Seattle Center Coliseum (right) are legendary.

Top left: Peggy Claire, KJR helicopter traffic reporter; Top right: Pat with sons Jerry (on left), Garry (on right), and Jeff (front); Bottom right: Tom Hulett & Pat; Bottom left: Annette Funicello.

Memories of the '95s in Seattle

'at's has been a fixture of Seattle's annual Seafair hydroplane race since 1968. One year he nlisted the help of his good buddy Wayne Newton (top left) to serve as color commentator.

Left: Brenda Jones is the only woman in history to compete in (and win) an unlimited hydroplane race. Above: The U-95 out for a spin.

Top: Pat and Dick Curtis teamed up on stage at EMP to lead the crowd in the singing of the KJR jingle. Above: Three of The Fabulous Wailers: Buck Ormsby, bass, the late Rich Dangel, lead guitar & Neil Rush, sax; Center right: Pat at EMP book-signing party; Bottom right: the late Rich Dangel.

Top left: Jim Clapp presents a check to Spencer Haywood at a Seattle SuperSonics game in 1973 as Pat assists; Bottom left: Pat O'Day emceeing at a Rolling Stones concert; Top right: Record promotion man Ernie Farrell, with Billboard Magazine Radio Editor Claude Hall, in Pat's office, 1974; Middle right: Pat and Dusty Springfield; Bottom right: Pat with Petula Clark and Bill Gavin

Right: Preparation for a concert on the revolving stage at the Seattle Center Coliseum started hours before the show itself began. Center: Impresarios Pat O'Day & Dick Curtis reviewing concert plans with staff; Bottom: Let the music play!

SEATTLE METROPOLITAN AREA   MONDAY-FRIDAY   JULY-AUGUST

Noon-1PM	Avg ¼hr Rating	MEN ADULTS	WOMEN ADULTS	3-4PM	Avg ¼hr Rating	MEN ADULTS	WOMEN ADULTS
KJR	7.0	6100	14000	KJR	6.9	5300	18100
KIRO	2.0	2600	6400	KVI	2.7	4200	7600
KIXI	2.0	3200	6100	KXA	1.8	3400	6000
KXA	1.9	2300	6200	KOL	1.7	2200	5200
KVI	1.8	2000	6000	KING	1.6	3200	4800
KOL	1.3	1500	3400	KIXI	1.6	2500	5400
KING	1.1	1500	3600	KOMO	1.4	1900	4700
KOMO	1.1	1500	3000	KIRO	1.2	1700	3800

1-2PM				4-5pm			
KJR	5.9	5200	11600	KJR	7.5	8800	20000
KVI	1.9	1800	6500	KVI	3.2	6000	8200
KIXI	1.8	2700	5400	KING	2.2	5400	5900
KXA	1.7	2400	5800	KOMO	2.1	4000	5800
KIRO	1.3	1800	3900	KIXI	2.0	3800	6300
KOL	1.3	1600	3600	KXA	1.9	4000	6300
KING	1.2	1800	4000	KOL	1.7	3500	4800
KOMO	.9	1300	2900	KIRO	1.3	2400	3700

2-3PM				5-6PM			
KJR	5.8	5100	11800	KJR	7.8	9400	21300
KXA	1.8	2100	5600	KVI	3.3	6700	8500
KIXI	1.7	2700	5000	KXA	2.3	5000	7000
KVI	1.5	1800	5300	KOMO	2.2	5100	6500
KIRO	1.5	1600	4500	KIRO	2.2	5000	5500
KING	1.3	2000	4700	KING	2.0	5300	5800
KOL	1.2	1500	3100	KIXI	1.8	3600	5600
KOMO	.8	1300	2700	KOL	1.7	3600	4900

SOURCE: Audience Composition The Pulse Inc Seattle Metro Area
July-August Monday through Friday

These rating are adults only. KJR was also carrying 80 percent of the teen audience. Pat O'Day's ratings are in the right-hand column. Note: KOL was KJR's rock competition.

Channel 95's on air team, circa 1965, listening to air checks. Left to right: Larry Lujack, Jerry Kaye, Lan Roberts, Dick Curtis, Lee Perkins, Pat O'Day

Two of Top 40 radio's finest: left, Dick Curtis; right, Lan Roberts

9 – You're My World

Cilla Black, 1964

BACK IN 1962, THE POWERS THAT BE excused me from the wasteful tedium of hiring research firms and listening to consultants. Given free rein, I ran KJR-Seattle according to my gut instincts, and those were as follows: Day and night, I wanted to have performing live on air at Channel 95 the most powerful and entertaining and unique disc jockeys alive. Every minute of every hour of every day, seven days a week, they must be better than any other jock working at any other radio station anywhere else in the region, regardless of format or target audience. If that caliber of polished talent couldn't be found locally or lured to town from outside, we'd recruit it in its raw form and develop it ourselves.

The same standards applied to KJR's news reporters. To seize and hold the giant market share I sought, we groomed our staff to deliver news with an urgent, exciting, flamboyant style, neutralizing any temptations our audience felt to switch stations when no music played during newscasts. We wrote news reports in the present tense and delivered them at a fast pace with genuine emotion and a keen sense of immediacy. Reporting on KJR became critical, factual and essential, offering a quality of information found nowhere else on the dial. Hourly, we delivered news and sports editorials, every one a compact, straight-to-the-heart dagger (no long or boring dissertations allowed!). Preceding those elements, dramatic intros jumped out of radios, grabbed listeners by their collars and commanded them: "Don't you dare go away! You must hear this!"

We applied a similar approach to music. Playing only Top 40 songs, even if you're the best-produced, most entertaining station in town, still leaves you vulnerable should a competitor decide to broadcast the same selection. They might not beat you, but by running fewer commercials and promoting them-selves heavily, they *might* carve into your dominance. To avoid this trap, at KJR we offered more than just the Top 40 songs while maintaining the illusion that we played only the big hits. National trade charts (like *Billboard*'s weekly list) included too much hype and were dominated by music primarily weighted with an East Coast appeal. Seeking that always-elusive advantage, I crafted our music selection to reflect the specific tastes of the Pacific Northwest. Admittedly, similarities existed between KJR's top-sellers and the nation's. Even so, there were great differences, some more subtle than others, and rec-ognizing them was critical to our success. To respond to those nuances, and to guarantee a precisely Northwest appeal to our music, we focused on regional record sales from then on.

Then, I expanded the current song library out to as many as 70 songs. This required careful selection as well as focusing some songs into certain parts of the day depending on what audience was available during those hours. Day-time school hours and late at night offered the opportunity to broaden the music scope without burning off the teens. During those hours, country western music and other rock-'n'-roll derivatives could be played with just the adult in mind. Also during those hours, oldies of the past eight or so years, especially oldies with great adult appeal, could be used to balance the top 40 or 50 songs on the hit parade. Records with heavy sub-teen appeal could be ignored during those hours.

One happy dividend from this approach with the disc jockeys having lots of music to choose from was the avoidance of redundancy. I had a slogan: Redundancy kills! This didn't apply to a hot new song on its way up the music charts with an audience demanding to hear it, but it certainly applied to songs that had peaked, as well as to oldies. Expanding on that thought, if I had a new record, just out of the box, that I knew was a hit, we played it once an hour for several days, based on my feeling that when a song is new and appealing, listeners just can't get enough of it. That is when the song is a high impact and emotional tool — as well as an exciting new experience — and should be used to its fullest. I treated a song in the opposite fashion once it achieved maximum upward popularity growth.

This approach was quite radical and helped us soundly defeat all attempts by other stations to establish musical inroads into our listening audience. Most stations never figured out that airplay cannot merely match record sales, because some people are slow to catch on to new music while others grasp it immediately. I wanted to program the station to appeal to those we felt were in the majority that were quick studies. In addition, many record purchases are for collection purposes and not for immediate listening satisfaction. Therefore, we held to our motto when it came to current music: "Be the first station on a record and the first station off of it." That way you can be perceived by listeners as being as "hip" as the next minute. And, in fact, you are! Putting all these elements together, coupled with jingles singing the call letters that had been carefully written and recorded, creative and innovative contests with attractive prizes, lots of outside activities in the community and the constant conversation piece such a station becomes, you began to realize how we increased our listenership to sometimes over 30 percent of the total radio audience in the Seattle Metro area. The station became an awesome, overpowering juggernaut of information, fun, music and companionship—but most of all, fun.

Fun, Fun, Fun
The Beach Boys, 1964

NONE OF THIS COULD BE ACCOMPLISHED without talent. I often said, "I don't care if they drink too much! I don't care if they kick their dog! I don't care if they've been married 20 times! I just don't care so long as they have loads of talent!

What do I mean by talent? It starts with a person that since childhood has been afflicted by a compulsion to entertain others. That, combined with the ability to do so adds up to raw talent! Many a time I was approached by young radio aspirants wanting to work for us who said their greatest broadcasting attribute was their love of music and their ability to really relate to it! That one would earn them a quick, "Gee, thanks for thinking of us and NO!" The mind and individual that would describe themselves in that manner was wired wrong for what I sought. But, if an applicant told me they could be funnier than hell. Ah! That got my immediate and full attention.

Funny wasn't the exclusive requirement. If the individual could be consistently and compellingly interesting, they could also be considered. The Casey Kasem approach speaks for itself, but must be the exception and not the rule on a station designed for fun listening. I traveled to other cities and listened to their radio stations, trying to find those deejays who could make me laugh. I searched for those news reporters who could nearly make me cry. Perpetual emotion, that was the goal.

My interviewing and searching brought great rewards. The growing legend of KJR was perpetuated by such radio stars as Lan Roberts, "World Famous" Tom Murphy (at least, that is what he called himself), Larry Lujack, Mike Phillips, Jim Hilliard, Dick Curtis, Kevin O'Brien (Metheny), Scotty Brink, Emperor Lee Smith, Jerry Kaye and many others. I mention these particular names because they effectively used KJR as a launching pad for their careers. I like to think that the training, the standards, the high levels of expectation and the peer pressure amongst the KJR air staff were partially responsible for their later successes as well as their great success in Seattle.

Lan Roberts came from Texas with Gordon McClendon-type inspirations, which meant "Be funny and famous!" So did Jimmy Hilliard. Lan, after several years of Seattle morning dominance, went on to become the morning giant on the only English-speaking station in Taiwan. That, after bringing me great success in the late '70s with the station I owned in Honolulu.

Hilliard before long showed stunning radio moxie and was sent to our Spokane farm club as program director to develop young talent. From there he went to a Canadian broadcast chain, then to WFIL-Philadelphia, then WIBC-Indianapolis, as manager, and finally to KVIL-Dallas where he created the new number one station there that endured for years. Hilliard is one of maybe two dozen of the greatest broadcasters ever.

I discovered Jerry Kaye when he was in high school and on my air staff at KLOQ during my Yakima days. Charming and smooth, at KJR he developed a sense of humor on the air that was devastatingly funny. He eventually went on, as did many others, to Chicago for large money. Jerry now sits by the ocean in his cabin at Seaside, Oregon just watching seagulls and counting his savings, which in his case is about 98 percent of everything he ever earned.

Mike Phillips went from Seattle to a big job as morning man at KFRC-San Francisco, eventually becoming the program director of K-EARTH 101 in LA. Mike had a powerful, commanding on-air presence and an amazing funny streak. Tom Murphy graduated to Chicago for a while, then settled in Los Angeles, where he is still heard on syndicated radio shows. Scotty Brink was already a star when I hired him from WLS-Chicago. One might wonder why Brink, with the world's greatest voice and style, would move from the Chicago market to KJR. Likely it was because true talent found total fulfillment at KJR.

Leaving on a Jet Plane
Peter, Paul and Mary, 1969

BY THE EARLY '70S, KJR WAS WHERE SO MANY TALENTS wanted to be, and the fact that Seattle was a smaller market was immaterial. Larry Lujack went the opposite direction. He wanted to be in a drive time slot but at KJR those positions were held by Lan Roberts and me. So, he found the on-air hours he wanted at WMEX in Boston. But soon, it was off to Chicago to become the deejay they were to call *Superjock*. He totally mesmerized the Windy City. Originally working for Kenny Draper at WCFL-Chicago. Larry was soon hired away by ABC's Chicago giant, WLS. In a short time, Lujack became one of the best-known and highest-paid disc jockeys in the US and deserved every penny of it.

Lujack had started with our company at our Spokane station, and I think we aided him in building the foundation of what was to be a totally different type of presentation. He was funny, but the laughs came from his creation of the most sarcastic, cynical, negative, arrogant, self righteous, irreverent personality imaginable. At KJR, I impressed on Larry, as well as the rest of the team, the importance of show preparation. I always told my staff that the greatest ad-lib is a well written, well rehearsed ad-lib. Know where you're going and what every word will accomplish. Then, you have head room for that spontaneity that may or may not be successful. Lujack took this to heart and spent hours planning his three hour show.

I was in Chicago for a concert and, naturally, was proudly listening to my protégé. It was the morning after the NCAA Final Four championship game. The following exchange had of course been carefully planned with the WLS newsman, as Lujack left nothing to chance. The newsman delivered the score from the game, and Lujack interrupted him, in the middle of his newscast, by saying, "I saw that game and I wonder, don't white guys play basketball anymore?"

The newsman cleared his throat and tried to continue, sounding embarrassed. Lujack just continued: "You know, I think I have it figured out! Those black guys have grown up in apartment houses that don't have elevators. They've been running up and down stairs from the sixth floor all their life and that's what makes them so good!"

I think that if any other air personality in the country tried a line like that, they would be tarred and feathered as well as fired—but not Lujack. His listeners, black and white, always found his cynical comments hilarious, and so did I. One night we had the Moody Blues at Chicago Stadium, and I asked Larry if he would like to come and be the emcee of the show. Typically, Larry mumbled that it was a terrible imposition....Where did it say he owed me something?...etc., etc., etc.—but agreed. Now that's Larry. He actually was thrilled to be asked to jump up in front of 18,000 Moody fans, but his adopted personality made him act like someone being put upon, even with me.

Just as the Moody Blues were ready to come on stage, from a backstage microphone I said, "Ladies and gentleman, your master of ceremonies. Let's welcome, from WLS, Mr. Larry Lujack!"

In keeping with his entire persona, most of the crowd loudly cheered, but a noticeable number booed. Larry slouched across the stage to the mike and began, "Nice to be here! For those that cheered when I was introduced, I want to congratulate you on your good taste. [Another big cheer.] And those that booed me, well, you can just go to hell!"

The cheers drowned out the boos, and you have a great example of Larry Lujack. Larry was living proof of an absolute fact when it comes to entertainers. The greats are either loved or they're hated. It might be Johnny Carson, David Letterman, Jay Leno, Bill Cosby, or Frasier. You will not find ambivalence in people's feelings. They either love 'em or hate 'em! I've always contended, Show me a performer who is neither deeply loved nor hated but, rather, inspires nice, neutral feelings and I'll show you a loser! Lujack, intuitively sensing this, burrowed further and further into his "Nasty Larry" personality, with total success.

During the early '80s, when I owned KORL radio in Honolulu, Hawaii, Larry and his wife came over on vacation, and he and I played golf. Larry and I played together a great deal when he worked for me in Seattle, so it was fun to renew the old rivalry. I took him out to my country club where at the end of our match I owed him 100 dollars, as he and I always bet on our golf games. We sat in the golf cart, totaled our scores and established his victory, and he said, "Give me my money!"

That night, he and his wife were coming over to my place for dinner, so I said, "I don't have that much cash. I'll pay you tonight!"

Larry nearly shouted, "No, God damn it, I want it now!"

I responded, "Okay, you slimy predator," pulled out my checkbook and, with the scoring pencil, wrote him his check.

We had a great dinner that night talking about old times. Fifteen years later, a Seattle radio station sponsored a reunion of former KJR deejays and, of course, Larry was invited. He declined, and I quote him as to why: "I'm not participating in any event where O'Day is involved. He wrote me a check in Hawaii and he wrote it in pencil because he knew the bank wouldn't cash a check written in pencil! I'm holding onto that check, and, until he pays me my 100 dollars, I refuse to go near him!"

This was wonderful. Can you imagine a sense of humor that intricate, complex and beautiful? I will always love this guy. And Larry, when you read this book, may I suggest that you take a pen, you moronic senile crank, and trace over the pencil with ink, then go cash it and shut up!

In closing on Larry Lujack, in his book, *Superjock*, he wrote: "With me, Jerry Kaye, Pat, Dick Curtis, Lan Roberts and 'World Famous' Tom Murphy, KJR was, in my opinion, the best rock-'n'-roll station that has ever existed."

Personally, I always felt that honor should go to Rick Sklar's WABC-New York with "Cousin Brucie" Morrow, Dan Ingram, George Michaels, Ron Lundy and others. However, if a credible source like Lujack actually believes it was us, I'll proudly settle for a tie!

My Guy
Mary Wells, 1964

DICK CURTIS WAS A DEEJAY AND NEWSMAN extraordinaire, and his story is somewhat covered elsewhere in this book. Suffice it to say here that he just recently retired from the air, 40 years after first coming to work for KJR. When he retired from KOMO and KVI in 2001, he was still the most exciting and professional radio newsman in Seattle.

Then there was Kevin O'Brien, now back to his given name of Kevin Metheny, who went on to serve as program director at WNBC-New York and many other successes. At this writing, he is a programming executive with Clear Channel, which has become the biggest radio group in the world. Kevin makes an interesting story on how we found the talent I so fervently sought. While driving downtown from the airport in Oklahoma City one Saturday evening (I had Three Dog Night scheduled the next night at the Memorial Coliseum in Oak City), I was listening to radio station WKY. I found myself fascinated by the young, fresh voice of what was apparently a weekend deejay (Saturday nights are almost always tended by part timers). This guy had something; I couldn't put my finger on it but I felt it was magic. His wasn't a deep voice, not your usual announcer type. He spoke with more of an Oklahoma twang, and there was something there that moved me.

The next night, following the Dog's concert, I was in the car again on my way back to the airport for a late flight out. I heard that deejay again, and now I was convinced. Upon returning to my office at KJR, I asked Vivian Anderson, my assistant, to discreetly call WKY (which was run by a friend named Lee Allen Smith) and try to get the home number of the young man who, on the air, called himself *Kevin O'Brien*. She used some excuse I thought up like, "We want to see if he would come to our school!"

This led to my finally reaching him at home, and he was shocked when I asked if he would be willing to fly to Seattle and talk with me about a career on KJR. I enjoyed the advantage of KJR by now being one of the most respected set of call letters in the nation, and this kid was in shock and nearly speechless in the face of my call. When he recovered, after asking several times if this was for real, Kevin agreed to come to Seattle that following Friday so he could be back for his part-time show on Saturday. What he didn't tell me was that to be in Seattle on Friday, he would have to skip school. Not college, high school!

Our meeting was to the point. My brief listening to him in Oklahoma City told me almost everything I needed to know. He graduated from high school six weeks later and immediately became my six-to-nine-P.M., Monday-through-Friday deejay. He was only 18 years old, with the poise to fit right in with one of the finest broadcast teams the country had known. He was perfect. Kevin O'Brien was funny, exciting and articulate, employing a superb vocabulary that he knew how to use and a cunning ability to make an individual listener believe he was talking just to them.

One year later, with no television or newspaper or *Billboard* advertising on Kevin's behalf, I ran a study through the Hooper Ratings Service to determine the recall power of the names of Seattle's deejays. I did this to confirm my hunches as to the relative strengths of the individuals on my staff compared to all other radio personalities in the market. Our current morning man, Emperor Lee Smith, was number one. Lan Roberts, now doing middays, was number two. I showed up as number three. (I hadn't been on the air regularly for three years, but Seattle apparently still either loved me or hated me!)

Number four in the survey, ahead of nearly 40 other Seattle air personalities, many of whom had been around and heavily promoted for years, was my new young star, Kevin O'Brien. I always felt it took a minimum of two to three years for a new personality to establish themselves in a city. Kevin had done it in one. Throughout the years since, Kevin has always fought to gain big executive programming jobs. In my humble opinion, that's a shame. I believe that, had he pursued his on-air career, he was destined to become maybe the greatest deejay in the history of radio. I think Kevin was given more natural radio talent than any of the hundreds of great radio people I have known!

All Day and All of the Night
The Kinks, 1964

ALTHOUGH THE FOLLOWING NAMES WILL BE UNFAMILIAR to most readers, I want to list them because these individuals were all part of any success I have enjoyed. Some of them were phenomenal talents, and I thank them for the part they played and for allowing me to mess with their techniques: Norm Gregory, John Maynard (still a big star in Seattle radio), Steve West, Gary Shannon, Nick Anthony, Charlie Brown, the late Bobby Simon, the late Robert L. Scott, Emperor Smith, Scotty Brink, B'wanna Johnny, Burl Barer, Robt O. Smith, Buzz Barr, Tom Larson, Lee Perkins, Gary Taylor, Steve Nicolet, Jimmy Rabbit, J. J. Valley, Terry Rose, Bob Bracken (Bobby Bee), Derrick Shannon, Chuck Bolland, Mike West, the late Lee Michaels, Paige Clair, Spencer Haywood, Steve Slayton, Joe Colburn, Les Parsons, Frank Thompson, Tim Burgess, the late Chuck Ellsworth, engineers Norm Fish and Lee Hurley and others I am sure I will never be forgiven for omitting! Even with all this talent we put together over the years — and we needed lots of potential in the wings because other stations, in Seattle and across the country, delighted in hiring away my stars — the station needed strong fiber and tradition to keep it consistent.

A key to our level of performance was the Wednesday deejay meeting. This meeting was mandatory, took place at 10:00 A.M. and included the news and production people as well as jocks. We listened to the new music we planned to play and discussed contests, promotions and the commercial campaigns of our clients. But, most important, we evaluated what we had done on the air the past week.

A rarity in radio, this method brought forth such accelerated improvement and growth with our stars that I will never understand why other stations haven't employed it. We played tape recordings, surreptitiously gathered, of selected shows from recent days. The assembled staff then critiqued those shows. Of course, it wasn't fun being on the hot seat and having your peers closely examine your work on the air. But, the cumulative opinions of the other deejays, coupled with my input and care to be sure no one was held up to ridicule, worked (and believe me, these guys, with their rapier-like senses of humor, were totally capable of same!). Most program directors keep such evaluations just between themselves and the air personality, partly because they wouldn't want their suggestions challenged by the other professionals in the room, and partly because most personalties think such discussions should be private. That's bullshit! The tape recording we critiqued was what the deejay had put on the air the previous week for millions to examine. Now you tell me, why should the weaknesses or strengths thereof be examined in secret? Why not take advantage of the rest of the air staff and let the individual correct and grow from their collective professional opinions? The other benefit that accrues from this approach is that everyone is also evaluating themselves while the other person is being critiqued. I believe this, more than my coaching, was responsible for the matchless group of entertainers we produced.

Other things we taught at KJR included the timing and actual production of every second on the air. How very tight cues and releases of the first note of a song or commercial can, in themselves, command the listener's attention and create a hypnotic effect with audio surprises. We taught how to show your deep respect for the music with subtlety. How to say a few important things over the front or back of a song without interfering with the song or its mood, thereby irritating the listener. How to pitch your voice to match one of the musical notes within the song, avoiding discord between voice and music. And, also, how to match the tone and tempo of your voice to the feelings and tempo of the music. I am stunned when I visit large, big market radio stations today and find that such absolute truths as these are never coached, never discussed, never requested, never considered and, quite probably, not even known. These are such important basics when hosting music, it's no wonder few people bother to remember the names of most deejays today. They tend to be just lovely voices, saying inane, empty, well-researched things the stations want them to say with no intellectual recognition or deep understanding of the ultimate place they could hold in their listeners' lives.

The air staffs at KJR-AM and KISW-FM. Left to right, front row: Rick Hanson, Joe Colburn, Lan Roberts, Garry Shannon, Kevin O'Brian (Metheny), Pat O'Day and Bob Bingham (FM Sales Manager); Back Row: Robert L. Scott, Lee Michaels, Emperor Smith, Norm Gregory, Steve Nicolay, Shannon Sweatte (AM Sales Manager).

Pat O'Day, Bill Gavin and Les Smith at a New York ceremony saluting Gavin, the powerful radio programmer.

At his/her best, a deejay is the frame around a picture, and the picture is the music! They have the option of making the frame fun, exiting, memorable and salutary to their music or making that frame a boring, unattractive, unimaginative distraction from the picture. Too often anymore, we hear the latter.

The development of a broadcaster's humor isn't necessarily that easy. It's a trial-and-error process with few specific rules or guidelines. One must first determine a style that fits the individual. There is nothing wrong with emulating a style that has been effective for other comics, hosts, etc. *if it works*. The entertainment business is heavily populated with those who have borrowed ideas from others. Robin Williams is just the new version of Jonathan Winters, Chris Rock has borrowed heavily from Bill Cosby and the late Flip Wilson. Carson was a whole lot of Jack Benny, as is Frasier. The secret is, If you borrow only that which matches your strengths and heavily insert your own personality, you just may be providing the world a fresh new entertainer! We are all products of our environment and a multitude of impressions. Musicians, comics, movie stars, deejays, painters, sculptors, and writers who claim to be totally original, lie. However, as close to original as an individual can come was Lan Roberts.

The Martian Hop
The Ran-Dells, 1963

LAN ROBERTS, BORN IN BONHAM, TEXAS, embraced the new radio of the late 50s like a mother embraces her newborn child. He arrived in Seattle from New Orleans at my competitor, KOL. After listening to him for a few days, I knew that situation had to be corrected. It took two evenings of explaining my radio dreams to him to convince Lan to join me at KJR. Lan has a voice that charms and a mind driving it that captures. He displays the wild thoughts and actions of a child with adult nuances. As is the case with Larry Lujack, the best way to explain Lan is to pass along stories of our adventures together, on and off the radio. To be a regular listener to Lan was to expand your acquaintances to include some marvelous characters he portrayed with his ability to create many voices and personalities for his morning "get up" audience.

There was Phil Dirt, an Oakie who operated a roadside sock stand. Phil was a total hick but a funny lovable reflection of so many in our southern Midwest states. Phil's wife was Radene. Phil readily admitted that Radene weighed in at about 300 pounds, but, in Phil's words, "Radene is good people and besides,

I always wanted a big woman that could give me a lot of love!" Phil also had political views, hated bureaucracies and drove a Chevy pick up.

Then there was Lan's Hollywood Reporter routine, in which he could flawlessly imitate Louella Parsons, well-known newspaper, television and radio gossip columnist. In Parsons' husky Camel cigarette-sounding voice, Lan delivered outrageous reports on Hollywood's stars. He never believed being clever was enough. His goal was to get unrestrained laughter. I fondly recall one morning when his Louella reported, "One of the world's great motion picture stars told me exclusively over lunch at the Brown Derby yesterday that she's coming out of retirement to do a couple of films. Yes, that great, talented and beautiful star of so many films, Lassie, wants to give movies another go! She told me, "Louella, tell my fans, in the words of Elton John, *The Bitch is Back!*"

Lan portrayed other characters as well, such as a voice he borrowed from a Stan Freberg character that Lan called *Clyde Clyde, The Cow's Outside*. You're no doubt wondering What in the hell is a Clyde Clyde, The Cow's Outside? It was just another hilariously unique character, and the name was the sort of thing you came to expect on Lan's show. It made starting the day with Lan Roberts on KJR-Seattle so much fun. Clyde often joined with my character, Granny Peters, doing comical helicopter traffic reports. With Granny piloting and Clyde reporting, they'd try to fly through tunnels, they'd nearly hit tall buildings, they'd drop down to spy on apartment dwellers showering and they'd crash to earth on a regular basis.

Clyde Clyde, The Cow's Outside also joined with Granny Peters in a long-running KJR feature we called *Wonder Mother*. ("Wonder Mother, fighting for victory / Wonder Mother, fighting to keep man free" was part of the song we played every time she appeared on radio.) Granny was cast as herself, eighty years old, a heavy drinker with a lust for life. She was a superpatriot and joined Clyde in a fight to preserve the American Way. New threats to our society appeared each Monday, and the solution was always happily found by Friday. These threats generally appeared in the form of a sinister individual who was trying to destroy our defense industry and military capabilities and, in various other ways, disrupt the American Way of Life.

How did Lan and I research and test market to determine whether our efforts were really entertaining? Simple. When we listened back to the shows we had just recorded, if we were convulsed on the floor laughing, we knew we were fine. If not, we erased the whole thing and started over.

One week, Wonder Mother was notified by the CIA that the dreaded Mr. Snow had been contracted by the enemy to perform a dastardly deed. She explained that Mr. Snow was planning to drop special pellets on top of Mount Rainier. These mysterious pellets were capable of immediately melting billions of tons of snow on the top of the mountain. This would then cause a massive flood as water rushed down the mountain and into the rivers which would presumably wipe out the Boeing Company, Fort Lewis and several other key defense facilities in Washington state. That sequence of episodes ended on my show on a Friday afternoon with Wonder Mother and Clyde sitting on the top of Mount Rainier in the Wonder Chopper, acting on information they received that the dreaded Mr. Snow was going to swoop over the mountain in his Learjet and spread his lethal pellets. Clyde brought along Fernaldo, his specially trained security chicken.

At 20 minutes past five we heard Mr. Snow's Learjet approaching the mountain. Wonder Mother and Clyde were standing beside the Wonder Chopper giving Fernaldo last minute instructions. As the Learjet made its dive to bomb the mountain with pellets, Fernaldo was released with a mighty cackle. You heard his wings flopping as he flew straight into the air intake of the engine on Mr. Snow's plane, then a loud explosion. Wonder Mother and Clyde described the plane's disintegration and accompanying dive into the side of the mountain. They cheered loudly, and Clyde was shouting "Thank you, Fernaldo, thank you! You're a great American hero!" as the final few lines of *America the Beautiful* wrapped up another week's adventures of Wonder Mother.

Lan had a weird side a mile wide. He held Wednesday Night Fish Fights at his home and invited over friends and local record promoters. In his living room he installed a tank filled with imported Piranha fighting fish. He developed a system using food coloring that gave them contrasting colors. When two were in the small space together, they attacked each other. Lan operated the parimutuel betting, while his guests wagered on who would survive.

Lan had a fixation on strange animals, and I have it on good authority that his first marriage failed because of a boa constrictor. Using his radio-developed influence—which was substantial—he had borrowed the snake from Seattle's Woodland Park Zoo. One morning, after he left home for his morning show, the snake escaped from its cage in the living room and couldn't be found. His wife, JoAnn, justifiably concerned that a boa constrictor might do harm to their children, called not only the police but an attorney.

There was always a fine line with Lan between fantasy and reality, and he seemed incapable of determining where one ended and the other began. Case in point was his relationship with Major Wayne Aho. Rumor had it that the Major had been a Section 8 when leaving the US Air Force. Section 8 has something to do with mental incompatibility with Air Force standards. The Major retired to the mountains southeast of Seattle and was the person who brought to the attention of the world the existence of flying saucers. In 1948, he spotted scooting around Mt. Rainier, some of the first flying saucers ever reported, and civilization has never fully recovered. To Lan, this made the Major a modern day Christopher Columbus. To more rational minds, it made him a "real package."

Aho published a magazine called *Saucer Intelligence* and used his prior Air Force affiliation to the hilt. This gave him credibility, and it could be argued that Wayne Aho did for flying saucers what the Wright Brothers did for airplanes. All of this was reinforced in the minds of his followers by his insistence that he had been hosted on a trip through the universe on board a saucer that picked him up on the flanks of the Cascade Mountains. It was during this exclusive tour that the *Saucer People*, as the Major liked to call them, fulfilled their mission to earth by teaching him the Intergalactic Peace Language, which he now spoke fluently. Lan Roberts, overwhelmed by the whole thing, became a devoted disciple of Major Aho.

It all struck me as harmless. The Major stopped by the station about once a week, where he huddled with Lan in a production room discussing I never knew exactly what. From those encounters, Lan passed along a few tidbits of insider saucer information to his audience in the morning. Lan's listeners yearned for more. Wild, funny, incredible stuff, and the fact that he did it with a straight face made it all the more enjoyable. I probed to determine the extent of Lan's actual beliefs where saucers were concerned and never once determined the true depth of Lan's convictions. Who cared?

One day, the Major and Lan approached me with a major idea. They were convinced that if we invited the Saucer People to actually communicate with Earth people, they would do so. Their idea called for a message to be broadcast to them each morning at a set time on the radio during Lan's show. We would give them our frequency, 950 kilocycles on the AM dial, on which to answer, then go silent for several seconds, allowing the Saucer People time to answer. I knew everyone in town would soon be talking about it, so I didn't let the fact that the Major and Lan were serious interfere with my decision.

Every morning at 7:00 A.M., following the 6:55 news, we broadcast a message to the universe. Lan's and Aho's pre-recorded announcement began with Lan saying, "This radio station, KJR, will now, as a public service, make an attempt to contact extra-terrestrials that we know are aboard flying saucers in the area. KJR will now go silent for 15 seconds to give you a chance to communicate with earth on 950 kilocycles. Here to speak to you in the Intergalactic Peace Language is the Chairman of Saucer Intelligence, Major Wayne Aho!"

The Major, in the goofy monotone space voice he had adopted, then shouted, "Ah donay vausooo! Ah donay vausooo!" which, according to Lan, meant, "We come in peace!"

If you were shaving, eating breakfast, riding on the school bus, driving to work or just listening in bed before getting up, you *had* to turn up your radio, just in case outer space answered. Maybe, just maybe, you would hear something. The general public never heard anything, but the Major did. At his home in the mountains, he had listening equipment with greater sensitivity than most folks, better than the station itself, for that matter. One morning, the Major excitedly called from his mountainside listening post with the news: The Saucer People are coming!

The Major stated that they had agreed to land their space ship and had given him latitude and longitude coordinates. These intersected a short distance from Seattle, east of Bellevue, near the town of Issaquah at the Issaquah Airport. The time of their arrival, according to the Major, was three days later at nine in the evening.

For those three days, Lan bordered on a nervous breakdown. It was too much for him, and I was beginning to re-examine my wisdom in approving the whole thing. Evidence of my questionable judgement appeared the next morning when I awoke to hear Lan berating the National Guard and the Boeing Company for not providing a circle of infra-red lights the Major said the saucer people had requested. I solved this problem by calling Lan on the phone in the studio to tell him I had been a tank commander in the National Guard and knew for a fact that, if they parked cars in a circle pointing inwards and covered their headlights by taping red cellophane over them, every benefit of infra-red lighting would be met.

Satisfied with this, Lan proceeded, abandoning his usual morning features (other than the music) and devoting his program totally to the upcoming arrival on earth of the Saucer People.

My next action Lan, to this day, still calls a big rotten lie. Maybe I didn't want to disappoint the thousands who, given the exposure this was receiving, would undoubtedly be at the airport. Maybe it was just my sick sense of humor. Regardless, I contacted the sky diving school at Snohomish Airport which is 40 miles or so north of Seattle. My instructions were simple. They would fly their Cessna 207 sky diving plane, lights out, engine idling, 6,000 feet over Issaquah at the appointed time. The skies would be dark in that it was Fall. Their diver, using a black chute and armed with a high power flashlight, would jump from the plane and float toward earth flashing something like Morse code with his powerful light. Then, at about 2,000 feet, he would turn off the light and slip his chute so as to drift over the I-90 freeway that bordered the airport and land quietly and undetected in a dark farm field on the other side. Total secrecy needed to be maintained. Everything worked to perfection.

That night, the freeway and surrounding roads were jammed with traffic as thousands came to see history in the making. Promptly at 9:00 P.M., the sky diver left the unseen plane and began his descent, pumping out Morse code flashes to the ground. At the airfield below, this created total chaos. There were the cars in a giant circle, cellophane red lights on, and, in the middle of the circle, a massive throng. With the first flashing light, they began to shout and scream, "The Saucer People are here!"

Lan was so excited, he was jumping up and down, fists clenched like he had just scored the winning touchdown in the Super Bowl. The Major was another matter. Watching the light as it descended, he was smitten. Falling backwards onto the wet grass, he was staring into the heavens, tears running down his cheeks, mumbling "Au donay vausooo. Au donay vausooo!" Meanwhile, my skydiver, right on schedule, shut off his light and, undetected, floated silently down into a field some distance away.

Lan's outrage the next morning on the air caused me to ask him to briefly leave the control room and come into my office. On the air, he was calling all Seattle television stations and newspapers irresponsible and worse for not delivering a single word of coverage of what he claimed was the most significant happening in the history of mankind. He was, live and on the air, throwing an absolute fit over the news snub of the phenomenon. It became serious, his accusations grew harsh and I had to do something. I told him what I had done, explaining the plane, the parachute, the flashing light and the elusive landing across the freeway. Lan looked at me after my revelation and said, "You're a #*&%/&@ing liar!" and that was that. He went back to the control room and, immediately, things returned to normal.

Years later, Lan resigned from the station and took a sabbatical in Tahiti. Later, Lan and I were reunited after I bought a radio station in Honolulu. Once again, we teamed with some other fine air talent, and the station that was rated number 18 in the market when I purchased it climbed to number one with a 14 percent share of all Hawaii listening.

Major Aho came to town and stayed at Lan's waterfront home out on Diamond Head, where Lan liked to throw what he called *reef parties*. He rented folding chairs and tables, took them 250 feet out from shore onto the reef where the water was about one foot deep, and there had catered a party for several dozen friends. Meanwhile, Lan himself never ventured out on the reef. He sat on a lounge in his front yard with the Major, looking out at the spectacle of what appeared to be a floating party, just watching and grinning. I would never have believed it had I not personally witnessed it.

Again in Honolulu, and again, aided and abetted by Major Wayne Aho, Lan decided to give Planned Parenthood a public service promotion. He talked the local distributor out of a couple thousand condoms, took a helium tank to the top of Oahu's Pali Pass to a peak they call The Tantalus, filled the condoms with helium, and released them, reporting the release live on the air and leaving the trade winds to blow them down to landings throughout the Honolulu community. Now, you may conclude this would be a rather vague form of promotion, inflated condoms floating through the sky. What wasn't vague was the amount of conversation and attention it received around the city. Like, how often has an inflated condom floated out of the sky and landed in your front yard? People said, "Is that Lan Roberts nuts or what?"

I forgot to check nine months later to determine whether there was a significant reduction in newborns in the Honolulu metropolitan area. I doubt that Lan or the Major checked either.

WKRP in Cincinnati (Theme Song)

Steve Carlisle, 1978

JUST GIVE ME TALENT! That was my motto, and, with KJR-Seattle, it allowed me to create one of the best rock-'n'-roll stations ever. Earlier, I wrote that Larry Lujack said in his book that KJR-Seattle was the best! I offer that title to WABC-New York, but one we put together in Cincinnati, Ohio might have beat them both. In 1965, Les Smith and Danny Kaye purchased an under-powered, low-achieving station from Scripps Howard, the newspaper people, and I was given the challenge of creating programming that would quickly turn it into something successful.

I knew that, to achieve this, we were going to have to be better than good, we would have to be sensational. We had acquired an FM station along with the AM, but this was before FM's time of success. The AM station had a very weak signal, and we were going up against an established force in Cincinnati's WSAI. I designed the station's overall feeling and direction and, to make it all work and win, we hired the best.

At Gordon McClendon's KLIF in Dallas, their morning man, whom I had met while in Dallas on business, was Kenny Dowe, and we had become friends. Kenny was the enormously popular, top-rated deejay in Dallas but yearned for a program directorship, and I just happened to have one. Kenny accepted my offer and, with him on board, we built a staff that was second to none. Rex Miller, the morning star of country music KBOX-Dallas and maybe one of the five funniest jocks in America, was signed on for the A.M. show. Kenny would do afternoon drive time. Frank Benny, unquestionably the most popular disc jockey on the air in Portland, Oregon, joined our team as the mid-day man. In the evening, Jim Hudson, who later became the Hudson of the powerful Hudson and Harrigan team in Houston, and Gary Corry from WQXI-Atlanta, rounded out the staff.

All were the top-rated guys in their markets, all were sensational and all were excited to be a part of the radio power play we were organizing. In my enthusiasm over recruitment, I forgot to consider one thing: Would the wives and families of these performers be content living in Cincinnati? They were not!

When our station went on the air with its new sound and lineup, one day of listening told you new levels of radio and entertainment greatness were in the offing. It all seemed to be spontaneous, exciting, fast-paced, funny from morning till night and totally cool. We had changed the station's call letters to WUBE. When spoken or sung, with a frequency of 1230 on the dial, it was *One–Two–Three–Double–You–Bee Cincinnati.*"

It was all working beyond belief, despite the burdens of families just arriving in town, operating out of the corner of a warehouse as new studios were being built, a miserable Cincinnati winter, and Cincinnati itself, which wasn't exactly the friendly, charming, cosmopolitan city of my radio team's dreams.

Cincinnati, Ohio is an acquired taste, with a strong German heritage. Not particularly warm to newcomers, it is a city steeped in traditions that are a bit vague and which, to newcomers, appear only semi-attractive. Cincinnati in 1966 wasn't similar to Dallas, Houston, Atlanta, Seattle, Portland or anywhere else, for that matter. Further complicating matters, our newly-arrived stars were trying to mitigate unhappy families disrupted by the move and not particularly thrilled by the prospect of becoming new residents of Ohio. Their husbands and fathers had seen this as a great move professionally and money-wise, but, there are some things a daddy's professional contentment and increased salary cannot reconcile. Within 90 days, the station was succeeding beyond my optimistic forecasts and was already approaching entrenched WSAI, when the exodus began.

It started at the top. Kenny Dowe's wife, Dottie, a beautiful, charming southern belle, was depressed—clinically depressed. She called me in Seattle, late at night, and said things like, "Do you know what you have done to me? Do you know how terrible this is? How could you have taken my Kenny away from beautiful Dallas and put us here?" (Actually, Dottie used stronger words than these.) Dottie has, over the years, apologized to me several times for her behavior in those days. She was young and suffering from serious bouts of unhappiness. Without expanding on the extent of Dottie's depression, suffice it to say that Kenny, out of great concern for his wife's health, resigned to take her back to her home town in Mississippi. The chemistry that was supposed to hold everything together until Spring arrived with its warm weather, new studios and successful adjustments to the town was now irreparably altered.

Other families re-evaluated the wisdom of their recent move, plus I was somewhat paralyzed. I was up to my ears in radio work out west in Seattle. While I had accepted the responsibilities of national program director for the company, this Cincinnati train wreck was beyond my long-distance persuasive abilities. I made trips east to visit the battlefield but was only able to slow the outbound flow of talent, not stop it. My dear friend, the late Jim McGovern, who had moved from management of our Spokane station to Cincinnati, tried his best as well to make the station work, but in vain. Within six months, our stars were gone, taking with them our dreams of quick success.

A short time later, Kenny and Dottie drove out to Seattle, and we had dinner at my house, where Dottie repeated that she was sorry about 100 times. She repeated again her tearful apology a few years ago when we met at a National Broadcasters Convention. She needn't have. I appreciated what she had gone though. Their first child, little Kenny, was a baby at the time and, in retrospect, the move set in motion events that defined big Kenny's career, which boomed. He went on to become everything I believed he was, eventually owning his own stations. He remains one of radio's truly brilliant performers and programmers.

This tale of our station in Cincinnati brings me to a story involving one of those unique individuals whom I talked into moving to Cincinnati, Mr. Frank Benny. Frank's adventures were related to me by mutual friends. I wasn't there to witness them first hand. Still, they make for a good story, which I will tell as though I really had been there!

The First Time Ever I Saw Your Face
Roberta Flack, 1972

WITH A STARTLINGLY LOW VOICE and childlike sense of humor, Frank Benny was Portland, Oregon's finest disc jockey in the late '60s. Working at Don Burden's KISN, he made listening great fun and seemed the perfect choice to join the staff at our new Cincinnati station, WUBE. I sold him on the idea but Frank, like others before and since, soon desired an exit from the shores of the Ohio River. The management at WKBW-Buffalo heard him and successfully recruited Frank there. Quickly and not surprisingly, he became a huge media figure up in Niagara country. In a brilliant move, WKBW made him their TV weather man as well. As years passed, Frank Benny became arguably the best known broadcast figure in the city of Buffalo. His face appeared on billboards, in the paper and on the most watched local TV news each evening. Everyone in Buffalo knew Frank Benny, by sight and by sound!

One mid-morning at a downtown bank in Buffalo, Frank walked in, strolled up to a teller's cage with his hand in a bag and told the teller he had a gun. In his deepest Frank Benny voice, he said "This is a stick up!" The teller, charmed to have a famous person at her cage, took a second bag from Benny and filled it with all the money in her drawer. Smiling, she handed him the bag and said "Thank you, Mr. Benny!" She never thought of hitting the alarm button. After all, what concern could there be? This was Frank Benny!

His bag filled with money, Frank retreated out the door while the teller turned to the other employees and said, "Frank Benny just robbed our bank!" Soon the branch manager was at her side, confirming her story. It was obviously a stunt or promotion of some kind, and the advertising manager was contacted to fill in the blanks. When he didn't know anything, a call went out to WKBW, and they didn't know anything either. Still certain it was some kind of stunt, the bank decided to err on the side of caution and called the police. Officers tracked the episode much as the bank had, contacting the advertising agency and Benny's employers and asking the teller again and again whether she was certain Frank robbed her. She insisted it was Benny, no doubt about it. It was time to talk to Mr. Benny.

Two hours after Frank's departure from the bank, Buffalo police knocked on the front door of his home. An ashen, trembling Frank Benny answered the door and said, "You've got me!" Arrested, he told investigators he was in debt a goodly amount to some local bookies as a result of his relatively new addiction to wagering on horse races. Unable to pay his bookmakers, who were threatening him and his family with bodily harm, he decided he needed cash quick! He could have gone to his employers for the money. Surely they would have helped such a valuable asset as Frank with his predicament. But no, this Frank did it his way! True genius comes in strange packages. The extreme brilliance we find in one lobe of the brain is often offset by illogical quirks in the other. Such was the case with our friend Frank.

At Benny's sentencing, the judge was mystified. Frank pleaded guilty, and the court tried to adjudicate a fair punishment. In a state of befuddlement, the judge addressed the defendant:

> Mr. Benny, I just don't understand it! You must know you have the most recognizable face in Buffalo, you must know your voice alone gives you away. Yet, you walk in and rob a bank, making no attempt to disguise yourself, no attempt to disguise your voice. And when the teller addresses you as Mr. Benny, you accept that. This whole thing is sui-

cidal! Frankly, Mr. Benny, I don't think I'll ever understand what made you think you could do this. I imagine I'll go to my grave still trying to figure out what you could possibly have thought would happen. However, my job is not to understand you but, rather, to make sure nothing like this ever happens again. Therefore, I am sentencing you to 25 years in the New York State penitentiary, but suspending the entire sentence and placing you on probation for a period of 15 years instead. You will report to your parole officer regularly and, if the court discovers that you have ever bet on anything, or had a conversation with a bookie, or gone near a race track—even once—your suspension will be revoked and you will serve every single day of your sentence.

Frank returned to his morning radio show and evening TV weather reports, and Buffalo fell more deeply in love with him than ever. Benny became a ratings monster! How could they not love a guy so naïve, so nuts, so charming, so funny?

Pat O'Day conducting the University of Washington Husky band at Husky Stadium in Seattle

Lee Perkins (standing), Pat O'Day, Dick Curtis & Jerry Kaye (head showing)

Wolfman Jack making a promotional appearance in Seattle for Pat O'Day

Pat O'Day & Jerry Kaye at the mike in the KJR control room

Left to right: Dick Curtis, Larry Lujack, Jerry Kaye, Tom Murphy & Lan Roberts

10 – Roll Over Beethoven

Chuck Berry, 1956

IT'S TIME TO LOOK AT THE START of Top 40 radio. It's important to do so because this form of radio, which generated the rebirth of radio broadcasting, wasn't so much an evolution as it was a creation. Nationwide, radio died in the early '50s when television took away its stars. Radio once meant network just as television does today. Radio was the center of life for the American family since its inception on KDKA-Pittsburgh in 1921. By the late '20s, networks evolved, and a big console radio became the central feature in the living rooms of American homes. Families gathered after dinner to enjoy a good selection of comedy, adventure, quiz programs and serials that poured forth nightly. Daytime radio targeted exclusively housewives who in those years were generally home. Networks entertained them with what have always been called *soap operas*. These long-running serials, anywhere from 15 to 30 minutes in length, contained the never-ending adventures of a host of fictional families and relationships and yes, they were generally sponsored by soap companies. The *Arthur Godfrey Show* was an exception, a talk and entertainment program, one hour in length, heard in the midday with a regular cast of musicians and lots of conversation, sponsored by Lipton Tea.

These programs quickly deserted radio when TV arrived, and the radio in the living room was moved to the garage and replaced by a TV set. It's important to realize that not all cars then had radio. A radio was extra equipment on autos and an option many neglected to add.

The portable radio was in its infancy as an appliance and the transistor still years away from reality. Portable radios for the kitchen, clock radios, radios for the bathroom — these were available but hadn't caught on because now, with television, who needed them? Even portable radios that could be taken to the beach or along on a picnic operated with big, pre-transistor tubes and required a large supply of batteries which the power-hungry tubes quickly exhausted.

A large industry was on the rocks. Radio's entertainers had deserted it, as had a large portion of its listeners. Radio still had sports, news and locally-originated programs, and radio networks lumbered on like dinosaurs, but vitality and relevance had escaped them. Todd Storz and Gordon McClendon owned several of those now-inert stations. There are several conflicting stories about how the new breed of radio actually began, but the reliable ones all center on these two men. The late Gordon McClendon personally told me his story of the birth of Top 40 radio, and it is the version I prefer. Both he and Storz are gone, but what they did was so significant, almost every radio station in the world today is programming a derivative of their idea. Here is McClendon's story:

He and Storz were having a drink together in a New Orleans bar, trying to figure out what to do about their lagging broadcast properties. McClendon's were mainly in Texas, while Storz's were in New Orleans, Kansas City, Omaha and another town or two. McClendon never took sole credit for the idea, insisting that the agreement was joint and mutual. They were discussing the evolving growth and strength of the juke box industry, as well as of the record industry in post-war America. They noted the ratings strength of a television show called *Your Hit Parade*, sponsored by Lucky Strike cigarettes and offering versions of the nation's top 10 songs on Friday nights. They projected that if a station, on a 24-hours-a-day basis, played the top 30 songs, number 30 right on down the list to number one, and then turned around and did it again, it might have appeal. Especially if this sort of program were hosted by this new thing that was evolving called a disc jockey — a man or woman who introduced and played records on the radio.

Between songs, McClendon and Storz concurred, commercials would play. The deejay would give the time and temperature and other germane information, say some funny, clever things and introduce the next song. Added to that, they felt offering news each hour would be important, with a five minute news-cast at the top of the hour and maybe just headlines at the half hour mark.

Up until then, a five minute newscast was unheard of; they were always 15 to 30 minutes in duration. That was the network way.

The new idea soon went on the air, initially (I believe) at Todd's KOIL in Omaha and, not long after that, on all of the other Storz stations. It worked; no question, no delay in response, it worked! Stations across the country soon began escaping the moribund by trying this exciting new concept. Radio was instantly transformed from a predictable carrier of just programs to an immediate, constant companion to keep you entertained and informed 24 hours a day, a companion you could turn on or off at your convenience without missing a beat. Top 40 radio was also called *formula* radio because it was a new formula, a new idea, a new service to America. It gave new life, fundamentally and financially, to the radio industry we rely upon today. This re-birth of radio, along with the birth of its exciting young companion, rock-'n'-roll, caused an instant surge in the sales of radio sets. The small kitchen radio, as it had been called, was suddenly being purchased, and those radios began being heard in the office, the shop, the bathroom, the basement; at the same time, sales of car radios skyrocketed. I was fortunate to enter the radio business while this new concept was in its infancy. What a thrill to take these gentlemen geniuses' ideas and help make them grow.

Leader of the Pack
The Shanglri-Las, 1964

WAS KJR THE GREATEST TOP 40 STATION IN THE NATION in the '60s like some people — Larry Lujack and Bill Gavin among them — have said? Possibly, but there is no way to really know. Every city is different and each region has its own particular likes and dislikes. Thus, two great radio stations in two separate cities, if properly programmed to appeal to the tastes of their local audiences, would sound different from one another. If you placed KJR-Seattle alongside WKBW-Buffalo, or KHJ-Los Angeles, or KLIF-Dallas, you'd be looking at apples and oranges, not apples and apples.

There's a different yardstick some people have used to compare KJR's success with that of others around the country. That measurement? — ranking an AM station's ability to withstand FM radio's withering attack in the '70s. Stations using frequency modulation — FM — eventually won that battle, helped by the technological superiority of a stereophonic signal that improved sound quality and reduced static. Which major-market AM station held off their inevitable defeat the longest? KJR. Until early 1975, we maintained ratings domination over all other Seattle stations, AM and FM alike. By this measure, KJR qualifies for consideration as one of the greatest Top 40 AM stations of all time.

I'm often asked What was your secret? The answer is simple: common sense. It doesn't take pages of ethereal radio programming jargon to explain it, so I'll not bore you with a phony attempt to appear erudite. My radio formula was as simple as a paper clip. As I explain it, I will try to follow the same rule we once applied to programming: "Keep it simple, keep it logical."

One hundred days following my arrival in January 1960, KJR took over first place in the Seattle market and basically remained undefeated for 15 years, the span of my deejay/program director/general manager years. As KJR's chief executive and later co-owner during that time, Lester M. Smith made the station's and my success possible. Les believed that if you hired talented people and gave them the tools and freedom they needed to excel, rewards would follow for all. That helps explain why Lester and I had such a wonderful relationship over the years. His thoughts mirrored mine and allowed me latitude to grow.

KJR was compellingly interactive and fun 24 hours a day, seven days a week. To merit being the constant companion of our listeners, we had to meet their expectations whenever they turned us on. The notion prevails in radio today that people wish to laugh in the morning until 9:00 A.M. and hear only music after that. That's stupid and illogical and defies common sense. You want to play music that better matches the moods of people at different times of the day, yes. But always remember: The overall companionship must remain the same.

We struggled to avoid boring listeners with our selection of music. Music was our message, and we needed that message to deliver thrills old and new, to inspire good feelings, to spark occasional memories and, above all, to satisfy our listeners' insatiable appetite for the latest sounds from the Northwest and around the country. Staying ahead of the competition meant always being first to play a new song even before it became a hit. While others furrowed their brows and feared playing records that might not quite make it big, I saw the pioneering of new songs as key to staying fresh and exciting in listeners' minds. If once in a while we missed, so what? Better that than put our audience to sleep playing the same little package of 40 safe songs over and over and over again. Pursuing and promoting new music relentlessly, KJR became known around the country as one of only a handful of radio stations capable of "breaking" newly released songs and helping them become national hits. We did it many times, and the following are a few examples.

Sukiyaki

Kyu Sakamoto, 1963

ONE SUNDAY IN 1960, I dropped in on a recording session at the fabled Joe Boles studio in West Seattle to listen to an unknown group from Tacoma cut their first record. Liking what I heard, I took a tape of the recording back to the station with me, and we began playing it once an hour just before the news. The response was immediate, and the Ventures, world famous today, had their first hit, *Walk — Don't Run*.

Another time, while vacationing in Honolulu, I visited my friend (and future co-promoter) Tom Moffat, music director at KPOI, then the leading radio station in Hawaii. We were sitting in his office chatting and listening to new record releases, when a number from MGM Records caught our attention with its strange pumping organ sound and unusual lyrics. After listening to it three times, I called Seattle and had it added to KJR's play list. I didn't care what anyone else in the business thought about the record or whether any other station in the country had tried it yet. My ear told me it was a hit. When Sam the Sham and the Pharaohs went gold with *Wooly Bully*, MGM gave me a gold record crediting KJR with discovering the song and the group. I hope Moffat received one as well.

Three years later, Ron Terry of our concert division was visiting London on business when he happened to listen to a recording by a new group he felt had great promise. He expressed an acetate (test pressing) of the song to me in Seattle and, after listening to the cut, I immediately put the song on the air. The response from listeners was so impressive, I told Ahmet Ertegan and Jerry Wexler, the heads of Atlantic Records in New York, that this new group they had just signed to a contract was about to deliver a sizeable hit. As it turned out, rock music fans around the world felt the same way as KJR's audience did about *Whole Lotta Love* by Led Zeppelin.

The strangest song I was credited with unveiling was *Sukiyaki* by Kyu Sakamoto. I mean, how in the world of rock-'n'-roll could a soft ballad with Japanese lyrics become a hit in English-speaking America? In Seattle in 2002, considering how the Northwest has embraced Kazuhiro Sasaki and Ichiro Suzuki of the Seattle Mariners, maybe; but nationwide, in 1963? Most unlikely. We were the first *major* station in America to play that song, but I must give credit to a young man whose name, sadly, I can't recall, who worked at a station in some small California town. He phoned me one day, described the surprising response from listeners when he played this song and suggested that I take a chance on it. I ordered a copy from the Capitol Records distributor and threw it on the turntable. Puzzled but sufficiently pleased after listening to it, I put *Sukiyaki* on the air, and the rest is history.

A tragic footnote: In August 1985, Kyu Sakamoto was a passenger on board a JAL 747 when the plane's steering system failed. The aircraft continued to fly out of control for some time before crashing into a remote mountainside in Japan, killing over 500 passengers and crew. Miraculously, four people survived. Kyu Sakamoto did not.

When listeners turned on KJR, they did so with a sense of anticipation, knowing they were going to hear something new, something different, something interesting that day. So it was with *From Me to You* from the Beatles, and *Angel of the Morning* from Merrilee Rush, and *Louie Louie* from the Wailers and so many songs from so many other acts. KJR was "cutting edge" long before the expression became popular. We modified J. P. Morgan's formula for success. Old J. P. allegedly said of investments "never be the first in or the last out." When KJR invested in music, we *always* tried to be the first ones in on playing a new hit record. As soon as listener demand for a song began to fade, however, we took it out of air-play and reinvested our time elsewhere, hoping to strike new gold. Our motto, in short, was "Be the first on it and the first off it."

I Heard It Through the Grapevine
Gladys Knight & the Pips, 1968 / Marvin Gaye, 1969 / Creedence Clearwater Revival, 1970

HOW IS IT POSSIBLE THAT SOME RADIO STATIONS make news sound so dull and boring? After all, isn't news the reporting of life as it's happening, and what can be more exciting and interesting than that? News turns dreary only when presented with the frequently-heard dullness some misguided news types confuse with journalistic integrity. We accomplished one major breakthrough in this area that remains unique to the KJR of the early '70s. That breakthrough earned us new respect from listeners and has not been tried since. It was a product of common sense, an idea so simple, I kicked myself for not thinking of it years before.

Back then, television news was usually broadcast four times a day: in the morning before work, at midday around lunch and in the evening around dinner time and again just before bed. Newspapers, meanwhile, were published for distribution in the morning or the afternoon. Television and press alike reported mostly on events that took place in the hours immediately preceding their deadlines. With those news stories selected as more important, their reporting grew redundant as the day progressed, especially on TV. Following standard operating procedure, every time a news department updated a story, they repeated the background as though you had no previous knowledge of those details.

Most radio stations played copycat, taking the bulk of their news from the same sources (Associated Press and others) used by television and newspapers. As a result, everywhere you looked for news, you found the same stale information being rehashed—repetition (television), repetition (newspapers), repetition (radio). In the "wake up hours," admittedly, it *was* important for radio to inform listeners as to what took place while they slept. *But what about the rest of the time?* I asked myself.

— *Why keep repeating the same news stories hours later?*
— *Why not capitalize on radio's great, unique strength—immediacy?*
— *Why not be the station that tells listeners what's happening the moment it happens?*
— *Why not leave the recaps, the repeats, the restatements to others?*
— *Why even have newscasts, save in the morning so listeners can catch up on overnight developments?*
— *Why wait for a newscast to report an important event if it has just taken place?*

Radio has flexibility. Radio can interrupt regularly scheduled programing at any time. Radio can build a mounting sense of urgency while enhancing its ability to create excitement.

I dictated a new approach; we called it "KJR Instant Information."

We gave newsmen on duty full authority to interrupt deejays and music any time they chose. What power to place in the hands of the news department at a rock-'n'-roll radio station! We attached strong provisos to this freedom to make sure it worked properly. Unless there was an earthquake or something similarly big, no news interruption could exceed 60 seconds. As well, no story could be repeated unless there was critical new information to report. Henceforth, we'd be the first radio station in western Washington to air a news story when it broke, and we'd be the first station to move on, never looking back, leaving excess coverage to others.

We turned our listeners into local KJR reporters by offering a television set, a motorcycle, or even a thousand dollars in cold, hard cash for the week's top news tip. Information poured in, and the news department picked and chose items they judged sufficiently gripping to air. We ran the same fine tooth comb through national stories. As a result, when a KJR newsman popped onto the air saying, "This is KJR Instant Information at 2:43 P.M.," you knew you were about to hear something big. My admonition to the news department was clear: "You have more power and authority than any other news people in the industry. Be alert, use that power wisely and don't ever bore me with a story."

Frank Magid, the respected radio news and research consultant from Philadelphia, was hired by KIRO-AM, Seattle's 50,000 watt CBS affiliate, to help determine whether they should become Seattle's first all-news station. After studying the Northwest market and delivering his report (KIRO went forward with their plan), Frank invited me to lunch to share some astonishing results from his Seattle study. After hundreds of interviews, he found that rock-'n'-roll KJR had the number one news image in the region. When asked questions like "Where do you tune first to hear a new story?" "What station's news do you really trust?" and "Which station do you believe is most dedicated to bringing you the news?" the leader every time was KJR. Unbelievable!

We had two full-time, one part-time reporters; other stations had dozens. Without news cars or writers or editors, with immediacy and excitement and cogency instead, KJR News created the happy illusion that we were the best.

Something's Burning
Kenny Rogers & the First Edition, 1970

OUR NEWS TIP AWARD CAMPAIGN resulted in one memorable incident. One night, around 9:00 P.M., I was listening to the station while driving from work to my home on the east side of Lake Washington when the music was interrupted with a listener report of a large fire at Bellevue's Newport High School. I was 10 minutes from the school at that moment, so I drove straight to the scene and found the school's library engulfed in flames. As I stood there watching, I heard the sound of approaching sirens and, minutes later, fire trucks arrived at the scene. Firefighters poured thousands of gallons of water on the flames in a futile struggle to save the building, but they arrived too late, and the school's massive, beautiful new library was destroyed. As the fire died out, I thought to myself *Something's fishy here! Something doesn't fit!*

I drove home and called the station, where the times of all inbound news reports were carefully recorded. I learned that the call reporting the fire came in 15 minutes before the report that I heard aired. If it took me 10 minutes to drive to the scene —and it did—why weren't the fire trucks there before I was? How strange!

First thing next morning, I called the Bellevue fire chief to determine what time the fire was reported *to them*. They checked their precise records and determined their units reached the scene eight minutes after the first report came in. That meant whoever called the station with the news—and we were offering a new motorcycle for that week's best tip—called KJR 17 minutes *prior* to the Fire Department's first alarm. It wasn't reasonable to assume that a good citizen, upon seeing the flames, would call a radio station first and not the fire department, regardless of the prize he or she stood to win. It also wasn't reasonable to assume that after one party saw the fire, 17 more minutes would pass before anyone else noticed it—the library sat next to a constantly busy highway. Unless…Unless the person who called the station had a hand in starting the fire. Eager to win, the caller that night gave his name, address and phone number when he reported the fire. Following those leads, investigators soon solved the case, and two young men went to prison, convicted of arson. Just 17 years old, having downed a few beers, they concocted a scheme to win the motorcycle, went to the school and threw gasoline-filled Molotov cocktails through the library windows. Both were Newport High students and both saddled their parents with an enormous long-term debt, restitution ordered by the court.

Even with the best intentions, radio sometimes sets forces in motion that go well beyond our ability to control. That certainly was the case with our motorcycle-a-week news tip promotion.

Do You Want to Know a Secret
The Beatles, 1963

ONE NEWS STORY WE AIRED FIRST AT KJR —and one that brought the station worldwide attention—provides me with one of my funniest tales. It all centered around the Beatles' third and final US tour and their return visit to Seattle in August 1966.

Strangers wanting to talk with me often dropped by the station unannounced. So, early on this one particular July afternoon, I wasn't expecting much when I was paged to the reception desk to meet with a young woman. Appearing nervous, she said she needed to talk with me in private. I led her into the station's lunchroom, unoccupied at the moment, and there she laid out startling evidence suggesting that Paul McCartney planned to marry Jane Asher during the Beatles' visit to Seattle in August. Rumors about Paul and Jane had been circulating for months, and London tabloids assured readers that marriage was a certainty. The girl before me explained that she worked for an answering service (very common in the age before answering machines and voicemail) and that she was assigned the duty of acting as Seattle liaison for a certain Brian Epstein of London. Brian Epstein was the Beatles' manager, and he gave her two private London phone numbers where he could be reached, as she was dealing directly and only with Brian. First making me swear never to tell anyone that she was the source of the story, she presented substantial evidence of a pending McCartney-Asher wedding.

A month or so earlier, Epstein had set up an account with the answering service, giving them duties ranging well beyond the normal services they offered. And he transferred a significant amount of money to their bank account to cover the costs of the tasks he gave them. Those tasks included making a deposit for rental of the large Spanish Ballroom at the Olympic Hotel for a reception, ordering finger food with great attention to detail and making cash deposits on tuxedos ordered from a local formal wear store. Epstein provided exact sizes for ten tuxes, each one to be individually labeled: *John, George, Ringo, Brian* and six other names I didn't recognize.

There was a series of calls and follow-up letters to the British Consulate arranging for an official to conduct the ceremony. The mailings included a copy of a marriage license issued in London to Paul McCartney and Jane Asher. Numerous other communications from Epstein assigned still more duties. The answering service was instructed to contact Seattle police to suggest that additional security be made available that evening, *that evening* being the night of the Beatles' scheduled Seattle concert. The hours designated for use of the Spanish Ballroom were from 10:00 P.M. until 2:00 A.M. Flowers were ordered in abundance, with plenty of money provided for advance payments to the florist and to a bakery which was enlisted to provide a large custom wedding cake festooned with *Paul and Jane* on top. Additional local security, a hairdresser and more were ordered, with advance deposits sent for all.

I was impressed, and perplexed. Why Seattle? Why on a tour? Why after a show? Why? Why? Why? But then, I had been around rock-'n'-roll performers enough years to know that logic wasn't always the key to understanding their behavior. In the world of rock, the unexpected and illogical were generally the norm. Nevertheless, I wanted more information. Clearly, the young lady was putting herself at risk employment-wise. She didn't want anything in return and stated that this was her town, that KJR was her station and that she thought her station should be the first to alert the world to this giant story. I made copies of several of her documents and told her to stay in touch. I decided to keep the whole thing to myself until I saw further evidence, until I grew comfortable with the thought that a wedding really was planned.

I had already met all of the Beatles at that point (they visited Seattle previously, in 1964), but it would be a stretch to say that we were friends or even casual acquaintances. More importantly, I was heavily involved in their upcoming Seattle concert and wondered whether this implied some fiduciary duty or moral obligation on my part. On the one hand, I was a deejay programming a radio station that was my city's Alpha and Omega of rock-'n'-roll. Being the advance source for earth-shaking news like this would be a major coup for our news department and would only enhance our image of being totally cool. On the other hand, there was the issue of protecting Paul's and Jane's privacy and respecting their wishes. I finally decided that a story of this magnitude would break sooner or later anyway and, considering the way evidence was flying around, probably sooner.

A few days later, my volunteer informer returned with additional verification: airline reservations for Jane Asher, her mother and brother (Jane's brother was Peter Asher, one-half of the famous British singing duo of Peter and Gordon). They showed the trio flying on TWA out of London to New York, transferring to Northwest Airlines Flight 2 from New York to Seattle and arriving on the morning of the concert/wedding. Limousine service from Seattle-Tacoma International Airport was on order as well as private security for their airport arrival. After examining other supporting bits and pieces of evidence, I conferred with my news director, Charles C. Bolland. *Chuck* Bolland, as he was known on the air, relished the thought of breaking this big a story, and I cautioned him to verify, verify, verify, to find corroborating evidence for every detail, if possible. Then and only then, when he was confident that his information was correct, fully confident that a wedding really was planned, *and* if he avoided any and all details that could point to the actual time and location, it would be his call what to do with the story. Having done what seemed to me to be the responsible thing, I sat back and waited to see what would happen. At 5:55 P.M. the day before the concert, Chuck personally broke the story on KJR.

All hell broke loose. Calls poured in from all three networks, from major newspapers, from every news service in the country. We offered them nothing but the copy we broadcast on the air, which said,

> KJR News has credible and documented information that leads us to conclude that Paul McCartney of the Beatles will marry one Jane Asher of London, England while the group is here in Seattle. We do possess further information that KJR News will not disclose to protect the privacy of the individuals, as we wish them well!

The next morning, the Beatles' traditional pre-show press conference was packed with reporters and cameramen, some of whom had flown in to town after hearing about KJR's "scoop." McCartney appeared baffled as reporters avoided the usual questions and pounced on him with one and only one inquiry: "Tell us about the wedding!" Standing next to the long, elevated table where the Beatles sat behind microphones, I fidgeted uncomfortably when, on several occasions, Paul turned his head and looked at me as if to say, "Pat, your radio station did this!" I just shrugged my shoulders.

After the conference, I avoided all questions directed at me by local news people. As I left the building, I was more than a bit puzzled, thinking that Paul's denials of the wedding certainly sounded convincing. But then, wasn't a convincing denial expected? One other disconcerting development surfaced that morning: Northwest Airlines Flight 2 from New York landed on time, and one of our newsmen, standing in the background, carefully inspected the face of every arriving passenger as they left the plane. None of them looked like Jane Asher.

That night, I emceed the concert at the Coliseum and departed the building immediately afterwards, gathering up my family and heading for home. The next morning's television news gave the show full coverage, repeated McCartney's wedding denials and said if there was a wedding, no one knew where. I worried that our reports might have thrown a wrench into Paul's plans. A huge wedding cake and platters of food lay uneaten, paid-for tuxedos hung unworn and a pre-rented ballroom sat unused. Who knows how many others were confused as they attempted to carry out their instructions. Also interesting was the fact that Brian Epstein, the Beatles' manager, whose phone calls and letters started all this, never appeared. As time went by, it became clear that no wedding took place. We knew that *something* happened, but what? Soon, I stopped worrying, as other matters occupied my time and attention. In November, I learned the truth.

I was invited to the Phi Gamma Delta fraternity house at the University of Washington to emcee their annual holiday awards banquet. I took with me my assistant, a young woman named Peggy Claire, who was also KJR's helicopter traffic reporter (ours was the first helicopter radio service in Seattle). Peggy was five feet tall, totally gorgeous and also a U of W graduate. Bringing her along on my appearances thrilled listeners—especially the men—who got to meet and see our "Voice from the Sky." I worked my way through the agenda and, when I introduced Peggy as an ex-Husky, the frat boys cheered loudly. The final event of the evening was identified in the program simply as *A Surprise*.

And what a surprise! The real reason those men invited me there that night was to present me with a special "Pigeon of the Year" award. I was the unwitting dupe in an award-winning con! These ambitious young fraternity men, with way too much time and money on their hands, pulled off a sham that won first prize. Their stunt? The Seattle marriage of Paul McCartney to Jane Asher.

They planned everything to perfection, down to the finest detail. The girlfriend of one of the house members was selected as the facilitator. They recruited her based on her naïveté, her position with a respected answering service, her love of KJR and her well-established inability to keep a secret. She performed flawlessly. Next, they held fund raisers to earn the money needed to support the fraud. During Summer break, one of the brothers already familiar with England flew to London and became "Brian Epstein." Operating from a relative's house, he arranged for a London address, ordered phone lines and became chief executive of the operation. His first call was to the Seattle answering service, where he requested the services of the pre-targeted girlfriend. His account was assigned to her, and the sting was underway. Everything hinged on the gamble that she would eventually call me up or go to the station with the story. She did. The men planned well and created an air of genuine authenticity. Their remarkable scheme worked to perfection. The UW chapter of Phi Gamma Delta richly deserved their national award, and KJR's program director richly deserved his. I stood there as the brothers applauded, holding a rather ugly trophy with a stuffed pigeon on top. Somewhat red-faced, I was in a semi-state of shock. The joke was on me, and God, was it funny.

Running Scared
Roy Orbison, 1961

RADIO, BEING THE MENTAL MEDIA, can trigger emotions, actions and reactions covering the entire spectrum of human behavior. If you're looking for proof of this, consider the following incident: It was a hot summer afternoon in Yakima, Washington in 1958, and I was alone in the station, doing my regular Saturday afternoon show (we worked six days a week in radio back then). With no air conditioning, I opened the back door of the control room to allow for some circulation. One minute, I was putting on a record; the next, I was lying on the floor, just waking up, my head throbbing. *What hit me?* I hadn't a clue! I felt a huge knot growing atop my skull and heard the record I was playing go click, click, click as the needle bumped around the inside track. I grabbed another record, put it on the air and tried to collect my wits.

Suddenly, the phone rang. It was my friend, Lee Hurley, deejay/engineer at another station in town. Earlier, a young man mistakenly came into his station looking for me. When told I was over at KLOQ, he shouted "I wanna kill him!" and ran out the door. It took Lee several minutes to find my station's private line number to warn me. Telling Lee the youth in question had probably already visited me, I hung up the phone and called the police, who quickly made an arrest.

The man had given Hurley his name, and I soon learned I was attacked by someone with a record of severe mental instability. The following week the head psychiatrist at the county hospital contacted me. He explained he had treated the young man before and feared that if I pressed charges now, a lengthy sentence was likely with no mental help offered. If I agreed instead not to press charges, the doctor would seek a court order to hold the youth in the security division of the hospital where, for the first time, he could receive the extensive treatment he badly needed. I agreed.

Two months later, the doctor called to report that his patient was doing well and that, as part of his therapy, it would be good if he came and apologized to me. The man was a paranoid schizophrenic, deeply in love with a young lady who had recently called off their relationship. When still a couple, they often parked in a vacant lot behind the Yakima Cement Products Company and made out. On the day they broke up, I delivered a commercial for this same company and followed it with their favorite song, by Elvis. In the darkest recesses of his poorly wired brain, he concluded that I was somehow responsible for their breakup. Enraged, he came after me.

This time, the patient would be heavily sedated for his visit, the doctor said, and a nurse would accompany him, so there was no cause for concern. We set the meeting for the following afternoon at 2:00 P.M., just before I went on the air.

When I returned from lunch the next day, I found the young man sitting in the station's waiting area, alone. Nice in appearance, with a pleasant smile, he said he was sorry and shook my hand. I told him all was forgiven, wished him well and thanked him for his apology. He headed out the front door while I headed for the control room to start my show. The absence of the promised nurse puzzled me, but the meeting went well, so what did it matter?

Five minutes later, the young man crashed through the control room door and, in a swan dive, flew over the top of the turntables and landed squarely on top of me. My chair toppled backward, and his momentum carried him across me and onto the floor. He landed on his back, and I jumped to my feet and buried my toe in his groin. He screamed in pain. One of the station's salesmen, Norm Statt, knowing the circumstances and seeing the youth run in the front door from the parking lot, had followed his rush down the hall. Norm now jumped on my assailant and pinned him to the floor while I ran to the engineering room and grabbed a spool of electrical wire, which we used to tie him up. A few additional kicks reminded him not to resist.

The police arrived, along with the missing nurse and an explanation. On the way from the hospital to the station, the young man asked to stop by his house so he could put on a special shirt. The nurse foolishly agreed and patiently waited in her car in front of his parents' home while he changed. Instead of grabbing a shirt, he grabbed his father's shotgun, loaded it with a single round and escaped out the back door to where his car was parked. Fully intending to shoot me, in his excitement and rage he forgot the shotgun when he rushed back into the station.

I pressed charges this time, and the young man was sentenced to serve time at the maximum security facility at the State Mental Hospital in Medical Lake, outside Spokane. I breathed a sigh of relief, believing I was safe. Wrong again!

Three months later, I received a call in the middle of the night from someone at the Yakima Police Department. He warned me that my attacker, whose name was Bach Stevenson, escaped from Medical Lake earlier that day. To his doctors he expressed a desire to kill me, and they thought he was headed my way. Within the hour, an officer appeared at my house to guard my wife and children. Another officer was assigned to stay next to me during the day. I went about my duties and did my show like nothing was wrong, with a policeman constantly beside me as a reminder that something *was* wrong!

Three days later, a break came in the case. At a barber shop in Wapato, some 10 miles south of Yakima, our young man sat in a chair and told the barber he had just escaped from Medical Lake and planned to return to the hospital as soon as he killed a certain disc jockey in Yakima. The barber listened carefully, took out his long blade razor, placed it against Stevenson's throat and told him "If you move one muscle, you're dead!" He yelled for his partner to call the police and, later that day, my guy was on his way back to the state hospital in handcuffs.

Years later, doctors deemed Stevenson healthy and released him back into society. His first day out, he made the very same doctor who tried so hard to help him his next and final victim. It never ceases to amaze me how, through radio, listeners can develop one-on-one relationships in their minds that impact their lives as much as any off-air personal relationship. That the broadcaster knows nothing of the listener and the growing relationship makes no difference.

Brother Love's Travelling Salvation Show
Neil Diamond, 1969

"K-J-R-SEATTLE, CHANNEL NINETY-FIVE," as the jingles sang, impacted people and events far beyond any reasonable expectation. Today, more than 30 years later, I am regularly asked to emcee high school class reunions, speak at seminars and make various other public appearances, all due to one and only one thing: a radio station that left an indelible mark on the minds of its listeners, a radio station they can still hear in their heads and quote verbatim, a radio station whose jingle they can still sing flawlessly.

It wasn't so much what we said that stuck in listeners' hearts and minds as it was the context in which they originally heard us—a context of close, careful listening as listeners feared they might miss something. What created such devotion and intense involvement? A talented staff that always left listeners with something worth repeating to family and friends.

To promote growth of our talent, we engaged in a fun exercise that I still use when addressing public speaking classes today. In a group meeting, we gave one of our talents a topic. It mattered not whether they knew anything about the subject matter. We allowed them 15 seconds to begin their address with the goal of convincing all present that the speaker had expertise in the field. This exercise worked wonders, greatly increasing the ad-libbing abilities of our staff. Obscure subjects like sewers came up, with some wonderful responses. On this topic, Mike Phillips, who went on to become the morning star at KFRC-San Francisco, convincingly told of a major problem deep beneath the streets in the north end of the city, where the glacial nature of the soil jeopardized the giant north trunk of the city's sewer system. One hundred years of secretion coupled with minor seismic activity created conditions making a massive cave-in a certainty. The trunk was constructed with a conical brick method of support, and the mortar had decayed more and more as years passed. The impending back up of raw sewage would make Seattle famous for something other than its rainfall. We all pounded the table and laughed over the enormity of the lie, but an important skill was being developed: If you can convince someone of something about which you know nothing, think how effective you will be when you actually know what you're talking about!

We also demanded that our deejays enter the control room with written scripts containing clever ad-libs prepared in advance for their shows. This preparation allowed head room for the unusual and unexpected.

Many humor segments were pre-recorded to assure quality, and one fact was certain: If you couldn't make someone laugh, there was no place for you at KJR! Strange to some, we never interviewed rock artists live on air out of fear they might be boring. Nothing was left to chance. Something was either very funny, very entertaining or it was nothing!

Games People Play
Joe South, 1969
CONTESTS AND PROMOTIONS WERE A BIG PART of the overall scheme of things at KJR. We buried the keys to new cars, including the hot new Mustang and even a Jaguar XKE, and gave clues on the air until someone figured things out and found them. Listeners dug up half the Puget Sound region in their searches.

Starting in 1970, we offered cash prizes hourly as part of an ongoing contest we called *Cash Call*. We phoned listeners and asked whether they knew the exact amount of money in the jackpot that minute (we broadcast that figure just before making the call). If they knew the correct answer, they won.

The kickoff to this promotion provoked an interesting joust with the owner of another station. The state's Attorney General had long espoused a strict interpretation of statutes pertaining to illegal lotteries. With an illegal lottery, they held that there had to be three elements involved: prize, chance and consideration. Washington State maintained that if someone had to listen to a certain radio station to win a prize, the station benefited, thereby enjoying something that amounted to consideration under the law. I disagreed, and asked our attorneys to chase down an ancient case from a federal court in Kansas that someone had told me about. Sure enough, a federal judge back in nineteen turtle-do had ruled that the mere act of sitting in a rocking chair, listening to the radio and contemplating great riches, did not constitute consideration.

Armed with a printed copy of that decision, and with Lester Smith's enthusiastic approval, I prepared to introduce Seattle's first big cash prize radio contest in over 20 years. We purchased flashy ads in the newspapers and ran exciting promo announcements on the air. A high energy billboard recorded by me announced the contest each hour: "Ladies and gentlemen, this is KJR and it's Cash Call Contest Time!"

Competitors whispered that I was breaking the law and that KJR was in big legal trouble. Monday morning the contest began; Thursday afternoon Chief of Police George Tiltsh called. Dorothy Bullitt, well-known owner of KING-TV and 50,000 watt KING-AM had called him. (KING was our closest competitor at the time, and struggling.) They must have really panicked to bring the respected matriarch of the powerful broadcast company down from her throne to call the cops. She told Chief Tiltsh that I was violating state law and that her station was about to suffer irreparable harm as a result. She suggested they arrest and charge me, giving them time to go to court for a cease and desist order that would formally stop our contest.

KING TV enjoyed awesome leverage in the Seattle community, as did the Bullitt family—its owners—and Tiltsh felt compelled to do something. He asked what authority I thought I had to run what appeared to be an illegal lottery. The last thing he wanted to do was get involved, but he felt it was his duty to do something based on what he was told was the law. Following Mrs. Bullitt's call, her attorneys phoned with urgent pleas of their own. Feeling squeezed, Tiltsh asked me, "Pat, what in the hell do you think you're doing?"

I told George that I respected him, the law and the position he found himself in. I assured him that we were standing on solid legal ground and that nothing would please me more than to have him come to the station and arrest me. (I pictured headlines reading *Pat O'Day Arrested for $100,000 Cash Give Away!*) The Chief noted my enthusiasm, recognized the love the community felt for KJR and said, "Pat, I'm sitting here thinking that's exactly what you want me to do!"

While I had no yearning to tangle with George, I told him that, if Dorothy Bullitt insisted on having a piece of me, "Come and get it!" In the meantime, if the city attorney wanted to discuss this matter with us, he was welcome to sit down with our station's counsel who could easily validate our position.

The Chief accepted my invitation, the lawyers met and KJR's Cash Call Contest continued for a three year run. At its next session, the state legislature re-worked the applicable laws, taking into account the decision of that wonderful federal judge in Kansas. Radio and television cash contests have enjoyed unfettered acceptance in the state of Washington ever since.

What Does It Take (to Win Your Love)
Jr. Walker & The All-Stars, 1969

IDEALLY, LISTENERS TOTALLY EMBRACE YOUR PROMOTIONS and station advertisers directly benefit from them. When I entered radio, rock-'n'-roll was new and slowly growing in acceptance. Early on, it was hard to convince merchants that rock stations reached valuable listeners, that we appealed to more than just teens, that our adult numbers were shockingly high. Television and newspapers tried to excuse us away by saying that the adult listening numbers shown by all surveys were due to kids in the house controlling the radios — a totally bogus argument. I have kept survey results showing KJR was number one in every age group, men and women, all the way up to age 45. Nevertheless, it was the brave merchant with vision that came to us for support.

Two such merchants were Bernie Brotman and Jay Jacobs. Bernie had men's stores in Tacoma and Seattle, Jay two women's apparel stores in Seattle. While at KJR, I was often called upon to personally deliver a pitch for the sales department because I could articulate what was going on with our new kind of radio and the community. I still tingle with excitement recalling when, over lunch, Bernie and Jay signed their first big contracts with the station. Those were major breakthroughs. Brotman and Jacobs were bell cows, so to speak, leading a herd of merchants to our door and making the sales department's job much easier. The huge spurt in business they enjoyed from their campaigns on our station made me realize we were, in fact, the real deal. I had already sensed it, but here was proof! I made numerous personal appearances at Bernie's and Jay's stores, passing out free records, our "lucky number" weekly music sheets, pictures of deejays, whatever we had. Crowds came, cash registers rang and another long stride was taken toward true credibility for rock radio. Later, we found ourselves happily enslaved by our advertisers' desire to have us help plan their promotions. Ironically, Bernie Brotman's son Jeff was a high school student while this was going on. He was later to continue his father's pioneering spirit when he founded Costco, of which he remains chairman today.

Rock the Boat
The Hues Corporation, 1974
EVERY SPRING IN THE LATE '60S AND EARLY '70S, the Seattle Boat Show ran for 10 days at the Seattle Center Coliseum, home of the Seattle Supersonics. On weekends, crowds jammed the place; on weekdays, you could safely roll a bowling ball down the aisles. Not surprisingly, exhibitors complained loudly to the show's organizers. In desperation, the association came to KJR for a solution.

The summer before, I had cruised Alaskan waters in a yacht with my friend, the late Jim Clapp, and his wife, Pam. We spent one afternoon at the face of a wall of ice in Glacier Bay just northwest of Juneau. On the outside of much Jack Daniels, we gleefully fired an AK-47 rifle, and the gun's sharp reports were all it took to dislodge huge chunks from the glacier and send them crashing into the water. We maneuvered close enough for me to reach out and snare some of the freshly dislodged ice, which we used for our drinks. That ice refused to melt. Due to enormous pressure, all oxygen is forced from glacial ice, leaving it substantially more stable than ordinary ice. It resists melting for hours and hours.

Donald McCowan, one of the great radio time salesmen of our generation, brought me to a meeting where boat show executives explained their problem. Somehow, that glacial ice came to mind, and we immediately offered them a concept that turned out to be a winner. Figuring that the glacier was x miles long from point of origin to its face, and that ice passed downward at a rate of y inches per year, we quickly calculated that a single snow flake falling at the glacier's head could well take 100,000 years to travel from there to Glacier Bay. That was all I needed to know! One never wants to be confused with unnecessary and possibly contrary facts when arriving at such brilliant conclusions.

Two weeks before the Boat Show opened, we began an exotic campaign using the incredibly believable voice of my news director, Frank Thompson. With the sound of a chilling, screeching windstorm in the background Frank read:

> One hundred thousand years ago, on a desolate mountain side, a snowflake fell. Did man even exist 100,000 years ago? What was the world like then? What was our planet like 100,000 years ago? Well, that tiny snowflake landed on that mountainside and was soon engulfed with other snow flakes that would become the head of the mighty Mendenhal Glacier just outside Juneau, Alaska. And for 100,000 years, it has inched its way, ever so slowly, down the side of that mountain until now. Because now, that snowflake has finally reached the face of that nearly eternal glacier. My God, what history has that snowflake seen and experienced!? KJR's Emperor Smith [our morning deejay then] has been given orders to leave Seattle for Juneau and see if that very snowflake can be captured and returned to Seattle. Alaska Airlines with its magnificent Boeing 727s has agreed, if the Emperor can cut two tons of the ice, which contain that precious snowflake, from the face of the glacier, they will then quickly fly it to Seattle in the belly of a 727 so it may be displayed, Monday through Friday, at the 20th Annual Seattle Boat Show. So all may come, see, touch, and thrill. Truly the experience of a lifetime, 100,000 years of history!

All-time attendance records were set those nights at the show. We placed the large chunk of ice on a purple velvet floor covering surrounded by stanchions linked by a velvet-covered chain. Glacial ice is crystal clear. Augmented by colored lights placed on all sides, ours was awe-inspiring. And, as projected, little of the ice melted during the promotion's five-day run. At night after the show closed, we covered it with an insulating blanket, and it suffered no more than 20 percent shrinkage that week.

Raindrops Keep Falling on My Head
B. J. Thomas, 1969

PERHAPS MY PROUDEST MOMENT IN MY YEARS AT KJR was our station's 50th birthday celebration. Searching for something meaningful, spectacular and memorable, I found the obvious answer: a giant fireworks show—but not just any fireworks show. Bringing in a fireworks consultant, we planned a program that proved to be everything we prayed for. We wanted innovation and refused to be ordinary. History validates that perfect August night in 1972 was the first time a fireworks show was choreographed to a music program broadcast on a radio station. We built a 30 minute radio show that was the history of radio, the history of KJR and the history of rock-'n'-roll. Then, to the split second, we planned the fireworks to take advantage of every nuance on the radio program. Details like an Italian shell specially designed to explode in a series of colorful bursts at the end of each musical measure when we played a portion of B. J. Thomas's *Raindrops Keep Falling on My Head*. Lots of cute little stuff like that.

That night the Washington State Patrol closed the Mercer Island Floating Bridge carrying Interstate 90 traffic across Lake Washington between Mercer Island and Seattle. Hundreds of cars had stopped on the bridge, turning it into a parking lot. Passengers and drivers left their cars and walked to the railing to watch the show. That's what I call audience participation!

They were not disappointed. The grand finale found a Cessna with rocket pods attached to its wheel struts flying in a large circle laying down a huge ring of green phosphorus at 10,000 feet. From just above that, two DC-3s disgorged 50 skydivers holding white flares who became candles on our cake in the sky. As they dropped through the cake and their flares began to flame out, we electronically fired 50 of those loud, exploding white salutes *simultaneously*! The explosion was heard clear across Puget Sound in Bremerton, over twenty miles away. Many windows were shattered, but no matter. The cheering from the crowd of thousands watching the show more than compensated for the damage. Traffic remained jammed for hours; people recalled the show fondly for years.

Camelot
Robert Goulet, 1960

KJR WAS MORE THAN A WAY OF LIFE for many of its listeners. It became their near-total life, providing daily rations of fun and laughs, music and news, adventure and sorrow. And, that important family-like feeling of inclusion. KJR was also more than just a way of life for those of us fortunate enough to enjoy its incredible internal chemistry. My eternal thanks to Lester Smith for letting me run wild. He made possible radio's version of Camelot.

Truly great three-dimensional radio may be a thing of the past. If you think this sounds fatalistic or like a plea for a return to the good old days, consider the following. The radio America embraced in the '60s and '70s grew from the days before television, days when radio people were schooled in the notion that radio was a dramatic and loving companion. They believed that radio was the consummate emotions delivery vehicle.

As radio expanded, its primary tools were music, deejays and news. Stations required knowledgeable, visionary program directors and artistic, entertaining disc jockeys, but radio grew too quickly and soon ran short of the talent it needed to sustain excellence.

Yes, there are some individuals in broadcast today that maintain the dreams of total entertainment, but they are few and father and farther between. Witness Howard Stern, now on hundreds of stations across the country. Why? Because the local station can no longer find competitive local talent and is doing nothing to create such talent for the future. I have always tried to hold on to the fundamentals that first made rock-'n'-roll and radio explode. I give speeches on the subject, teach classes, (write books), but I fear it is all in vain. When the Federal Communications Commission stupidly waived regulations limiting the number of stations one company could own, any chance that local ownership would again develop great local talent went out the window — at least for now. Can a station like KJR happen again? Of course it can! But only if people are once more willing to dream, to dedicate themselves, to find out what thrills listeners, and have the courage to follow those dreams tirelessly. Yes, it can happen again, People remain the same; only radio has changed.

KJR Fabulous Fifty
SURVEY

NO.	TITLE	ARTIST	No. Last Week		NO.	TITLE	ARTIST	No. Last Week
1.	HE'S SO FINE	Chiffons	3		26.	Surfin' USA	Beach Boys	36
2.	YOUNG LOVERS	Paul & Paula	2		27.	Our Winter Love	Bill Purcell	17
3.	END OF THE WORLD	Skeeter Davis	1		28.	Boss Guitar	Duane Eddy	28
4.	TWENTY MILES	Chubby Checker	7		29.	Watermelon Man	M. Santamaria	37
5.	GRANNY'S PAD	Viceroys	5		30.	Follow The Boys	Connie Francis	24
6.	PUFF THE MAGIC DRAGON	Peter, Paul & Mary	4		31.	I Got What I Wanted	Brook Benton	33
7.	CAN'T GET USED TO LOSING YOU	A. Williams	12		32.	Hey Paula	Paul & Paula	21
8.	I WILL FOLLOW HIM	Little Peggy March	19		33.	Our Day Will Come	Ruby & Romantics	22
9.	OVER THE MOUNTAIN	Bobby Vinton	9		34.	Do The Bird	Dee Dee Sharp	25
10.	YOUNG AND IN LOVE	Dick & Dee Dee	14		35.	On Broadway	Drifters	38
11.	Maria Madrid	Tijuana Brass	8		36.	The Folk Singer	Tommy Roe	45
12.	Blame It On The Bossa Nova	Eydie Gorme	16		37.	Mecca	Gene Pitney	43
13.	Charms	Bobby Vee	20		38.	Sting Ray	Routers	Debut
14.	Country Boy	George McCurn	6		39.	Hes Got The Power	The Exciters	44
15.	They Remind Me Of Your	Elvis	10		40.	Genesis Through Exodus	Dennis Weaver	DJ Pic
16.	Reverend Mr. Black	Kingston Trio	31		41.	Walk Like A Man	Four Seasons	29
17.	Sun Arise	Rolf Harris	18		42.	Foolish Little Girl	Shirelles	49
18.	Out Of My Mind	J. Tilotson	13		43.	So Long Lucy	Wayne Newton	32
19.	Yakety Sax	Boots Randolph	11		44.	So It Always Will Be	Everly Brothers	47
20.	On A Merry Go Round	Jerry Wallace	26		45.	Skip To M'Limbo	Ventures	Debut
21.	In Dreams	Roy Orbison	15		46.	Cry On My Shoulder	Johnny Crawford	Debut
22.	South Street	Orlons	27		47.	Bony Moronie	Appalachians	Debut
23.	Sandy	Dion	23		48.	The Guitar Player	John Laudermilk	50
24.	The Bird Is The Word	Rivingtons	30		49.	Don't Say Nothin' Bad	Cookies	Debut
25.	I Wanna Be Around	Tony Bennett	34		50.	If You Wanna Be Happy	Jimmy Soul	Debut

KJR PIC ALBUM OF THE WEEK: "THE BEST OF THE DRIFTERS"- ATLANTIC Label

LIST YOUR OWN FAVORITE KJR "FAB 50" TUNES
KJR P.O. Box 3726, Seattle 24, Wash.

1._____
2._____
3._____
4._____
5._____
6._____
7._____
8._____
9._____
10._____

NAME:_____
ADDRESS:_____

WIN ALL THE "FAB 50" RECORDS — EVERY WEEK

Listen to "Name It and Claim It" every hour

Channel 95

In the '60s, any station worth its salt published a weekly Top 40 list. At KJR, Pat O'Day had the station publish a weekly Fabulous *Fifty* Survey and proclaimed it "Seattle's **OFFICIAL** Music Survey." The above example, preserved through the years by Robby Robinson, barkeep at Haggerty's at the Washington Athletic Club in Seattle, is from April 1, 1963 and lists *Granny's Pad*, by Seattle group the Viceroys, in the number five spot for the second week in a row.

11 – Thank You for Being a Friend

Andrew Gold, 1968

THERE IS AN OLD SAYING, "You're a lucky person if you can use all the fingers of one hand to count your good friends. "Well, I have a rather different take on friendship. To me, this view is short-sighted and self-defeating. Too often, people impose meaningless criteria on their friendships, denying themselves the riches of one of life's greatest treasures. In contrast, there aren't enough digits on my hands and feet to tabulate all my friends. I don't judge my relationships by geographical proximity or frequency of contact. Such elements have no place in determining the quality of a friendship, especially when ours has become such a transient society, where people no longer visit over backyard fences.

I also subscribe to a law of nature as true as the sun rising in the east and setting in the west—the *Law of the Speed of Relationships*. It works like this: We meet someone we find fascinating. Magic fills the air and we thrill in their company. Joy marks every moment spent together, and we can't get enough of each other. Then, somewhere along the line, something happens, things start changing, and we can't put our finger on exactly why. The person may have told the same story once too often. Or maybe they failed to return a phone call or answer an e-mail. When we meet, the magic has vanished. We speculate that the relationship never was quite as "neat" as we thought. Soon we drift apart and seek new acquaintances. What a shame, when all that is wrong is, we failed to recognize the Law of the Speed of Relationships.

That law holds that we can meet a person for the first time only once, get acquainted with them, once, grow accustomed to their mannerisms, their sense of humor, their many characteristics, once. We were exhilarated by the relationship, by the blinding speed of our coming together. Again, these are things that can only happen once. The problem is, we have evaluated the entire relationship based on things that could happen only once. In truth, there was nothing wrong with the relationship. It could have endured for a lifetime had we recognized the law and responded properly.

If they obey the law, the two people will recognize that the rush of discovery they originally felt cannot be repeated. They will realize that their relationship can go forward and prosper if they look outward for new experiences to share and enjoy. Clearly still there, their original chemistry will be renewed by their fresh adventures, and their friendship will grow. Failure to obey the law often leads to short-term, shallow relationships.

I have often thought that Carole King was puzzling over the Law of the Speed of Relationships when she wrote her great song, *It's Too Late*:

> It used to be so easy being here with you
> You were light and breezy
> And I knew just what to do
> But one of us is changing
> Or maybe we just stopped trying.
>
> And it's too late, baby, now, it's too late
> Though we really did try to make it.
> Something inside has died
> And I tried, but I just can't fake it. Oh, no…

I think of this when I recall dear friends from past years whom I rarely if ever see or talk to. Whether they are as fond of me as I am of them is immaterial. I am the rich beneficiary of the warm feelings I still carry for them.

I now live with my wife, Stephanie (we have been married for almost 22 years), and our dreamy daughter, Kelsey, age 11, on San Juan Island in the far northwest corner of Washington state. We moved to this paradise believing it would be an ideal place for Kelsey to enjoy her childhood—and it's exactly that. Stephanie is a land use attorney, while I made a late-in-life career change and became the owner of a John L. Scott real estate brokerage. We are not isolated by any means, but I am no longer "hanging" in the city—Seattle—or constantly traveling the country and the world, where I would have contact with my many friends spread hither and yon. This doesn't dilute my appreciation of those relationships for one moment. I value them as the greatest treasures on earth. Most valuable of all are my family: Stephanie and Kelsey, along with my three sons Jerry, Garry and Jeffrey (now in their 40s) and my grandkids, Jacqui, Jessie and Colby.

I would now like to introduce you to some of my other extraordinary friends. I think you will enjoy them.

Fly Like an Eagle
Steve Miller, 1976

WITH A COUPLE OF NOTABLE EXCEPTIONS, many of my closest relationships have come from outside the radio and music business. Exception number one, from the radio business, is Dick Curtis. You met Dick earlier in this book—he's my former deejay colleague, business partner and, later, manager of one of my radio stations. He's a friend for life—and a friend of great quality. Although I rarely see him, I don't have to for our friendship to endure. Our chemistry is so strong, as is our trust in one another, we always know the other is there. We run on different tracks in different towns, but what matter? Great friendships, as I tried to explain earlier, don't require frequent contact or constant cultivation. They simply need the respect of one individual for the other, and the mutual recognition of the good fortune of knowing each other.

Another individual, this time from the music business, whose friendship I have come to enjoy is Steve Miller. I have known Steve for 25 plus years, and his ability to absorb fame and fortune with his Steve Miller Band and stunning career—and yet remain unchanged as a human being—impresses me the most. Steve is married to the former Kim Smith, daughter of my one-time boss/business partner Lester Smith and his lovable wife Bernice. Two winters ago, my wife Stephanie, Kim and I were happily skiing the runs at "The Valley" in Idaho, and my mind wandered back some 34 years to when Kim and her sister, Laura Lee, were young teenagers, and I helped teach them how to ski. And now, here we were, true friends after so many years, still skiing together. The old adage, "The more things change, the more they remain the same," came to mind. So much time and so much great history later.

About six years ago, I nudged Steve and Kim into purchasing a waterfront estate here on San Juan Island, and now they divide their time between here and Sun Valley. When schedules permit, we have dinner at one another's homes, play some golf or do something else, and it's always such fun. Steve's musical brilliance has never shaded his personality, as he personifies the well-rounded individual. This, despite carrying the burden of greatness.

Steve's father was a doctor in Dallas, Texas, and Steve was a young boy when his father introduced him to an acquaintance, Les Paul. For those of you who don't know, Les Paul is to the electric guitar what Henry Ford was to the automobile. Not only a virtuoso *playing* the instrument, he was a pioneer in developing new ways to *record* the instrument. Some readers will recall the team of Les Paul and Mary Ford (his wife). Back in the mid-50s they had hit after hit, huge Capitol Records hits like *How High The Moon*, *Vaya Con Dios* and others. Les Paul's wild manipulation of old single-track tape recorders—overlaying track-after-track—broke barriers and created new recording vistas for vocals as well as for electric guitar sounds. All this was a guiding light for a young Steve Miller, who surpassed his idol in many ways, but idolizes him to this day.

Steve remains deeply in love with music. He recently took a few years off from his very successful touring to concentrate on exploring new directions in music and feelings. He writes and writes, plays and plays, sings and sings. From *Fly Like An Eagle* to *The Joker* to *Abracadabra* and so many other songs recognized around the world, Steve's hits "just kept on comin'," and there are more on the way.

Steve created a recording studio at his home in Idaho, and it brings him great fun. He often invites fellow musicians to drop by, experiment and develop new ideas. A few years back, Paul and the late Linda McCartney stayed with Steve and Kim for several days. The boys locked themselves in the studio to have their fun, which was, getting better acquainted musically.

The God-awful condition of today's recording and radio industries limits our exposure to new recordings and keeps us from enjoying artists like Steve that have much more left to give. How strange, when one stops to think that here is a performer who can still easily sell 15,000 tickets in any major city. The record industry has been paralyzed by the accountant mentality and a fear of exploring new, uncharted waters. Stations are limited to playing music mainly from highly forgettable urban acts to the exclusion of quality rock-'n'-roll mainstays. Today's radio has departed from the objectivity and pioneering spirit that once served it so well. Lately, much has been written about accounting misdeeds at Enron and WorldCom and elsewhere. What accountants and corporate suits have done to the music and radio industries may not be criminal in the eyes of the law, but it's a crime against art and creativity.

True art and "the accountant mentality" will always be enemies. I hope the success of the sound track from *O Brother, Where Art Thou*, with its refusal to conform to pre-conceived notions, will take the blinders off some record executive somewhere. I hope that unchallenged greatness, like that of Steve Miller, can again enjoy the exposure and freedom that once made rock-'n'-roll so great. Today's music industry environment would have disallowed everyone from Elvis to the Beatles. Someone please tell them: Great art resists practical analysis!

I'm not an accountant, so Steve is my friend. I admire him and his music. But, most of all, I respect his humility and kindness. He has a grand boat moored at the dock in front of his San Juan Island home, bearing the name *Abracadabra*—the floating symbol of a great imagination and talent capable of writing, playing and singing such a song. And, in the "it's a small world" department, speaking of accountants, another friend, Irv Karl, comptroller with Kaye-Smith for years and a major part of Concert West' business success, now serves as Steve's business manager.

At the release of the first edition of this book, Paul Allen's Experience Music Project in Seattle kindly turned their facilities over to me for the grand kick-off. I was having lunch with Steve and Kim at their house and told them of the up-coming event, which was to include the original Wailers and Merrilee Rush. Steve said, "Can I come and play at it?" I replied, "God, are you kidding me? Do bears poop in the woods? And so Steve put together a 12-piece band and stunned a sold-out crowd that historic evening in 2002. How lucky can I get, and what a friend! I think Steve made my book *Fly Like An Eagle*.

Nights in White Satin
The Moody Blues, 1967

TWO CLOSE FRIENDS FROM OUTSIDE the music/radio world are Chuck and Pam Lyford. I met Pam back in the '60s when she was dating my buddy, the late Jim Clapp. As I explain elsewhere in this book, Jim was the businessman who believed in my dreams and provided financial support for Pat O'Day & Associates in our early days. Jim and I also raced jet hydroplanes together, and Chuck was chief engineer and designer on the project. When Jim died rather suddenly, I assisted in the financing of the racing team by going to the Air Force and gaining their sponsorship of the racing boat. In its maiden season, during the Seattle Gold Cup race, the boat, which had already become the fastest boat in unlimited racing history, exploded and sank. Sometime thereafter, Jim's widow, Pam, and Chuck fell in love. Twenty-eight years later, they remain happily married. Pam and Chuck are both extraordinarily brilliant. She likes to do interesting things. A year or so ago, the phone rang and it was Pam. She was calling from her satellite phone. From somewhere in northern India. From the back of a camel. Recently, I confessed to Pam that I was writing this book, and she said I simply must include the story of an unusual evening in 1973. So, here it is.

That year, I was in Orange County staying at the Airporter Hotel for two reasons. First, Concerts West had the Moody Blues playing in Long Beach, and I was needed at the show. Second, for our jet-turbine-powered hydroplane that was being built, the hull was coming out of the Ron Jones Boat Shop in Costa Mesa. As such, Pam and Jim Clapp, Chuck Lyford and some others arrived in town for a boat-christening ceremony, and I invited several friends as well. Knowing a party was in order, I secured the hotel's presidential suite, featuring a large indoor swimming pool in the center of the room. Pam and Jim, being huge Moodies fans, attended the Long Beach show the first night of their stay. The second night was the party.

The celebration started rather calmly. A good friend named Perry Dickson was in town on business and dropped by, along with several former Southern Cal Trojan football players with whom he chummed. Adding to the mix were a couple of dozen boat-types, and things appeared mellow. Once the sun went down, however, the enthusiasm level went up, way up. One early indication of looming mayhem came to my attention when I noticed that one of the couches from my suite was floating in the swimming pool. Another appeared when I realized that an unknown artist in the group had acquired some paint and embellished the ten-foot-long seascape mural that adorned one wall. It now prominently featured our new racing boat skipping over the mural's waves. I made a hurried visit to the hotel manager, told him our group was becoming unpredictable and assured him that I would pay for any damages. He was content with my promise.

Midway through the evening, Perry Dickson, who was single, went patrolling for female companionship. During his several trips to the hotel bar, he noticed an attractive young lady sitting in the lobby. Finally drawn to her after two hours, Perry inquired as to why a pretty girl like her was just sitting there all alone. She explained that she and her husband were in town for a convention, and that he was nearly three hours late picking her up for dinner. She made her disgust known to Perry, who suggested that maybe they should go into the bar and have a drink together, which, he opined, was only fair under the circumstances. She agreed, adding she was not much of a drinker. But why not? Two hours later, they appeared in my suite, where they announced their intention to get married for the night. Both were clearly intoxicated and giggling at the thought of their pending matrimony.

It was suggested that I serve as the minister, and I complied. I took off my dress shirt, turned it around and put my suit coat back on, creating a priest-like collar. Just then, Pam entered the room, saw what was happening and ran out onto the hotel grounds to pick flowers. Returning with a handsome bouquet of very fresh flowers, she fashioned a bridal veil and cape out of white towels from my bathroom. Nothing fancy, just functional. With that, all was ready.

Next to the shimmering pool with my lovely floating couch, a charming, moving, simple service was held. Once the "I do's" were out of the way, the happy couple disappeared in the direction of Perry's room, presumably for their honeymoon. I never asked Perry whether their brief marriage was consummated. Nor did I inquire as to the quality of their brief hours of married life. I didn't want to know, partly because I had other things on my mind, but mainly because Perry revealed upon his return to the party that his bride was the disgruntled wife of a regional director of Youth For Christ.

As the party continued, the deterioration of the celebrants accelerated. By midnight, critical mass was achieved and manifested itself at the expense of Costa Mesa's finest. As an ex-Trojan football player stood by the pool, holding a beautiful, heavy, one-gallon glass decanter of Jack Daniel's bourbon given to me as a gift by Jim Clapp earlier that day, someone from across the water yelled that he needed another drink. Our football star, who was intolerably drunk and whose name I choose to omit as a personal favor to him, decided to play quarterback. Picking up my decanter, he sent it spiraling across the pool in the direction of his thirsty friend. Sadly, the intended target—another USC football great—disappointed his fans in his role as wide receiver. Instead of catching the pass, he jumped out of the way, and the decanter sailed through a giant plate glass window overlooking the courtyard. The window shattered, the decanter broke and bourbon and glass shards showered down upon a Costa Mesa police officer who had been hiding unnoticed in the dark, peering through the window, spying on us.

The call went out on the police emergency band: "Officer down!" and within minutes my suite was swarming with deadly-serious Costa Mesa police officers, all assuming that one of their fellow officers had been attacked. They were decidedly unfriendly, and handcuffs were quickly placed on several of my guests, including all the football types. At last, a police captain arrived, and I tried to calm things down by explaining that the accident with the officer had occurred through no ill intent on the part of my friends. It was quite late, and after a long day I had already climbed into my bed, which sat directly in the middle of the suite. Wearing nothing but my jockey shorts, (I forgot to pack pajamas), I was trying to negotiate a peaceful conclusion to the misunderstanding. For a time, it looked like I would succeed.

The police captain sat down on the edge of my bed, where I propped myself up with pillows and explained the entire evening. I told him about the new race boat, about the Moody Blues, and finally about how and why the decanter had been chucked at the window. I made it clear that none of us had realized his fine officer was peering in from behind the potted plants. The captain accepted my explanation, ignored the couch floating in the pool, and ordered his men to uncuff my guests. That was a mistake.

Upon the removal of his handcuffs, my favorite Trojan All-American doubled up his fist and delivered a Batman Comics-like "POW!" to the nearest policeman. Now we had a second "officer down," and all hell broke loose. One of the officers yanked me from my bed, handcuffed me and marched me out the door. We proceeded down the hallway and into the lobby, where I spotted my friend, the hotel manger, standing behind the check-in counter. I was deeply disturbed, and why not? I had done nothing wrong and, dressed only in my jockey shorts, I was being paraded through the lobby toward the front door with several people staring. The manager immediately jumped over the counter and shouted, "What's going on here, anyway?"

As I was being assisted/pushed/marched/dragged down the hall, I indicated my shock and indignation by telling the officer who had painfully jerked me from my bed that I thought he was an asshole! The Costa Mesa police that night all wore white shirts, and I suggested to my officer friend that an ink rubber stamp with the word *Asshole* should be applied to the front of his shirt, right over the pocket. That way, I explained, everyone who came in contact with him would know what he was. *An Asshole*! I repeated my suggestion several times.

Meanwhile, the manager was telling the captain that I was a dignitary, a respected and valued regular guest of the hotel, and that they simply were not going to remove me from his establishment. He asked the captain what I had done, and the captain replied that I was part of the group. Finally, their discussion turned into a private conference between the two of them in the manager's office. All that time, I was held in the lobby, standing in my jockey shorts, humiliated and reminding my officer that he was an asshole while Jim, Pam and Chuck stood in the background, laughing.

To my relief, I was released and not hauled off to jail. At the insistence of the police, I was placed in a separate room with an officer assigned to guard me. He sat in a chair outside my door, determined to prevent me from leaving my room or entertaining any more company that night. (My original suite was now locked, with tape on the door saying it was a crime scene. The couch still floated in the pool.) Meanwhile, the football players had their own issues to resolve, mainly dealing with the unhappy insistence by the police that they "come downtown." The Trojans had not gone peacefully. Brave to the end, but badly outnumbered, they were finally clubbed, wrestled and maced into submission, thrown into paddy wagons and transported to the Costa Mesa jail, where they spent the night. The next morning, they were charged with various and sundry infractions. That same morning, I met with the manager, thanked him for intervening on my behalf, settled up the room charges and damages and caught a plane to Seattle.

I had forgotten the entire incident when, on Christmas Eve that same year, Jim and Pam Clapp came by the house for our annual exchange of gifts. When I unwrapped my gift, my wife at the time immediately began probing as to its meaning. Having neglected to tell her of the Costa Mesa party, it was all a bit awkward. But it was also very funny, because when I unwrapped my present, there was the large cut glass bulb and cork that had once adorned that ill-fated Jack Daniel's decanter. That night at the hotel, Pam had retrieved it from the crime scene. Ingeniously attached thereto was a three-inch-wide rubber stamp that bore the word *Asshole!*

Have Gun, Will Travel
Fred Steiner, 1957

WHAT ABOUT CHUCK LYFORD? Well, let me tell you about him! Here is the real package, and a fascinating book could be written about Chuck and his exploits. He started flying while still a boy and later became one of the world's greatest pilots, which he remains today. Chuck has won every major air race out there, save for the famous Reno race, where he has twice finished second. His abilities flying a p-51 Mustang are unmatched, and he has done a great deal of test flying for many airplane manufacturers, including Lear. There was a period of time when he barnstormed between air shows in a World War ii-vintage Lockheed Lightning p-38. He enjoyed performing a trick maneuver not seen before or since. Roaring down the runway in front of the grandstand at 400 mph, he would shut off his engines, pull up the nose of his plane and execute a complete inside loop. Swooping down, power off, he would continue up into a second loop, impossible to complete without power. At the apex of the second loop, upside down, he would restart his engines, flip the plane back over and narrowly miss hitting the runway as he plummeted earthward. Ask any pilot. That's good stuff!

Chuck's pilot's license has been suspended on more than one occasion, as many of his efforts to entertain have run afoul of regulations. Like the time when stunt flying had been temporarily suspended over Seattle's Lake Washington during the big annual Seafair hydroplane race and extravaganza. Undaunted, Chuck was determined to show off the versatility of Lear's new business jet. He came in low over the lake—barely higher than the mast tops of the hundreds of sailboats moored along the log boom—then pointed his nose straight up, doing several snap rolls as the Lear climbed into the heavens. This particular stunt cost him has ability to fly in the US for a year, so Chuck detoured to Central America and formed his own air force. He took with him his p-51's from his air racing days, equipped them with guns, rockets and everything else available on the black market in Manila and soon was fighting small wars out of El Salvador. There was more than enough unrest through-out South and Central America in those days to keep Chuck busy, and many countries, or opponents of same, needed air power. Chuck offered a solution, and his business card, copied from the '50s television show starring Richard Boone as Paladin, read "Have Guns, Will Travel." And travel he did.

Soon, his operation came to the attention of the cia, who put him on their payroll with one provision: Henceforth, Chuck could only fight for the side approved of by the Agency. Not a bad deal, really. It provided welcome new income and still left him with a strong customer base: one side or the other of any country with internal friction. The full story of the demise of his air force I will leave for Chuck to write in *his* book.

Chuck was and remains a premier air race pilot, stunt pilot, you name it, as long as it moves fast. None other than hero-and-flying-legend Chuck Yeager has said that the three best pilots living today are him, California's Clay Lacey—and Chuck Lyford. He will also say that the best of the three is Lyford.

Chuck and I have had great fun together—nothing of the scope or as hazardous as his military excursions, but close. One mile from my home on San Juan Island sits Henry Island, and the two are separated by that world-famous yachting destination, Roche Harbor. Chuck and Pam have a place on Henry and spend much of their summers there. One clear, calm summer night at the Lyfords' it came time to, as Chuck put it, "go play with the freighters."

Just off Henry Island lies De Haro Straits, which divide the US and Canada. Some of the world's largest ships move constantly up and down the Straits on their way between the Pacific Ocean and Vancouver, British Columbia. Have you ever noticed that these giant vessels have a large bulb up front at the bottom of their bows, just beneath their waterlines? This protrusion gives the hulls certain hydrodynamic efficiencies, and all large vessels now have them. Precisely what the bulbs physically do for a ship, I can't describe, but I can tell you that as the ship moves through the water, the bulbous nose raises the water in front by about 10 feet. This phenomenon is an important element in "playing with freighters."

All credit for inventing this game must go to Chuck. I am merely the enthusiastic ally of almost any idea he hatches! On the evening in question, we took off in a 16-foot-long Boston Whaler with a 40 horsepower motor and shadowed the freighter until we were positioned just right. At that point, Chuck jumped to maximum speed and maneuvered the Whaler up and onto the platform of water raised by the ship's bulb. With precision timing and deft handling, he reduced power, and our craft surfed along on the elevated wall of water. The real rush came when I looked upward. The prows of such vessels extend many feet forward from their waterlines, and I saw that we were actually riding *under* the bow of this massive 400-foot-long iron leviathan as it sliced through the water at top speed just a scant few feet behind us.

With our boat under the control of Chuck, maybe the world's greatest pilot, all went well. Escaping from this precarious position, which is required to win this game, is no small feat. It's accomplished by applying full throttle to the small boat, then making a precisely-timed quick turn to one side or the other. With just the right acceleration, and a straight and true run to the side, you remove yourselves from harm's way. I refuse to consider what would have happened had the small boat's engine quit. Surely, Chuck has that all figured out. And, besides, I don't care to dwell on such unhappy thoughts.

Chuck told me a funny story recently. I really like a guy named Joe Clark, and he and Chuck are close friends. Joe heads Aviation Partners, the firm that invented and builds the winglets, those small vertical fins you see on the wing tips of Boeing and other big jet planes. Joe and Chuck have been pals since high school and have enjoyed many adventures together. This time, they were on their way to a wedding in San Francisco, and Chuck had elected to fly them down in one of his fighter planes. Lacking luggage room, they folded up their suits, shirts and ties and carefully placed them in the port that once had held the machine guns. Just after takeoff, before they could climb above the clouds, they flew through a heavy rainstorm. The machine gun ports had no semblance of protection from water, and the rain poured in on their formal wear. As they climbed higher for their cruise south, they encountered sub-freezing temperatures. Upon arrival in the Bay Area, their clothes for the wedding were frozen into two impenetrable blocks of ice! They had no choice but to go to the wedding dressed as they were. They set the blocks of ice on the tarmac next to their plane in the sunshine and returned to Seattle with thawed out, but badly wrinkled and shrunk, garments.

Tapestry
Carole King, 1971

ANOTHER TREASURED FRIENDSHIP OF MINE is with Bruce McCaw. Bruce and his brothers, led by Craig, pioneered the cellular telephone age with their company, Cellular One. Back in 1988, I was doing some business with an associate of Adnan Kashoggi, the Saudi billionaire part-time arms dealer. Kashoggi was also interested in the new cell phone industry and wanted to have a base in Texas. Craig and his brothers were then owners of the cellular licenses for Houston, San Antonio, Austin, Galveston and some other cities. The price of such licenses were then based on "per pop," meaning, a certain dollar amount for every adult in the population base. Kashoggi's agent hired me to go to Craig and offer him an unheard-of price of 21 dollars "per pop." This would have been a record transaction at a price nearly double anything ever offered before for such a license (and offered a hell of a big commission for me!). I smiled, as rarely does one have a chance to make someone an offer they simply can't refuse. Except,

Craig did! He told me, "Pat, you're going to think I'm absolutely crazy, which I may be, but I have this plan I'm working on, and for it to really work, I have to hang on to every single license I can acquire. The offer is outstanding, and I'm sorry, but we just can't do it!" It wasn't long until we saw the big picture. Craig amassed licenses and, as the cell phone business began to mature, he and his brothers, Bruce, John and Keith, sold out to AT&T for about 17 billion dollars.

Whatever the gene is that triggers "the visionary," it runs rampant in the McCaw family. The patriarch, the late J. Elroy McCaw, was one of many modern-day radio pioneers, starting with a small radio station in the little town of Chehalis, Washington and moving forward to the purchase of WINS-New York. There, he was an early proponent of hit-music-oriented radio and cultivated the career of that preeminent program director and my friend, the late Rick Sklar. Rick was for years the PD of rock-'n'-roll powerhouse WABC-New York. Elroy McCaw put the Big Apple on its ear with the nation's most exciting, innovating radio station of its time. He hired the inventor of the term rock-'n'-roll, Alan Freed, to do the night show. Murray the "K" was on his staff, and he had the famous team of Bob and Ray in the mornings. When the Dodgers and Giants departed New York for the West Coast, he capitalized on the broken-hearted baseball fans by purchasing the teams' broadcast rights for New York and, with legendary Les Keiter doing the play-by-play recreations of their games on the West Coast. This built late evening audiences that far exceeded those of the Yankees broadcasts. McCaw had purchased WINS during that transition period between network programming and independence. He bought WINS for under a half million dollars and sold it short years later to Westinghouse for 10 million, over 20 times what he had paid for it. J. Elroy McCaw was a visionary who, in the early '60s, was years ahead of Ted Turner as he foresaw and began preparations for the day when cable TV would become a massive national web and provide its own programming.

J. Elroy's passing was unexpected, very premature, and coupled with mass confusion as to what he did and did not own (brilliance, oftentimes overshadows details). Before finally establishing that he was in excellent shape financially, lawyers plowed through vast sums of the families cash in a needless and unforgivable fashion. I have expanded on this because there was one asset he held that was unattached from greedy attorneys: a small TV cable company he had built and held from his original broadcast efforts in the adjoining towns of Chehalis and Centralia, Washington. His sons, with the same roll-the-dice-on-your-dreams spirit as their father, coupled with the frugal accounting sense of Marion, their mother, began to build. They quickly turned that little cable company into a massive national cable empire, then converted it into their new cellular phone development (Cellular One) which is now the foundation of AT&T Wireless.

The McCaw family, led by their mother, has been remarkable in their generosity and contributions to the Seattle community. This year, the city's opera house enjoyed a total renovation, paid for in large part by millions of dollars donated by the McCaw sons, and is now named for their mother. A stunning facility, it is known today as *The Marianne Oliver McCaw Opera House*.

Back to Bruce. He was very successful in his own right. Even before the cable empire grew and their cell phone efforts came to fruition, he owned a large insurance agency that specialized in aircraft and airports. His big fun, other than his wife Jolene and kids, Skye and Wynn, has been car racing, as he formed and ran Pac West Racing with two cars on the Championship Auto Racing Teams circuit. There, during recent years, he joined with Chip Ganassi, Bobby Rahal, Roger Penske, Newman, Haas, and others in presenting the fastest car racing in the world. Now, here is a touch of coincidence. Bruce and Jolene live in Medina on Lake Washington across from Seattle and just doors down the lake from Chuck and Pam Lyford. Chuck and Pam's next door neighbors are my former boss and partner, Lester Smith, and his wife, Bernice. They bought their house from my close friend Bob Crossetto and, of course, Lester and Bernice are the parents of Kim Miller, wife of my friend, Steve Miller, and they are close friends of Chuck and Pam as well as of Bruce and Jolene. Also, Chuck and Pam live in the home originally purchased by Pam's late husband, Jim Clapp, with whom I had a close business relationship and friendship, and who had been responsible for my moving to Newport Shores in 1963, also on the lake, and meeting my neighbor, one Lennox Scott.

Another happy coincidence (probably selfishly speaking) is that I have been able to, in my capacity as a real estate guy, find summer homes for all of these folks here in the San Juan Islands. Now, I see Bruce about as often as a full eclipse of the moon, but that's okay! He's very busy, and I much admire what he does with his money. Just like his father and mother, he and Jolene give more to charitable causes in a single day than most of us give in a lifetime.

I think Jolene is still unhappy with me because, upon receiving my invite to Bruce's 50th birthday party, I failed to notice that somewhere on the invitation it said it was a surprise. I guess I said to Bruce, "See you next week!" and Bruce that night said to Jolene, "Why does Pat think he is seeing us next week?" Jolene went skyward, but it was all covered well, as Chuck and Pam Lyford came up with an excuse. I flew off to Bruce's next car race that weekend and, in the pits, we held a mini-surprise birthday thing. Thus, the big surprise was maintained. And, besides, for God's sake, Jolene, I'm a broadcaster! What do you expect?

And I must include amongst these ironies that, after the death of Elroy McCaw, Marion, the boys' mother, married a recent widower and Seattle real estate magnate, John L. Scott. John's son, Lennox, back in the 60's built a house by me on the lake in the Newport Shores neighborhood of Bellevue, and we became big buddies. He replaced his father as the president of the firm, but also died young. His son, Lennox Jr., was a little older than my sons and baby sat for us. Lennox Jr. was to eventually attend the University of Washington and become well-acquainted with another student, named Stephanie Johnson, who in 1981 became my wife, Stephanie O'Day. Meanwhile, Lennox Jr. has assumed the presidency of John L. Scott, now the most powerful chain of real estate agencies in the Northwest, of which I own the franchise here on San Juan Island. Oh, and one final note to this. When I was starting my radio career and working in Yakima, the second station that employed me, KLOQ, was owned by J. Elroy McCaw's brother, John McCaw. And when I purchased KORL radio in Honolulu in 1976, that station had originally been built and owned by J. Elroy McCaw. And then their was my first hydroplane broadcast I anchored in Seattle back in 1967. It was on J. Elroy's television station, Channel 13, and a young man was at the controls in the truck helping his father's station with the telecast. That young man was my friend, Bruce McCaw. I guess I should have created a chart to help you picture this whole amazing maze!

Sadly, since the release of the first printing of this book, Keith McCaw died of an accident at his Seattle home. He was deeply loved by all for his kind spirit and philanthropy and is very much missed.

The "In" Crowd
Dobie Gray, 1965
WE WERE ALL FROM DIFFERENT VOCATIONS, but found energy and synergy of all sorts in our close ties. My next-door neighbor on Lake Washington, the late Dick Peterson, passed away from bone cancer this past year. Dick and I set several world records in various fields of misbehavior. Bob Crossetto, a life insurance pro. Dick Koopmans, who was with Touche Ross accounting firm and

eventually became the chief financial officer of my radio stations. Jerry Horn, whom I met when he was advertising manager for Sears in Seattle. He later moved to management of their San Francisco store, which was failing and which he quickly corrected. Then he became president of REI Co-op, and then he was hired to the lofty position of president and chairman of the board of General Nutrition Corporation in Pittsburgh, PA. Another card-carrying member was Lyle Anderson, now of Phoenix, a developer who can safely be labeled the most successful golf course community developer in the world today.

Every once in a while the group would decide it was time for a summit meeting, and we would work our schedules to get two or three days free. The summits were almost always held in Las Vegas, where we would golf and play all of the Vegas games. Most important, though, was the time that we all sat together and talked. It was time to do personal mind dumps with friends, trusted friends — dumps of our thoughts, dreams, goals, frustrations, disappointments — and give one another input. Input that could be trusted because it came from knowledgeable, caring friends. If you think this sounds boring, you should have been around us in the evenings.

I remember one time when the summit was held in Reno. It was there one evening that the highly-respected and usually very conservative Jerry Horn ingested an excessive amount of scotch. In a very loud voice, he was urging the rest of us from across the casino to come join him at the craps table where, in the words he was shouting, "I'm hotter than shit." We were avoiding Jerry at this point, but I didn't escape entirely. Jerry, it seems, wound up and threw the dice, this time entirely missing the dice table. The errant die flew across the floor and under the curtain into the lounge and bar where the entertainment is staged. The entertainment that night just happened to be Paul Revere & the Raiders. Noting they were there when we checked in the hotel, I had intended to drop by after their show and say hi. Paul and I have enjoyed a superlative relationship for years. Jerry Horn's dice hurried the meeting.

As Jerry's dice flew under the curtain, he said "Damn it! I'll get them!"

Too late, the casino pit boss said he would take care of it. Jerry was already through the curtain and crawling around on the floor in the darkened lounge, filled with customers, and with Paul and the band in the middle of a song. Paul, always looking for humor to further enliven his show, stopped the music, peered out at Jerry, crawling around between and under tables, and said, "Sir, on the floor there, what in the hell are you doing?"

Jerry, realizing he had been noticed (the stage spotlight was turned on him), got to his feet and said, "I lost my God-damned dice. Hey, your buddy Pat O'Day is here."

Paul said, "Pat O'Day from Seattle?"

Jerry said (and I quote him accurately), "Hell, yesh. He's right outside at the blackjack table!"

Paul said, "Go get him and bring him in here!"

Jerry stumbled into the casino and found me at the blackjack table. Grabbing me by the arm he dragged me into the lounge and said, "Here he is!"

Paul, on stage, said, "Pat, where in the hell did you find this guy?" He's been crawling around on the floor in here looking up ladies' dresses!"

The crowd seemed to love it, so Paul brought me up on stage, briefly told the audience we were old friends from Seattle where I was a deejay and promoter, and had me join him and the group for a spirited rendition of *Louie Louie*. In the end, I imagine those in the lounge that night thought the whole thing was planned and rehearsed! If you are part of any of the many corporate boards on which Jerry now serves, don't judge him harshly based on that one evening. Even super-execs get to have a little quality R & R from time to time.

Drag City
Jan & Dean, 1963

SO MANY WONDERFUL RELATIONSHIPS have developed over the years, but my relationship with one man in particular should make for very fun reading. His name is Bill Doner.

Bill moved to Seattle in 1968 to take over the operation of Seattle International Raceways—a mile-and-a-half road race circuit and, more importantly, a drag strip. He came experienced with such operations in southern California. He developed a powerful string of drag race venues from Orange County and Fontana, California to Portland, Oregon and Seattle. Bill and I had a great deal in common since we both felt that life was a great deal of fun and we both relied, to some extent, on receipts from ticket sales for success. In short, we were promoters!

Our relationship was a natural in many ways and began when Bill came to my station, KJR, to promote his racing events. Through Bill, I became acquainted with Evel Knievel, race driver Dan Gurney, dragsters Don Prudhomme, Tom McKeun, Kenny Burnstein and many more. Introductions also included the brilliant car designer, Caroll Shelby. (I introduced Shelby to my assistant, Peggy Claire, and they became an item of nearly a 15-year duration. Peggy, in addition to running my desk, was also Seattle's first helicopter traffic reporter.) Shelby was a hero of mine from college days, when I watched him drive his Ferrari to victories in West Coast sports car races. Of course, everyone knows of his wonderful Cobras, Shelby Mustangs and, most recently, the Viper!

How good a promoter was Bill Doner? When it comes to creating excitement, he had no equal! Bill created a giant drag racing event he called *64 Funny Cars* which doubled any attendance known of at that time. (Funny cars are the stubby, Camaro- and Mustang-looking cousins of dragsters and just as fast.)

It was Doner that brought a guy named Evel Knievel out of the dust of small stock car race tracks and put him in the spotlight. This was long before Knievel's famous accident in Las Vegas. It was Doner who brought Linda Lovelace to his tracks to sing a throaty rendition of the National Anthem. (If you don't know who Linda Lovelace was, never mind.) Doner simply took a stumbling Seattle International Raceways and turned it into the giant success that it remains today, some 33 years later.

Bill became bored, sold out, and bought a Marlin fishing fleet in Cabo San Lucas, Mexico. He called it Fleet Tortuga, and it was there that the following wondrous story begins.

A Seattle travel group hired me to participate in a Carnival Cruise Line tour to Mexico. It was one of those deals where we advertised "Cruise the warm waters of Mexico, visit the Gold Coast with Pat O'Day as your host!" Two hundred people purchased all the available tickets, and we were having a splendid time except for one thing. In a spasm of excitement, I said on the commercials that when the ship anchored at its last stop in Cabo, I would arrange for the group to go marlin fishing with my friend Bill Doner. However, three days into the cruise, I was contacted by the cruise director who had heard some rumor about a fishing excursion. In no uncertain terms, he told me that there would be no such event. That because of insurance, liability, blah, blah, blah, he would not tolerate it and told me to inform my party the fishing event was off! In reading this book, I imagine you have come to know me well enough by now to realize I wasn't a bit discouraged!

I arranged for my wife Stephanie and I to have dinner the next night with the good Captain Francola of Carnival Cruise Lines ship, the *Carnivale*. Captain Francola was a likable native of Genoa, Italy whose broken English didn't slow the conversation flow! For half the dinner we traded cruise-type chit chat. Then I addressed my issue. Confirming that Francola had the ultimate authority while on the high seas (which he assured us he did), and that his authority exceeded that of the cruise director (which he more than assured us it did), I presented my case. I told the captain of my excitement over the cruise and how I had this nearly lifelong friend who operated the fishing fleet in Cabo. Of how we had concocted the idea that his fleet could come alongside the *Carnivale*, once the anchor was set, and take my two hundred guests for the fishing experience of their life. After all, I pointed out, these are advertised as the "fun ships," and what could this be but a lot of fun?

The Captain looked off across the dining room for a few seconds, then hit the table with his fist and said, "I agree!" Thus, the cruise director's dictate was overturned and, following an all-night run from Puerto Vallarta to the harbor in Cabo, we dropped anchor. I alerted Doner by ship-to-shore phone immediately after our dinner with the captain. (Doner and I discussed some other things as well) and, as the gangway was lowered alongside the ship, Doner's Fleet Tortuga came along side, and my friends began piling into his boats. We had an outstanding morning of deep sea fishing. No marlins, but big tuna in abundance, and it was a happy bunch of Seattle-area tourists that returned to the ship that afternoon. Holding up their catches so the big crowd that lined the rails of the ship could see, they were even more excited when it was announced on the ship's speakers that our tuna, freshly caught, would be featured for all at the dinner that night. For all, that is, except Stephanie and me!

You see, in my conversation on ship-to-shore with Bill, he asked whether I was having fun, and I told him I'd had about all the fun I could handle. So, as I returned to the ship from fishing, Stephanie had stealthed our bags down onto the gangway. They were quickly slipped on board the fishing boat I was on and, as the last fisherman stepped off the boat, Stephanie stepped on and we pulled away waving goodbye to our friends. Simple as that, we jumped ship.

Within the hour, we were sitting by Doner's pool, sipping cordials and looking out into the harbor at a departing ship, the *Carnivale*. Also significant in our decision to forgo any more ship-board excitement was the final game of the Final Four that, thanks to the miracle of satellite television, was on the tube at Bill's house. We stayed with Bill and his girlfriend, Georgiann, for a few days, but the highlight of the stay for me was an activity Bill arranged for the following evening. We were going to La Paz for the cock fights.

La Paz is about 40 minutes north of Cabo San Lucas if there are no trucks slowing you down. We stopped for dinner on the way up and, just after dusk, arrived at the cock fights. Little did I know this was going to be a Bill Doner promotion. Or sort of. Bill had scheduled himself to embark on a gainful activity at the expense of the cock fight operators who, Bill said, were crooked as hell. He told me the whole thing was a fix. I want to inform you here of another of Bill's talents. He has a gambling instinct that parallels the nose of a blood hound. He is just a human calculator when it comes to games of chance. But the time between our arrival and departure puzzled me. We were seated in a large, open-sided, tin-roofed building in the center of which sat the fenced cock-fighting ring and, surrounding the ring, seating for probably about 500 on what we call "circus blues." These are the wooden, portable grandstands like the circus used to cart from town to town. No backs, just bench seats.

Just outside the fighting ring, there was an elevated table with a fight official. Men circulated through the crowd taking the fans' bets. They would bet on the red chicken or the green chicken. When the red light was on you could bet on the red chicken, and same with the green light. This way, the house could exercise some control over the amount of money wagered on any given chicken.

Bill inquired and was sent a touter. This was a man who would give Bill, in exchange for cash tips, inside advice on which way to bet. (It's assumed stupid gringos need touters.) The action soon began and, once I became numb to the bloody carnage in the ring, I began to notice that Bill was losing almost every bet. Now, these were not small bets. These were wagers of from $250 up to $500 per fight. His touter kept saying, "Oh, señor, we must stay with it! Increase your bets, we will get them!"

Bill finally whispered to me, "I'll explain in the car!"

What Bill was to explain took place a few nights later. What Bill was doing was casing out how the fix worked. Naturally, Bill was losing nearly every bet because he was the largest bettor in the barn. One chicken or the other is doped before each fight, leaving it vulnerable and insuring its death in battle. In that all odds are 50-50, the operators simply insure that the chicken with the most money bet on it loses. Doner studied the movement around the house, watched carefully when his touter went for his so-called information, noted who talked to whom, and perfected his plan.

When he returned a couple nights later, his touter was nearly delirious with excitement. Another night of big commissions from the house off the money of the stupid gringo. Bill, who was very involved in community fund-raising events in Cabo and who had durable, lasting friendships with the local federales (Mexico's federal police), brought four of them along in case he had a collection problem. Then, along with two other accomplices, he brought a new order to the chaotic world of cock fighting. Bill would place his bet, a sizeable one that would assure a fix in the opposite direction. Then, at the last possible moment, once certain that the chicken destined for chicken heaven had been fixed, the accomplices loaded a huge bet on the other side. This worked three times, then Bill calculated they would now adjust. He was right. So this time, the accomplices placed smaller bets and Bill, seemingly in deliberation, at the last moment, made a very large bet on the other chicken! Too late for the operators. They had already hit the chicken of the accomplices, and Bill had another touchdown! That was all it took. The score was large. Bill's friends, the federales, spent the night with the cock fight operator in his hotel room and the next morning accompanied him to the bank where, after a great deal of complaining and squirming, many, many thousands of pesos were handed over to the police. I called it the agricultural version of *The Sting*.

It wasn't too many months later that Bill sold Fleet Tortuga and left Mexico to become Vice President in charge of marketing at Caesar's Palace, Las Vegas. A few years later, Caesar's was sold and, with new management coming in, Bill became the commissioner of the Unlimited Division of the American Powerboat Association, overseeing the same sport I have been voicing on radio (and, this year, television) for the past 37 years.

Bill soon married Georgiann while in Hawaii for the national championship race in Pearl Harbor. Wanting this wedding to be the very best for two good friends, I contacted my dear old friend, Don Ho, whom I now owe, and big time, for so many favors. He came over to the Outrigger Hotel where the wedding was being held in the courtyard next to the water and provided the music, including singing the *Hawaiian Wedding Song* as the couple said "I do."

Doner currently does consulting for the National Football League and also with the group selling luxury boxes and suites at Churchill Downs. We still talk frequently, and he agreed a few pages of this book must be dedicated to his long-time associate whom I became acquainted with through Bill, one Father Duffy.

Ventura Highway

America, 1974

DUFFY WAS RAISED THE ONLY BOY in a family with ten sisters. Father Duffy was defrocked! Not because of the sins we read of these days, but rather, because he liked to party. Although, as of this writing, he has been dry for several years, Duffy formerly drank a bit and, if I ever write another book, I will tell many Father Duffy stories. But this book is primarily about rock-'n'-roll music and radio, so I will limit my Duffy tales to one.

Father Duffy was married and living in Ventura, north of Los Angeles. Over the years, he had accumulated powerful friends, being one of the most charming and lovable men on earth. Ronald or Nancy Reagan, numerous California politicians, movie stars and sports figures would pick up the phone if Duffy called. He had worked as a publicist for Caroll Shelby when Shelby was running the Grand Prix Circuit across Europe for Ford Motor Company. Duffy had accompanied Doner to Seattle when Bill operated and owned the car race track there, but now was living back in California.

Father Duffy was charged not only with drunk driving, but with assault on officers of the law and assorted other violations. County of Orange, State of California, was upset and wanted Duffy punished to the fullest extent of the law. This trial was presided over by a lady judge. Duffy requested and was granted a jury trial. Here is the story the prosecution told the jury.

Duffy was apprehended on Christmas Eve, about 10 in the evening, driving on the median that separated the north/south bound lanes of Interstate 5 just north of Costa Mesa. Sworn testimony held that he was driving at a speed of approximately 20 miles an hour and weaving all over the median. The officer stated that after the stop, while he was trying to remove Duffy from his car, Duffy pitched the contents of a glass he was holding at the officer. The liquid, the officer testified, which soaked his shirt, smelled like gin. The officer further testified that Duffy resisted attempts to place him in the rear of his patrol car, and there on the grass next to the freeway, a wrestling match ensued.

Further testimony was provided by the booking officer at the police station, a young lady who told the jurors Duffy asked her several obscene questions and also offered to participate with her in what is sometimes called "the love act" on the police department counter. She went on to testify that Father Duffy had, in addition, picked up a bicycle, leaning against the wall, which had been impounded and thrown it through a police department window.

The officer who administered the Breathalyzer test could not verify the content of alcohol Duffy was transporting in his body because, while the officer was attempting to administering the test, Duffy jerked the breath-capturing balloon from the device, then picked up the machine and threw it against the wall, rendering it useless. With this all on the record, the county made way for the defense. Duffy's defense was unique.

Character witnesses by the dozens appeared. All stated what a wonderful person was Father Duffy. Sports stars, retired judges, television personalities, all called Duffy kind, loving, polite, caring, generous, nearly God-like. There was important and interesting testimony by an individual who freely stated he was a heavy drinker and a regular customer at the bar in Costa Mesa where Duffy was said to have spent the evening. He was very credible, with a bulbous nose and blotchy red face. He was introduced as an expert on Costa Mesa bars, and he kept eye contact with the jury as he told how Duffy might have been the victim of circumstances beyond his control. He went on to describe how, at this particular bar, on special occasions like Christmas Eve, the bartenders would often pour a drink they called *The Triple*, in which the unsuspecting celebrant might think they had ordered a single, only to be served three times that amount of alcohol. If repeated several times, Triples had significant consequences.

There was testimony from the Goodyear Tire Company, provided by their racing representative. It was a rather vague—but possibly relevant revelation—that under certain circumstances, if running at reduced pressure, the new steel-belted radial tires they were building showed tendencies capable of causing a car to swerve. Allen Green, a Chevrolet dealer from Seattle for whom Duffy briefly worked, flew down to testify. He stated that Father Duffy was reliable, warm, gentle, and incapable of anger, much less violence. At this point, the Judge stepped a tad over the line of judicial conduct, interrupted Green's testimony and asked, "Mr. Green, now this is just fine that Mr. Duffy is kind, gentle and all that, but isn't that only when he's sober? Isn't it a fact that he can go totally out of control and become almost animal-like when drinking? Whereupon, Alan Green brought the house down by turning to the judge and asking, "Duffy drinks?"

There is an important element in the American legal system: A defendant can choose to speak or not to speak in his own defense. Duffy chose to speak and did great harm to the prosecution's case. This was a jury trial, and Father Duffy's simple, childlike charm is more than any prosecutor should be forced to deal with. Finally, Duffy took the stand and told a most moving story.

He testified how his family had recently moved from the Seattle area back to California so he could be near his many friends. How, this past Christmas Eve, he had driven all the way from his home in Ventura south to Costa Mesa so he could wish his many friends there Merry Christmas. That is how he ended up in a bar in Costa Mesa, and it was within the realm of possibility he might have accidentally encountered one or two of those Triples, as previously testified. But even if he did, he assured the jury, they had no discernible impact upon him. He continued that he was heading home, driving up the freeway, when he sensed the weaving of his car and knew that behavior meant a tire problem. This being Christmas Eve, and knowing that his family was waiting by the tree for him (I think they were actually up in Seattle at the time), he was frustrated. But he certainly hadn't wanted to be the cause of an accident on Christmas Eve. And so, he elected to drive in the median.

He went on to describe the flashing blue lights and the arrest. The liquor thrown on the officer. A misunderstanding. The glass had been handed to him as he had said good-bye to friends when leaving the bar. He was just holding it so it wouldn't spill. The officer tried to pull him from the car, and somehow it had slipped out of his hand. He was very sorry it had dampened the officer's uniform. And his behavior at the police station? Again, a big misunderstanding. He was actually telling the clerk how sorry he was she wasn't home in bed with her husband on Christmas Eve and how he wished he were in bed with his wife. Somehow, she had totally misinterpreted his kind Christmas thoughts.

Now, he said, what with all the confusion and everyone mistaking his every gesture, he became very frustrated. He was suddenly realizing that he, Father Duffy, was going to be in jail for Christmas. At that point, he said he did what most people would probably do. He vented. He didn't hurt anyone, he would never do that, and he would gladly pay for the window and the Breathalyzer machine. Besides, they hadn't needed it for him anyway because he was totally sober. He apologized for any hurt feelings. He deeply regretted it if he had caused any of the officers to have to work late that night. He closed by saying he was going to buy the even-newer steel-belted radial tires for his car because they were safer and, above all, safety on the highway was paramount to him.

The jury was out for 20 minutes and returned. Upon reading their verdict, the judge broke the pencil she was holding in two pieces, threw them into the air and stomped back to her chambers.

The verdict? Father Duffy, innocent of all charges.

12 – *Beginnings*
Chicago Transit Authority, 1971

OCK CONCERTS STARTED shortly after rock-'n'-roll first emerged. With origins in the South, the music took root primarily on the East Coast, where disc jockeys like Alan Freed built careers around it. Black performers recorded many of rock's earliest songs on small independent labels. Soon, white performers began duplicating their songs for mainline labels. In the beginning, though, rock was primarily an East Coast/black artist phenomenon.

A big national breakthrough came in 1955 when the Oscar-nominated movie *Blackboard Jungle* featured the music of Bill Haley and His Comets. Ruth Brown, the Penguins, Fats Domino and other artists added their names to a growing list of rock talents. Touring with acts like these, Freed and others began renting theaters and small auditoriums where they presented as many as 10 recording artists on the same bill. New York, Philadelphia, Boston, Cleveland—these cities and others hosted rock shows. Those shows were not yet a significant force, save in the wrong direction. Small riots marked performances in several cities, reinforcing the notion held by elders that rock-'n'-roll was dangerous, demented and detrimental to America's youth.

By 1957, some of these rock variety shows went out on tour, with mediocre results. They played mostly in small theaters, and many cities lacked full time rock-'n'-roll radio stations where promoters could advertise to a targeted audience. Instead, they plastered posters around town and ran small newspaper ads as their only advertising. The shows rarely delivered a deep musical experience. Their attraction was more the novelty of seeing the musicians in person and hearing them do two or three of their songs. The acts found these tours torturous, traveling the country jammed into a couple of chartered buses. Conditions were especially difficult throughout the South, where black performers were about as welcome as boll weevils.

Not even Colonel Tom Parker's huge success taking Elvis on the road in 1957 could trigger a substantial movement in the direction of a cohesive rock concert industry. Two years later, Ricky Nelson mounted a relatively successful national tour, but much of that success was due to his stature as a weekly television fixture on the *Ozzie and Harriet Show*. A pair of Philadelphia singers—two-hit wonder Fabian Forte (*Turn Me Loose* and *Like a Tiger*) and Frankie Avalon, both beneficiaries of extensive exposure on *American Bandstand*—went on the road that same year, but in some places selling their tickets was like pulling teeth. The Kingston Trio, with multiple hits, went on the road about this same time, but they didn't fall into the rock-'n'-roll category of things, as they primarily drew customers college age and up. Most rock acts contented themselves with playing at dances—when they could find the work. State fairs had not yet dreamed of hiring rock acts. Allowing evil rock-'n'-rollers on the same grounds as God's chickens and cows was apparently unthinkable.

I had now operated successful rock dances for four years. Then, in 1962, I agreed to help promote a concert we called the *World's Fair Opening Twist Party* at the old Orpheum Theater as part of the opening of the World's Fair. Zollie Volchok and Jack Engerman owned Northwest Releasing, an old-line promotion firm mostly handling mainline performers and touring Broadway shows. An out-of-town promoter contacted Zollie with the idea. He had purchased several dates for Chubby Checker and a new young singer from Philadelphia, Dee Dee Sharp (*Mashed Potato Time*), who, like Chubby, recorded on the Cameo label. The Dovells (*Bristol Stomp*), another Cameo-Parkway act, and Joey Dee and the Starliters, who had a big hit titled *Peppermint Twist* and were a hot new group from New York, were also part of the package. Zollie agreed to underwrite the event and brought me in to promote and handle the show. Together we presented two shows a day the weekend the Fair opened.

The Orpheum Theater once stood where the tall towers of the Washington Plaza Hotel now stand. In those two days in 1962, that grand, ornate old building saw more excitement than it ever saw again in its lifetime. Every show was a sellout or near, partly because of the stars, partly because of the synergy of the World's Fair opening the same weekend.

My next step in the field of live rock-'n'-roll entertainment was now clear to me. Also clear was the fact that rock concerts were risky business. About this same time, representatives for a troupe on tour in Japan contacted me, wanting to book them in Seattle upon their return to the States. The headline act was Del Shannon, whose most famous song was *Runaway*, along with an assortment of marginally successful rock acts. Eight performers in all, all of whose records had enjoyed some airplay. Three weeks out, I stuck my toe in the water, rented a theater, printed some tickets and started advertising. One week later, I pulled the plug. We'd sold 10 tickets, and the ticket agency said sales were starting to slow down. Slow down! What could be slower than an average of 1.25 tickets a day?

That aborted attempt taught me a lesson I never forgot and caused me to create and adopt a slogan, one I repeated often to partners and associates in the years to come. Sometimes it was heeded, sometimes not. Its validity, however, was never proven weak. The slogan : *A show with many small acts doesn't add up to a big show. It's still just a show with many small acts.* Promoting concerts looked appealing at first glance, but the opportunity to lose a great deal of money was there, too, if you weren't careful.

In late winter/early spring 1963, Dick Curtis and I cautiously expanded our horizons and announced the *1963 Seattle Spring Spectacular.* We scheduled our initial concert effort for the Seattle Opera House, a facility that sat only 3,200 —no workable economics there. We decided to run three shows in a single day, bringing total capacity up to nearly 10,000.

It just might work! I speculated. *Maybe it's time to bring the rock concert business into the present. Make it classy, prestigious, conversation-provoking. Put the ushers in tuxedos. Give the tickets an upscale price. Back the performers with a full orchestra instead of the usual three or four musicians. Let's put together a show the fans will never forget! If we do it right, they'll come back for our shows again and again. But it all starts with the first one!*

We brought to town April Stevens and Nino Tempo, whose current smash record was *Deep Purple*, and George McCurn, who had a West Coast hit with *I'm Just a Country Boy*. We added Mel Carter (*Hold Me, Thrill Me, Kiss Me*) and, to close the show, the Four Seasons. We included Northwest bands as warm-up acts, wanting to support local efforts and give them a chance to share the stage with the biggies. We sold out. Plain and simple, we sold out! I floated on cloud nine for days, not because we grossed $30,000, which paid the bills with a little left over, but because Dick and I had tried something totally different —rock-'n'-roll with a mass of class—and it worked!

That was the first of a string of concerts for us in the Opera House, and they all sold out. The Beach Boys headlined our next show, and Roy Orbison the one after that. Over the span of our Opera House run, we marched across the stage Stevie Wonder, Dee Dee Sharp, Freddie Cannon, Johnny Rivers, Trini Lopez, Bobby Vee, Jerry Lee Lewis, the Cascades, Jan & Dean, Bobby Vinton (*Blue Velvet*), Ray Stevens (*Ahab the Arab*), Terry Stafford (*Suspicion*), Jimmy Gilmer and the Fireballs (*Sugar Shack*), H. B. Barnum (*Lost Love*), Jackie DeShannon (*Needles & Pins*), Dorsey Burnette (*Tall Oak Tree*), Bobby Bare (*Abilene*) and oh so many more acts. All this did nice things for our pocketbook, for my radio station and for my on-air program. I emceed all the shows, brought my fellow deejays on stage for introductions and, in general, turned the concerts into pep rallies for KJR. The setup was as close to perfection as anything could be. Even more significant, rock-'n'-roll concerts were here to stay.

Those Opera House shows were great fun for everyone involved. We put the acts up at the Edgewater on the Seattle waterfront, and the hotel became the setting for a regular rock-'n'-roll convention. Local musicians came down to "hang" and were never disappointed. They might find 15-year-old Stevie Wonder dining in the coffee shop, or Glenn Campbell—at that time a Beach Boy playing Brian Wilson's role on stage—relaxing in the lounge. Dennis and Carl Wilson, Bruce Johnston, Mike Love, Roy Orbison, Johnny Rivers, the late Bobby Hatfield and Bill Medley (the Righteous Brothers)—they all were there. Not until the Beatles came to town and stayed at the Edgewater, and the surrounding publicity blew our cover, did the general public discover where we sequestered visiting stars. After that, the Edgewater wasn't nearly as secure and private for those wonderful and informal music business get-togethers. Nevertheless, they continued for years with an ever-changing cast of characters. Later it was Led Zeppelin and the Who and the Rolling Stones instead of Bobby Vee and Bobby Vinton and Bobby Goldsboro.

How did we manage to get that many acts on and off the stage in one show? We began by limiting each act to maybe four or five songs or at least to their hits. Songs back then were shorter and tighter, usually less than three minutes long. Even that was not enough to fit it all in, so we employed a "two band

Stars shine in Seattle: middle left: April Stevens, O'Day & Nino Tempo; middle right: 14-year-old Stevie Wonder & O'Day backstage at the Seattle Opera House; bottom left: The Righteous Brothers at the Edgewater Hotel; bottom right: Johnny Rivers

setup," taking advantage of the Opera House's extensive staging capabilities. While one band played at the front of the stage, a second band's equipment was set up at the rear of the stage. When they finished and the curtain closed, a crew of 10 worked feverishly behind the curtain removing one set of equipment and pushing forward another, while I entertained the audience on the other side of the curtain with humor and shtick. Three minutes later, the next band was ready to go. When we used the orchestra, they sat in the orchestra pit, and no changeover time was needed for them. It also helped that bands in 1963 had nowhere near the amount of sophisticated, massive equipment seen at concerts today. Another factor worked in our favor: the Opera House's excellent concert hall acoustics.

Please Please Me

The Beatles, 1963

ON THE GROUNDS OF THE SEATTLE CENTER stood a spacious structure built to house the "World of Tomorrow" Exhibit, a massive futuristic display that was part of the 1962 Seattle World's Fair. The city long dreamed of building a large arena to house NBA basketball, NHL hockey, home shows, car shows, revivals—meeting the demands of affluent people wanting to get out and go do things. When the Fair closed, a major renovation was undertaken, converting the building into a 15,000 seat arena. This conversion took place while we were operating our concerts in the nearby Opera House. Upon its completion, along came the Beatles.

The timing was perfect. Here was a brand new building we hoped to use for our shows. But to successfully move our concerts from the sophisticated confines of the Opera House to so vast a facility as the Coliseum, there needed to be a weaning process. Who better than the Beatles to initiate it? Several questions needed answers first, and those answers weren't readily apparent. We saw Elvis fill small ball parks and stadiums eight years earlier. The Beatles seemed the equivalent of Elvis, but Elvis didn't open the door to ballpark-type concert events. His concert was a one time deal. Could the Beatles' success be a portend of new and bigger shows in new and bigger buildings?

The Beatles sold out everywhere they appeared, and several things became obvious: (1) We could raise our prices; (2) A coliseum-type building was acceptable, and the energy of the larger crowd became a significant part of the show; and (3) Something had to be done about sound systems. The

Seattle audience heard hardly a single note the Beatles played because of all the screaming. What's more, even without the screaming, the opening acts (the Righteous Brothers, the Exciters, Jackie DeShannon and others) had trouble making themselves heard in the giant building. Delivering enjoyable music proved impossible. If big buildings like the Seattle Center Coliseum were going to work as concert venues, something had to be done about the sound systems they used.

Nothing readily available on the market offered an acceptable solution. Sound engineers for different companies drew up all sorts of mathematical formulas proving their equipment was adequate, but all their math went out the window once reality set in. The reality was, rock-'n'-roll was best presented at far greater volume levels than any music before it. Look at the behavior of people listening to rock on their radios. They want loud. Another factor was the guitar, the basic tool of rock-'n'-roll, which needed power and amplification. Drums, keyboards and other instruments also demanded boosting. Added to that, how could you get the singers' vocals to exceed that volume? Unless you managed that, *they* wouldn't be heard.

Following the Beatles, we brought the Beach Boys with a great supporting cast into the new Coliseum. Again, even minus the intense screaming inspired by the Beatles, the sound was miserable. I told the city's sound engineer to join me at the show and took him to the back rows of the building to prove to him that his system was entirely inadequate. His answer was about what I expected: "Well, they're playing their instruments too loud!" That's the equivalent of saying, "We couldn't show John Wayne's head in the film, only his body, because he's too tall!" Something had to be done, and done quickly, if these events were to grow in stature and quality, let alone endure.

Bridge Over Troubled Water
Simon & Garfunkel, 1970; Aretha Franklin, 1971

WHEN FIRST ELVIS, AND THEN THE BEATLES, filled stadiums and auditoriums with screaming, swooning fans, those events were not quality music presentations. They weren't really musical presentations of any description; they were more public appearances than concerts—chances to see superstars in person, often for the first time. Maybe for the only time.

If a person went to hear the music, they were disappointed, and not just because of the screaming of the girls in attendance. The performers would barely have been heard even without the screaming. Theoretically, the ball-parks, stadiums and big auditoriums were carefully engineered for pleasing sound, but there was a big difference between what looked good on paper and what worked in reality, especially with rock-'n'-roll.

Sound engineering is little different today. Although sound system problems were basically solved 30 years ago by those of us in the rock music business, many elite sound engineers still refuse to accept obvious truths. They go on trying to reinvent the wheel, as though the level of excellence achieved in rock-'n'-roll and concerts in general somehow isn't valid.

For example, a few years ago Husky Stadium at Seattle's University of Washington was re-engineered for sound at staggering expense and in good faith, courtesy of Seattle Seahawks owner Paul Allen. It was a thank-you gesture by Allen, whose team used the university's facilities while waiting for their new stadium to be finished. Those well-paid sound engineers made a mess of what was already a serviceable system by hanging multiple small speaker boxes from the stadium roof. These strategically placed boxes replaced the existing battery of giant speakers installed within the end zone scoreboard which had pleasantly served fans for years. The results are pathetic! When the sound is turned up to a comfortable listening level, it becomes distorted and the speakers are overdriven.

Last season, from my top-priced seats directly beneath one speaker installation, I heard about half of what I should have heard. Stubborn engineering is all it is.

Stadium speakers must pack enough punch to overcome ambient noise, wind, cheering crowds and that noisy fan sitting behind you. Speaking of wind, with outdoor systems, wind can have a dramatic effect, effortlessly moving sound away from intended listeners. The only worthy opponent for this natural phenomenon is brute force. Nonetheless, sound engineers continue to draw you indecipherable diagrams, print up computerized models and get out their calculators, all to prove to you that their numbers and fancy systems work. Except, in the real world, they don't! Good sound in outdoor stadiums is possible only when pure intentional sound is transmitted to giant speakers in giant boxes and fed from giant amplifiers with thousands of watts of power. The struggle of real versus theoretical sound engineering seen today was also part of the music scene in the late '60s. It was a problem that stunted the growth of the rock-'n'-roll concert business.

In the '60s, the strongest speakers were the University horns, a design dating from the '30s. Manufactured by University Electronics, those horns can still be seen in old photos of auditoriums, stadiums and grandstands at fairgrounds, racetracks, auctions and political conventions. They were even mounted on trucks and driven through neighborhoods and down highways with someone using a microphone to promote one or another candidate or event. Made laughable by today's noise abatement ordinances, this promotion technique was once pure Americana.

Those durable, all-weather speakers looked like giant trumpets or trombones. Inside their metal bell (about four feet long and three feet across at the mouth) was mounted a speaker. Incapable of handling bass notes, these sound blasters had a crisp, shrill sound that carried for miles in one direction.

Some auditoriums in the '60s were equipped with University horns. Prone to feedback, the horns could not be pointed at the front rows lest the microphones on stage picked up the transmission from the speaker and began retransmitting it in that familiar feedback squeal we've all heard. New engineering replaced "the Horn," and soon you saw auditoriums hanging two or three small speaker boxes over the stage instead. These speakers could barely be heard by people sitting in the rear of an auditorium and were really only suitable for speeches, not music.

Don't think that I'm criticizing the grand old University Horn! On the contrary, I don't know what the early days of rock-'n'-roll would have been like without them. From Conway Twitty to Bobby Vee, from Roy Orbison to the Wailers, rockers in the early '60s traveled with U-Haul trailers packed with guitar amplifiers, drum sets, sometimes a Hammond organ and, of course, a couple of those big University horns with tripod stands for mounting. Crowds heard the drums acoustically, the guitar amps spoke for themselves and pianos, if used, had placed near their open lids a microphone that fed into the Universities along with all the vocals. It worked for roller rinks and other dance venues, but not for concerts.

Crude by today's standards, back in the '60s that setup was the best we had. Until rock-'n'-roll came along, music was not nearly as beat and bass oriented, so speaker systems that lent themselves primarily to high notes were acceptable. But with rock-'n'-roll 's drums and big bass beat, and the frequencies required for rock vocals, traditional systems were woefully inadequate.

With screeching systems that served only narrow bands of sound to the audience, most in attendance were happy with the music at rock concerts, not understanding that it could be so much better. We all thought the typewriter was just great — until we sampled the word processor. We thought the rubber eraser was satisfactory — until someone handed us a bottle of White Out. And we all thought television in black and white was amazing until we saw TV in color. Those innovations added greatly to the pleasure of writing and viewing — and it was the same with improvements in sound and rock concerts.

I'd heard clean, powerful sound in recording studios employing new equipment and knew how wondrous sound can be. I knew that if we found a way to overpower the audiences with a crisp, full-spectrum system of unlimited power, we'd be able to sell many times the number of concert seats we'd sold before.

As we moved forward, scheduling frequent concerts at the Coliseum, I was deeply troubled by the handicaps of the speaker systems installed there and disappointed for both the audience *and* the performers. Audiences knew nothing better, and performers, having struggled with crude systems in city after city and building after building, *expected* nothing better. It was a problem we had to solve. If and when we did, the emotional impact of our shows would be magnified greatly.

We needed to find a way to produce live performances that equaled the musical quality and emotional experience of sitting in front of a stereo. We knew it had to be done. But how? We gave up talking to engineers, who always offered the same mumbo-jumbo. The answer, instead, came from an unexpected source.

Danke Schöen

Wayne Newton, 1963

THE UNDISPUTED CAPITAL of the entertainment business in the '60s was that little oasis in Nevada, Las Vegas. As showrooms there increased in size and hotel casinos flourished, more and more talent was needed to meet the demand for first-class entertainment — mainly musical entertainment. Entertainers began receiving dramatic increases in pay as competition for first rate talent increased. Along with all this came demands for better and better sound to support the quality music experience the hotel/casinos were striving to present. In Las Vegas, they wouldn't settle for second best.

Showrooms struggled to duplicate exactly the sound that came from your radio and record player at home. How ironic, since today, fancy, high-priced "surround sound" music systems struggle to duplicate the sound of performers in concert!

When Frank Sinatra, Sammy Davis Jr. or Paul Anka appeared on stage at the Sands Hotel, customers were treated to sound like they'd never heard before from live entertainers. The sound systems used by the Sands and others weren't yet of sufficient horsepower to work in truly large auditoriums, but tremendous strides in quality had been made.

Much of what Vegas did speaker-wise, they learned from movie theaters, which for some time had employed what they called the *Voice of the Theater* system. While movie theater audiences are generally hushed, and movie houses are tiny by coliseum standards, the systems built by the engineers at Altec were a sizeable improvement over previous sound systems. Altec systems faithfully reproduced music—and at great volume. Basically, they were giant heavy boxes, each one containing a 15-inch speaker for lower frequencies and a tweeter horn for high notes.

I employed a similar approach in my early rock-'n'-roll dance days when I hand-built two heavy cabinets and mounted a 15-inch JBL speaker in each. Jerry Lee Lewis, Roy Orbison and others commented it was one of the best speaker systems they ever encountered.

I also used amplifiers with "equalization," which allowed various frequencies, like bass and treble, to be lowered or raised. This enabled me to cancel out those frequencies specifically causing feedback. I could thus safely crank up the volume. These elements today are absolutes—back then, they were breakthroughs!

Go Where You Wanna Go
The Mamas and the Papas, 1966

OUT OF DESPERATION, WE CAME UP WITH a unique formula, more physical than scientific, that somewhat solved these annoying sound problems. The formula? If you can't bring the sound to the audience, bring the audience to the sound! We decided to move the performing stage to the center of big arenas, creating the opportunity to hang speakers over the stage pointed in all directions and at the foot of the stage. This shortened the distance to the ticket buyers' ears and was nearer the sound system's capabilities.

Some buildings already had the cables and pulleys needed for hanging large clusters of speakers. They were installed for ice shows as well as for NBA basketball games. This setup actually cut in half the distance sound needed to travel to reach the back rows and tended to overcome the deficiencies that accompanied the current state of the art! People before us had used center stages; we didn't invent them. Dick Clark, for instance, ran a tour back east with some of his Bandstand acts and put the stage in the middle. For the most part, though, those early center stages caused more problems than they solved.

The basic problem with a center stage was that half of the arena was *behind* the stage, and bands were neither prepared for nor accustomed to playing to crowds on all four sides. Everything about their routines, their setup, their shows themselves called for them to play to their front. To solve this problem, we created the first *revolving* center stage. Six feet in the air, riding on eight automobile tires hidden beneath, this 30-foot-diameter monster was powered by electric motors that reversed direction after two complete turns to avoid tangling the power and sound cords. The stage was geared to make a complete revolution every 60 seconds; after two cycles it reversed and went back the other way.

One happy consequence of using a revolving center stage was it gave us many more good seats to sell. It was simple: The back row now sat 50 percent closer to the stage and the stars, the front row offered twice as many premium seats and the quality of sound was greatly improved. If revolving stages could talk, what stories our first one could tell. But, since it was sent to stage heaven many years ago, let me relate some of the history it otherwise might have shared, starting with the first major concert appearance for the Mamas and the Papas.

They had already performed on television and in clubs and small auditoriums, but they were still quite new. Their hit, *California Dreamin'* was in the Top 10, and somehow I convinced their manager, the great Lou Adler, that it was time for them to hit a big venue.

So a young and beautiful Michelle, and a fun and very rotund Mama Cass, along with John and Denny, came to Seattle for the stage's inaugural. After the most stunning of introductions by me, and an awe-inspiring reception by the packed house, and only two songs into their set, Mama Cass ran off the stage and made it halfway down the stairs before she threw up! That's right! Right in front of the good folks in the front row, she heaved.

Michelle looked down and back as the stage rotated away and said, "Come on, Cass, we can't make it without you!" Fortunately, they didn't have to try. Someone handed Cass a handkerchief, and she wiped her face, remounted the stage and finished her first big auditorium concert like the pro she was.

It has been my contention ever since, based on a conversation I had with a very anxious Mama Cass just before she went on stage, that her problems that evening were due to nervousness. To the very end, Cass disagreed. She insisted that her problems were due to the fact that our stage, which she thought was spinning at no less than 40 miles per hour, had made her dizzy!

(I Can't Get No) Satisfaction
The Rolling Stones, 1965

THE AUDIENCE, AT LEAST, ENTHUSIASTICALLY RECEIVED our new stage on its first go-around. On its second spin, it carried a musical cargo without equal: Paul Revere & the Raiders, the Wailers, the Sonics, Ian Whitcomb, Patty Labelle & the Bluebelles and starring—yes, all of this and starring Mick Jagger and the Rolling Stones! It was just after Thanksgiving, 1966, and the Stones were in the middle of their fourth North American tour when they arrived in Seattle. I was worried that Jagger and the group might not take well to a 360 degree stage that went around in circles.

Only one thing about the stage bothered Mick, and he solved it in typical Mick Jagger fashion. After rehearsal, he told us that, in one song he usually grabbed his balls for a few seconds, and the girls really loved it. Looking at the stage as it revolved around, Jagger said, "My God, I think I'd better hang onto me balls for the whole circle. I don't want to disappoint anyone!"

Groovin'
The Young Rascals, 1967

OUR REVOLVING STAGE WAS PORTABLE. We could disassemble it, pack it in a truck and take it to Vancouver, Portland, Spokane or wherever. After a few concerts, Rex Beatty, supervisor of the Seattle Coliseum's stagehands, pointed out that our stage was bulky and hard to assemble and could be improved. Thus came revolving stage number two, not quite as tall as number one and easier for performers to access. It ran on smaller airplane tires and was slightly larger in circumference. The design took 60 percent less time to assemble and disassemble, saving us a great deal in labor costs. Like Revolver Number One, it had its share of adventures.

The Young Rascals, a red-hot American group, had enjoyed a string of big hits (*Groovin'*, *How Can I Be Sure*, *Good Lovin'* and others) and we were looking forward to hosting their first tour of the Northwest. Seattle, Vancouver and Portland were scheduled. We planned to use the revolving center stage, and all seats were reserved. The shows were nearing sellouts when I received a call from the agency handling the Rascals. Although it was in the contract, they had omitted telling the group that they were going to be playing on this new mobile center stage.

Have you ever noticed how good news travels slow and the facts remain unchanged while bad news, on the other hand, travels fast and the facts rapidly grow more grave? Such was the case when the Rascals learned about the revolving stage. By the time the story of Mama Cass and her embarrassing encounter with our revolving innovation reached the Rascals, it had grown to cataclysmic proportions. They were told that Cass was thrown from the stage by the high-speed centrifugal force it generated! It's a good thing *National Inquirer* and *Star* paid little attention to rock-'n'-roll in those days. If they had, supermarket shoppers would probably have read how poor Cass Elliot was cyclonically launched into outer space!

Sid Bernstein, an artist management genius from New York who later developed New Kids on the Block, managed the Rascals and was a good friend. He and the boys were taking a break at a rented home in the Diamond Head area of Honolulu after a couple of Hawaiian concerts when I learned there was trouble brewing. I immediately reached Sid by phone and tried to straighten out the situation. The Rascals were telling their agency that either we switched to a conventional stage or they wouldn't play the dates. Changing stages was impossible by then because we had sold the tickets based on a center stage configuration.

When it comes to concert seating, levels of expectation are critical. To rearrange 15,000 seats and avoid a riot with disappointed fans was an impossibility. I begged Sid to reconsider, but he said the boys were firm in their position. It was time for a top level overseas diplomatic mission by our company's chief ambassador, me. Getting fellow KJR disc jockey Tom Murphy to cover my show for me for the day, I jumped on the early morning Pan Am flight to Honolulu. With daylight savings time and a three-hour time difference, I arrived in Hawaii at noon. Met at the airport by Tom Moffat, deejay, promoter and longtime friend, I headed out to Diamond Head with him for a face-to-face with the group.

We spent the entire afternoon together, and all went well. I brought pictures from concerts with the Stones, Paul Revere, the Vibrations, the Shangri-las and others. I closed my pitch with a phone call to New York, where a friend at the Allen Klein office (they managed the Stones) confirmed that performing on our stage had been a happy and professional experience for the Stones. The Rascals seemed convinced. They retreated for a brief private meeting, took a vote and made it unanimous: They would come to Seattle after all, as originally scheduled, and perform on the Pat O'Day & Associates revolving stage. Thinking the crisis over, I made my scheduled 6:00 P.M. return flight on Pan Am to Seattle. The cocktails on the plane tasted so good. I had done it again, almost.

Upon my arrival late that night in Seattle, my partner, Terry Bassett, met me at the gate. My first thought was, *How nice of Terry to meet me after my long day—11 hours in the air and a victory!* The look on his face said something else.

Back in Honolulu, no sooner had I climbed into Tom Moffat's car at the Rascals' house and headed for the airport than Felix Cavaliere, organist, lead singer, lead everything for the Rascals, after shaking my hand and saying, "See you in Seattle," jumped on his rented Honda motorcycle, intending to follow us out the driveway and take a spin around the Diamond Head neighborhood. As Felix pulled out behind us, one of the cycle's wheels caught on some loose gravel and sent him skidding into a tree, breaking his arm. Felix would be in a cast for weeks, and only after that could the group begin rehearsing again and return to the road.

We cancelled the shows and refunded all the ticket money. The Rascals paid us back by making the Northwest the first stop on their next tour. The big arenas we usually used weren't available for the makeup concerts, so we put them into smaller buildings in each town and left our revolving center stage at home.

Tiny Bubbles
Don Ho, 1966

THE FINAL NOTE TO MY RASCALS' STORY came some months later with a guy I've been close with for many years, legendary Hawaiian entertainer Don Ho. Don was in Seattle with his Honolulu cast doing a concert with us. As he performed, he was mounted on a riser in the middle of the revolving stage.

Between songs, Don sipped on a scotch, played softly on his organ and visited with the audience. During one of those mellow interludes he looked around at his band and said, "Are any of you frightened?"

The band all shook their heads no.

Don continued, "Do you remember when Felix Cavaliere of the Young Rascals hit that tree out on Diamond Head and broke himself up?"

The band all nodded their heads yes.

"Well," Don continued, "he hit that tree on purpose because that poor little rock-'n'-roller was afraid to come to Seattle and play on this stage. Well, let history show that Don Ho and the Aliis were proud to play on this stage!"

I doubt that there were many in the crowd that night that got Don's joke (the people who listened to Don Ho's *Tiny Bubbles* were seldom the same people who listened to the Rascals' *Good Lovin'*). But my staff certainly thought it was funny.

We invented our revolving stage in an effort to improve sound quality at concerts. With this stage and somewhat improved speakers and amplifiers, we were making progress, but we still had a way to go before our system would be satisfactory. It would require about three more years, and take events like Woodstock, a large investment by Concerts West, efforts by production companies like Clare Brothers from Pennsylvania and Showco from Dallas, and the contributions of rock entertainers like Elton John and Led Zeppelin to pioneer the future of rock-'n'-roll sound.

13 – Joy to the World

Three Dog Night, 1970

ONE OF THE ALL-TIME GREAT rock-'n'-roll bands if judged by their live concert performances was Three Dog Night. The Dog, with Danny Hutton, Cory Wells and Chuck Negron sharing the lead, filled the stage with excitement, enthusiasm and great music. The three top Dogs showcased contrasting styles, trading lead vocals and crafting tight harmonies on a score of hit records: *One* and *Joy to the World* [Negron], *Try a Little Tenderness* and *Mama Told Me (Not To Come)* [Wells], *Black and White* and *Never Been to Spain* [Hutton] and many others. Not only were they great singers, musicians and performers, they were constant fun to be with out on the road. They brought joy to my world. No book I wrote about concert tours would be complete without some stories recounting my adventures with the Dog. So, here goes!

One

Three Dog Night, 1969

THERE'S AN EXPRESSION ORIGINATING FROM the Australian Outback that describes sleeping outdoors in the extreme cold. Aborigines used their dingoes for comfort and warmth, and an exceptionally frigid evening called for the companionship of not one, not two, but *three* canine friends. Thus, they called such an evening a *three dog night!* This was the name chosen by Danny Hutton, Cory Wells and Chuck Negron for the trio they formed in LA in 1968.

Backed by drummer Floyd Sneed, keyboardist Jimmy Greenspoon, guitarist Mike Allsup and bass guitarist Joe Schermie, the group catapulted to stunning popularity in the early '70s, running off a string of 21 hit records over a brilliant six year stretch. Stable mates with John Kay and Steppenwolf under the management of Burt Jacobs and Reb Foster of Los Angeles, they chose Concerts West to handle their appearances.

The two camps married with a simple handshake, begetting a long, spectacular and happy relationship. At Concerts West, we offered a simple-but-oh-so-attractive formula to our performers. We advanced the money needed for tours and arranged all the details. This variously included everything from trucks and equipment to lights and sound systems, airplanes and limousines, hotels and food and security. In addition, our staff handled every aspect of the shows themselves. This comprised renting auditoriums, printing the tickets, advertising events and much more. In short, by plighting their troth to Concerts West, all a group needed to do was show up at the appointed hour at a nearby airport and board the plane.

All proceeds from the concerts went to our office in Bellevue, Washington. After a tour ended, income and expenses were tallied, every bill paid and the remaining profits split. Splits varied from act to act, but generally 80 to 90 percent of the profits went to the performers, the balance to Concerts West.

It seems so simple when you look back on it today, but at that time, this approach was revolutionary. Jimi Hendrix, Glen Campbell, and Three Dog Night embraced our formula early; before long, Elvis, Led Zeppelin, Chicago, Creedence Clearwater and the Moody Blues signed up, too. With signature acts like these for clients, we found ourselves besieged by other performers anxious to jump on the Concerts West bandwagon. As our business burgeoned, we began to feel the strain of a pledge we made to these stars who placed full confidence in us. We promised to have one of the three principals of our company present at every performance. Those original principals were Terry Basset, Tom Hulett and me.

Initially, by creatively juggling schedules we were able to keep that promise. When we were handling shows for Elvis, Jimi Hendrix, Led Zeppelin, the Moody Blues and a few others, their tours usually ran for a period of 30 to 45 days and, with creative staggering, it could be done. Three Dog Night was an exception: They chose to avoid long tours with many venues and performed only on weekends, returning to their LA-area homes on Sunday night after their last show. This often created scheduling conflicts with our other tours. To deal with this challenge, I drew the Three Dog Night assignment.

One problem loomed—I served as general manager of two Seattle radio stations, and that required my presence all through the week. As a result, my life came to personify 24/7 decades before the term became popular. I wasn't a workaholic; I was simply a healthy young man, highly motivated, who found his relaxation from the satisfaction of doing a good job on all fronts. When called, I could goof off with the best! A typical week found me returning to Seattle on the red-eye from some East Coast or Midwest city early Monday morning. My routine for the week proceeded something like this: Home for a quick shower and some time with my sons before they left for school. Then off to my office for a few days of radio. They were long, intense days because my work weeks were abbreviated by my need to depart for weekend concerts by early Friday morning at the latest. The one saving grace was that the Dog only wanted to work three weekends a month. That left me one free weekend every lunar cycle for taking my family skiing, boating or off to pursue whatever activity they found fun.

On a typical weekend, I'd catch the Thursday midnight United flight out of Seattle to Chicago and arrive at O'Hare, weather permitting, in time to jump on a connecting flight to whatever East Coast, Midwest or Southern city I was supposed to be at that week. (Thankfully, I fall asleep instantly and comfortably on planes, so sleeping in a real bed on Thursday night was unnecessary.)

In those days—the early '70s—concerts such as Three Dog Night's had not yet reached the level of complexity that later emerged in the industry. The sound systems, the mixing boards, the guitar amplifiers, the rudimentary lighting and everything else—all were designed to fit into the luggage compartments of most passenger planes (except for the DC-9, whose cargo doors weren't big enough). Accordingly, road crews made arrangements well ahead of time, reserving sufficient space so they could travel on scheduled flights with all their gear on board with them. The day was still in the future when I would have assistants to help me once I arrived in a city for a show. In my time with the Dog, yours truly mostly flew solo.

Home office staff made my hotel and car reservations and left everything else to me, and I was busier than a one-legged man in a butt-kicking contest once I stepped off the plane. Arriving at my destination around noon, I'd dash to the rental car counter, grab a vehicle, race to the hotel (speeding tickets I considered one of the costs of doing business), check in, rush to my room, throw my bags on the bed and jump on the phone. (Remember, this was back in the pre-cell phone days, and the hotel room phone was critical to my mission's success.)

Always first, I called the ticket office for the latest tally on sales. If any seats remained, I made hurried trips to local radio stations to update commercials with some tried-and-true copy which invariably produced a sellout by show time. (I often recorded the new commercials at the stations myself to make sure they conveyed the required sense of urgency.) Then it was on to the auditorium to meet the building manager and staff, inspect the staging and dressing rooms and introduce myself to the stagehands. The latter task usually included a conversation with the union shop steward, who carried on at length about what his members would and would not do. Every shop steward in every city felt compelled to establish firmly that *he*, not I, held total control. The song they sang rarely varied: "By God, this here's a union hall and my men ain't gonna take shit from no one!…By God, they can shut you down in a heartbeat if anyone shits on 'em!…By God, everything'll be just fine so long's you understand that!…By God, if this thing runs into overtime [which meant double-time pay] it sure won't be our fault!…No, by God, it'll be your fault 'cuz all my men are professionals, they ain't no sand baggers!…" Blah, blah, blah!

The auditorium's box office generally doubled as the accounting office where I reviewed projected expenses for the evening. Some costs were deducted from the cashier's check I received after the show's final accounting. Others were prepaid by our home office. The rest were settled in cash, of which I always carried a goodly supply. That same union boss usually became a lovable pussycat after receiving a small advance token of Concert West's appreciation for a job to be well done.

By now, the equipment had arrived from the airport, and the road crew was wrestling it into position. It was time to prepare the dressing room for my stars. (I stated earlier that things were simpler early on. We prepared comfortable dressing rooms for the Dog, understanding that these were generally sports arenas, not theaters. Usually we operated from a team's dressing room. Backstage excesses—insane indulgences ranging from slate pool tables and pinball machines and ping pong tables to cases of chilled Dom Perignon and tanks full of fresh lobster—had to wait for Elton John and others to develop). About now, I'd jump back in my car and speed off in search of a deli. In most cases, I phoned them in advance from the hotel and ordered the food which should be ready: sandwiches — big ones and lots of them — to match the tastes of the individuals in the band. Cory Wells wanted turkey with loads of lettuce. Floyd Sneed was a pastrami kind of guy. Also, gobs of extra condiments like pickles, mayo and mustard, plus cartons of chips and cases of soft drinks.

Then on to find a liquor store for beer, wine and whatever other forms of fortified refreshment the entourage required. A couple cases of beer pleased the road crew, and it didn't need to be some fancy microbrew, as long as it was cold. This I accomplished by buying plastic garbage cans at a nearby Kmart and filling them with ice. One more stop for that all-important ice, some paper table cloths and a couple of candles with plenty of cups and Pat's Custom Catering Service opened for business. Then it was back to the auditorium or stadium or gym, grab a roadie to help set up the dressing room tables, put the ice in the garbage cans and fill them with beer and pop. Finally, I sped off to the airport.

Every airport has a general aviation section where private planes can park, refuel, embark and disembark passengers and so forth. Butler Aviation is the best known national chain. Such an operation is referred to as an FBO, which means "fixed based operator." Typically, the Dog's Falcon Jet taxied, stopped and disgorged the group down the stairs at a local FBO. Usually, I brought along a modest press representation to greet their arrival, not so much for the ink as for the inspiration and motivation of the group. Sometimes, the head of the local fan club or maybe even a local dignitary joined the welcoming committee. There, on the tarmac, as the group exited the plane, band members tried to appear cool, wearing "I'm totally bored" looks on their faces.

I stood at the bottom of the steps waiting to greet each one as they came down. Of course, they looked at me as though I had flown on the plane with them. Nary a glimmer of surprise or recognition was permitted if you wanted to retain your membership in the Cool Regime. They displayed the same feigned indifference toward the other people welcoming their arrival. The stars paused briefly for a few pictures, then hastily retreated to the security of the back seats of the limos waiting nearby.

Why did I even bother to go to the airport if indifference greeted my presence there? The answer is quite simple. Were I not there, it would have instantly become an issue. An affront! A full-blown calamity: "Jesus, where's Pat?…Where's Concerts West?…What's going on here anyway?…Didn't he know what time we were landing?…Do you think he's okay?…God, can you believe this?…No one at the airport to meet us!…Pat always meets us!"

Within seconds, the limos whisked the Dog off to their hotel and suites. They already had keys for their individual rooms—I picked them up at the hotel earlier that morning and handed them to each member of the group as they left the plane. At the hotel, they unwound until the limos reappeared for the evening ride to the back door of the auditorium.

Meanwhile, I returned to the auditorium to make sure everything was set and under control. I confirmed that security was in place and stopped by the box office to find out how last-minute ticket sales were progressing. (A sellout prior to greeting the group at the airport always helped. If the Dog asked me one question as they got off the plane it was either "Are we sold out?" or "How are ticket sales?") My clients always found comfort when I smiled and told them that "this evening one more American city will be participating in your careers to the fullest extent allowed by the building's capacity." That allowed them to conjecture that, had only enough seats been available, every man, woman and child in the area would have been there that night to worship them.

You see, there is a big, big difference in the performer's mind between "We're sold out" and "We might have a few unsold seats but things look great." It's the difference between "tens of thousands more people wanted to attend but couldn't" and reality. Hence, if we were within a thousand seats of a sellout, my tarmac report read, "We're all sold out. Congratulations!"

Any discrepancies between my declaration of a sellout and the actual attendance figure appeared only sometime later, if anyone in the group bothered to check on the final numbers. But I never worried about that, knowing (a) they wouldn't check and (b) they really didn't want to know anyway.

Bang A Gong (Get It On)
T. Rex, 1972

THE FIRST PERSON OFF THE DOG'S PLANE was always Bob Tomaso, their road manager, who immediately would ask whether everything was in order. After updating him, I would repair with Bob to the venue to go over security arrangements, determine how the group could best enter the building, inspect dressing room locations and discuss all the myriad details of a Dog performance. Then he hustled to the hotel to oversee his flock until the limo ride to the concert site.

Concerts always began with an opening act, a group carefully selected to help sell a few extra tickets, create the correct mood, offer some contrast to the headliners and, above all, not upstage the stars. Generally we were successful, but there were exceptions, like one night in Chicago. Hints of an impending problem surfaced the night before in Detroit. For that particular weekend's package of shows, we hired England's T. Rex as the opening band. Lead singer Marc Bolan headed the group. Though huge in the UK, hey enjoyed only one significant hit in the States, in 1972, and you may remember it: *Bang A Gong (Get It On)*. Since then, however, they suffered through a drought. Bolan, a bit out of control by this point in his career, plotted to steal the show from Three Dog Night. His intentions first manifested themselves in Detroit when T. Rex squeezed an encore out of the crowd, something unacceptable from an opening act unless the ovations were so strong there would be resentment if the performers did not return for one more number. And such *was not* the case.

Nothing about the Detroit audience's response called for a T. Rex encore. Frustrated by this, Bolan hatched a new plot to distinguish his band in reverse. Few who suffered the effects of his machinations realized exactly what was happening to them at the time. The setting was the grand old Chicago Stadium, since torn down and replaced by the new United Center. In 1932, FDR was nominated for president there, and in the '80s and '90s, a basketball player by the name of Jordan made it his personal playground. But on this night in the early '70s, Chicago Stadium belonged to Three Dog Night, with T. Rex as their invited guests. The Dogs' headquarters for the show were the Chicago Bulls' dressing room, and the tables were festooned with food, paper cups, buckets of ice and beverages of every kind. I poured myself a Seven-Up, and many others also used cups for their beverages. The roadies joined us and were helping themselves to drinks when, just before show time, strange sensations overcame many of us. I found myself flat-out hallucinating!

I asked "World Famous" Tom Murphy, a former deejay colleague of mine at KJR in Seattle now working at WCFL in Chicago, to emcee the show and introduce the Dog that night. I turned to Tom, standing nearby, and said, "Something's happening to me, and I can't figure out what it is!"

One member of our crew had the responsibility that evening to stand side stage with earphones and microphone and direct the operators of the big spotlights in the far rear of the building. When it came time to go on stage, he was missing. A quick search found him wandering around the parking lot announcing at the top of his lungs that his sister lived somewhere in the Chicago area and asking people whether they knew exactly where. Clearly, I wasn't the only one who was a mess. To varying degrees, other members of the entourage were similarly taking unplanned trips to la-la land.

With the light man judged totally out of commission, I was drafted to take his place, and a long night began. Boy, did I mess up the lighting pattern for that show! How could I have done otherwise? First, I'd never done it before and second, I couldn't remember what city I was in. Though far more experienced with mind-altering substances than I, two band members were complaining before going on stage of an inability to focus. Chuck Negron performed glassy-eyed, while Cory Wells and Danny Hutton, who sipped only bottled beer that night, were unaffected.

Meanwhile, Bob Tomaso conducted a backstage investigation. When pressured, a T. Rex roadie spilled the beans. Bolan had slipped into the Three Dog dressing room just before his performance. Once inside, he secretly laced the paper cups with mescaline, hoping to render the Dog useless. With the headline act thus disabled, he figured that T. Rex would be called back on stage to finish out the night for the 18,000 Three Dog Night fans in attendance.

That evening the Dog lived up to the words of their 1974 hit, *The Show Must Go On*, and Bolan's scheme failed miserably. Mescaline be damned, the band played anyway, and Murphy told me it was a great performance. Two encores! The Windy City just loved it. All this despite two rather goofy instrumentalists, one spaced-out singer and an out-of-his-mind promoter/light man who was so far gone, later that night he insisted on standing through his entire flight from Chicago to Seattle. (I finally returned to earth late the next morning, long after my plane landed at Sea-Tac Airport.)

Nice try Marc. Bang a gong, get it on!

Black and White
Three Dog Night, 1972

I WANT TO SHARE ONE ESPECIALLY MEMORABLE WEEKEND with the Dog, from early February 1971. We faced a tougher-than-normal schedule: Winnipeg, Manitoba on Friday evening, University of Tennessee in Knoxville on Saturday night and St. Louis on Sunday.

Winnipeg greeted us with a severe winter chill. After the show that night, we planned to gather in the hotel bar to celebrate Cory Wells' birthday. Leaving the auditorium after settling with the box office, I tried to start my rental car, only to discover it had other ideas. Running late, I decided to ditch the car and walk the mile back to our hotel. Upon entering, I commented to the doorman about the nippy weather outside. "Well, yes, it is cold," he said. "It's minus 22 and supposed to drop to minus 28 later."

Heading for the bar in search of antifreeze, I arrived just as people came down from their rooms to join in the celebration. The band, a few groupies, Tomaso and Ron Berry, their publicist, who was traveling with us this trip. I should point out that I rarely saw Cory drink alcohol. Being his birthday, this night was an exception. Cory made a special request of everyone in attendance. He had recently learned of a cocktail called the *Velvet Hammer* and was determined to have all of us share in his discovery.

A Velvet Hammer is constructed with two shots of vodka, two shots of creme de cacao and one shot of bourbon mixed in with some cream. It's tasty, smooth and deceiving. The first one ingested makes celebrants feel better than ever before in their lives, and the second only enhances the euphoria. The problem is, two Hammers take on the characteristics of a well-swung billy club. Most of those attending the Cory Wells birthday gathering, myself included, experimented with a *three*-Hammer program with nearly identical results.

Cory and his Three Dog cohorts planned to travel to Knoxville the next day on their private Falcon Jet while I intended to travel with the equipment and road crew on scheduled service. This called for us to depart at 7:00 A.M. on Northwest to Minneapolis, go through customs there and take another flight to Knoxville. Knowing this, I tried to excuse myself early from the party, but Cory would have none of it. Instead, he suggested that Ron Berry, the publicist, go on the scheduled flight and I ride with the band on their plane. All parties agreed, and I gave Berry my tickets and told him he could travel as me. (It didn't occur to me that going through Customs posed a potential problem, as Velvet Hammers tend to lessen the importance of such small details.)

At eight the next morning my phone rang. Due to my precarious physical condition, some time passed before I awoke and answered. On the line was Ron Berry, whose urgent message went as follows:

"Pat, are you awake? Pat are you listening to me? Pat, now listen carefully. You have a faulty pacemaker in your heart and you've got to contact your doctor immediately. Pat, they say it's serious. Are you hearing me?"

Picture the scene: I'm totally hung over, the room is dark, I'm not sure whether it's day or night and I can't figure out what it is that Ron Berry is talking about. "Ron," I said, trying to collect what little was left of my wits, "What in the hell are you saying? I don't wear a pacemaker. I have no heart problems. Where are you?"

Berry became frantic and tried to explain himself:

> Pat, your doctor called the airline. They stopped the plane as it was taking off from Winnipeg. The pilot came back to my seat and said they were returning me to the terminal building because my doctor said it was urgent, that my pacemaker was faulty and I shouldn't be allowed to take off. I freaked out because it would have meant going back through Canadian Immigration, and here I am using your name and ticket. So I told the pilot my doctor's getting senile. I said my pacemaker works perfectly. I told them there's no way I'm going back to the terminal building, that this is ridiculous and please, let's just head for Minneapolis. Well, they held a hurried conference and talked to me some more and agreed to take off. But they made a stewardess sit next to me with an oxygen bottle the whole way. The plane's just landed, and I ran to the first phone I could find because you are in trouble, and please, please, please Pat, call your doctor right now!

Gradually regaining consciousness, I was, with some effort, able to satisfy Berry that someone was badly mistaken, that I didn't have, never had, a pace-maker and that I was in perfect health.

"Who knows what all of this is about?" I remarked, a bit confused myself. "I sure as hell don't. But don't worry, Ron, I'm just fine!" I said I'd see him in Knoxville and hung up.

I sat up in bed as my injured mind spun wildly. Something happened, but I couldn't figure out what. *Can three Velvet Hammers erase one's memory?* I was checking my chest looking for a pacemaker when someone knocked on my door. It was Bob Tomaso, who walked in, sat down on the bed and said, "Shit, we've got to charter a plane to get the equipment to Knoxville!" Bob explained that the entire road crew was so hung over they all slept through their wake-up calls and were very late getting the equipment and themselves to the airport. So late, the departure gate was closed. Seeing that, Bob ran to a phone, called the airline (knowing that Berry was flying on my ticket), told them he was my doctor and spun the pacemaker tale. He said the plane actually stopped on the runway for a few minutes, but then went ahead and took off. The mystery was solved. Bob was the man who told Northwest I had a faulty pacemaker. Pretty resourceful!

Our adventures that day had only just begun. Bob found an old DC-3 properly licensed to cross into US airspace and chartered it. The band's equipment was loaded on board along with our groggy road crew. That evening they told us that the flight to Knoxville on that grand old plane made them wish that Cory Wells had never been born. I'll leave out what they said about participating in his birthday celebration. The plane's heaters were not designed for subzero temperatures, and the aged-but-sturdy veteran of World War II bounced, bucked and rolled all the way from Winnipeg to Chicago and from Chicago to Knoxville. Once in Tennessee, the roadies thawed themselves out, unloaded the equipment and somehow managed to get it to the University of Tennessee Field House in time. Employing a wide selection of four letter words, the crew indicated it was not a happy experience.

The rest of us boarded the Dog's plane at noon. A quick flight to Chicago from Winnipeg was anticipated, then a short hop to Knoxville. What optimists we were! As we landed in Chicago, snow fell heavily. At the Customs office, Bob Tomaso confirmed that the DC-3 had cleared and continued on its way south. A different fate awaited us. Due to a long backup caused by the storm, we weren't going anywhere for a while. We scouted out the remaining seats in the large square waiting room. The customs people occasionally called out the names of some party or group and kept repeating that, due to snow blocking the freeway from downtown, they were way understaffed, and that all of us would just have to wait our turns.

Years of experience had taught me that boredom and rock-'n'-roll musicians made a dangerous combination. They are creative individuals—artists—who have already shaken loose the social restraints that confine most of us. Freed from such burdens, they viewed their tours as giant, profitable, heady safaris across a land they believed would forgive them for almost anything. Confine a collection of such types in a small room with nothing to do, and watch out! Something out of the ordinary is bound to happen.

On this particular February afternoon, in the General Aviation/US Customs office of O'Hare International Airport, Jimmy Greenspoon and Floyd Sneed decided to put the public's tolerance to the ultimate test. Jimmy, from a well-known show biz family (his mother was actress Rhonda Fleming), was gifted with a brilliant sense of humor and flair for high drama. His appearance that wintry day belied his roots, education and wealth. Six feet tall, light-complected, sporting two feet plus of red and rather kinky hair, strangely-tinted glasses and a long, flowing green overcoat, he presented a most striking package. In contrast, Floyd was the perfect character actor—a giant black man, strikingly handsome, with the ability to instantly flash the world's greatest smile, or send tears running down his cheeks, or do both simultaneously. A lovable individual when behaving normally, Floyd greatly expanded on his good-naturedness when he acted.

The co-conspirators disappeared down the hall together, concocted an impromptu one-act play and decided to try it out on the assembled travelers crowded impatiently in the Customs waiting room—an actor's dream, a captive audience. Floyd returned and found a seat. The play opened with Jimmy strolling into the area, bag slung over his shoulder, reading a newspaper. He circled the room and finally stopped several feet in front of where Floyd sat, also reading. In a loud voice Jimmy said for all to hear, "Has anyone here noticed that there's a black man sitting in a chair while a white man has to read his newspaper standing up?"

A sudden, deafening silence filled the room. Conversations stopped, reading material was put aside and all eyes traveled first to Floyd in sympathy and then to Jimmy in scorn. Floyd looked up, fidgeted a bit and went back to his reading. After a pause, Jimmy spoke again, this time in a voice with a biting edge at a volume which made it impossible to ignore his words: "Listen to me, a white man is standing while you are sitting. Now get out of that chair!"

This was 1971, and years of violent racial clashes had recently rocked America. Everyone heard of the abuses and cruelties blacks suffered, but few whites ever experienced them firsthand. Now, in the Customs Office at O'Hare, a room-full of white men and women were witnessing racial hatred up close. They didn't recognize it as theater; they heard only horrid insults, saw only the cruel abuse of one human being by another. Anyone in that room not yet in total shock was soon taken the rest of the way.

Floyd continued reading his magazine and didn't even look up when the next indignity came. His silent, stoic response captured the heart of every soul in the room. Sitting quietly with his magazine, Floyd epitomized everything good and noble in humankind; standing menacingly with a snarl on his face, Jimmy represented pure, unrepentant evil. He symbolized the world's every wrong.

Having brought their audience to the edges of their seats, the two actors moved to the finale of their play. After staring at Floyd for the longest time, Jimmy walked over to him, said "I warned you" and reached for his wrist. He tore off Floyd's watch, which Sneed surrendered without complaint. Throwing the timepiece on the marble floor, he stomped on it with his high-heeled leather rock-'n'-roll boots. After a few blows, the watch lay in pieces on the floor.

Looking up at last, Floyd put aside his magazine, quietly rose and walked over to his totally-destroyed watch. Every eye was riveted on him as he slowly bent down and picked up the remains. Holding them gently and lovingly in his cupped hands, he returned to his chair only to find it taken, now occupied by Chicago's new Public Enemy Number One, Jimmy Greenspoon. Without a word, Floyd picked up his coat off the floor where Jimmy had dumped it. With tears streaming down his cheeks, he stumbled out the door into the howling blizzard. By now, many women in the room were also weeping, and some of the men were discussing joining forces and doing Jimmy bodily harm. Had this not been a Federal facility with armed guards milling around, they just might have done it. Most witnesses were too shocked to do anything. As everyone else in the room seethed, Jimmy sat calmly reading his paper, while Floyd stayed out of sight.

Finally, our turn came, our names were called and we were processed through Customs. Floyd returned, cautiously remaining separate from the rest of the band. After a two hour delay, we at last re-boarded our plane and took off through falling snow for Knoxville. After the plane leveled off, Danny Hutton stated a belief that Jimmy and Floyd had likely just set a new world record for pissing people off! He pointed out that generally, in any given situation like this, you have x number of people who are ambivalent about whatever is going on around them. His contention was that their theatrics that day had defied all equations, that there had been no ambivalence, that they had genuinely and totally pissed everyone off. Jimmy nodded in agreement and smiled; Floyd just went to asleep.

Three Dog Night in Concert, The Cotton Bowl, Dallas, Texas —1972

14 – *Try a Little Tenderness*

Otis Redding, 1966 / Three Dog Night, 1969

BURT JACOBS CO-MANAGED THREE DOG NIGHT and was as interesting an individual as anyone in the group. A New York native, he grew up on the streets and worked at a young age as a numbers runner. As I came to understand, this involved something called the *numbers racket*. At a secret location hidden from the eyes of the law, someone ran a game similar in many respects to today's lotteries. Numbers runners fanned out through the neighborhoods collecting bets. Following the drawing (or whatever it was that determined winners) they again scattered to report the results, distribute the winnings and take new bets.

In time, Burt graduated from running numbers to bookmaking, eventually moving to Los Angeles where he continued to ply his trade. His partner from New York joined him in LA, and in time a local crime family confronted them, insisting that the newcomers had an obligation to share their take with them. When the two failed to hand over a cut of their action, bullets flew. Burt's partner and partner's wife were shot and killed while sitting at their breakfast table. Frightened by this development, Burt prudently retired from the gambling profession in favor of a less deadly, more lawful occupation.

He became involved in some dance halls and graduated from there into the artist management business. This progressed into a partnership with an LA deejay, Reb Foster, managing two major rock groups, Steppenwolf and Three Dog Night. I have occasionally been credited with having above-average street smarts—in other words, being able to quickly evaluate people I come in contact with. Whatever such smarts I possess, they are feeble to nonexistent compared to those of Burt Jacobs. Burt and I traveled together on several business trips, and he never ceased to astonish me with his accurate perceptions. While developing survival instincts in New York in his youth, he learned to see things in people that totally escaped others.

With just a glance, Burt could spot a woman vulnerable to a proposition. I witnessed the accuracy of his appraisals many times. Gays were immediately identified by him, and they didn't have to say a word. His calls were uncannily accurate, remarkable.

Burt displayed the same talent gauging truthfulness. He could detect a lie the moment it was uttered. In the world of rock-'n'-roll in the early '70s, veracity was a scarce commodity, especially when dealing with record companies, club operators, some promoters and all hangers-on. I always felt that the Dog was in good hands with Jacobs. Later it dawned on me that Burt, by placing the Dog with my company, Concerts West, and allowing us to handle all their concerts as well as their money, was paying us the ultimate compliment. Burt Jacobs trusted Terry, Tom and me, and the rest of our firm as well. We were given a clean bill of health by a man I considered a human polygraph machine. In those years, we deserved that sort of trust.

The Show Must Go On
Three Dog Night, 1974

OUTDOOR STADIUM ROCK SHOWS REMAINED A RARE NOVELTY in 1972. Continuing to innovate, we arranged three outdoor shows for Three Dog Night. The first show was held in the Rubber Bowl in Akron, the second in Three Rivers Stadium in Pittsburgh and the third in the Cotton Bowl in Dallas.

With 50,000 seats sold deep in the heart of Texas, we wanted to make that last show special. We booked a phenomenal opening act, a new group called The Faces with a dynamic lead singer named Rod Stewart who went on to enjoy some serious fame of his own (Rod is on my all-time top-five list). Earlier that year, they released their classic album *Every Picture Tells a Story* featuring *Maggie May*, and we figured the crowd would love them. We figured right.

To make these outdoor shows as spectacular as possible, we developed an elaborate fireworks show to introduce Three Dog Night when they went on stage and timed it to fade perfectly into the first notes of their opening number. We contracted with a reputable fireworks company to have one of their accredited pyrotechnicians (the guys responsible for shooting off the fireworks) travel with us to all three cities. In Akron and Pittsburgh, the results were everything that we hoped for. In Dallas, however, we bumped into a problem which produced results far beyond what we intended. The city's ordinance dealing with fireworks shows required the exclusive use of pyrotechnicians licensed in Dallas, of which, it seemed, there was only one.

Our meeting with him the day before foreshadowed trouble to come. He showed up half drunk, seemed disinterested in our fireworks plan and basically said this was nothing new to him, that he had been doing this sort of thing for years. His response to every question was a soon-to-be-famous line, "Pahdnuh, I got it all handled!"

The planned fireworks were to consist of waves of rockets of every color growing in size and altitude and reaching a crescendo just as the band left their dressing room backstage. At the exact moment the band approached the stage, an array of white phosphorus fountains would trigger a multicolored, animated display of the Three Dog Night logo. As that wall of fire faded, a riot of flashing lights and spots would bathe the group as they simultaneously hit their first note.

Not totally trusting our Dallas compatriot, we went over the program again and again and again with him and his assistant. Each time we pointed something out, he reminded us, "Pahdnuh, I got it all handled!"

As an insurance policy, we gave him two of our walkie-talkies—one for him and one for his assistant whose obvious lack of mental dexterity was discouraging. We told them we would transmit a password over the radio—*Fire away!* repeated three times. Under no circumstances, we emphasized strongly, were they to ignite *anything* until they heard those six words. Bob Tomaso, the Dogs' road manager, was given the task of sending the password from their dressing room when they were ready to go, and not a second earlier.

As expected, Rod Stewart turned the crowd on and earned an encore. During intermission, the usual equipment changes took place. Thirty minutes later, the crowd was back in their seats waiting in anticipation for the entrance of the stars of the show. Afterwards, we pieced together fragments of what happened. I noted earlier in the evening the distinct smell of liquor again on the breath of our Texas pyrotechnician. Whether this impacted subsequent events remains a distinct possibility. Afterwards, he blamed his assistant, at whom he was then shouting, while the assistant said he had simply misunderstood.

The fireworks were set up at one end just outside the stadium, which is located on the Texas State Fairgrounds in Dallas. Near that end of the bowl stood several dozen wooden shacks that served as booths during the State Fair. A series of racks were set up on the ground to hold the rockets and various displays. Parked nearby was the tractor-trailer rig used to transport the fireworks.

A torrent of some kind of pyrotechnical shouting initiated the chaos that followed. Before anyone realized what was happening—and before the Dog was ready as well—the assistant hit his button and fired the first rocket. Seeing this, the head pyro raced to the truck, attempting to remove it from harm's way. Due to the truck's close proximity to the fireworks, he had planned to move it prior to the start of the show. Now it was too late.

Switching on the ignition, he mistakenly jammed the transmission into reverse and backed into two racks filled with lovely-but-extremely-potent Italian-made sky rockets, knocking them over. His assistant, gazing heavenward at the explosion of the first shells, was unaware of the accident behind him and continued with the firing sequence. Next in line to ignite were the Italian shells which, thanks to the truck-driving error, were now levelled directly at the stadium and surrounding buildings instead of pointed vertically at the dark sky.

I will never forget my partner Terry Bassett's words as we stood on the stadium floor at about the 50-yard line. We thought the first rocket was premature because stage hands were still moving the last of the gear into place. At that very moment, the now-horizontally arrayed rockets were ignited. Terry's simple and moving words were, "Holy shit!"

Rockets flew in every direction, the force of their blasts spinning the fallen rack around in circles like a blazing top. One rocket arced over the stadium wall and landed at the 30-yard line. Others streaked crazily every which way around the Fairgrounds. A few strays embedded themselves in the frail sides of the wooden concession shacks, setting off an instant conflagration. In seconds, a warm red glow formed over the area.

When the ill-timed firing stopped, we decided the Dog should start their show before anything else went wrong. They rushed to the stage and began playing. No sooner did they start than Captain Pyro decided to set off the giant Three Dog Night display and white phosphorous fountains behind the band. Adding more drama to that astonishing scene, just then a fleet of fire trucks came roaring onto the Fairgrounds, sirens blaring.

The crowd roared its approval, thinking this was all part of the show. Behind the band, the Three Dog logo burned brightly as smoke from the blazing concession stands drifted across the stage. The light from the phosphorous candles rippled through the plumes, creating a spectral, surreal effect. How perfect. The group was singing *Mama Told Me (Not To Come)*.

Terry and I stood at the 50-yard line, laughing at the improbable spectacle playing out before us. I thoroughly enjoyed imagining the scene outside the stadium behind the stage. I pictured our licensed and accredited Dallas pyro-technician telling the fire chief, "Pahdnuh, I've got it all handled!"

The Family of Man
Three Dog Night, 1972

IN JULY 1972, I FACED A LONG, TIRING WEEKEND AT BEST. Shortly before, Milton Shapp, the governor of Pennsylvania, called with a special request. In late June, the entire Susquehanna River Valley took the brunt of torrential rainfall in the northeast (courtesy of Hurricane Agnes) and Harrisburg, the state capital, was transformed into a waterlogged wasteland. When the greatest flood in the river's history crested, water ran deep throughout the city; when it finally fell, it left behind a muddy, stinking mess and a shaken populace.

Governor Shapp wanted to light a fire of optimism with a community cleanup of the National Guard Armory capped by a major concert in the building. Several feet of mud coated the inside of the Armory, the only concert facility in town with reasonable capacity. We agreed to provide Three Dog Night for a two-day, Friday/Saturday event. This came just after my secretary, Phyllis Walker, truly my right arm for years, suffered a brain hemorrhage at her desk. An outstanding assistant and outwardly the very picture of good health, in an instant she was gone. Phyllis joined me when I moved into the general manager's slot at KJR. For much of the time since, I ran two radio stations while globe-trotting for rock on weekends. She was my human *le cabinet*. Also my dearest friend. Without Phyllis, Vivian Anderson, my new assistant, now made my travel arrangements, and they were complicated: Out of Seattle on Thursday night and into Harrisburg early Friday morning to check on the condition of the Armory; then a quick flight back to Chicago for a meeting, followed by an immediate return to Harrisburg by six that evening for the first show.

When I landed at the Harrisburg airport, the runways were mud-free, and cleanup continued inside the terminal building. A day or two before, hundreds of Mennonites from across central Pennsylvania had arrived unannounced with their horses, wagons and entire families and gone to work. As I made my way out, many of them were on their hands and knees scrubbing the terminal floor. Others were washing windows, polishing fixtures, cleaning out mud-filled toilets. By the time I departed on Sunday morning, those angels of peace were gone and the terminal building stood spotless. A true miracle took place right before my eyes, and I vowed to never entertain an unkind thought about members of their faith. Mennonite women wear long black dresses, the men strange-appearing (to me, not to them) black suits in keeping with their rejection of luxury and modern vanities. Sometimes the subject of ridicule and misunderstanding, the Mennonites demonstrated giant hearts filled with kindness in the flooding's aftermath.

I can't begin to describe the odor permeating Harrisburg. Falling waters painted this lovely city with mud, strewing everywhere a now-rotting accumulation of everything the river swept up in its rampage across the state: dead animals, garbage, human waste, wrecked cars, uprooted trees, you name it. Despite the long odds, the Armory was ready by Friday. The young people of the area teamed with the National Guard and did an amazing job. The old building was immaculate, gleamed like new, and everyone felt justifiably proud. Both shows sold out, with ticket prices reduced as an expression of support from Three Dog Night. Before or since, I have never seen a crowd that so much appreciated a show. Great idea, Governor! I only wish that a weekend I spent in Baltimore the previous Fall had gone so well.

I Fought the Law
Bobby Fuller Four, 1967

IN LATE OCTOBER 1972, WE SCHEDULED THREE DOG NIGHT for a Sunday night show at the old Baltimore Civic Center. Sunday morning, I deplaned at Washington National and took a cab into Baltimore. I avoided my usual rent-a-car routine, knowing that I had to depart right after the show that night to make a meeting scheduled for noon the next day in California. I wouldn't have time to bother with auto check-in. My travel plans allowed me to make three concerts and two meetings in one weekend, one of the meetings in Chicago, where I was interviewing a potential KJR disc jockey, the other out west in Beverly Hills with Burt Jacobs and some advertising execs. I planned to be back in Seattle in time for dinner with my family Monday night and work in my office Tuesday morning. (How's that for efficiency?)

Earlier, I described my road duties at Concerts West in the early '70s. In 1972, our days of sophistication and ample manpower had not yet arrived. Looking back, what we accomplished with limited staff seems impossible. Not knowing any better, we just went ahead and got it done.

In Baltimore, in blissful ignorance, I commenced my regular pre-show rounds: Checked into the downtown Hilton, took a shower, made a few phone calls, laid out my clothes, grabbed a cab to the Civic Center, reviewed preparations and ticket sales. Everything seemed to be in order. The building, still home to the Baltimore Bullets, held an enchantment for me. I pictured future Hall-of-Famers Earl "the Pearl" Monroe and Wes Unseld running the floor, as had so many other great NBA stars. Little things like that meant a lot, and made those antiquated structures very special to me, historic and emotional landmarks. On this Dog day, thousands of chairs covered the floor, awaiting the evening concert a few hours away. I chatted amiably with the head of the stagehands, who seemed an exception in the trade. He was anxious to please, and when I told him I came from Seattle, he wanted to know more about a city he visited briefly while in the service. When the equipment began to arrive from the airport, I left him to his work and continued with mine.

I called a cab from a backstage pay phone and, a few minutes later, slid into the back seat of Veterans Cab Company car № 113. It made good sense to get a cab's number because, if you liked the service and the driver, you could call for them if you needed something later. Normally, I would have forgotten the cab's number by the next day, but subsequent events embedded it in my mental software forever. Our first stop was a deli recommended by a local for sandwiches, of which we ordered about three dozen, plus a big bowl of potato salad. After securing a promise from the deli to deliver the sandwiches within two hours, we sped off to find the balance of what was needed in the dressing rooms.

My cab driver wanted to show me Baltimore once he determined who I was and what I was doing. While picking up plastic garbage cans for the ice and beverages, plastic plates, cups, napkins, cases of pop and beer, chips and all the rest, I took a private, guided tour of a city only a resident could love. When I returned to Baltimore years later, I was delighted to note that civic leaders also saw what I saw that day: a run down, cluttered cityscape, block after block, building after building at some level of decay. Even better, they did something about it. The rebirth of Baltimore into the vital, vibrant city we see today makes one a believer in miracles.

With our car and trunk filled with items from my shopping list, we drove back to the Civic Center. I ordered the Center's rear truck door opened so the cab could drive across the backstage area and park next to the dressing rooms. There, with the driver's assistance, I unloaded the supplies. I prepaid the driver $150 for his efforts, so it came as no surprise when, after carrying the last load into the dressing room, I returned to find the cab gone, leaving me with one small problem: I left my briefcase in his car!

May I explain the importance of that briefcase? It served as my traveling office and contained everything necessary to make the show work, and I mean everything. What did I miss most? Was it the $15,000 in cash, or the checks pre-written by our home office to pay for many of the services? Or maybe it was all those contracts, agreements and licenses, to say nothing of my credit cards? The cards were critical. We carried high limits, including an Air Travel Card with a Q clearance with which you could charter a 747 if that suited your fancy. It was a toss-up, I missed them all, and the reader can safely assume I was very concerned over my bag's unexpected departure.

I ran to the pay phone and called Veterans Cab. Thank God I remembered the car number! The dispatcher failed in his attempts to raise car 113 and said the driver must be out of his vehicle. When I heard those words, all sorts of totally unhappy possibilities entered my mind. Then I spotted a potential solution: several Baltimore police just then entering the Civic Center for show duty.

I ran up to the first officer I saw with a radio on his belt, explained my problem and its implications for the event and asked whether he could use his radio to try to find Veterans Cab car № 113. The sergeant listened to my impassioned story with little apparent interest and responded, "Look Mr. Rock and Roll, the Baltimore Police Department has better things to do than run around looking for your God-damned bag. I don't care what's in it!"

"Hey, look, I admit it, it was my dumb mistake!" I responded. "But that bag has the payroll for lots of men in this building. If I don't get my bag back, how am I going to pay them? I would certainly appreciate your help."

The sergeant laughed and said, "Find the fuckin' bag yourself!"

I turned to again use the pay phone, but a burly policeman stepped into the booth just then, so I rushed to the offices in the front of the building. There, I was back on the phone with my friends at Veterans Cab when a police captain who entered the office behind me overheard my conversation. He stepped over and asked, "You left your bag in a cab and can't find it?"

I briefed him on the situation and told him that the dispatcher couldn't contact the car. When I explained the value of the bag, he immediately pulled his radio from his belt and called headquarters. Within minutes, an all-points alert went out over Baltimore's police channels, and the captain said, "Let's just sit here and listen for a bit. They should come up with something."

I walked over to the desk of the building manager in the rear of the room. We were discussing alternate ways of paying the various parties after the show when the radio crackled with good news: The cab was found, my bag was still in the rear seat and the car was on its way to the auditorium! The captain asked that the bag be brought to the front office, but his request somehow got lost in the communications. About 10 minutes later, a call came from my friend at the rear of the building, the manager of the stagehands who witnessed the scene where the sergeant refused to cooperate. He said the cab had arrived backstage and the policeman at the door held my bag in his hands.

Enormously relieved, I retraced my steps down the aisles and back to the rear of the auditorium. Along the way, I asked myself, *How could you be so stupid?* and felt undeserving of such good luck. At the back door, the same sergeant who refused to help me stood holding my bag. I walked up, said "Thank you very much!" and reached for it.

He pulled it away and said, "Not so God-damned fast, fella. I don't know who you are. You're not getting this bag without some identification!"

"Identification!" I screamed. "It's all in the bag, you know that! If you want, I'll tell you everything that's in the bag. What's going on? You know damn well it's mine!"

The sergeant stared at me for a moment, then said, "Sorry, no ID, no bag!"

I angrily responded "I'll just go up front and get the lieutenant, and he can explain to you who owns that bag!"

As I turned to go, a short little man in a bright green sport coat, who, I came to understand later, was a plain clothes detective, grabbed my arm, pulled me aside and said, "Look man, don't make this difficult. You're not showing this officer any respect. Here he's gone to the trouble of finding your bag for you and you're not showing any appreciation."

"Oh!" I replied. "And just how do I show him my appreciation!"

Detective Ugly Green Coat enlightened me: "Why not just give him a few dollars, you know, like a couple of Honey Bees, you know, to show appreciation?"

Why hadn't I figured out his deal? Kicking myself, I reached in my pocket and took out what remained of my pocket cash, peeled off two 100-dollar bills, walked over to the sergeant and handed them to him. Finally, he gave me back my bag. It felt so wonderful to have it in my hands again. As I turned to head up to the front office, my buddy the stage manager was standing off to the side, having watched the whole episode. He wore an ear-to-ear grin, and I shrugged my shoulders as if to say, "What in the hell are you going to do?"

Clutching my precious bag tightly, I left for the airport in one of the limousines to meet the band. All was set, and it seemed like everything that could go wrong was behind me. Wrong again, Pat!

After the opening act (I don't remember who) was through and the equipment reset, I went on stage and did my usual introduction of Three Dog Night. The crowd stood screaming their welcome, and the first bars of their opening number echoed throughout the building as I returned to the front office to close out the business affairs of the evening. This typically included checking the ticket printing manifest against any deadwood (unsold tickets are called *deadwood*) and reviewing all invoices (covering security officers, stagehands, ushers, ticket takers, spotlight operators, ticket sales commissions, any advertising paid for by the auditorium, ticket sales taxes, et cetera, et cetera, et cetera). After distributing checks and cash, I usually received a large cashier's check with Concerts West's and the Dog's share of an evening's proceeds. This whole process, along with double-checking the auditorium's accounting, generally took a little over an hour. With all that done, I normally shook hands with everyone, thanked them for a good job all around and retreated backstage just about the time the group came off after their encore. If it all went well, I would leave the auditorium with them in their limo and we would return to the hotel together. That is, *if it all went well*—and if the city in question wasn't Baltimore.

This was Baltimore! That night, having finished my accounting chores, I was collecting my paperwork, stuffing it in my bag, and was about to thank everyone when the kindly captain who earlier had helped retrieve my bag with his radio came into the room and said, "Would you please come into the next room with me? I would like to have a private conversation with you."

I agreed, finished thanking the office staff and joined him in the conference room next to the main office. He wore a stern look on his face, and I had no idea why.

He quickly filled me in: "Did you give some cash to one of our officers backstage before the show?"

I said something dumb like, "Why?"

> Why?! I have a witness, the head of the stagehands, who tells me that two of our officers hit you up for some cash before they would give you back your bag. He says he saw you give them the cash. This is serious business. I am in charge of this auditorium, and those officers are not in my battalion. But God damn it, if you gave them money, I want to know about it!

Isn't this a cute mess I've got myself in? I thought as I explained exactly what took place, adding, "Look, this seems to be your problem, not mine. We play by the rules, and I don't want to be involved in some internal squabble. Yes, that sergeant is a jerk, but I want nothing to do with this. It wasn't my fault! I had to have that bag immediately. Please, just leave me out of it!"

The captain responded with a rather lengthy discourse on the importance of this episode. He explained that there was an internal investigation currently being conducted into alleged police department corruption and that little things like this shakedown were only the tip of the iceberg. Little things added up to big things, and if it took him forever, this department to which he had dedicated his life was going to be straightened out! He wanted me to come down to headquarters and give a sworn statement describing what had happened with the sergeant backstage.

I tried to defer, I tried to beg out. I told the captain I had a plane to catch from Friendship Airport to Dallas at half past midnight so I could be in Beverly Hills for a meeting the next morning, that I still had to go to the hotel and get my things and that I couldn't possibly afford to miss that flight. I suggested that he let me call him back on the phone after I returned Seattle, and that we could discuss it more then.

The captain listened, then played his big card, and it was truly a big one, the musical ace of spades. He said, "I see on the schedule that your company is planning to bring Elvis here to Baltimore the end of next month."

I held as how that was true.

He said, "Well, I have the power to stop that show if I choose. All I have to do is say that I have some security concerns, you know, like crazy old Elvis groupies making threats on his life or something like that and that show will be cancelled. Or at least postponed until I'm comfortable with everything. Much as I'd hate to do it, I'll shut you down if you don't help me out on this!"

I agreed to go downtown on the condition that, after that, he would take me by my hotel and out to the airport in time for my flight. No sooner did he agree than the conference room door banged open and my two least-favorite Baltimore cops, Sergeant Scum and Detective Ugly Green Coat, stormed in screaming things like "What's this bullshit about someone giving us money?…What's this lying mother fucker telling you?…He never gave us a thing!…What's this bullshit about?…" and so on and so on.

Captain Good (I never knew his last name) said, "You men don't work for me. Now please excuse us!" as he took me by the arm and led me out the door and across the parking lot to his squad car.

On our way downtown, he busied himself on his radio with ordering a stenographer to meet us in the interrogation room. Arriving at Baltimore's shockingly rundown police headquarters, I followed the captain up a couple of flights of old wooden stairs winding up the sides of the main waiting room. We arrived in the windowless interrogation room, sparsely furnished with a long table, some chairs and a small desk with a phone. The stenographer sat waiting for us in front of a typewriter he had rolled in on its stand from somewhere, and I began dictating my statement.

It wasn't tough, except I wished the stenographer took shorthand. He typed fast and said he would clean it up later, but even with that, he had no idea how quickly I wanted out of there. My watch read nearly eleven, 90 minutes to flight time. I kept telling myself, *That cocktail on American to Dallas is going to taste so good!*

I factually related the events surrounding my lost bag and the recovery of same. As I described the final moment, when the sergeant refused to surrender my bag, the door flew open and all hell broke loose. In came Sergeant Scum and Detective Ugly Green Coat along with a new player, the lieutenant of their battalion, a large, swarthy, dark-complected gorilla. I heard this thundering voice as he came up the stairs, and now he filled the room with his wrath. He didn't bother to turn down the volume, and his first words indicated things were about to go downhill fast. "Where's the fuckin' son of a bitch that says he paid off my officers? Where's that rock and roll son of a bitch?" I astutely surmised, he was referring to me.

It occurred to me that, in Baltimore, rock-'n'-roll connoted some sort of social disease, at least in one division of the police department. I shrunk down into my chair as far as I could and attempted to continue my dictation in a lowered voice. In the meantime, Captain Good and the newly-arrived lieutenant conducted a shouting match, interrupted occasionally by Sergeant Scum and Detective Ugly Green Coat. The two were pretty much saying the same thing over and over: "We never took a fuckin' nickel from the mother fucker!"

Finally, Lieutenant Nasty (that was a good name for the recent arrival) said, "I'm telling you one God-damned thing. Mr. Rock and Roll here is going into our fuckin' jail in protective custody for the night. He ain't leavin' this town accusing my men like this. We can have ourselves a little hearing in the morning and get to the bottom of this!"

As if this weren't bad enough news for me, Detective Ugly Green Coat worked his way around the room and stood behind me. Each time the conversation reached a volume where he figured he could get away with it, he whispered in my ear, "You a dead man, mother fucker! You shut yo' fuckin' mouth or you dead. You'll never leave this town alive, fucker, so you better shut the fuck up!" (*Fuck* and various derivations thereof appeared to be a communications mainstay of the Baltimore Police Department on this evening.)

Realizing how quickly the situation was deteriorating, I had to do something fast. I jumped up and said to Captain Good, "Give me the phone. I'm here of my own free will and I don't like what's going on. Give me the phone. Now!"

The captain pulled the phone over to the table where I sat, and I dialed my attorney in Seattle. His name is Joe Holmes and he has been a friend nearly all my business life. It was approaching midnight Sunday in Baltimore, almost nine in the evening on the West Coast, and I hoped and prayed I'd find him home. His phone rang once, twice, three times...*God, no answer*...four, five, six times. *I've got to do something.* Pressing the receiver so hard to my head it nearly punctured my skull, hoping this would eliminate any chance that those in the room could hear the phone still ringing, I began a one-sided, imaginary conversation with my attorney (who, knowing Joe, was probably at some lovely waterside restaurant having dinner): "Joe! I hope I didn't wake you up, but you know I'm in Baltimore and I've got a hell of a problem going here." After a short pause I went on:

"Well, here's what's happening, Joe," and I quickly recited recent events. I paused occasionally, seemingly interrupted, said some things which sounded like I was trying to calm my attorney down, then finished by telling the receiver:

> There's one lieutenant here who thinks he's going to throw me in the slammer for the night… Joe, I know you can call the senators, Maggie and Scoop, but how about your buddy Ehrlichman over at the White House?… Look, don't do anything right now!…If you don't hear back from me in an hour, put your plan to work. Okay?…Yeah, I'm okay. But don't go to sleep!

Just as I hung up the phone, the door opened again and who should walk in the room but Baltimore Police Commissioner D. D. Pomerleau himself, who was roused from his night's sleep and looked grumpy as he shouted, "What in the hell is going on in here, anyway?"

First, Captain Good gave his perspective of events along with a ringing endorsement of me and my willingness to cooperate. Then, Lieutenant Nasty delivered a profanity-laced defense of his officers and restated his position that I should be held as a witness in that I planned to leave town within the hour and would probably never return. (Sounded good to me!)

The Commissioner listened carefully to all reports, read the statement he took from the stenographer's typewriter, thought for a while and said, "Look boys, this is kind of confusing. Now why don't you all just run on back to duty or home if you're off duty and let me figure this thing out for a while. Mr. O'Day, you just sit still here with me for a spell, and let's discuss this whole thing."

He turned to the gathering and said, "Now leave us alone!"

After the assembled multitude filed out, the chief closed the door and said, "So, you've got Elvis coming to town?"

I confirmed that was the plan.

"Hmmm," he said. "That'll be a good show, and we sure don't want to do anything to mess up your plans. Now, you said you've got a plane to catch?"

I confirmed such, and the Commissioner offered to drive me to the hotel to pick up my things and take me to the airport. We walked down those rickety wooden stairs together and out to his squad car which sat with about two dozen other identical vehicles in the lot behind the station. When we reached his car and got in, he said, "Dammit! I threw my keys on my desk when I walked in! Excuse me, I'll be right back."

No sooner did he leave the car and head back into the station than, to my surprise, who should appear standing next to the chief's car but Sergeant Scum and Detective Ugly Green Coat. The detective opened the door on my side as they delivered a parting reminder. I can still quote them. I say *them* because they were saying the same identical thing: "You dead, mother fucker, we're following you, you keep yo' fuckin' mouth shut, you hear us?" Despite the similarities in their messages, Detective Ugly Green Coat proved to be the more persuasive of the two. The small caliber revolver he waved in the air in front of my nose gave him the nod.

They disappeared as quickly as they had appeared when the Commissioner came out the door, walked across the lot and climbed in the car. As we pulled out of the lot, our conversation went something like this:

"Young man. Did ya' ever hear of a thing called a flim flam man?"

I said, "I guess I've heard the term before."

He continued:

Some people call 'em con men, but I like to call 'em the ol' flim flam men. You take a good flim flam man and he can pull off just about anything and make you believe it was completely different than it really was. The reason I tell you this is that here in Baltimore, we seem to be having a little run of these guys. I think they come up from Florida but lately, we've seen a lot of this flim flam stuff going on. And I just wonder if there isn't a chance that's what happened to you. You don't suppose that maybe you ran across a couple of old flim flam guys that took your 200 bucks? I mean son, I want you to think about it! I mean, don't you think that, now knowing what you know about all the flim flam men around Baltimore, that that's maybe what happened to you? I mean, lot bigger chance it was a flim flam man than one of our good officers. What do you think?

I responded, "Well, Commissioner, I certainly hadn't considered that. My prepared statement is the truth, but if you think I might have been fooled by an old flim flam man, well, who knows?" (The Commissioner was giving me a road map out of town, and by God, I was going to follow it carefully!)

"Well!" the Commissioner exclaimed. "I'm sure glad we had this here little talk before you left town. Looking forward to Elvis coming. You know, this whole thing got me out of bed, and I've got to get up early in the morning. Would it be okay if I just drop you at the hotel and you take a cab out to the airport?"

I assured the Commissioner that was fine with me as we pulled up in front of the Hilton. I'll always treasure his parting words, spoken as I stepped from the car. Closing the door, he said, "You take care now, son. Have a good trip. And keep an eye out for that ol' flim flam man!"

As the Commissioner pulled away from the curb, I quickly looked around to see whether we had been followed by another car. With none in sight, I ran into the hotel and up to my room, threw my stuff in bags, phoned for a cab and told them to meet me at the rear entrance of the Hilton. When I stepped from the elevator, the taxi drove up almost immediately. I said "Friendship, and quick, please!" It proved impossible, and I arrived at the American counter 10 minutes late for my flight. Not only that, it was the last flight of the night heading anywhere west. I was frightened! I genuinely felt that those two cops wanted me floating in Chesapeake Bay and would see to it themselves if they had a chance. *What do I do now?* I wondered.

I literally ran through the terminal to the north end, flew out the door and darted across the street to the first hotel I could reach—I couldn't afford to be picky. I quickly checked in, paying cash for the room under the name of *Igor Smith*. (Not very creative, I admit, but I didn't have time to invent a more exotic name.)

After a fitful night of attempted sleep, I awoke early and caught the first flight of the morning out to LA, looking over my shoulder every few seconds, feeling lucky not only to be out of Baltimore but to be alive.

Upon my arrival back in Seattle, I related my tense hours in Baltimore to Joe, my attorney, as well as to Bill McKenzie, our concert business comptroller. I recommended that we set a procedure to fall back on if any of our people ever ended up in a similar mess in the future. At home, when I told Joni what happened, she couldn't relate. The concert side of my life was so vastly different from the balance of my career, her disbelief was understandable. In Seattle, I was a respected entrepreneur, radio broadcaster and business man. It was hard for my wife to fully understand the seriousness of the predicament I had just experienced. It was hard for her husband, too.

Within a couple of days, I was fully occupied with what's next, and my Baltimore adventure was cached in my memory bank. Two weeks later, I received a letter from the Internal Investigation Commission of the Baltimore Police Department informing me that they were conducting an on-going investigation of alleged police misconduct and enclosing for me to finish filling out the nearly-completed and still-unsigned statement I gave the stenographer at the police station that night. I waited a couple of weeks, until the day after the Elvis concert in Baltimore, then gleefully finished the statement, had it notarized and sent it back. I figured it wouldn't matter for much, but what the hell, after what they put me through, I had to give Sergeant Scum and Detective Ugly Green Coat a token of my appreciation. I hoped it wouldn't bring the Commissioner, D. D. Pomerleau, too many additional headaches, what with his big on-going investigation of all those flim flam men!

About five months later, one of the most hilarious letters I ever received came in the mail. I plan to preserve it for posterity. The letter, from the Baltimore Police Department, is reproduced on the following page.

Old Fashioned Love Song
Three Dog Night, 1971

I WISH TO DEDICATE THESE PAST TWO CHAPTERS to Cory, Danny, Chuck, Floyd, Mike, Jimmy and Joe who, without exception, always treated me with the greatest of kindness and respect. I remember the fun we had together, things like water skiing at my house on Lake Washington and bumming around New York. Most of all, I remember their professionalism and dedication to their trade. I remember, too, Joe Shermie, their talented bassist, who passed away not long before I began writing this book. And especially, I salute Chuck Negron, who fought all the way back from the bottomless pit of drug and alcohol addition to become the fine gentleman and performer he remains today.

POLICE DEPARTMENT ··· CITY OF BALTIMORE

FALLSWAY and FAYETTE STREET   BALTIMORE, MARYLAND 21202

Mulberry 5 - 1600   Area Code 301

DONALD D. POMERLEAU
Commissioner

RALPH G. MURDY
Administrative Bureau

FRANK J. BATTAGLIA
Operations Bureau

THOMAS J. KEYES
Services Bureau

Deputy Commissioners

March 8, 1972

Mr. Patrick O'Day
#6 Crescent Key
Bellevue, Washington 98006

Dear Mr. O'Day:

      The Internal Investigation Division of the department has sustained a misconduct allegation made by you against members involved in an incident of October 24, 1971.

      Please be advised that I have approved the recommended discipline of the members made by their supervisory and command officers.

      I am taking this manner and means of sending you a check of the department in the amount of **two hundred dollars** ($200.00), enclosed herewith, which was the amount as I understand it, you tendered a member of this department on the date in question.

      I wish to thank you for bringing this matter to my attention.

Sincerely,

D. D. Pomerleau
Commissioner

Letter received by Pat O'Day from Baltimore Police Commissioner D. D. Pomerlau

15— Taking Care of Business
Bachman-Turner Overdrive, 1974

BACHMAN-TURNER OVERDRIVE WAS ONE of the most brilliant rock groups of the '70s. Randy Bachman, formerly with Burton Cummings and the Guess Who, teamed with his brother Robbie, with Fred Turner, an outstanding guitar player and great vocalist, and with Blair Thornton. Together they comprised BTO. The group, from Vancouver, BC, recorded their hits for the Mercury label at our company's recording studios on Fourth Avenue in Seattle. In the mid-'70s, *Taking Care of Business* and *You Ain't Seen Nothing Yet* were on every contemporary radio station's play list in the States and were played once an hour on Canadian stations.

Our musician friends from up north enjoy intensive airplay at home when they score big with a hit. Their government dictates what percentage of a station's music will be Canadian in origin; that percentage, specified by law, is sometimes higher than Canada has hits of its own. Thus, when an Ann Murray, Paul Anka, Guess Who, Steppenwolf, Gordon Lightfoot, BTO, Rush, Bryan Adams or, more recently, Alanis Morissette or Celine Dion has a hit, their air exposure in Canada is guaranteed to be extensive. Bachman-Turner richly deserved all the airplay they received, and I mention these regulations because of the helpful role they play in getting Canadian groups off the ground. Record sales are record sales, regardless, and increased sales translate into increased North American attention, since record sales drive the music charts.

Despite BTO making our recording facilities (Kaye-Smith Studios) their session home, our concert division somehow overlooked them when they needed help. I was busy at the radio station when this happened, but was told that the group's manager, Bruce Allen, contacted us when they needed a big start, and we sort of yawned. Understandably, this caused hurt feelings. When BTO started climbing the charts, Tom Hulett from our Seattle office made a pitch for Concerts West to become their exclusive promotion firm and was firmly rebuffed. BTO found success with independent promoters willing to gamble on them, and Bruce Allen, as well as Randy Bachman, had no time for the "big guys" down in Seattle who had shunned them. It seemed like it was always on deals like this that Tom decided I was really important to the company.

He called me and came over to the radio station for a meeting. I already knew what he wanted, but sat back and listened as he explained that BTO, these guys from Canada, were giving us a hard time and refusing to return his phone calls. He said he was personally offended by their aloofness, but that Terry in Dallas was screaming to patch up whatever was wrong and try to get them for at least *some* dates. Tom asked whether I would take charge of the project and see what could be done.

I was already up to my ears in work running the radio stations plus spending many of my weekends on the road with various concerts. But, if I could be of help, of course! I felt like I was a kick return man seven yards deep in the end zone without a single blocker in front of me!

I phoned a not-too-warm Bruce Allen, business partner of my friend Red Robinson, Canada's greatest disk jockey ever and also from Vancouver, and asked whether we could sit down and talk. Bruce said of course we can talk, but cautioned me not to expect anything to come from it. He offered that he hoped I didn't mind the trip north because he couldn't see where it would accomplish anything. (He immediately knew what I was attempting, and his disinterest was established and valid.)

Bruce and I had quiche at a little restaurant in the wonderful Gas Town section of Vancouver. He patiently explained to me why he and Randy Bachman thought we were arrogant butts. Our office had rudely dismissed his efforts to get our attention at a time when their first hit was rapidly jumping upward. He finally took the group on the road himself with little or no money, maxing out his personal American Express card, to get them live exposure. Later, as we continued to show disinterest, other promoters came to his assistance and gave him tour dates. He said he was eternally grateful to them and planned to give those promoters, not Concerts West, his future business.

Bruce said he knew his partner Red Robinson was fond of me, and that I was probably a good guy. Even so, one of my concert partners was a rude jerk, and Bruce wanted nothing to do with us.

I thanked him for taking time to meet with me, told him I wanted to think about the things we said today and promised to come back to see him again. Bruce gave no indication that there was any reason for me to return. As I drove back to Seattle from Vancouver, I felt total sympathy for his and the group's point of view. Concerts West had become the reigning monster of international rock promotion, and I already saw slipping from our demeanor as a company humility and a commitment to our relationships with artists. We were busy, very busy, on our way to producing 500 shows that year from Australia to Tokyo, from New York to Manila. Nonetheless, here was a nearly-local band that busted out big after patronizing our recording studios and spending thousands of dollars with us. And we turned our backs! Alarming!

I waited a week before returning to Vancouver for an office meeting with Bruce, who was polite but indicated at the offset that another talk was not the best use of his time or mine. I thanked him for seeing me again and said the only reason I was there was to apologize for our entire company. I told him that he was right — we *had* treated him poorly, unfairly, rudely — and I was ashamed of our conduct, which was atypical of our firm's behavior. I told him that, had they approached me, I would have embraced them like long lost brothers and that, with the records they were producing, anyone who short-sheeted them was out of their mind, and that I was stunned by our stupidity.

Although it was still a secret, I told Bruce that, after 15 years, I was retiring from KJR at the end of the year. I added that if he and Randy could somehow find it possible to give us a second chance, I would personally handle every date they worked for us. I would be there with them every night, every step of the way, and they would never have to talk to anyone from our company but me. I would be their personal concert slave driven only by my desire to make each and every date with us the greatest and most comfortable of their careers.

I pointed out that Concerts West always offered the best opportunity for sell outs: we advertised more heavily than other promoters; we negotiated rates with radio stations across the country that other promoters couldn't match; our rental deals in buildings were better; our insurance costs were less; and, in general, nearly all costs associated with our shows were lower due to the volume of business we conducted.

We were beyond effective at selling seats, and no one could match our performance. Such savings, and greater grosses, allowed us to pay talent more money than could our competitors. And, perhaps most important of all, image-conscious acts knew they were in safe hands with Concerts West. We were concert perfectionists, and talent needs to be free of all outside worries so they can concentrate totally on the performance itself. Our reputation in this all-important area was impeccable.

Bruce asked whether I was ignoring his commitment to promoters that had helped him when he and the group needed help.

"Not for one minute!" I told him. I respected loyalty, it was the foundation of our firm. Wherever he requested it, I promised, promoters who had helped them in the past would be made a 50-50 partner with us. I closed by saying, "I would be proud to work with you and Randy, and if anything I've said today is of interest, let's talk some more."

I always considered Bruce Allen the ultimate of managers because he invariably put the interests of his group first. Too often, that was not the case in our business. His next move typified his management style. Our early rebuff of his attempts to approach us had made him look ineffective. Although he resented our actions deeply, Bruce put Bachman-Turner Overdrive's needs above those of his own ego and decided they should try working with us, or at least with me. I felt that he trusted me, and this seemed verified when, after another couple weeks went by, he called and said, "We need to go out again soon. Let's sit down and see what you can do."

Thus began a relationship that was unique in rock-'n'-roll in 1974. Randy and Robbie Bachman are Mormons, Fred Turner and Blair Newman very straight, and there were no excesses associated with their tours beyond lavish meals served every night in the dressing room following the show. The men of BTO were enthusiastic eaters and did not take well to mediocre meals. We tried our best to meet their standards and usually scored. If you don't have to buy cases of Dom Perignon and Chevas Regal, or assorted drugs, popping for a catered gourmet dinner is a pleasure. Mormons tend to be cheap dates in this regard.

What really amazed me was, everyone that was part of the band, Randy and Fred included, traveled on regularly scheduled flights riding in coach. We always had to charter a custom interior Boeing 707 for Elton John, and for many other acts as well—Learjets, Gulfstreams, you name it. In contrast, here were these guys, at the top of their game, riding coach. They even shamed me out of my first class seats (begrudgingly, I might add!).

The really pleasant feature of a BTO tour was that every night was a good night. Intending no criticism of the other acts we handled, in the world of rock concerts there was a direct, distinct connection between sobriety and tour consistency. With this troupe, I felt guilty about slipping away to sip a little Jack Daniels after the show. I was, however, able to overcome that guilt.

Our first tour together picked up in Chattanooga, Tennessee. Thence to Johnson City/Bristol, Memphis, Greensboro, Charlotte, Charleston and, finally, Terre Haute (Indiana State University). True to our word, we included as a partner Phil Lashinsky, the promoter who booked them the first time around. Phil traveled with us on many of the dates.

Phil comes from one of America's great show biz families—his uncles operated the Ringling Brothers, Barnum & Bailey Circus while he and his brothers owned the Lippizan stallions that annually toured and thrilled American horse lovers. We drove from Chattanooga across Tennessee to the Tri-Cities, telling concert stories all the way. My original partner, Dick Curtis, who was back with the company and now running our Atlanta office, was in the car with us, and we set a new world's record for laughs per mile. One story I remember from that day was my telling of how Dean Torrence of Jan and Dean lost his sneakers on a plane ride from LA to Seattle. He went to the police department upon arrival and reported the theft, which naturally made the TV news that night! Dean claimed, with a straight face, that the sneakers were worth millions in that he sang better when wearing them!

I had the joy of presenting BTO to audiences in Los Angeles, New York, Boston, Hartford, Buffalo, Chicago, Phoenix, Houston, San Antonio and Dallas/Fort Worth, to mention a few of the cities we visited. One episode sticks out in my mind, a special event connected with our stop in Dallas/Fort Worth for a performance at the Terrant County Convention Center.

Traditionally, the last night of a successful concert tour called for a party. Such a party for, say, Led Zeppelin, demanded the appropriation of a variety of entertainment, refreshments and activities (nothing wholesome would be achieved here by explicitly identifying what those items were). When it came time in Dallas to celebrate the conclusion of Bachman-Turner Overdrive's tour, the band was delighted to learn I had rented a new, high speed go cart track in nearby Arlington for the occasion. We took over the facility at midnight for an event I titled *The* BTO 500.

The track was an immaculate new facility, and I arranged for a big scoreboard, checkered flags, time trials, a Texas-sized barbecue and special commemorative shirts printed front and back. I did, however, make one significant mistake which provided me with scars I still display today and nearly proved fatal at the time. With additional money, I enticed the army veteran who built and operated the track to remove the speed governors from the carts. They sported powerful McCulloch engines and were fast enough already, but nothing was too good for the BTO 500! *Faster,* I reasoned, *is better.*

The event proceeded flawlessly until around quarter to four in the morning when, in the last lap of the last heat of this wondrous motor sports epic, my best-laid plans backfired. I was on the outside and Bruce Allen was on the inside, and we were fighting for the lead. In the final turn, side by side, engines racing at full power, checkered flag waiting, we collided. At a speed in excess of 50 MPH, I rode my cart through a chain link fence.

When I regained consciousness, I found myself sprawled flat on my back amidst some sage brush outside the track, with worried faces hovering over me. I heard the siren of an approaching ambulance, remembered last seeing that steel fence coming at me and wondered whether I was still alive and, if so, for how long.

"Where's all the blood coming from?" someone shouted.

No answer.

"Are my legs moving?" I asked.

"Yes!"

"How about my arms?" I inquired next, feeling great pain as I flexed them.

"Yes!"

"Oh, shit!" someone in the ambulance crew exclaimed as they converged on me. His colleagues muttered similarly encouraging words as they loaded me onto a stretcher.

Within minutes, I was in the emergency room of Arlington Hospital.

Ten days later, I flew out of Dallas for Seattle fully reassembled thanks to the remarkable surgical skills of a team of Texas doctors. I wasn't the prettiest of sights, having sustained deep gashes, a concussion, a smashed elbow and

more. My most serious injury was losing a thumb in the wreck. Thankfully, someone at the racetrack had noticed that one of my digits was missing, and a quick search located the lost appendage.

A lengthy medical stay was needed to successfully reattach my thumb, replace a few tendons, add some skin grafts and insert a few bone screws to hold everything together until I regained (hopefully) use of my right hand. I'm not a southpaw, so that made it the thumb of my writing hand. Of course!

My cast was unique. I had so many broken blood vessels, arteries, etc. in my right arm, it had to be kept over my head to reduce pressure from the heart. Also, I had steel wires extending through my so-glad-to-have-it-back thumb straight up my hand and out through the end of my pinkies! This contraption allowed no movement whatsoever until healing was complete. My arm was supported by a rod that extended up from my waist and held my elbow firmly in place.

I promise you, I didn't care. I must have ducked my head just as I hit the fence. Otherwise, it would have meant decapitation or, at the least, a broken neck. (No, none of us wore helmets.) Racing BTO band members in go carts suddenly made Led Zeppelin's tour-ending parties look attractive!

The picture on the previous page tells the story. I took five more days off before returning to the road. This photo, shot at the Nashville airport, indicates the quality of sympathy I received. Bruce, Randy, Robbie, Blair and Fred all had big fun at the expense of their dedicated and nearly-mortally-wounded promoter. Even worse, my job included doing the accounting, check writing and book balancing at the end of each show, and I had to learn to write legibly using my left hand. There were those, like my family, that hoped I learned even more lessons than that. The jury is still out.

Let It Ride
Bachman Turner Overdrive, 1973

IN THE SUMMER OF 1976, the band wanted to do something really big in Seattle. Another show in the Coliseum wasn't enough. This was nearly home turf for them, and they sought a defining moment for their careers. It came in the form of an idea I hatched called the *Seattle Summer Jam*. I was particularly excited about the concept because partner Tom Hulett had told partner Terry Basset it was a dumb idea and would probably loose a lot of money. Hearing something like that always inspires me, especially from Tom, who a year and a half earlier had begged me to mend fences with BTO. This was what the group wanted and this was what it would be.

I rented High School Memorial Stadium, under the Space Needle, which had never been used as a concert venue. The lineup? The J. Giles Band. The Charlie Daniels Band. The red hot Bob Seger & The Silver Bullet Band. And, as headliners, Bachman-Turner Overdrive. There were some problems to overcome, but they seemed manageable. The school board demanded that I cover the stadium's Astro Turf to guard against cigarette burns and other stains. Scouting around, I discovered that Arrowhead Stadium in Kansas City had just such a cover which they used on the field between games during periods of snowy weather. They were happy to rent it to me, and trucks were hired for the transport of the giant tarp out to Washington state.

I needed a special sound system because the Seattle Symphony was performing some kind of program that same day in the Opera House next door. The thought that the slightest whisper of BTO rock might filter into the symphony's hall was unbearable to them. I knew that Bill Graham in San Francisco had a highly directional system that could be used to target the sound away from the symphony lovers. I made arrangements with Bill for its use so none of our music would invade the Opera House.

Ticket sales boomed, and 28,000 fans soon made it a sell out. You no doubt have heard of Murphy's Law: Whatever can go wrong will. There's also O'Toole's Law, which states, Murphy was an optimist. It's long been my contention that Murphy and O'Toole wrote those laws specifically for the outdoor concert business. Just then, both came into play. When the trucks arrived at the Kansas City warehouse on the Wednesday morning before the show to pick up the tarp, the drivers noticed smoke coming from the structure. I'll spare you the details except to say the building and the tarp inside were destroyed.

A touching plea I delivered to Seattle school administrators fell on deaf ears. I thought I had pretty good juice in my town—usually my requests were granted—but I was unable to "con" them into believing that for one Sunday afternoon, we could convince the crowd to avoiding smoking or engaging in other activities that might harm the big green carpet. When our insurance company sided with the school officials, it was time for serious innovation.

I told you earlier of my good friend Bill Doner, he of 64-Funny-Cars/ Mexican-cock-fights fame. Bill and I were inseparable companions when we were in town at the same time. I always figured that, between Bill and me, we could solve any problem in the world. A few cocktails on the waterfront that evening led us to a solution. One thousand eight hundred pieces of three quarter inch thick plywood, in four-by-eight foot sections, would cover the 120-yard-long, 50-yard-wide field. There remained the problem of how to hold them together, and another round of drinks produced the answer: Duct tape, plain old duct tape, more than two miles of it.

By evening's end, I forged an agreement with Bill that he would bring his crew from the race track, along with some local casual laborers, and get it done in time for Sunday's concert. I insisted that a job of this scope and genius required his personal supervision and, after another round or two, Bill agreed to that, too. Our over-the-top idea required scouring every lumber yard in western Washington to find enough plywood sheets. We accomplished that and, by two o'clock Saturday morning, the field was covered. Then, we were again visited by either Murphy or O'Toole. I'm not sure which.

If you ever look closely at Astro Turf, used in so many stadiums in the '70s and '80s, you'll notice that it's really millions of tiny green bristles made to look like grass. Those bristles are stiff and stand upright, much like the bristles on a toothbrush. Characteristic of these fields are slopes from the center to the sidelines to promote drainage. The laws of gravity being what they are, tons and tons of plywood and duct tape placed on those little Astro Turf bristles began to slowly slide down the slopes toward the sidelines. They slid in no orderly fashion. The duct tape had held for a short time, but now the plywood advanced across the running track surrounding the field, finally piling up against the grandstands. Bill Doner uttered profanities.

At times like this, pure, unadulterated brilliance can truly be measured. Together, Doner and I were confident we possessed such brilliance, and within two hours, our new plan was in place. The concert was now sold out, and if anyone thought I would cancel the event and take a loss after being subjected to skepticism from within my own company, and with Doner at my side, they didn't know me well.

We called back to Minneapolis to the headquarters of the 3M Company and, on a Saturday morning, actually raised an executive. He confirmed our guess that they possessed a special duct tape that absolutely would not come loose from plywood, regardless of pressure. It was, however, in Minneapolis, and we were in Seattle. Then someone from our office remembered that John Denver's Learjet was sitting in Chicago with a pilot. After short telephone negotiations, pilot and plane were on their way to Minneapolis.

Another engineering problem we solved while standing and viewing the wreckage of our floor: A retainer collar of 6"x6" wood beams was stretched along the sidelines, end to end. Holes were drilled though the running track's surface deep into the ground, and long bolts were run through the beams and into the ground. At two o'clock that Saturday afternoon, the magical 3M tape landed in Seattle and was applied as the plywood was replaced. By nine o'clock Sunday morning, the job was complete and, one hour later, the gates opened.

Around 6:00 P.M. that beautiful summer afternoon, Bachman-Turner Overdrive was celebrating their greatest victory ever with a second encore. No fewer than 14,000 of the 28,000 people in attendance were on the stadium floor, jumping up and down to the final song. Just then, the 3M tape line down the center ridge of the field finally grew tired and popped. As the band played on, the crowd and flooring on both sides of the center line began moving toward the grandstands like two mighty glaciers slowly heading down to the sea. The hefty 6"x6" collar and its deeply imbedded bolts were ripped up and joined the crowd and the 1,800 pieces of plywood in that slow slide. It didn't matter; who cared? The show was ending. And it had been perfect!

The next morning, on my favorite Seattle radio station, KJR, commercials were heard announcing "The greatest plywood sale in Seattle history, today and today only! Bring your truck, 4'x8' sheets, only five dollars each! Hurry, it's all just one block east of the Space Needle at Memorial Stadium!"

If
David Gates & Bread, 1974

A SOURCE OF GREAT PRIDE FOR ME was the development of not only the many young groups we handled but also of our own Concerts West people. Such was the case with David Gates and his eternally-famous Bread, and a man named Willie Leopold, who handled all their appearances for Concerts West. Willie was the former brother-in-law of Terry Bassett, who cut his teeth at Pat O'Day & Associates with out region-wide teenage dance business. Willie went on to personify the character, concern and business astuteness that makes for success on the road for performers. (At this writing, he manages Melissa Ethridge, David Lanz, Kenny Loggins, David Koz and others.) However, there came a time when Bread decided to disband.

It wasn't that David Gates and the group couldn't keep on pumping out the hits. God, could they pump out the hits. Stresses, however, accompanied so many young groups, stresses like too much money, too many drugs and too little maturity. Sometimes, combinations of musicians, seemingly put together by the gods of sound, but blinded by success and youth, broke up. Such was the case with Bread. I will always be so sorry that their string of hits, which included *If, Baby I'm a Want You, The Diary, I Wanna Make It With You, Aubrey* and *It Don't Matter to Me* ended prematurely. The group could have given themselves and the world so much more music to enjoy.

I want to tell you the amazing story of their final concert. It defied all odds—a calamity that threatened to end the reign of Bread on a sour and premature note. It was the catalyst for one of the most remarkable efforts ever by Willie Leopold and Concerts West. I have used the following true story many times when some individual told me something couldn't be done.

Bread decided to break up following one last tour. Thirty cities and dates, and there would be no announcement of their disbanding until the final night, which would be in Salt Lake City. They didn't want their last tour to turn into a day-by-day, tear-jerking farewell festival that would distract from their final performances as a group.

Their shows sold out every night, and we were down to the final weekend: Friday night in Phoenix and Saturday night at the Salt Palace in Salt Lake City. Friday night's show ended with lots of encores, and the group was in great spirits. Now, if only they could emotionally make it through their final show the next night in Utah! That night, everyone accepted an invitation to an informal party some young lady had put together at her home for the group. Don't ask me how that happened. You don't just put together a big bash for a group with which you have had no prior contact and that doesn't know you! The last thing they are going to do is to go out to your house in some strange town simply because you have put a party together. In short, things like this never ever happened … except, on this one night, it did.

To start with, the young lady that somehow got back stage and passed out her own invitations was gorgeous. Then, it must have been the emotional toxins of the group's imminent retirement that eliminated normal constraints. Anyway, by intermission I heard that everyone was going out to this young lady's house in Scottsdale after the show. The group, the road crew, our people —everyone was planning to attend. Haste in arrival was not an issue; the hostess said the party would go all night. I attended for a while and then headed downtown to the hotel for some sleep before a noon departure for Salt Lake. The group planned to head north by private jet, so they had no reason not too kick back and enjoy. David Gates, however, rode back to the hotel with me in the limo. He was in a pensive mood, and I could tell he was taking these last dates together with his group very hard.

My sleep was interrupted shortly after seven the next morning by Willie Leopold pounding on my door. "You're not gonna believe what's happened!"

I was by now a seasoned veteran in this business. Openers like that exposed a vista of possible occurrences that ranged anywhere from some key person being imprisoned to an unexpected death.

Willie came in, sat down on the bed and began relating his news. The driver of the giant double trailer truck carrying all the equipment from the show had attended the party, got pretty drunk and left around three. Shortly before six, while driving at high speed, he lost control on the southern outskirts of Flagstaff, Arizona, left the highway and rolled the truck and trailer over several times. An Arizona state trooper told Willie it almost looked like there had been an explosion.

The trailers had split completely apart after the first roll. The driver was in the hospital in stable condition, but the massive array of sound equipment, speakers, lights, frames, pianos, guitars, drums, amplifiers and everything else was spread in pieces across the desert floor. Willie had just come from David's room, and David was very decisive. Cancellation of Salt Lake City was out of the question. His group had yet to have their final show, and a final show they must have. It could not be delayed, not even for a day, because everyone had made reservations, chartered planes, formulated big plans to leave the country on Sunday in several directions. We had no option but to somehow, someway put on that show!

What happened in the next 12 hours is the difference between an average company and a great one. In a hurried meeting up in David's room, we agreed that the purse strings were off. It would be a little expensive but, after all, there was a $70,000 check waiting for us in Salt Lake. If we failed …? We knew we would go down trying!

My Air Travel Q Card was a powerful weapon to wield in such a situation. With it, I could buy anything any airline had for sale. I was immediately on the phone with the local supervisor of, at that time, Hughes Air West. After some checking, he found that he had a Fairchild F27 twin engine turboprop passenger plane that would be idle for several hours.

"Great, we'll take it!" The plan we developed worked like this. We would go back to David's room and bring in the road crew. There, we would construct as best we could a list of everything that was on the truck. Then, Willie would head out to the airport with two of the road crew and fly to Flagstaff. Before arrival, they would call the local Salvation Army, which often has men looking for casual labor. They would rent two Hertz trucks at the airport, pick up the men and head out into the desert to see what could be salvaged. Of particular importance were guitars, custom made foot pedals, uncommon microphones to which the group was accustomed and a maze of wiring that was critical to Bread's production scheme. Hopefully, portions of the overhead light frame and connections had avoided demolition and could still be employed. Little hope was held out for the piano, the other keyboards, the drums and the giant overhead speaker racks with their multiple sound boxes and JBL speakers.

Whatever could be salvaged would be rushed to the airport, stuffed into the F27, flown to Salt Lake and trucked to the auditorium, where repairs would be attempted. This all had to happen quickly because, in the worst case, we had a nearly impossible task of rounding up replacement equipment on a Saturday, none of which we were going to find in Salt Lake City.

I assigned myself, along with Mike Crowley from our Seattle/Bellevue office, the task of trying to replace all of the group's heavy essentials that, it was reasonable to believe, had already done their final show. Step one was a call to Western Airlines in Los Angeles where, after some strenuous negotiations, I arranged for the use of a Boeing 737 and the removal of most of the seats within four hours. I told them to have the plane ready and standing by.

Now, it was really action time. We started down the list of every contact we could think of in Los Angeles and San Francisco. By 10:00 A.M. things were starting to take shape. A sound and lights company in Santa Monica had a light frame that would work. A recording studio in Hollywood that Gates recommended had some microphones and foot pedals that would fill the bill. An expensive set of drums was ordered from some Hollywood music store. We were also in luck in that the engineer from the recording studio had several friends with an assortment of keyboards, amps and guitars that he would assemble and get to the airport on time. The late Bill Graham in San Francisco came up with a replacement sound system and mixing board. No small item, way too late to truck, it would have to somehow be squeezed into the 737. Bill's guy said he would have it at San Francisco International at the Western Airlines hangar by three that afternoon.

It was time to get ourselves to the Phoenix airport and catch a scheduled flight to Los Angeles to coordinate the loading of the equipment we had secured. Somehow, we needed to be out of LA and on our way to San Francisco by 2:00 P.M.

We called the Salt Palace in Salt Lake, as well as the radio stations, and told them to announce that the concert's start would be delayed one hour, until nine that night. We had a one hour time difference to make up. It was already mid-morning in Phoenix. We arrived in Los Angeles on time, I confirmed that our 737 was ready for loading, confirmed also that the San Francisco gear was on its way to that airport, left Mike in charge and headed for Salt Lake City. I arrived there just in time to greet the Hughes Air West F27 as it arrived with Willie Leopold from Flagstaff. God, what a mess. They hadn't been able to take the seats out of that plane, but it didn't matter. There wasn't a piece on board big enough to make any difference. When the truck began its sideways roll across the sagebrush north of Flagstaff, internally it created a sort of 18-wheel Mixmaster for a few hundred thousand dollars worth of equipment. There wasn't much left except for one very important wiring harness that had everything to do with the special effects used by Bread. I thanked God we had arranged for nearly complete back up gear. We were going to need all of it!

With the help of the auditorium staff, we hired extra help because when the 737 set down from San Francisco around six, we would have a job on our hands that normally took six hours, and that's working with equipment, plugs, bolts, pulleys, etc. that everyone was familiar with. This was a whole new lash-up on the way, and the new nine o'clock starting time was looking overly optimistic. Safe to say, nothing like this had ever before been attempted.

However, if you really believe you can do something, and if you have a group as inspired as Bread's road crew was that day, as well as all the local help we could find, miracles can happen. Miracles only happen if you give them the chance to happen. "Believe and it might come true" was one of my favorite sayings. Willie created absolute magic! I was at the radio stations giving interviews, explaining what had taken place and why the show was being delayed. We still weren't telling anyone that this would be the final performance of Bread.

To make a long story shorter, Bill Graham came through in San Francisco and sent a couple of his equipment people along on the plane, which arrived ahead of schedule just before six. David Gates and the group were still in Phoenix (they saw no reason to come to Salt Lake if we weren't going to be able to pull it off). Willie kept David informed of progress and, by 6:15, he called them and said, "Get your sweet retiring butts on your jet. We're gonna have a show tonight!"

Following the opening act, Bread came on stage at quarter past ten for the last time as a group. We decided beforehand that I would introduce the group and then reveal to the audience that they would, this night, be a part of history. For, when the show ended, Bread the group would be no more.

I recall bringing them on by saying, "Ladies and gentlemen, this is a special night, as Bread has selected Salt Lake City to be their final performance ever. The group has decided to disband. After tonight, the group will be only a memory. So, on this very special evening, let us all sit back and enjoy as, for the last time anywhere, we proudly give you David Gates and Bread!"

Many in the audience were too stunned by the announcement to know what to do. Of course, the greeting was warm, but the usual craziness wasn't there as the crowd concentrated, listened, tried to take home with them every delicious moment and note of this rock-'n'-roll finale. In turn, Bread delivered as fine and emotional a farewell show as any Bread fan could have hoped for.

After the show, we went to the Hilton by the Salt Palace and had dinner. We not only relived the show. For the first time, the band heard all the intricate details of the amazing events and accomplishments of the day. Having checked and found that the driver of the truck was going to be just fine, we roundly toasted him for being so stupid.

Reading the Sunday Salt Lake City newspaper while flying back to Seattle the next day, I made another toast to another truly stupid person. In the review of the show the night before, the paper's music critic said that, overall, it was a good concert despite the long delay because of equipment problems. He then went on to say that the only unfortunate part of the evening was when some jerk from Concerts West tried to make a big teary-eyed deal out of this being the last city on the tour. He called it disgusting and a "juvenile disruption."

That writer, that clown, who probably told himself he was a person of great intellect, that moron, had totally missed the significance of the entire evening. I almost became furious, but then I tried to remember that God also loves "the small guys with their small thoughts." If I were to let this bother me for another moment, it would only take away from the smile pasted on my face, the smile of knowing how lucky I was to have been a part of one of music's truly great and historic moments. I occasionally put a Bread tape in my car stereo and take myself back to that weekend. As I hear David singing *It Don't Matter to Me*, I have to look upward in thanks for my truly blessed life. There must be a law somewhere against having so many wonderful and exciting experiences!

16—Viva Las Vegas

Elvis Presley, 1964

*L*ET'S GO BACK TO 1970. We were a young, growing company when we first became acquainted with a talent manager out of New York named Jerry Weintraub. Jerry had managed the Four Seasons, and I had met him years before when we brought the group to Seattle. Soon he was also handling the affairs of Geraldo Rivera, Ed McMahon of the *Tonight Show* and others. He was well connected, and we talked of different ways we might do business together.

Jerry introduced our company to Colonel Tom Parker, Elvis Presley's manager. Jerry knew the Colonel, we had the credentials and, with my new partners, Les Smith and Danny Kaye, we had the resources and ability to handle the largest of tours. Elvis was just out of seclusion and wanted to perform again after his grand re-entry in Las Vegas.

The Colonel told Jerry he would meet with us in Vegas and, if we wanted to take Elvis out on tour, we should "bring along" a cashier's check for one million dollars made out to him personally as a token of our good faith. Not surprisingly, this caused strong debate within our firm. It wasn't our usual way of doing business. No contract, no guarantee, just, "Hey, give me a million dollars and we'll talk!"

We did it.

Tom Hulett delivered the check to Vegas and joined Jerry in the Colonel's suite at the Hilton. A deal was struck, and every single Elvis performance outside of Las Vegas for the rest of Elvis's life was handled by Concerts West in partnership with Weintraub. This deal made Tom Hulett's concert career, as he became our Elvis specialist.

Tom and Jerry walked into the Colonel's suite, and the first thing Parker said was, "Did you bring the money?" When Tom produced the cashier's check, the Colonel looked at it, threw it on his cluttered hotel suite floor and said, "Okay, let's sit down and talk!"

Hours later, they decided to go downstairs and eat. As they left the room, Tom nervously looked back at the check still lying on the floor. Should he pick it up for the Colonel—a million dollars? Tom kept his mouth shut, and they went for dinner.

So began a profitable, high-profile, unbelievable run for our company with Elvis. This was a typical stunt by the Colonel, and many more like it followed. My experiences with him went back to 1962. Elvis was in Seattle filming *It Happened at the World's Fair*, and Parker called and asked whether I wanted to be in the picture with Elvis. What more could a deejay ask for than to be in a Presley movie? Parker said I could include a couple of other deejays if I wanted, so I brought along Lan Roberts (KJR's morning man) and Lee Perkins (middays). As per the Colonel's instructions, we wore coats and ties—what we normally wore at the radio station in those days. Arriving at the Paramount Studios' set on the Fairgrounds, we were put off to the side and told to wait. After about an hour, the Colonel came over and grabbed me. Lan and Lee followed, and Parker herded us over to where Elvis was standing between takes. I had met Elvis before, so we shook hands and exchanged a few words. Then a photographer said, "All of you stand around Elvis."

We complied, and flashbulbs popped. Colonel Parker, who had been standing to the rear of us, elbowed his way through the group, shook my hand and said, "Congratulations, Pat. You've just been in a picture with Elvis."

There's No Business Like Show Business
Ethel Merman, 1954

COLONEL PARKER CUT HIS SHOW-BIZ TEETH on the carnival business and remained the consummate hustler all his life. He created a famous sideshow attraction called *Colonel Parker's Dancing Chickens* and sold it as a ready-to-use package to carnivals from coast to coast. They would hang a big banner across the gayway, showing two chickens dancing. After customers paid their money and entered the tent, recorded music began playing. With great bravado, the barker announced

Pat O'Day "in a picture with Elvis" on set of It Happened at the World's Fair —*1962*

that their senses were about to be stunned by the finest-trained chickens on earth. The curtain opened and, there before their very eyes, two chickens were hopping up and down to the music. Minutes later, a satisfied audience left the tent amazed that someone had actually taught chickens to dance.

In truth, no training was involved. Parker instead developed a small trailer that could be pulled behind a car. The trailer contained a stage, a sound system, curtains that folded down for travel and, last but not least, a large, kerosene-heated hot plate. Shortly before the show, the operator turned on the gas and warmed up the plate. Once the plate heated up, the show began. Chickens were dumped onto the plate, the curtain opened and, as the music played, the chickens naturally jumped up and down to avoid burning their feet. The only way for the act to fail was to not have the plate sufficiently hot. During the great carnival years of the '30s and 40s, tens of thousands paid their money and thrilled to the Colonel's famous dancing chickens.

Parker's carnival days manifested themselves in many little quirks and sayings. For example, when arriving with Elvis on tour in a new city, he would tell people, "We better go pawn the tires!"

This harkened back to a time when traveling shows arrived in town too broke to make the up-front payment any wise hotel demanded from carnival folks. They parked their trucks at the show site, removed the tires and rims, took them to the local tire store and borrowed money against them. Monday morning, with cash from the weekend's take, they would retrieve the wheels and head for the next town. The sums involved were never great, and the interest rates were probably high. That's show biz!

Don't Be Cruel
Elvis Presley, 1956

ANOTHER ONE OF PARKER'S QUIRKS resulted from his once being caught in a late night hotel fire caused by faulty electricity. From then on, in his own home, he pulled the circuit breaker at exactly eight o'clock every night, his usual bedtime. Fine for the Colonel, terrible for Charles Stone from our Dallas office, road manager of the Presley tours. At the Colonel's insistence, Stone spent endless weeks at the Parker home while they planned tours together. The Parkers lived in Palm Springs and, during the heat of the year, staying in their home at night with no air conditioning was a less-than-pleasant experience. Poor Charles spent his evening hours reading books by flashlight and talking to his wife on the phone from his stifling hot bedroom. Charles deserved a Medal of Honor for the services he provided our company.

The Colonel's twisted sense of humor showed itself one morning when His Highness called our home office in Bellevue, Washington with an odd request. There was a farm outside Portland, Oregon that raised three-foot-tall miniature horses, and Parker wanted us to go down there and buy two of the horses and ship them to Barron Hilton in Las Vegas. Dan Fiala drew the lucky number and was soon on his way to Oregon.

Every year, the Las Vegas Hilton hotel and casino—the International—made millions off of Elvis, and Elvis and the Colonel formed a relationship with Barron Hilton based on mutual respect and need. That left Hilton vulnerable to the Colonel's imagination. The tiny horses arrived in Vegas while Hilton was away and were delivered to his palatial office on the top floor of the hotel. The Colonel prearranged for a great deal of straw and a small wooden fence to be installed in the Barron's office, and the horses were placed inside their new home. When Barron returned, he found his beautiful office half filled with tiny horses and hay and smelling of fresh manure and urine. Waiting there, too, was a lovely birthday card offering the hope that these horses would mean a great deal to the Barron. It was signed by Elvis and the Colonel. What was Hilton to do? He dared not offend Elvis and the Colonel.

Barron Hilton moved to a small office and left his big, palatial one to the horses. A month or so later, Parker arrived unannounced, noted the horses were still there, and headed for Hilton's temporary quarters. He walked in, told Hilton "Barron, you still have those dumb horses in your office! For God's sake, get rid of them! Can't you take a joke?" and walked out.

Colonel Parker pulled another of his creative, nasty tricks on RCA Records. Elvis had been with RCA almost from the beginning and, suffice it to say, RCA was indebted to the Colonel and his star. This time, the occasion was Parker's birthday, and he waited until 9:00 A.M. came, then called RCA in Hollywood from his home in Palm Springs and demanded to speak to the president of the record division. Once he had his target on the phone, Parker unloaded on him:

> This is Colonel Parker. You know, Elvis and I, for the past 20 years, have shown great loyalty and love for RCA. We have been reliable and honest and done our best to make our relationship with you one that could be a model. So why, after all I have always done for you and for your company—why, in God's name!—would you stoop so low? This is an obvious attempt to humiliate me!

The RCA exec was stunned! What could Parker possibly be talking about? He needed to get to the bottom of this quickly, so he began to gently probe: "Colonel, you're our dearest friend and client. I can tell you're very upset, and that upsets me. Please tell me—What happened?"

The Colonel then went on and on about how he had never asked RCA for a single thing, about how generous he had always been toward them, blah, blah, blah, about how he had not asked anyone to do anything special for his birthday because his birthday wasn't that important. But, to have someone from RCA call and tell him that a giant billboard was going to be erected along the highway from Los Angeles as it entered Palm Springs that would read "Happy Birthday, Colonel Parker," and then to drive out there that morning with his closest friends to show them how much RCA loved him and find no billboard—that was more than he could take! He was so humiliated, so embarrassed. The Colonel pretended to be weeping as he said goodbye and hung up.

Panic struck the Hollywood offices of RCA. No one knew who had planned the billboard or who had contacted the Colonel and told him about it, but answers to those questions could wait. First things first! A billboard company in the Palm

Springs area was contacted and offered any amount of money they wanted to get to the outskirts of Palm Springs and paint "Happy Birthday Colonel Parker, RCA Loves You!" on the biggest billboard they owned.

The company promised to have it finished by noon and, with that pledge in hand, RCA called the Colonel back. In a voice dripping with sympathy and empathy, RCA's head man fell on his knees before the Colonel. He blamed the billboard company for the snafu—and himself for not sending his personal representative to Palm Springs to see that it was done right. Expressing again and again RCA's eternal love for the Colonel and appreciation for all he had done for RCA, he closed by once more begging the Colonel's forgiveness and telling him his billboard would be in place by noon.

Continuing with his weeping act, Parker mumbled, "I accept your apology. I never asked for anything, you know, but thank you. I feel better!"

The Colonel hung up the phone and fell on the floor, laughing. He called his three best friends in Palm Springs, picked them up in his Cadillac and drove with them to the outskirts of town where he told them the story of what he had done. Parking the car near the billboard, they all laughed loudly as the Colonel's outdoor birthday card was painted.

Suspicious Minds

Elvis Presley, 1969

THE SIDE OF THE COLONEL THAT WASN'T SO FUNNY found him doing next to nothing as his golden goose slowly killed himself. It was no mystery what was going on with Elvis. When I visited with him in 1970, I met with a shy, thin, dynamic, proud, energized icon of rock-'n'-roll. Six years later, we were dealing with a bloated, overweight, shockingly pale, psychotic mess. On stage, he even required an imitator's voice behind the curtains to sing the notes he could no longer accomplish—on nights that he could stand and make it to the stage.

Colonel Parker continued to book one tour after another for a desperately ill man. Never has someone needed intervention more than Elvis did then, and the Colonel had the power over him to accomplish it if he so chose. One is left to wonder whether Parker feared he would lose that power over a sober Elvis. We'll never know.

That Elvis of the early '70s was the finest single performer I ever witnessed, with one of the world's most wonderful voices, little boy charm and a certain charisma God has gifted to so few. If you want to see Elvis at the zenith of his career, watch the video of his round-the-world live satellite concert that we, along with Tom Moffat, put on at the H.I.C. Arena in Honolulu. All proceeds went to the Kui Lee Cancer Fund. (Kui Lee was a brilliant young Hawaiian musician who wrote many great Hawaiian love songs and died far too young of cancer.) That night, Elvis achieved a level of showmanship, talent and greatness never seen before or since from a rock performer on stage.

Watch it and realize what might have been. We might have had this wonderful entertainer for many more years had someone close stepped in and helped. The only person close enough was Colonel Tom Parker, who chose to do nothing.

Viva Knievel

Theme song to the motion picture Viva Knievel, *starring Evel Knievel, 1977*

IN THE PREVIOUS CHAPTER I MENTIONED an acquaintance with the world famous motorcycle stunt man, Evel Knievel. If you have never heard of him, he was a motorcyclist from Butte, Montana who began jumping his motorcycle over cars at the Spanaway and Graham, Washington race tracks. These small stock car ovals, in communities east of Tacoma, employed Evel (whose real first name is Robert) to augment their racing programs. The fans loved it, and Evil expanded his stunts to match their affection. First it was five cars with a ramp built up one side, the cars parked sideways, then a ramp down the back side where he would complete the jump. There was always a pledge that next week, he would increase the risk by adding more cars and greater distance to the jumps. Before long, he was reaching into the 20 car regime and the fans loved it even more.

Evel was in demand at tracks all over the West. Seattle International Raceways' owner, Bill Doner, one of the world's greatest promoters in his own right, joined with our radio station to present an epic Knievel jump. I think it was a jump over something like 20 Peterbuilt trucks. (The jumps varied from time to time. Sometimes it was 30 cars, other times 24 school buses, whatever would sell the tickets.)

Evel Knievel's career came to a turning point one Sunday afternoon in Las Vegas. He was scheduled to jump over the entire front yard fountain complex outside of Caesar's Palace. This was to have network coverage and was certainly Evel's most important jump to date. With success, a host of clients willing to write big checks to him was waiting in the wings for their turn. I had been a distant observer of his jumps and noted the margin of safety he always provided himself. Evel was a promoter of major league status and had no intention of getting hurt. The jumps he had been making were well-practiced and uncomplicated given his experience. He left little room for error, despite the image he imparted that every jump could be fatal.

He proudly boasted that insurance was unavailable to him because the insurance underwriters were convinced that, if he ever missed, even by a foot, it would be fatal! He proclaimed that his next jump, over an ever-expanding number of something-or-others, was probably impossible and would likely bring his death.

Factually, the distance from the one side of the jumping ramp to the down ramp rarely changed a great deal. Just the number of vehicles parked between, as perception is everything. If you perceive that it's harder to jump over 20 Greyhound buses than it is to jump over 30 cars, well, then it is! Especially if Evel or the announcer on the radio commercials tells you so.

The Caesar's Palace jump took Knievel out of his safety cocoon and put him in a new world over which he had less control. When all was set, he determined that, due to the distance, he would leave the ramp at greater speeds than normal to insure reaching the downside of the ramp beyond the water fountains. I watched on the evening news as they replayed the accident that occurred that day. It was gruesome! You saw him streaking to the take-off ramp, seemingly levitating into the blue sky, passing the tall evergreens that surrounded the fountains, then the trip back to the ground. The jump was perfect! the form was perfect! He had more than enough momentum to safely reach the other side. He also had *too much* momentum!

The motorcycle landed at the bottom of the down ramp which was angled upwards in the direction of the jump. The flat ramp than ran out from the bottom of the landing ramp, presenting, in degree of impact, a substantially different reception than the sloped ramp. (The slope made the return to earth more gentle.) He had never encountered landing on a flat surface before.

The impact twisted the handle bars from his hands, and the bike slammed onto its side before bouncing, twisting and gyrating for several dozen yards. Evel was pitched from the bike, across the driveway and away from the relative comfort of the run-out area. There, his body hit a curb.

I was sickened as I saw his legs turn outward at a strange angle as his pelvis was crushed. Head injuries and numerous broken bones accumulated as his body, still at high speed, tumbled across the parking lot. I figured it was "Annie Annie Over" for our friend Evel.

He was in the Las Vegas Hospital in grave condition and, having seen the tape of the accident, I figured he'd never leave Vegas alive. But he did! There followed months of therapy, months of painful, discouraging therapy that most could never endure. Pins in his bones, casts and supports on his legs, crutches and, eventually, a cane to aid walking. Evel came back, all the way back! This was a remarkable display of determination by anyone's standards.

Having written all these things, I think you know I cared for the guy and admired his courage and chutzpah. I also stood in amazement and amusement of his ability to self promote. This ability was unburdened by concern for any over-statements or falsehoods. Evel said and did whatever was necessary to get ink or TV time. When it came to contorting truth to his advantage, he knew no equal.

Evel was also a hard drinker and partied with equal dedication. He was truly a three ring circus to be around. Now, after his Las Vegas accident, he had a new shtick: his triumphant return from the dead. Such a happenstance could not have been placed in more capable hands. Evel was off and running again. Soon he was on a sort of lecture circuit. It started with a couple of TV interviews in which he stated, with tears in his eyes, that God told him he was born to jump. He had experienced hospital visions in which God told him to get up and jump again. He explained that this was a gift given to him exclusively by the Father Almighty and that, as long as he was given air to breathe and could somehow pull his crippled body onto a motorcycle, he would continue to jump! It's not necessary to delve into how much of his spiritual awakening was the result of a divinely inspired vision and how much was the creation of one man's fertile imagination. It's immaterial. What is noteworthy was that Evel was soon back frequenting bars, attending parties, going wherever there were people, regaling them with stories of his greatness. About this time, Knievel discovered that he was in demand as a speaker. People wanted speeches. Inspirational speeches. Speeches that freed the timid from their bonds of fear and sent them out to accomplish great things.

The late Royal Brougham was the dean of Seattle sports writers, having headed up *The Seattle Post-Intelligencer* sports department for more years than anyone could remember. (The street separating Seattle's new football and baseball stadiums is named in his honor.) He was also a very religious man. Royal called regularly, putting the arm on me for a donation to one or another of his Christian projects. We had a simple deal: He gave me ink on a subject if he could possibly make it fit on the sports page and also included my name on an artistic Christmas tree, made up of hundreds of names of important sports figures, that appeared every Christmas Eve day in the *P-I*. It was an entirely workable arrangement for me.

I would have made the donations anyway, but he offered tokens of appreciation, and I was not in the business of turning down publicity.

Royal also staged an annual *Seattle Post-Intelligencer* Man of the Year in Sports banquet. (Today, they select a Woman of the Year as well as a Man of the Year.) Over the years, such luminaries as University of Washington running back Hugh McElhenny, baseball's Fred Hutchinson and Seattle University forward Elgin Baylor were saluted at the $100 a plate event. All proceeds went to some worthy entity chosen by Brougham. The banquet featured the announcement of the winner of this coveted title, as well as noted speakers and famous guests, everything designed to give the attendees their money's worth. One year, Royal decided to invite as a featured guest that now nationally-famous motivational speaker, Mr. Evel Knievel. Evel delivered his typically moving, teary eyed, challenging address that night, complete with showing in slow motion the film of the destruction of his body in the parking lot at Caesar's. Grown men were in tears. I know, because I was there. Evel had the audience spellbound, and Royal's voice quavered notice-ably when he arose after the speech and thanked Evel for coming. A week later, Royal called me at my office.

> Pat, this is Royal. Thank you for buying those tickets for the boys from the school for the banquet. I know they really appreciated it and I told them personally that you paid their way. Now Pat, there's another matter I want to discuss with you. Robert Knievel told me that he and you are good friends. Is that true?

[When pronounced, Knievel's first name sounds exactly like "evil." That made it impossible for Brougham, a born again Christian of considerable enthusiasm, to utter "Evel." He therefore introduced Knievel at the banquet as *Robert* Knievel, and that was the name he used in his conversations with me.]

Royal went on,

> Pat, there seems to be some terrible confusion, and I am trying to straighten it out. When Robert came to town, we agreed to pay him his speaking fee and also agreed to pick up his expenses at the Olympic Hotel. However, when the bill came in yesterday, it contained charges of over $3,000 from the bar. I was shocked and called the bookkeeper over there at the hotel, but she says that Robert actually signed for all the charges,

and she has a letter from me saying I will pay for Robert's expenses. But Pat, how can this be? I called for Robert, and his wife said he isn't expected soon. Pat, can you help me get to the bottom of this?

I had dropped by the Olympic Hotel's bar the night before the banquet to say hi to Evel and found him in rare form. Waiving his cane in the air, he was describing his death-defying trade to all, adding lurid stories of young ladies that were smitten by his charisma. Evel was entertaining and maintaining a large audience in the bar, partly because he was Evel Knievel, partly because he was funny and fascinating and partly because he was regularly announcing loudly for all to hear: "Drinks are on me!" I wasn't at all surprised by the size of Knievel's bar tab.

What I told Royal didn't make him feel any better, but I figured the greatest service I could offer him was the truth. I said,

> Royal, you want to get to the bottom of this? Well, you're already there. You hired Evel, you told him you would cover his expenses and then you forgot to put a limit on them. You should have called me and asked me before you made your deal with him, but you didn't. You know this is my business. I'm sorry to have to say this to you, Royal, but just pay the bill. That's how it works with Evel. You said you would cover his expenses, and he's very expensive! Gave a good speech though, didn't he?

Royal didn't think it was at all funny. I went on to explain that it had cost me nearly $1,000 at the Westin in Vancouver to learn about Evel and his expenses. I told Royal to just pay it and forget it: "You're at the bottom of it, and nothing's going to change." I told Royal that it would be easier for him to jump 100 cars on a motorcycle than to get his money back.

I'll never forget our parting words that day. Royal said "Pat, all this money is supposed to go to a worthy cause!"

I replied, "And you know, Royal, Evel would assure you that it went to a very worthy cause! It's always been one of his favorites!"

As we hung up, Royal was still muttering, "I just don't understand it. I've got to get to the bottom of it."

The following summer, Royal and I were co-Grand Marshals of the annual Lynnwood, Washington Little League Parade. As we rode through that town, sitting on the rear seat of a convertible, Royal said, "Pat, I've sent several invoices to Robert Knievel, but I've never heard a word back."

I said, "Royal, and you won't. Why don't you just save the story of the whole thing and put it in your book when you write it?"

Royal never wrote that book, so I decided to include this story in mine. My take on the whole thing is likely a lot funnier than Royal's would have been, anyway!

New York, New York
Lisa Minelli, 1974, Frank Sinatra, 1976

FOR MY FREQUENT BUSINESS TRIPS TO NEW YORK CITY, my headquarters became the Lombardy Hotel. There were certain things that Danny Kaye saw as imperatives, among them eating at the right restaurants and staying at the right hotels. Les Smith always followed Danny's thoughts in these regards, as did I. As such, in Los Angeles I commenced staying at the Beverly Wilshire Hotel on Santa Monica Boulevard and in, New York, at the Lombardy on 43rd between Lexington and Park Avenue. The Lombardy is quite the opposite of the Beverly Wilshire. While the Bev Wilshire offers the ultimate in hospitality facilities, with extravagant rooms and equally-extravagent shops, services, pool, etc, the Lombardy would be best described as funky, old, charming, very secure, family-like and low-key. It didn't take long before I came to understand that there were other, rather significant people that shared Danny's point of view where the Lombardy was concerned. I would see recognizable faces in the little lobby and on the elevators. Danny had his own special room at the Lombardy that was always made available for him. The same was the case with Elizabeth Taylor.

I was to have dinner across the street from the Lombardy at the Benihana restaurant with Evel Knievel. He was an acquaintance from the Northwest, my radio station had sponsored some of his famous jumps (24 school buses, as I recall), and Concerts West had presented "Evel Jumps" in Vancouver, BC and Portland. He was staying in the Lombardy as well, and we were trying to have a dinner that, I had a hunch, he wouldn't remember. I was no angel in those days, but Knieval was a drinker of Olympic status. Midway through, he simply got up, took his drink, and began a conversation with some customers at a distant table. Evel was certain everyone in the world wanted to meet him. ABC Wide World of Sports was enthusiastically aiding and abetting that notion, as they gave live coverage to nearly all of his jumping efforts. Even Mr. Credibility, Keith Jackson, along with Jim McKay and Chris Schenkle, would breathlessly describe his feats. Evel had the world at his feet, and he wanted to share the thrill of knowing him. In most cases, that was true, although enthusiasm over the acquaintanceship could wane if he hung around too long or had too many cocktails. After a period of time, I finished eating, paid the tab, and crossed the street to the hotel. Why interrupt him?

As I jaywalked through the Saturday night traffic inching up 43rd toward Park Avenue, I noticed some television crews complete with bright lights in front of the Lombardy. I had elbowed my way past some news people and onlookers and was about to enter the hotel when a reporter grabbed my arm and asked "Are you a guest here?" When I confirmed I was, he asked, "What floor are you on? If you see anything of the argument, would you come down and tell us?" I think my reply was something like, "What are you talking about? See what? What argument?"

Well, it turns out that there was an international crisis taking place right there in the good old Lombardy. Not a crisis of great diplomatic or political impact, but one of great "show biz" and domestic significance. It seems that Elizabeth Taylor had debarked a flight from London late in the afternoon. Previously-alerted reporters were on hand to meet her and heard her say to a person in the terminal at JFK, "Let's go to the Lombardy. I'm gonna catch that son-of-a-bitch cold!" Well, it turns out that son-of-a-bitch was none other than the world-famous motion picture and Shakespearian actor, her fourth husband, Richard Burton. It seems that Richard had taken up at least temporary residence in their apartment at the Lombardy with one Susan Hunt, wife of Formula One racing driver Jimmy Hunt. Miss Taylor, who had been in London, somehow heard of her movie-star husband's activity in New York with the absolutely stunning Suzie and jetted in.

Burton was apparently caught totally by surprise. An upstairs maid had witnessed a marital jihad in the hallway outside the apartment shared normally by Richard and Liz. Abnormally, it appeared to be occupied by Richard and Suzie. Reporters, responding en masse to the JFK comment by Liz, had arrived at the hotel the same time as Elizabeth. It turned out that the Taylor/Burton apartment was on the floor above mine. A maid had witnessed the "shootout," slipped downstairs, and shared her limited insights with reporters, but nothing had happened since. None of the parties to the squabble had come out the front door, and the reporters were standing vigil, left only with the maid's description of seeing Miss Taylor throw a bottle of whisky in the direction of Mr. Burton's head. Thus, the reporters, hungry for additional details, saw me as a possible insider, hotel-wise, who might bring them the information for which they hungered. I told the reporter I doubted I could be of help, but if they stuck around long enough, they might get to see Evel Knieval jump over a car or two. I went to my room, climbed into bed and watched the late night news on the New York channels. Sure enough, they offered live reports from the front of the hotel. They said that, other than the maid's information, there was nothing new to report. (God, what did they expect, a Burton confession?) I turned it off and went to sleep.

The incident wasn't even on my mind the next morning as I punched the elevator down button heading to the lobby for breakfast. The elevator door opened and there, before my very own little eyes, stood Richard Burton and Suzie Hunt. I entered the elevator, the door closed, and I said "Good morning, Richard Burton and Suzie Hunt, stars of last night's news on several channels." Burton looked very hung over and just grunted. Suzie, looking like she had just come from an *Ingenue* photo session, giggled! I was, at that moment, shocked! There before me was the real Richard Burton, but nothing could have prepared me for how short he was. I couldn't believe it! I had been around movie stars long enough to know that we carry the illusion from the movies that many of these people are physically larger than they actually are, but nothing had prepared me for Burton. This powerful man, this hunk with the swarthy face and bulging muscles from Cleopatra and so many other films, this man was in real life only about five-foot-five or -six inches tall! I seemed to tower over him, and I'm only five-foot-nine. My first thought was, "God, it's a miniature Richard Burton!" Suzie seemed to be about my height, and she, too, towered over Burton.

Looking at Suzie, I was inclined to believe that whatever poor Richard was going through, it was probably worth it. There are value judgments one must make in life. After all, Richard Burton wasn't a priest, a president, or some other noble role model. He was just Richard Burton. Liz was supposedly in London, and I concluded that the opportunity to share their apartment with Suzie was really more than any man should be forced to refuse. I, of course, factored into this instant moral judgement call a recollection of Miss Taylor's rather recent statement about certain mediocre aspects of her marriage to Burton. The elevator arrived in the lobby, and Burton stepped out to survey the horizon for any sign of reporters. Suzie said she hoped I would have a nice day, and they were gone! The couple hopped into a waiting limousine and away they went. I went to breakfast to contemplate what I had seen, concluding that, for an overnight stand, Richard and Suzie were probably just fine, but, in the long run, he and Liz made a better couple. Liz is reported to be only four-feet-eleven. I never did get to see Miss Taylor, who has survived so many adventures, not the least of which must be those resulting from her close friendship with Michael Jackson.

Ben

Michael Jackson, 1972

FACT IS FUNNIER THAN FICTION. Life daily offers so many laughs if we will just stand back, watch, and listen. Case in point.

During a financial drought experienced in college, I secured a construction job at the Hanford atomic plant in the central part of Washington state. It was 1954, the Soviet menace deeply concerned the free world, and this giant nuclear complex was undergoing rapid expansion. Through a friend and his father's union contacts, I was hired at the nuclear reservation as an insulation engineer. My qualifications for such a position were absent, but they needed lots of people on the job, so I became one of hundreds the union sent in to fill hard hats. The work they asked of me required little more than carrying buckets of magnesium mud, used to cover steam pipes, up ladders, and stay out of the way of those who knew what they were doing.

The demand for construction workers in general, and experienced insulation workers in particular, brought hundreds to the plant from all parts of the country. Two such workers came from the mountains of Tennessee. They were Ben Hartung and Rayford Cox. Ben and Rayford were inseparable companions and had worked construction together for years. They drove identical cars and towed identical house trailers for their families' residences from job to job. Ben was a tall, heavy-set, round, happy-faced, very congenial man in his 40s whose two claims to fame were his success at repairing the automatic transmission of his Oldsmobile by himself and, even more important, his ability to flawlessly recite the names of all forty-eight states and their capitols. Ben was justifiably proud of his accomplishments and, when asked to confirm these stunning attributes, he would give a nod, a big grin and a knowing wink.

Rayford Cox, was quite the opposite—about five-foot-five in height and slight of build, with flaming red hair and a disagreeable streak a mile wide. Little effort needed to be expended to send Rayford into a rage. On construction jobs, conversations between workers are nearly constant. The conversations generally focus on automobiles, sports, women, working conditions, occasionally politics, then back to women. Rayford considered himself an expert on all the above subjects and more. However, he couldn't seem to get himself more than five minutes into any discussion before finding a point of disagreement. This was a big problem in that Rayford could never intelligibly articulate his differing viewpoint and would simply fly out of control. He seemed to have a standard approach to such occurrences, which were frequent. Turning beet red, he would drop his tools, double up his fists and scream, "Blow it out your ass!" Then he would head out in search of his buddy, Ben. At Rayford's insistence, Ben would then put his work aside and dutifully follow for an encounter with Rayford's adversary. Rayford would reopen the conversation with "Okay. You think you're so God-damned smart. Ben, ask this dumb sonofabitch Arkansas." Ben would grin, wink, and say, Arkansas? If one answered "Little Rock" Rayford would stab again. "Okay. Any idiot knows Little Rock, but how about Illinois? Ben, ask the dumb sonofabitch Illinois" Ben would then say, "Illinois?" The opponent might respond, "Chicago?" at which point Rayford would collapse in laughter. "Jesus, Ben" he would scream, "How stupid do you have to be to not know Illinois?" Ben would then grin at Rayford's opponent, wink, and say, "It was Springfield, friend!" Rayford would then grab Ben by the arm and say, "get on back to work Ben. Don't waste your time with him, he's too God-damned stupid anyway!" Rayford would then go back to work, grinning smugly over what he perceived to be a stunning triumph.

One day my high school chum from Bremerton, Jerry Ecklund, whose dad had helped us get the Hanford jobs, ran afoul of Rayford. It came about during a discussion with Rayford where Jerry was evaluating Rayford's favorites, the Tennessee Volunteers football team. Jerry projected a losing season for them, and Rayford totally lost it! He ran screaming for Ben, who arrived shortly, out of breath, apparently equally upset over Jerry's Volunteers appraisal. Pointing a pudgy finger at Jerry, Ben shouted, "Vermont?" Jerry was laughing so hard he didn't respond in a timely manner, and Rayford pressed the attack. "Any stupid sonofabitch that don't know Vermont oughta keep his fucking mouth shut!" Ben turned to Rayford, winking knowingly. Jerry just kept laughing, and Ben headed back to his post. Rayford caught me by the arm later in the day and said, "Hey, I would stay away from that friend of yours if I were you. He's so God-damned stupid, he's dangerous. That dumb sonofabitch don't even know Vermont!"

While it was hard to challenge the genius of Ben Hartung, I suspected the depth of Rayford's knowledge and intellect. A few days later, as I delivered Rayford a fresh bucket of magnesium mud, I asked, "Rayford, help me out on one. What's the capital of Montana?" To Rayford's everlasting credit, he didn't hesitate for a moment replying, "Any stupid sonofabitch that don't know Montana shouldn't be working here!" Rayford Cox then quickly walked away, confirming my doubts!

17 — Surfin' USA

The Beach Boys, 1963

THERE WILL NEVER BE ANOTHER GROUP that united young Americans the way the Beach Boys did. Their music found a certain common denominator in a majority of our citizens' brain receptors that made their songs a joy. Yet, their struggles, their family tragedies and the challenges they faced confronting life itself robbed them of the fun that should have accompanied their stunning success. Many writers have tried to get a wrap around the complicated, contorted, on-going saga of their lives, but it's a tough one to fully grasp. Still, it's important to try because, in a sense, what happened to them can happen to any family where effort and talent bring great success. Maybe studying the Wilsons' story will help someone avoid the same all-too-human pitfalls the Beach Boys faced. Probably the safest ground to stand on, as a Beach Boy, was to not be a Wilson. Mike Love, their phenomenal lead singer, and Al Jardine and Bruce Johnson, their talented instrumentalists and vocalists, have best survived the emotional twister that was constantly ripping at the structure of this wonderful, gifted bunch of guys.

Murry Wilson, father of Brian, Carl and Dennis Wilson, was, as sometimes can be the case, the best thing and worst thing that could happen to his sons and the other members of the group. It wasn't just the fact that he was their father. He must be credited for his vision, for he astutely sensed the depth of the group's talent and potential. The problem was, he coupled that with a domineering, controlling and manipulative personality, aided and abetted by excessive drinking.

I knew from first meeting Murry, he was protective of his sons and the group. With him, a promise made was a promise kept. During my early pioneering days with the Beach Boys, Murry pledged to remember my loyalty. He kept that promise, and they moved dates around and did whatever else they could to accommodate me whenever we wanted them for a concert. Murry was always careful with concert scheduling, wanting to avoid putting undue strain on *the Boys*, as he liked to call them. Most times, he seemed to operate with only their best interests in mind. Other times, he easily rationalized vicious moves contrary to their interests. In the end, one might summarize it as a messy combination of love, ego, pride, money, power, insecurity and alcohol.

There was the Murry Wilson who called me in the middle of one of my trips to Texas and tearfully begged me to stop at their house in California on my way back to Seattle to mediate a serious dispute between him, Carl and Dennis. Dennis announced that he was leaving the group after a squabble over money grew out of proportion. Carl, a wonderful, soft, caring individual who was impacted heavily by brother Brian's spasms of drugs, hearing problems and withdrawal, considered Dennis' departure the last straw and said that he, too, would go his own way.

When I arrived at their home, I determined after a little probing that the problem was centered on money. Murry had secretly slipped goodly amounts to Brian and Carl, but nothing to Dennis. He justified his actions by rationalizing that Dennis would have wildly spent it anyway. (Dennis was already drinking impressively.) When Dennis found out, he concluded—probably accurately— that his own dad had screwed him.

I talked at length with Dennis in private, then with Carl who was, as usual, terrified and heart broken. Next, I sat down with Murry alone, and finally spoke with Murry and Dennis together. I coaxed Murry into making an unusual admission of wrong-doing and explained to Dennis that one source of the misunderstanding was his father's concern over his recent behavior. A verbal peace treaty of sorts was reached, along with a pledge to balance the books and bring equity to Dennis. Such treaties, as all Beach Boy biographers would agree, were always short lived, and long-term resolutions to their problems were generally unattainable. Too much money, fame and pressure were involved. Plus addictions and more.

A couple of days later, I received another tearful phone call from Murry. He kept saying over and over how much he loved Dennis. He kept repeating how proud he was of him and how he was afraid he had lost his relationship with him. He thanked me repeatedly for my efforts.

There was the Murry Wilson who, out of anger with his boys, created a new group he called The Sunrays and, with help, absolutely duplicated the Beach Boys' sound with a recording called *I Live for the Sun* which became a fair-sized hit. Murry brought his new group to Seattle to play at our dances and told me he was teaching *his boys* a lesson. Of course, *his boys* were deeply hurt by what their father was doing.

There was also the Murry Wilson who came to Seattle just to sit and talk with me about Brian, expressing repeatedly his love for Brian, saying that he only wanted to help his son find happiness. We talked about Brian's hearing problems, his drug problems, his various associations and their impact on his creativity. A soon-to-become-famous-himself Glenn Campbell had replaced Brian on the tours, as Brian claimed his ears hurt on airplanes. (Brian's brilliant song writing and arranging remained, however, the fountain from which the group drank their magic potion.)

And there was the Murry Wilson who turned around and sold, behind Brian's back, Sea of Tunes, their publishing company, which owned all of Brian's brilliant and valuable songs. That totally broke Brian's heart. Even so, I still believe today that Murry somehow meant well.

Do It Again
The Beach Boys, 1968

TEN YEARS LATER, AT THREE O'CLOCK IN THE MORNING, at Chicago's Whitehall Hotel, Dennis Wilson and I sat talking in my room. It had been quite a week. The Beach Boys had just rebounded from near oblivion and were once again one of America's hottest selling concert tickets. It was truly a surfing, Beach Boy love song revival: they were doing it again with all their old tunes. Some months earlier, Jimmy Guercio, the musical production genius of the group Chicago, took them to a studio in Boulder, Colorado and locked them inside, bringing a fractured group back to its roots. With some added musicians to fully recreate their original recording studio sound, the Beach Boys went back on the road with Concerts West. For special effects, they recreated the hull and mast of a sailboat on stage, tying in to their most recent hit, *Sail On, Sailor*. Several musicians and the keyboards were stationed in the boat during the show. (Their percussionist was Billy Hinsche, formerly the *Billy* of Dino, Desi and Billy. Dino Martin, son of Dean Martin, and Desi Arnaz Jr., son of Lucille Ball and Desi Arnaz, were the other two members of that trio. They had worked for me several times, and I was always fond of Billy.)

Their timing was perfect. The world had missed the Beach Boys and their fun, forever young sound, and the tour was sensational. This particular week was beyond sensational, it was stupendous. We put a package together for a series of shows at Chicago Stadium pairing the Beach Boys as the opening act with the town's favorite group, Chicago, as headliners. Chicago would perform on stage for an hour, and the Boys would join them for any encores. The two groups, playing as one, would alternate between performing each others' biggest hits. There had been nothing like it before or since, and the shows broke the world's indoor attendance record for a series of performances.

Previously, that record had been held by Madison Square Garden in New York, where the Ringling Brothers, Barnum & Bailey Circus played five consecutive sell out days right after the end of World War II. The late Arthur Wertz, then owner of Chicago Stadium, the NBA Bulls and the NHL Blackhawks, decided that his Chicago building should hold the record instead. After five straight sold out nights, at 20,000 tickets a night, midway through the last show Arthur met with me and Larry Fitzgerald, Chicago's manager, to state that the new indoor record was within reach and that he wanted it. Would we be willing to try for one more show the following night?

This was during intermission, so we headed to the dressing rooms to discuss the idea with the two groups. It was entirely up to them. They had already made popular music history that week with 100,000 tickets sold for shows in one building. Both the Boys and Chicago were exuberant over their victories, but somewhat exhausted. There loomed the clear and present danger of a flop. We had only 20 hours to sell tickets, and maybe the town had already maxed out. Anything less than a sell out would put a negative ending on what was already an ultimate success.

Uncertain about what to do, both groups asked me for my thoughts. I provided a different perspective:

The shows were so electric, so devastatingly, emotionally effective, people left the building each night wanting nothing but more. If we made the announcement from the stage right after intermission *and*, if we immediately alerted Ticketmaster to be ready to sell tickets all night and into the next day *and*, if we got WLS, the sponsoring Chicago radio station, to trumpet the news, we would sell out with ease. We didn't need any new customers. The musical experience that week was so significant for those who had already attended, we would sell out with just those that wanted *one more such evening.* I was gambling, giving such a strong endorsement to the idea, but I believed what I told them.

The decision by the musicians and their managers was unanimous. "Let's do it again!"

I was appointed to go on stage and make the announcement. Once the crowd was seated after intermission and the house darkened, the spotlights illuminated me as I walked to the center of the stage, where I took the microphone and said. "Never before in music history has a town shown so much love for two groups as you have shown this week for Chicago and the Beach Boys!"

This brought a rafter-shaking roar, and I continued. "A meeting was held back stage during intermission, as the groups wonder if you have really had enough."

I didn't make it a question, and now the crowd grew very silent, listening intently. "There are those who are disappointed because, as you know, every night this week has sold out, leaving many who wanted to see this show but couldn't. Also, we think that many of you might even like to experience another night like tonight!"

Now the rafters really shook.

"So, I am pleased to announce, as they are announcing this very second on WLS, we are going to do it all ONE MORE TIME!"

I am always reluctant to use an expression like "The place went absolutely nuts," but right then, Chicago Stadium did exactly that.

When the crowd had quieted a bit, I added "So it's tomorrow night and tomorrow night only, tickets go on sale at Ticketmaster at midnight tonight. If you can come again, Chicago and the Beach Boys would love to have you!"

Saturday night's 20,000 tickets were all gone by 2:00 A.M.

As Dennis and I sat in my room in the Whitehall, we should have been celebrating, but Dennis was sad. He said his wife Karen was supposed to have met him for dinner after the show, but had stood him up and taken $10,000 in cash from the bag in his room. He was depressed, and I tried to cheer him up, but he just wanted to talk about the past and about life's strange turns. Eventually, the conversation drifted into his involvement with Charles Manson.

Dennis was the unwitting link between Manson and the entertainment world that led to "Charlie's" murder spree, and he wanted to talk about it. Clearly, it was a heavy burden on him, and he told me the intricate details in an ironic, "what if" sense. He explained how, one afternoon, he picked up two young women hitchhiking on West Sunset Boulevard and squeezed them into his Corvette. They immediately put sexual moves on him, and he took them to his home. One thing led to another, and they sort of moved in. The quality of their physical contributions to his sexual appetite were such, he carelessly let matters expand. More girls arrived, and they were joined by a couple of guys Dennis chose to include in the sexual smorgasbord. After a few days, the girls invited over some friends who were part of their Spahn Ranch family, including their leader, Charles Manson.

Manson soon expressed to Dennis a desire to record some songs he had written and actually showed some ability to play the guitar, although his efforts with the instrument were amateurish. The brief relationship, which seemed fun for a few days, was now becoming a serious problem for Dennis. Manson indicated that he and the group were staying until Dennis helped him. He now demanded that Dennis assist him with his music. Dennis, who was a bit frightened by Manson, turned to a friend, Terry Melcher, for help.

Melcher, the son of movie star/singer Doris Day, was a red hot record producer at the time, having created an impressive string of hits for various groups. Melcher undertook the Manson project as a favor to Dennis, and Charlie and the girls moved out. All this led to some recording sessions and demos that never amounted to anything.

Charles Manson's anger with Melcher for not making him into a music star led him to order Melcher's death. The Manson family thought they were visiting Melcher's home that fateful, bloody evening. Except, Terry didn't live there anymore. He had had only been renting the house. When Melcher gave it up, movie producer Roman Polanski, husband of Sharon Tate, leased it for one year. Thus, Tate and some of her friends, not Melcher, died that gruesome night.

Dennis continued to carry a big load of guilt and was trying a regimen of cocaine and alcohol in an attempt to off-load the pain, but with little success. I told him he needed to get some treatment and see how he felt about things from a sober perspective. I know many others had told him it wasn't his fault, but his addictions had plowed a fertile field in his mind, where depression always builds strong roots and grows.

After a while, I changed the subject to a comical event that had occurred the previous night. It had quite an international flavor and lightened the atmosphere for a time.

Wild Honey
The Beach Boys, 1968

MANY MONTHS BEFORE, IMELDA MARCOS, wife of Ferdinand Marcos, the "President for Life" of the Philippines, called our office. She asked whether we could arrange for the Beach Boys to come to Manila and put on a concert in their big stadium "just for the young people of Manila." Without boring readers with all the intricate details, Imelda stiffed the Beach Boys financially following a sold out show in Manila. However, one Beach Boy in particular enjoyed some measure of revenge. For the sake of his family and friends, as well as my relationship with him, I will refer to him as Beach Boy "X."

While in Manila, X became acquainted with Imee Marcos, the lovely and treasured daughter of the President and his wife. Imee was smitten by X, but was still in high school at the time. Other than her meeting him and hanging around with the band, it remained an acquaintanceship and nothing more. Following graduation from school, Imee made an extended trip to the United States, along with a friend and four of President Marcos' security men. During the trip, she caught up with the touring Beach Boys in Chicago.

I will not speculate on the extent of Imee's relationship with X, but will point out that nights were spent together in his room. It became quite amusing. The affair was driving the four dedicated, trusted Marcos security men crazy. Likely, they feared for their lives. Wearing long dark raincoats on hot Chicago summer days, they reportedly carried Uzi submachine guns, and big bulges in their coats supported that hypothesis.

Before the show, they followed the limousine carrying Imee and X out to Chicago Stadium in rented Ford Fairlanes, then tried to park their cars so that Imee and X couldn't escape and lose them afterward. Once the security men were in position, X ordered his driver to turn the limo around. This made the couple's after-show departure from the rear door of the Stadium look like a chase scene out of an old Burt Reynolds movie: A streaking limo pursued by Fords jumping curbs and squealing in circles, trying unsuccessfully to tail them.

Then, there were their nights together at the Whitehall. Concerts West always used the Whitehall Hotels in Chicago and Houston; they were small, very private, secure and discreet and, in Chicago, the property was conveniently located just off Michigan Avenue. Those nights at the Whitehall witnessed four anguished Filipino agents sitting in the lobby, knowing Imee was upstairs but feeling derelict because they didn't know exactly *where* upstairs. Several times, they rang my room for assistance, and I assured them that she was perfectly alright and promised them I couldn't help them any further. Two o'clock Friday morning, they gave up calling, came up to my room and knocked on the door.

Obviously frightened, they told me in the best English they could muster that Imelda Marcos, their president's wife, was on the phone demanding to speak to

Imee. Imee wasn't in her room; her friend was, but she wasn't. They told me they were sure she was with X in his room, but no one would tell them which room that was. The agent who seemed to be the boss of the four indicated with a slashing movement across his throat what their fate would be if they failed to bring Imee to the phone. They were genuinely frightened.

Four men, each of them about 5´7˝ tall, still wearing dark raincoats with big bulges, all white as sheets in fear, were more than I could again deflect. I told them that, if they went down to the lobby and waited and didn't try to follow me, I would try to bring Imee to them so she could talk to her mother.

They promised, and entered the elevator. I watched the lights as it descended straight to the lobby. Satisfied that they couldn't follow, I went up the fire stairs to the floor of X's room and knocked on his door. When X answered, the room behind him was dark. I apologized for the interruption and explained the predicament facing my four friends. I asked if Imee could please come downstairs and talk to her mother. Leaving the door open a crack, X retreated into the recesses of the darkened room, and I heard him explaining the problem. I also heard a young lady respond in a shrill voice, "Screw her!" My friend X returned to the door, holding out his palms in a sign of helplessness.

"Thanks for trying!" I said as I turned and headed down to the lobby.

I again took the fire steps until I arrived at my floor. Only then did I board the elevator, lest my friends in the lobby were watching the elevator lights. I was on my way to deliver bad news, but was feeling that, this very night, I maybe could find a new meaning for my life. Maybe, although probably only temporarily, I could become a great international peace keeper. My fertile imagination, enhanced by years on the radio where the mind is required to manufacture fresh ideas quickly, had developed a plan by the time I reached the first floor. I stepped from the elevator and, with a big smile on my face, walked over to the security men and said. "Señores, I have good news!"

I told the assembled group that Imee and the Beach Boys had gone out for an all-night church barbecue and celebration. I explained that it was way north of Chicago by the lake at a park, that it was an event sponsored by the Catholic Church and that it was fully chaperoned. I added that it would last all night, as everyone there sang songs, enjoyed barbecued food and had a nice, wholesome time. I kept emphasizing that the all-night picnic was a chaperoned church event, repeating the word *chaperoned* several times to make sure they understood, which they eventually did. I told them that Imee and the group would be back about nine in the morning, and that I would make sure Imee got the word to call her mother.

Sighs of relief were emitted by all four agents, but they still looked worried, and why not? Their precious charge had escaped their grasp, even if it was to a church picnic. Still, I had them halfway out of trouble, and their apparent boss ran off to pass the word along. One of the others indicated that Imelda, or *the wife of el Presidente*, as they put it, was still waiting on the line.

Years later, I thought of that night after reading how, against her mother's and father's wishes, Imee announced plans to marry a young movie producer from Hollywood. Over parental objections, the wedding was properly held in grand fashion at the palace in Manila. Just a week after the wedding, the groom disappeared while swimming in the ocean. Truly a shocking tragedy, and sharks were suspected, but only by the gullible.

Laughing about X's fling with Imee lightened the atmosphere for a moment. Dennis finally returned to his room in the wee small hours of the morning, still a lonesome, sad man on what should have been one of the happiest nights of his life. The next time I saw him was in Honolulu, where the Beach Boys teamed with Heart for a concert at Honolulu's big outdoor stadium. We visited for a bit, but he was very drunk and only did half the show before giving way to a replacement on the drums. That was the last time I saw him before he dropped his car keys into the water one night while walking the docks at Marina del Rey, just outside Los Angeles. He dove in after his keys and never resurfaced alive.

I simply loved that kid, and his brother Carl equally. Carl Wilson, genuinely kind, generous and sincere, a wonderful singer and talented guitar player, was also taken by death at a ridiculously young age.

Mike Love, Al Jardine and Bruce Johnston still tour with a cast that replaces the Wilsons. With them, the sounds, the voices, the arrangements that gave America so many thrills and so much fun, continue. The Beach Boys' music will never die; sadly, only the kids that brought it to us did.

You Can't Do That

The Beatles, 1964

MANY BROADCASTERS CONSIDERED the recording industry's promotion people the equivalent of the plague. On the contrary, I found them one of the keys to the success and growth of radio as well as rock-'n'-roll in the '60s and '70s. Their job was to get their company's songs played on the radio and to make sure those records were in the stores for consumers to purchase. This was no easy job since, out of every 100 records released, no more than 20 or so ever received serious consideration by radio stations, and even fewer actually became commercially attractive. Promoters awoke daily trying to figure out ways to overcome those odds.

These hard-working, generally young people made my life in radio and music pleasurable. They were a constant conduit for information and help in my goal to get new music on the radio while, at the same time, avoiding playing records that the public would not embrace.

Promoters became my personal friends and allies in my work. In the Pacific Northwest, we enjoyed the services of nearly two dozen promotion people, hired by distributors or the record companies themselves. Music selection was an every day activity at KJR, but became more focused on Wednesdays when we invited all promotion people to attend our music selection meeting. Promoters played their new products and made their cases for airtime. Competitors were welcome to comment on each other's new releases, while my staff and I tried to gain a consensus. In the end, it wasn't a democratic vote, it was a one-person decision—generally mine—about what to add to our air play list. The participation of promoters in this process was critical to our success.

Camaraderie developed as part of these relationships. For a long time, we staged Wednesday night slot car races. Everyone involved purchased and brought with them miniature electric race cars and a supply of track. We rotated from one home to another and combined our track and ran it throughout that week's house. In this way, some of the greatest grand prix races of our time were staged.

We created our own Seattle Friars Club which met for lunch once a month following one of the KJR music meetings. With no holds barred, everyone stood to deliver speeches with a principal objective of identifying the shortcomings and peculiarities of other members in attendance. The speeches were hilarious and, despite my relatively exalted position in the scheme of things, I always received my share of suggestions and ridicule.

There were also the national promotion directors who visited the city from time to time and were frequently on the phone making requests for airplay of their company's products. It took a strong individual with great sales and public relations acumen to accomplish this role and actually have their calls answered by busy program directors around the country. Often, these people were extraordinary characters like a young Jerry Moss, who visited me one day from New York begging for consideration of a record by an unknown artist named Little Eva —*Loco-Motion.*

Jerry went on to found A&M Records with his friend, Herb Alpert, building the company around Herb's Tijuana Brass. Joe Smith of Warner Brothers, one of my all-time favorite people, could always coax me into giving Connie Stevens's records a chance, which we did with *Sixteen Reasons* and *Something Beautiful*.

And there was Ernie Farrell. Ernie came to the West Coast from Cleveland and worked for Frank Sinatra's Reprise Records when I met him. Soon after that, I was in Los Angeles when I received a call that my youngest son Jeff, age two, had fallen through the bannister at the baby sitter's home, landed on the lower steps and broken his collar bone. It was late in the evening when I got the word, and no flight was available to Seattle until five the next morning. Ernie Farrell and I spent those hours at a coffee shop near LA International. After I boarded my flight, Ernie headed for home, only to fall sleep behind the wheel and suffer a head-on collision with another car. He was seriously injured, and guilt-tripped me for years to come. Nearly every call from him requesting airplay on a song was coupled with his reminder that he had nearly died while helping me get back to Seattle to see my injured son.

Ernie was not one to separate reality from hype, nor did he ever pretend he had my best interests at heart. I enjoyed him because he was honest; what you saw was what you got. And he was funny.

Ernie was good friends with Sammy Davis, Jr. and did promotional work for him. Sammy and I were acquaintances, and all this led to a golf game one afternoon on the Tropicana Course in Las Vegas. The foursome consisted of Ernie, Sammy, George Rhodes (Sammy's musical director and conductor) and me. We tee'd off at noon, but the round went slowly, mainly due to Sammy. Frank Sinatra had given him a new golf cart for his birthday that was unique, featuring a TV and sound system, a well-stocked bar, an ice chest and more. It was boldly painted in red and white with the name *Smokey The Bear* emblazoned on the front and sides. Sammy was fond of inviting other foursomes on the course to join him for a drink at his cart, and our progress around the 18 holes was slowed greatly. This didn't prevent us from gambling on the match and, when we arrived at the eighteenth hole, winning that hole was crucial for Ernie. He was way down on several "press bets," and requested we offer him double-or-nothing on the last hole.

Sammy, George Rhodes and I all hit excellent approach shots as we neared the Tropicana club house, with all three of our balls landing near the hole. Ernie, meanwhile, found himself one or two strokes down to everyone when he finally arrived on the green. His wisdom in going double or nothing appeared faulty, and the amount of money he was about to lose was unattractive.

Ernie walked onto the green and said, "We've held up these other groups behind us long enough" and, with that, picked up his ball, then quickly walked over and picked up the other three. Sammy was dumbfounded! It was an astonishing break in established golf course etiquette and a bold-faced attempt to avoid the monetary loss that faced him. Once balls are picked up, they cannot be returned with accuracy to their previous position, as any golfer knows. It instantly becomes a frustrating imponderable.

Sammy went nuts. He jumped up and down, screaming, "You picked up the balls! Are you crazy? You can't pick up the balls! No one has ever picked up the balls before! Pat, George, have you ever heard of anyone picking up the balls? Ernie, how the hell can you pick up the balls? He picked up the balls! He picked up the balls!"

Sammy kept repeating these things as he went to his cart, threw his putter into his bag, climbed behind the wheel and headed for the club house. George Rhodes and I were laughing so hard, we could barely walk. Ernie climbed in the other cart and drove away, leaving us standing there.

That night I was at the dinner show at the Sands Hotel and Sammy, on stage, told the story of what had happened that afternoon. He never forgot it. Years later, he was performing in Seattle at the Paramount Theater, and I went backstage to greet him. The first thing he said after I gave him a hug was, "Do you believe that God-damned Farrell picked up the balls!"

Candy Man

Sammy Davis Jr., 1976

IT WAS ONE OF THOSE NIGHTS ONE NEVER FORGETS. After a lengthy drought, Sammy Davis Jr. was on the national music charts again with a record called *Candy Man*. Sammy had enjoyed great success in the mid-to-late-'60s with Frank Sinatra's Reprise Record label and some great songs like *Shelter of Your Arms* and *What Kind of Fool Am I*, but it had been a while. Now, MGM had gone for this rather cute little song, and it had quickly become a big hit. My station had been one to take the lead on the song, and Sammy was most appreciative. He had his promotion man call and invite me to Vegas, if I could make it, as Sammy was playing the Sands and wanted to thank me as well as have me take in his new show. He'd added a singer/dancer named Lola Falana to his act, and business for Sammy was booming.

I always loved Sammy. He was a genuinely wonderful human being. How could anyone dislike him? He was energetic and funny, he always seemed to be "on," and he was so respectful of his friendships. Equally as gracious and warm were his wife, Altavese, and his music conductor, George Rhodes. Sammy had seen it all. He had grown up as the teenage star of his father's musical group, The Will Masten Trio. Sammy had spent most of his early life living out of a suitcase as the Trio traveled from club to club, town to town, night after night. It was in the late '50s that Sammy went out on his own and became the big star in his own right we now know. Sammy paid his dues. He experienced the cruelty heaped upon blacks in those days and, as a traveling musician, was exposed to the brunt of such behavior, barred from so many hotels and restaurants and other facilities. If he harbored any bitterness, he never let it show; he gave and gave and gave. If you were a friend of Sammy Davis Jr., you were indeed blessed to know this man of great and enduring quality.

He faced criticism early in his solo career. An instant Las Vegas hit, he married May Britt, a Swedish actress, and the inter-racial marriage was something that America was ill-prepared to handle in those early '60s days. Also, Sammy lived with a rumor that would not die. He lost an eye, reportedly in a traffic accident while driving from Las Vegas to Los Angeles. The rumor, however, held that his eye had been gouged out by a New York mafioso as a warning to stay away from movie actress Kim Novak. Novak, a stunning blonde that Sammy had been seeing, was also the target of the affections of a kingpin of the crime mob that ran Vegas in those days. After wearing a patch for many years over the injury, Sammy eventually replaced it with a glass eye that was remarkable and only occasionally seemed to be looking in the wrong direction.

It was 1973 or there-abouts, and a seasoned Sammy was back on top. He was always on top in Las Vegas, but now, he again was feeling national momentum. I was thrilled by the opportunity to go see him and his show. About then, my sales manager at KJR had been asking me to please try and do something special for a young lady named Barbara Vested who was the all-important time buyer at a San Francisco advertising agency (I believe it was Gray Advertising). She was the officer making the decisions as to which radio stations received that agency's advertising dollars, and several big buys were coming up. It was one of those perfect opportunities to achieve two objectives with one move.

I called Sammy and told him I would be there Thursday night. Barbara in San Francisco excitedly agreed to accompany me. As things worked out, she was able to board the same plan I was traveling on that afternoon from Seattle to Vegas with a stop in San Francisco. We arrived in Las Vegas, played a little blackjack, then had dinner at the old Desert Inn Hotel and Casino, referred to as the *D.I.* if you were cool. We had a table by the moat that ran around the restaurant. There, a harpist in a white gown that looked like what any harpist would wear two thousand years ago if she were floating on a raft down the Nile River playing a harp. Anyway, the moat had circulating water that caused her to float by every five minutes or so. After dinner we went to Sammy's sold-out show with our table in the front row.

Following the show, we went off to an "after show party" upstairs in Sammy's suite. George Rhodes was there, and Altavese and Sammy, of course. But, if my client Barbara wasn't already impressed, try this on for size. As the party was growing in size, in walked singer Eddie Fisher, former husband of Debbie Reynolds and Elizabeth Taylor, accompanied by Barbara Perkins, who had been a big star on the television series, *Peyton Place*. Soon, Rona Barrett, the LA newspaper and television gossip reporter, appeared and, shortly after that, Frank Sinatra and his then-wife, Mia Farrow. Tagging along with them was Dean Martin. There were others in attendance that acted pretty important, but I didn't recognize them.

My guest joined the girls, who were visiting at a big round table. It was obvious that Frank and Mia were having a spat of some kind. At the table with the girls, my client got the lowdown. It seems Mia had wanted to go dancing, while Frank had wanted to attend this party. She was quoted as saying, "Frank can be such a drag." Funny, the rest of the world never thought of Frank that way. I guess you had to marry him to discover that secret!

We had a flight back up to San Francisco booked for 2:00 A.M., so after an hour or so of schmoozing, with my thanks and congratulations to Sammy, we slipped out the door. My guest was simply in shock! God, there she had been with all the biggies, sitting and sipping cocktails with some of creation's biggest stars and visiting with them. She was speechless in the cab to the airport. Once on the plane she said, "Did tonight actually happen?" I looked at her and said, "I'm relatively sure!" in a tone that indicated such experiences might be mine every day. (Are you kidding? No one was more thrilled than I was!) In addition to a lovely thank you card that I received later that week, KJR enjoyed its (at least what I considered to be) fair share of business from Barbara. There were those in Seattle radio who thought my idea of a fair share for KJR was excessive, and I was always consistently subjective in such matters. Regardless, Barbara was an honest and fair time buyer. But it never hurts to show such a person they are appreciated. Also, I have found, the more things you try, the luckier you get!

Candle of Life
The Moody Blues, 1970

A FRIENDSHIP I WILL ALWAYS TREASURE went away when Jim Clapp died at an early age. Jim was the son of Norton Clapp, President and Chairman of the Board of Weyerhaeuser Timber Company. Admittedly from a wealthy family, Jim had a successful business career of his own, and he participated in such projects as the building of Seattle's famous Space Needle.

Jim and I became acquainted in 1962 when, one day on my show, I mumbled something about looking for a waterfront house for next to nothing. (One never knows what a little ad-lib like that might produce!) It brought a call from Jim, who introduced himself and asked me to join him for drinks at their corporate club when I got off work. At that meeting, he told of a Lake Washington real-estate development they had put together where sales were slow. He felt that selling to a high profile person such as myself might start a trend that would help get the development off the ground. He offered a partially-completed house a home builder was having trouble financing, and I bought it and moved my young family to the lake.

As the years passed, Jim and I grew ever closer as friends. We cruised the waters of Alaska together, our families played together and he became a participant in the early on financing of Concerts West. He built an extravagant jet turbine-powered yacht that caused me to convince him he should build the first jet turbine-powered racing hydroplane, the U-95. He hired the brilliant test pilot and engineer, Chuck Lyford, to spearhead the project. This was a development that changed that sport forever, as nearly all unlimited hydroplanes are now jet turbine-powered. Jim's team, which named me a vice president, paved the way.

Until the time of my company's merger with Danny Kaye and Lester Smith, it was Jim who believed in me enough to keep us afloat with capital to support the enormous up-front outlays a business like Concerts West required. The basic funding came from me, but Jim's deep pockets were always there when needed. When you have 20 or 30 concerts upcoming, that need was often.

Spencer Haywood was an NBA All Star, playing forward for the Seattle SuperSonics. That great super star from the University of Detroit was also one of my disc jockeys on our Seattle FM station, KISW. Spencer had a compassionate streak a mile wide, and it caused him to undertake the challenge of raising money to combat sickle cell anemia, a disease that strikes particularly hard at African-Americans. Jim was in the University of Washington Hospital with not long to live and, while I was visiting him one day, he said, "Pat, why don't we figure out a way to help your friend Spencer raise a bunch of money for his sickle cell fund?" That day, we enthusiastically created a plan.

Paul Anka and I have enjoyed a long and wonderful relationship. Paul is humble, likeable and generous, a totally charming musical genius. He is unaffected by the worldwide fame he has enjoyed since hitting the consciousness of the nation as a teenager in 1957 with his hit *Diana* and so many others after that. Some years later, Paul and I tried to purchased K-101 FM San Francisco together, but that's another story. Paul, who for years now has been one of the hottest tickets in Las Vegas, was appearing there when I called his secretary, Mary Rizzo. Mary immediately put me through to him.

I explained Jim's and my plan, and he simply said Yes! Our approach, which also was enthusiastically supported by my pal, Dave Watkins, then Vice President of Public Relations for the Sonics, called for a special halftime fund-raising show. Jim Clapp would come out and present Spencer Haywood with a check for $20,000 for the sickle cell fund. Then, Paul Anka would be introduced and, backed by an orchestra I put together, he would sing a song that had never failed to arouse emotions and provide inspiration. The song is one Paul wrote for Frank Sinatra called *My Way*. Being the song's author, Paul felt free to take liberties with his original lyrics and promised to customize them to fit the occasion. The thrust of his song then became one of, "Spencer Haywood does it his way, Jim Clapp does it his way, now reach into your pockets and do it your way."

Paul planned to fly up from Las Vegas for the halftime show but would have to leave immediately afterward to do a midnight show in Vegas. He made a call to Bill Harrah, who within 60 seconds agreed to loan Paul his Learjet, making the brief visit to Seattle possible. Probably because I had spent so many hours of my young years in church, the rest of the formula came naturally. As Paul sang, collection plates would be passed through the crowd, attempting to match the amount of money Jim Clapp donated. The "collection plates" would be in the form of a couple hundred cardboard Kentucky Fried Chicken buckets that were donated, in addition to a couple thousand dollars the local KFC folks threw in for good measure. Perfect! However, like Dan Jenkins' great line in his book, "There just ain't nothin that's dead solid perfect."

The Baltimore Bullets were the guest team. My orchestra was on the floor seated beneath the basket at the end of the floor, ready to play. Jim Clapp had been brought from the hospital by ambulance and was court side in his wheel chair. I was the emcee of the effort, and everything was set in Seattle. In Las Vegas, Paul's plane left on schedule but ran into unexpectedly severe head winds on its way north to Seattle, and he was running way late. I sent my KJR program director at that time, Nick Anthony, to Boeing Field near downtown Seattle with a police escort to ensure a quick transit to the Coliseum the moment Paul arrived. Paul's plane landed one hour and 15 minutes behind schedule.

The crowd in the arena had been told of a very special halftime event, and they patiently waited. I got on the microphone and did some artful ad-libbing, which inspired a degree of patience on the part of the audience that was impressive. But halftime had already lasted 30 minutes, and Paul's plane was just setting down. I decided to use the microphone to give a play-by-play report of his progress, which seemed to build the anticipation. The police lieutenant in charge of game security agreed to use his police radio to stay in contact with the caravan as they left the airport, and we gave accurate progress reports.

The teams had long before returned to the floor and were in their warm-up outfits practice shooting. Darrel Garretson, well-known veteran NBA official, came over to the bench and said, "You know, there is an absolute, not-to-be-exceeded 30 minute halftime limit league rule!"

I just said, "This is for Spencer and sickle cell anemia, Darrel. I'm not sure we should do anything that will mess up this deal!"

Garretson looked around at the crowd and said, "I guess I agree."

It turned out to be the longest halftime in NBA history.

Paul's entrance into the Coliseum a few minutes later was greeted with thunderous applause and cheers, and the program began. I told the crowd of Jim Clapp's desire to aid Spencer Haywood in his quest. With that, Jim was rolled forward to the scorer's bench in his wheelchair, where he gave Spencer the check. Then, I asked the crowd if maybe we could reach down and try to equal the gift Jim had just given. I then formally introduced Paul Anka, who simply mesmerized the 14,000 fans. He sang with great emotion, and the new lyrics he prepared for the occasion were brilliant. He kept singing and singing as the crowd kept passing the buckets back and forth along the rows of seats. I'm sorry, but I can't recall the amount of money given to Spencer's fund that night. However much it totaled, it far exceeded the doubling of Jim's contribution. Paul finally brought the ceremony to a giant, emotional finale. I gave him a hug and a thanks, and he headed back to the airport. Luckily, he enjoyed tail winds on his return flight to Las Vegas.

Halftime that night lasted one hour and five minutes. Spencer Haywood took away a giant check for the fight against sickle cell anemia, and Jim Clapp was elated. Seven weeks later, he passed away.

Good Vibrations

The Beach Boys, 1966

I HAD A WONDERFUL RELATIONSHIP with the Seattle SuperSonics when they were owned by Sam Schulman. Veteran Seattle promoter Zollie Volchok was President of the club, and Dave Watkins, mentioned earlier, headed public relations. So, when Seattle hosted the 1974 NBA All Star game, I was named to a committee of locals to help with the planning and presentation. At one of the committee meetings, I was given responsibility for the entertainment at the banquet the night before the game as well as for the pre-game ceremonies. I was not one who would be inclined to shirk from such challenges.

I made a list of ideal performers for the banquet and started inquiring as to availability. Of my final list of six who were available, the right answer was obvious to me, Dionne Warwick. At that time, she was enjoying hit after hit, and her albums were giant sellers. With the production and musical wizardry of Burt Bacharach, everything she sang turned to gold! Another plus: she was represented by a long-time acquaintance, Peter Golden at the William Morris Agency in Los Angeles, who had been the first agent for the Beach Boys. We didn't have a big budget to spend but, knowing that Dionne was a huge Lakers fan, Zollie Volchok of the Sonics talked to the Lakers and, for the good of the NBA banquet, they agreed to give Dionne a pair of prime Lakers season tickets.

To hire Dionne for the event at a price we could afford within the banquet budget, we couldn't pay to bring an expensive conductor or musicians from California. That was no problem.

In our Kaye-Smith/Concerts West power sphere were two gentleman, bountifully equipped to do the job. One was Jimmy Kirk, an accomplished writer, conductor, singer, you name it whom we imported from Dallas to head up the commercial production side of our Seattle Kaye-Smith recording studios. The other was maybe the greatest single musician the Northwest has ever produced. His name is Norman Durkee. How talented is Norman? At the age of 14 he was the head pianist at my father's church in Tacoma. Over the years, he became the most respected of composers and pianists. In current times, 2003, he is the musical director of Teatro Zin Zani, that smash production that has sold out month after month in Seattle and San Francisco. (Norman played at our wedding when Stephanie and I were married.) Anyway, back to 1972. Norman teamed with Jimmy Kirk, and Jimmy conducted while Norman put together a 36-piece orchestra and, of course, did the all critical keyboard work. Who needs Burt Bacharach?

What to do about the pre-game presentation was an awesome opportunity. Basically, the pre-game program boiled down to one thing, the National Anthem, and the direction to take was obvious. The game was to be played on Martin Luther King's birthday. Whatever we did had to focus on the late Dr. King. With a national television audience, and considering the image of the event itself, we needed a tasteful approach. Having just anyone perform the National Anthem never crossed my mind. We needed someone special, and I had a hole card: Dionne Warwick.

I called an old friend, the late Bill Bissell, head of the music department at the University of Washington and conductor of the Husky Marching Band. I knew Bill from when he was band director at my alma mater, Bremerton High School. He loved my idea, and agreed to bring the Husky band to the game where they would play during the pre-game as the fans were coming in. The highlight would be a softly played, 60 second rendition of *America the Beautiful*.

My next task was to assemble the greatest speeches of Martin Luther King, taking those powerful messages and pulling from them 60 seconds of the most memorable phrases. Among them, "I've been to the highest mountain," "I've seen the promised land" and "Free at last. Free at last. Thank God Almighty, we're free at last." In the meantime, we contacted the NBA, and they were happy to invite Coretta Scott King, Martin Luther King's widow, and the King children to the game, where they would be honored and sit in court side seats directly beneath the basket. Coretta accepted the invitation, and all was set.

I am happy to report, everything went perfect on this one. Before a sold out banquet crowd of 800 VIPs and players, Dionne and the giant orchestra were stunning. She performed every single one of her many hits, and the evening ended with an extended standing ovation. The following night was equally magnificent. The announcement from George Toles (a KJR account executive and also the Sonics' public address announcer) was scripted and simple: "Ladies and gentleman, to honor America, and to honor the late Dr. Martin Luther King, this being his birthday, the NBA is proud to have with us this evening, Coretta Scott King and her family. Please welcome them!"

They stood and, as the applause began to subside, Bill Bissell was given the signal and the Husky band began to softly play *America the Beautiful*. Simultaneously, the tape of Martin Luther King's speech highlights I had lovingly edited and produced at the radio station began to play. With those final words, "Thank God Almighty, we're free at last" the final notes of *America The Beauti-*

ful from the Husky band were heard. Silence followed, then George Toles said, "Ladies and Gentleman, Dionne Warwick!"

The King Family had stepped forward to near the foul line for the ceremony. Now, an American flag on a stand like what one sees in a courtroom was brought out and placed before them. Dionne, dressed in an immaculate faded denim pant suit, walked out, faced the flag and the King Family and delivered a stunningly powerful a capella *Star Spangled Banner*. There it was, right before our eyes, the very best of America.

Having spent so much of my radio life in the limelight, it was gratifying to stand in the background and thrill to the response given that emotional production. If you didn't have a tear in your eye that night when Dionne's final note faded, you were probably brain dead.

Smoke on the Water
Deep Purple, 1972

THERE IS A COLORFUL, DANGEROUS, EXCITING yet weird spectator sports event that is annually hosted by Detroit, Seattle, San Diego, Honolulu and several smaller cities. It is called an unlimited hydroplane race. This sport, which has tried in vain for years to gain wide national attention, faces one large, stubborn obstacle. It's very difficult to find a place capable of handling such a race. These boats, weighing about three tons and nearly 30 feet long, go about 200 miles an hour. They demand smooth water and a big enough course to provide a safety margin should they lose their steering or for any reason go out of control.

The sport is nearing 100 years of age and dates back to such names as Horace Dodge, Gar Wood and other pioneers of speedboat racing who founded the sport on the Detroit River. Detroit remained the capital of the sport until 1950, when a boat designer from Seattle named Ted Jones teamed up with a local auto dealer named Stanley Sayres and brought forth a new concept. Their engineering breakthrough produced a boat designed more like an airplane than a boat, in that it relied almost totally on aerodynamics to keep the boat out of the water. The only contact between the boat and the water would be two tips (called sponsons), one on each side of the boat. Believe it or not, the rear of the boat rides on the propeller, which supports the rear due to its high speed. This idea shocked the racing world, which up until then believed that any self-respecting racing boat must be designed to slide quickly *through* the water. Suddenly, racing speeds were increased by 50 miles an hour as this innovation rode *atop* the water. The new Seattle boat, called the *Slo-Mo-Shun IV*, headed east in search of fame.

That search took this new boat and crew to Detroit for the annual running of the Gold Cup, which was, and is, considered the World Series of boat racing. The arrival of the new craft from Seattle was greeted with giggles, despite rumors of *Slo-Mo's* speed. One look told the seasoned boat racing fan this had to be a bad joke. Constructed of plywood, instead of planking as one would have expected, it was, by comparison, stubby, frail looking, ugly—just another bad idea. Detroit was stunned the following Sunday when the ugly vessel from Seattle broke every existing world record for speed on the water. The *Slo-Mo* ran away from the Detroit fleet like they were toys. Even worse for the Detroit fans, as was the winner's right, with the victory the Sayres/Jones team stole the coveted Gold Cup from Detroit along with the rights to stage such a race and moved both to Seattle.

In the early 50s, Seattle could best be described as a nice town that was very Northwest. Since the end of World War II, when the defense industry closed down, many of those who had invaded western Washington during the war moved elsewhere in search of employment. Not all of them, mind you, but a goodly number, and this left this scenic region with its old standby industries of lumber, fishing and some manufacturing, as Boeing had survived and was still building bombers and some passenger planes. Equally quiet was the scene when it came to anything beyond scholastic sports. Oh, yes, the University of Washington football team would win a Rose Bowl berth about once every 50 years but, for the most part, Seattle had to settle for being a minor league town. Minor league baseball, a regional hockey team and that was about it.

Then, suddenly, some local citizens went to Detroit, a big major league city, and won something with a world title attached. Seattle wasn't too sure what they had won, but it sure sounded good, and by the following summer, the staging of the Gold Cup race on Lake Washington turned the town upside down. No less than 500,000 people lined the shores of Lake Washington, of which 100,000 were on their yachts tied up side by side along a length of water that comprised the back stretch of the three mile race course. There, on that sunny August Sunday in 1951, with Mt. Rainier looking down curiously, Seattle went nuts over hydroplane racing. Do I exaggerate? Fifty-one years later, and the race is still being held, with a live local television audience and over 200,000 paid attendance along the shoreline. The race became the foundation for Seattle's big annual festival called Seafair, with multiple facets and its giant parade that captivates a regional population of now over four million.

Why am I telling you all this, you ask?

To understand my whole story, realize that I was a kid of 16 when that first race was held, and I traveled from my home across Puget Sound in Bremerton to see the event. To me, this was like being at the Indy 500, and it impacted me in the same manner as the races at the brickyard in Indianapolis impact the millions who annually watch Indy's Memorial Day classic. Sitting on the beach that day, I dreamed of somehow becoming involved.

My involvement commenced several years later, when I was well into my career as a Seattle disc jockey. It was 1968 and, by this time, the race had grown in importance to a point where all three local network television stations were carrying the entire event live. I was in Texas with Jimi Hendrix on a Saturday night when I got a call from Seattle's independent television station, Channel 13. The voice of the sales manager on the phone told me that all three network stations had been hit that day with an engineers' strike, and that their race coverage was by necessity canceled. The independent station had decided to jump into the void and wanted Seattle's top-rated deejay to do the play by play. I had done a little play-by-play announcing of football and basketball when I was first starting out in radio, but was not thought of as a sportscaster. Nevertheless, my decision-making process took about five seconds. "Yes! Yes!" I screamed down the line. "But first, let me figure out how to get out of Texas." The race would start in only 14 hours but, thanks to a Braniff Airlines red eye flight, I arrived bright eyed and bushy tailed at Sea-Tac airport the next morning where I hopped into a waiting limo outside baggage claim.

God, I get to be a part of the hydroplane race! was my principal thought. With my position in radio, I already knew most of the drivers, some of them very well, and had remained a huge fan of the event. There were still, however, some little surprises awaiting me.

Once I arrived at the race site and viewed the start/finish tower, I discovered that time had been short and we would not be well-equipped to handle the telecast. This is an understatement! We had a total of two cameras and two microphones. The station, Channel 13, is now a very successful Fox Network affiliate. But at that time, it was struggling, as were most independents during television's early days. It was owned by the father of the now-famous McCaw boys, who are discussed in another chapter. McCaw planned to bring the station forward to a state of competitiveness, but that day had not yet arrived. Then I asked the critical question: "Who do I have to assist me, you know, color commentary and all?" (Understand, this race lasts for five hours, and one needs lots of help to effectively fill every minute.) The answer was shocking. "It's all up to you, Pat, but we just feel you can somehow do it!"

Suspecting that we were going to be short on replay and visual effects, while still in Texas I had called my son Jerry who was 11 years old and already an excellent artist. He came through like a champ with a 4′x8′ sheet of plywood painted to match the race course. From the official race program I had left on my dresser at home, he had duplicated each of the racing boats out of cardboard, right down to the smallest detail. This would serve as my primary prop between race heats. With it, I could manually demonstrate what had happened in the previous heats and explain possible strategy that might be employed in the next heat of racing. But I still needed a co-anchor!

Then it struck me. My buddy, singer Wayne Newton! I'd had lunch with Wayne on the Thursday before I left for Texas. He was in town doing a special concert in association with Seafair. I liked Wayne as a talent and an individual and had gone out on the limb for him on a song of his called *So Long Lucy* that never became much of a hit elsewhere. *Damn it!* I thought. *Like they say in Vegas, "Time for Seattle to call in that marker!"*

I reached Wayne by phone at his hotel, telling him, "Wayne, you're not only a great singer and a wonderful person, but potentially the greatest boat race TV color commentator in history!" Even if that weren't the case, I offered that he owed me one, and it should be fun. "Besides, Wayne, how can you beat all the prime time television exposure you're going to get?"

I told him chances like this come along once in a lifetime, and I would send the limo immediately to pick up him and his wife.

There was this long pause, then he started to laugh. Wayne said, "But Pat, I paid for lunch!"

With Wayne Newton at my side, with two cameras and my son's virtual plywood story board at hand, we hit the air at 11:00 A.M. on a day that was to be prolonged by several serious racing accidents. Wayne had to excuse himself about 2:00 P.M. to catch a plane, and I finally signed off at 20 minutes past six. Exhausted beyond words but, more than that, wondering whether I had destroyed my credibility with over seven hours of ad-libbing, shouting, rambling and generally trying to keep the telecast from bogging down, I went home and, for the only time in my entire career, I vomited! Now that's nervous exhaustion!

I turned on the TV and watched a little of the replay they were running late that evening, but was too wrung out to judge whether my performance was tolerable. I was genuinely concerned, and ignored the nice things people at the radio station were saying about the telecast, figuring they *had* to stroke me. I didn't smile until noon the next day when the *Seattle Times* came out. Their radio-television critic, Chet Screen, who had always gone out of his way to diss anything I did, wrote that "Pat O'Day has finally found his calling. As disturbing as he is to me as a disc jockey, his all day coverage of the hydroplane race was exciting and a work of art!" I sent the review along to Wayne Newton, noting he might also have received a good review had he stayed for the whole show!

That's how my involvement with hydroplanes started. As I work on the second edition of this book, it's August 2003. Earlier this month, for the 37th year, I was active in the broadcast coverage of this epic Seattle race. This year, I joined the broadcast team at Seattle's KIRO-TV Channel 7. Their station gives the event all-day live television coverage. It was a fun change for me after doing the radio broadcast as the official voice of the race for the previous 36 years.

My involvement with these unlimited hydroplanes has on occasions gone beyond the microphone. In 1972, I talked Jim Clapp into building the first turbine jet-powered boat, the U-95. Then, in 1981, I got a bee in my bonnet and bought my own unlimited hydroplane. With the boat sponsored by KYYX, the radio station I then owned, I recruited, trained and introduced to the sport its first woman driver, Brenda Jones. She was 21 years old and gorgeous, a fabulous physical specimen, being at the time the world's women's sit-ups champion. Her record at that time was 2,000 sit-ups in 21 hours. She had not only strength, but great powers of concentration, and was able to do what had been thought impossible, and that was to control one of those screaming, bucking monsters as they battled side by side around the waters of lakes and rivers. She not only was the first woman to qualify as a driver, she was the first woman to win a race! Her victory on Mission Bay in San Diego quieted a host of critics of my racing effort. They had already noticed that crowds around the nation dramatically increased as people flocked to see this 110 pound blonde-haired woman drive one of these dangerous machines.

After two years, I sold the boat to pursue other things less expensive and time-consuming. I assumed that another team would pick up Brenda and put her in the cockpit of their boat. In this macho sport, sadly, it never happened. The big mistake is all theirs. She was dynamite for sponsors, for the news media, for fans that came just to see her and for the sport itself. She never drove again and settled into life as a hair stylist. Today, she carries with her the knowledge that she, and she alone in all the world, is the only woman who has ever done it, the only woman in the sport's 100 years to not only drive an unlimited hydroplane, but to drive one to victory. Words cannot express how proud I am of her.

18 – Good Times, Bad Times

Led Zeppelin, 1969

HOW I LOVED LED ZEPPELIN, despite the fact that they were a pain in the ass! Not Robert Plant, not Jimmy Page and not John Paul Jones. These three were totally dedicated and professional artists that I count myself fortunate to know. I found them to be sensitive, responsible, gentle, splendid human beings. This was in sharp contrast to their drummer, John Bonham, and their manager, Peter Grant.

Richard Cole, Peter Grant's assistant, wrote his own book on the subject of the group's meteoric rise to fame and told many stories of the darker side of things. However, he gave Peter Grant nearly a total free pass. But then, Peter was still alive when Richard wrote his book and Peter would probably have broken him in half had he published the true story. Peter was totally capable of physically accomplishing this, having been a professional wrestler weighing over 300 pounds with an oft-stated desire to exhibit his wrestling skills.

Peter's intentions were to be protective, efficient, cautious and professional in all matters concerning the group. Unfortunately, he had a cocaine habit of proportions bigger than his own, and it left him argumentative, volatile and dangerous. Loving and caring one moment, paranoid and devoid of compassion the next, he was about as much fun to be around as a Cuisinart full of nitroglycerine. Whereas Robert, Jimmy and John Paul tolerated his behavior (although I know it was often troubling to them), letting it roll off their backs and ignoring it, Grant's real impact was on John Bonham.

Bonzo, as he was affectionately nicknamed, showed only infrequent signs of the individual who formerly inhabited his body and mind. Drugs and booze, namely cocaine and bourbon, which he used jointly and in generous proportions, gradually transformed him into a socially unacceptable package. His work on the drums was still superb, and he could arguably be called the best drummer in rock-'n'-roll history. It was following and between these superb performances that he would get himself remarkably screwed up. Bonzo accepted Peter Grant as his leader, and Peter aided and abetted Bonham's every excess. Together they made a darling pair.

Concerts West saw the potential of this group from the "git-go" when Ron Terry first put us together with them. We were proud to represent Led Zeppelin and did so right up until the time of their final, forced departure from America. Led Zeppelin convinced us to follow Terry Bassett's suggestion and invest in Showco, Inc. Productions of Dallas in creating the first of the big concert sound systems that were so needed to get their powerful music across. Zeppelin opened our eyes to the true potential of outdoor, football stadium-sized concerts, which we had been doing for a couple of years already. Led Zeppelin took us to a new and higher level. Braves Stadium in Atlanta, the Bowl in Tampa Bay, these were monstrous shows from a technical, visual, audio and audience perspective. We were all off on a wild, wondrous adventure, where every idea seemed to work, every ticket was always sold and true musical and entertainment destiny seemed ours.

Yet, I would often confide to friends that for me, 30 days on the road with Led Zeppelin was like one year with any other group due to the tension, unexpected surprises and highs of elation. To be in charge of such tours tested the extremes of all one's senses.

A very young Cameron Crowe, writing for *Rolling Stone Magazine*, accompanied us on many such tours. His great movie, *Almost Famous*, effectively and brilliantly tells the story of what a rock tour is like. We tried, with minimal success, to shelter Cameron from the darker side of things. His job was to write about what he saw and, for his age, we thought he saw too much as it was.

There was Atlanta Braves Stadium with special jets filled with guests flying down from New York. Ahmet Ertegan and Jerry Wexler were among the Who's Who of the recording industry in attendance, and many celebrities joined them. Then, sold out Tampa Stadium, with a thousand doves released during the show as a sign of love and peace.

In the midst of this great moment, a police officer was killed as he tried to hold a timber against a fragile gate to keep out hundreds of fans who hadn't been able to purchase tickets. When their pressure broke down the gate, the officer was crushed to death as the crowd outside surged in.

There were moments like a show in Greensboro, when the performance was so overpowering, the crowd would not let the group leave the stage, physically blocking them and forcing them to go on playing until late in the night. There were also moments of trauma like when Bonham was drunk, angry about who knows what, and tried to open the passenger door on our custom Boeing 707 flying at 30,000 feet over Indiana. And Bonham, with the fire department's nets extended below, walking around the twelfth floor ledge of the Continental Hyatt House in Hollywood. He had carved chunks out of a thread spool, slid it over a pencil and wrapped it with string. By placing the spool against a window and yanking the string, it made a frightening racket in the room. John not only jolted every guest on the floor from their sound sleep, he somehow, while very intoxicated, made it all the way around the top of the tower on a ledge not more than a foot wide. We were certain he would fall.

These were mild incidents compared to many others. In New Orleans, he set his room on fire and, before it could be extinguished, destroyed one entire floor of a treasured and historic hotel. (John faulted it on a hooker, posing as a women, who turned out to be a man!) And then there were the adventures at the Edgewater Hotel in Seattle.

Early on, it was clear that Bonham and Grant, occasionally aided by assistant group manager Richard Cole, were incompatible with most cities and their hotels once the group left the stage. Often, the damage they caused was not just expensive but criminal. In addition, Zeppelin attracted hangers-on who themselves often attracted the law. There was very little about this traveling caravan that would pass the scrutiny of even the most casual investigation, and adjustments had to be made before the worst, which seemed inevitable, happened. We came up with a "three cities, three hotels" formula that, until the end, saved the day.

By negotiating agreements between Concerts West and the hotels, and by hiring local police to provide constant security, we were able to protect the group from themselves. We used the Whitehall hotels in Houston and Chicago and the Edgewater Hotel in Seattle. Using a customized Boeing 707 complete with beds, a big bar and an organ, we flew to shows all over the United States and Canada and returned afterward to the sanctity of our guarded, understanding, patient and well-paid hotels Actually, everyone behaved quite well at the Whitehalls, and the group's pent up desire for destruction was mostly focused on the Edgewater in Seattle. The Edgewater had long been the headquarters for rock-'n'-roll musicians visiting Seattle since that practice was established by Pat O'Day & Associates in the early '60s. The Beatles gained national attention for the facility during their visits to Seattle as the Edgewater, which hangs out over a pier above Seattle's Elliot Bay, provided guests the opportunity to fish out their windows. Maids were accustomed to finding a large cod, rock fish or mud shark in the bathtub when making their morning rounds.

Members of Led Zeppelin did fish while there, but also introduced a new custom. The Edgewater back then was not exactly a five star accommodation, and Zeppelin felt that the furnishings needed upgrading. So, at the end of each tour, prior to leaving Seattle, they threw the entire contents of their rooms out the windows and into Elliot Bay. Carpets, televisions, couches, lamps, bedding, everything went sailing into the ocean. In that Zeppelin's entourage usually occupied a dozen rooms, there would be a remarkable clutter of furniture floating in the surf come check out time (to say nothing of the televisions and small refrigerators and other non-floating items that went straight to the bottom).

The natural question I was always asked after describing the ceremony was, "Why would the Hotel continue to tolerate this?" The answer is found in fundamental American business acumen.

The hotel would prepare a bill for all the damage and send it to our office. Then, the repairs and replacements would be deducted as an expense from the revenues of the tour and paid. The Edgewater could then freshly refurnish the affected rooms, funded in full by Led Zeppelin. I remain suspicious to this day that The Edgewater always put the group in rooms that were overdue for re-decorating. Others are puzzled by the logic of such excesses by the group, knowing they must pay later. Although I heard some of their money went to Barbados, most of it was subject to Britain's 90 percent income tax, the bracket they faced. And so, in essence, those were dimes, not dollars, that Led Zeppelin pitched into Puget Sound.

Cadillac Motor Cars now features Led Zeppelin in their television commercials. I find this to be so funny in that these guys represented everything Cadillac wasn't when they were at their peak. Their Cadillac commercials are powerful, and I'm sure they're selling lots of new cars as Page's guitar, Bonham's drums and Plant's indescribable voice cut through the clutter of today's advertising and force you to pay attention. That is the same power that captivated the imaginations and spirit of our Baby Boomers as they were growing up in the '70s.

For me personally, they bring back one memory I treasure. It was on an afternoon before flying to Vancouver, BC for an evening performance, and Robert Plant had been asking me to take him out in my boat. I had an ocean racer, converted to a cabin cruiser with a couple of special V8 engines that traveled through the waves at about 65 MPH. I invited the band, Peter Grant and Richard Cole to join me on the water.

It was going to be a special day, anyway, because I was able to thrill Robert Plant with a surprise. At a stadium show somewhere back east, a ring that he treasured had flown off his finger while he was singing and disappeared. Telling me of his loss in the dressing room, that it was a gift from his son, he was very sad. I returned to the field and, after carefully examining the stage, went underneath to the turf over which the stage had been constructed. Searching with a flashlight for about 15 minutes, I found it. Before his ring slid through the stage cracks, however, Plant had stomped on it, as he is an active singer. It was badly damaged, and I decided to give the story a happy ending.

When I arrived back in Seattle, I gave the ring to my son Jerry, an aspiring jeweler at an early age, and he brought it back to better-than-new condition while adding a couple of extra stones. I decided to surprise Robert with the ring, and make it a fun day as well. We went to Ivar's Famous Seafood Restaurant, purchased baskets of fried clams, clam chowder, fish and chips, etc. and headed in my boat out to Blake Island.

Blake is a state-owned park in the middle of Puget Sound about five miles out from Seattle, and generally very private and quiet, as it was that day.

It was the only time I felt a sense of reality and humanity within the group. After eating lunch sitting on beach logs in the sun, we walked around the entire island and talked, Peter about his family, Robert about his son. When he concluded, I stopped, pretended to look down in the sand, then reached down with a movement like I was picking something up. I handed Robert his missing ring. He started crying, and so did Peter.

Peter said, "Pat, you have no idea how important that ring was to Robert. We are all so happy he has it back!"

We walked and talked some more. Dreams, wives, futures were discussed and the afternoon, by necessity, ended way too soon. We boarded the boat and headed back for the Edgewater Hotel. As the members of Led Zeppelin climbed off the boat, I said, "See you at the airport!"

I saw Jimmy and Robert and John Paul Jones again, and they never changed. But I never saw the same Peter Grant and John Bonham that were there on Blake Island with me that day. My brief acquaintance with the real Peter and John was not to be repeated. They were undergoing severe personality transformations and their new personas were successfully overtaking and overshadowing normality.

Dazed and Confused

Led Zeppelin, 1969

DURING THE 1975 TOUR (I THINK), a few days were left mid-tour for R&R. Terry Bassett, through our good friend, the co-grandfather of Top 40 radio, Gordon McClendon, arranged to rent a large ranch north of Dallas. There, Terry figured, the group would be isolated, free of concerns over the behavior that would likely occur—in short, secure. On paper, the plan looked foolproof, but the realities of Zeppelin could make the best-laid plans of mice and men look foolhardy.

So it was that the fun began. What started out the first day as planned soon mushroomed into the sort of chaos for which our stars were by now famous. By the second day, unplanned, uninvited guests began to arrive, and they constituted a dangerous package: groupies, hangers-on, a few record industry types, hookers, and some without definition. Soon, the outcome of the little vacation we had created for the group was in doubt. Industrial-strength contraband was generously distributed. Alcoholic beverages were being consumed as though Prohibition were starting the next day. Obscene activities became prevalent and, in general, it quickly became a world-class event where sin and illegal conduct were the measures of success. However, given the isolation of the ranch, and our efforts to keep any prying eyes away, it could have ended with the only really serious impact being on the attendees. Unfortunately, the owner of the ranch, an elderly Texan with pre-conceived notions of what should and could take place on his property, made a surprise visit to see how things were going. To his way of thinking, things were not going well. As he drove through the electric gate and approached the ranch house, I guess the first thing that caught his attention was one of his horses in the swimming pool.

Parking his truck, the shocked rancher raced through the rooms of his home, and found around nearly every corner another surprise. Furious, he ran to a phone and called the sheriff. Then, he went to his gun rack, grabbed a rifle with a supply of ammo, and attempted to line the guests up—I assume in preparation for an orderly and efficient mass arrest when the police arrived. Fortunately, no one cooperated with his commands, and everyone, sensing impending doom, selected a method of escape. Some jumped in vehicles and went out the gate at high speed. Others, less fortunate, simply exited on foot running across the fields that surrounded the ranch house complex. To our good fortune, the sheriff's men were slow to respond, and we were able to get the band and crew into the limos and out of harm's way before law enforcement arrived. The next day, Concerts West met with the ranch owner's attorney. The damages were calculated and paid, and alternate plans were executed for the remainder of the group's vacation.

An American Band
Grand Funk Railroad, 1969

ROCK AND ROLL GAVE BIRTH TO THE GROUPIE. The big concert tours were generally followed from town to town by these devotees of music. Some, like those depicted in Cameron Crowe's great movie, *Almost Famous*, were devoted to the music but also to having a serious — if only short term — relationship with the young men that provided the music. Others just wanted to party, share in any drugs that were on hand and make themselves available should anyone even slightly associated with the show seek abrasive affection.

In that this movement grew to the point of becoming nearly an occupation, I think it's only right that we mention one individual who climbed to the top of this profession. Her last name, for purposes of this story, isn't important. I don't believe the hundreds who clearly remember her ever knew her last name, anyway. They only knew she was "Sweet Sweet Connie," and that seemed to be enough.

Sweet Sweet Connie had set one major goal in life and wasn't shy about proclaiming her quest. She had vowed to administer a non-intercourse-but-popular type of sexual gift to all rock-'n'-roll musicians in general and to the big stars in particular. To put it conservatively, Connie was extremely successful!

I have, while with groups we represented, overheard many a conversation where experiences with Connie were discussed. Those who hadn't enjoyed Connie's efforts were not belittled, but they were clearly outsiders as far as contributing to those conversations. I've told you that we handled nearly every major rock act from the Stones to Led Zeppelin and Elvis and the Beach Boys. I offer an honest (although not an eye-witness) estimate that Connie attained her goal with nearly 75 percent of the rock stars of the day. Her success was heralded in Grand Funk Railroad's great song, *An American Band: Out on the road for forty days/Last night in Little Rock, put me in a haze/Sweet, sweet Connie, doin' her act/She had the whole show and that's a natural fact.* Clearly, Connie became more than "almost famous."

I personally remember an evening in St. Paul, Minnesota when Connie just about wrecked a show. Concerts West had one of rock's most famous groups playing in the old St. Paul Civic Auditorium. This group, whose members generally hailed from a city not all that far away, were in their dressing room prior to the show and being visited by none other than "Sweetness of Constance," who was helping the guys relax before their performance. Suddenly, one of the group's roadies burst in the dressing room door and screamed, "Jesus, the wives are here!"

Earlier, we mentioned that the group's home town was not distant. With the noted exception of Paul McCartney, who was always accompanied by his first wife, the late Linda McCartney, and Jose Feliciano, whose wife was always present, bringing wives on tour simply wasn't the rule in the '70s. However, the spouses of this band had decided to get together and drive to St. Paul to surprise their husbands. They were successful!

The roadie had spotted them as they entered the back stage door. He had done all he could to alert the group to the imminent disaster, but the ladies had quickly proceeded around the back stage area and down the hall to the group's dressing room. Just as they arrived at the door, Connie, at the urging of the band, burst out. This might have been explainable had it been anyone but Connie. Her fame had already caused *Rolling Stone* and other rock publications to publish her photograph. Connie was blonde, attractive, and very recognizable to the visitors. As if this wasn't trouble enough, once entering the dressing room, the guilty looks—as only a wife can detect—on the faces of their husbands told the rest of the story. I entered the dressing room shortly thereafter, and one could sense great unhappiness. This mood carried forward to the performance of the group that night. They were subdued, distracted, gloomy and seemingly unawares of the 6,000 fans screaming their salute to the band. The wives had angrily left the building, telling the boys they would see them at the hotel after the show. It was apparent the boys feared those meetings. That night, the group ignored their fans clapping and screaming in demand of the usual encore. Instead, they left the stage after their initial set, not to return.

I never inquired as to what took place later that evening at the hotel, but imagined each of the suspects had his value as a husband evaluated. Nor did I bother talking to Connie, who kept asking everyone backstage if she had caused a problem. Daaahhh!

Deep in the Heart of Texas

John "Dusty" King, 1942

IN THE MID-'60S, MY RADIO DUTIES OFTEN TOOK ME to Dallas, where Pams Production Studios recorded many of our station's jingles. On visits to the Big D, while attending concerts, I noticed shortcomings in the area's concert promotion and production. The business changed quickly, and Texas, at the time, had fallen behind the curve. At Pat O'Day & Associates, we had expanded from our original Seattle-Tacoma base north to Victoria and Vancouver, south to Portland and east to Spokane. We learned as we grew and were years ahead of the rest of the country in technique. Our buying power increased, too, and I wanted all that to continue. Knowing the more dates we offered, the better, I constantly thought about where to go next. My trips to Texas convinced me that the best place was Dallas. An office there would open a vast new market for us: Dallas-Fort Worth, Houston, Austin, San Antonio, El Paso, Oklahoma City, Tulsa and a host of medium- and smaller-sized cities. With added venues to offer, we could aggressively pursue major acts. Managers for the Rolling Stones would follow us almost anywhere, and other acts felt the same way. The Lone Star State beckoned. Who would lead the charge?

One possibility was Frank Bloebaum. A singer at Pams Studios and boyfriend of Patsy Thompson, daughter of one of the owners of the Dallas Cowboys, Frank seemed to have the skills and contacts needed. On a trip to Texas in 1967, I told him about my desire to open a Dallas office, and he asked to run the operation. Returning to Seattle, I consulted with my partner, Terry Bassett. I laid out figures for auditoriums across the South, estimated our chances for success against Wynn and suggested we bring Bloebaum on board to open a Dallas office. Terry sat quietly for a long time, then uttered five words that changed our lives forever: "Why don't I do it?"

I was shocked. Terry hailed from Wenatchee in eastern Washington and never once had indicated an interest in moving elsewhere. Noticing my surprise, he quickly added "I have always wanted to try another part of the country."

Terry Bassett first appeared earlier in this book when I wrote about the expansion of my dance business. A loyal and trusted partner for four years, he became even more valuable when Dick Curtis left the company for financial reasons and returned to radio in the summer of 1967. With Dick gone, Terry picked up the slack. A natural genius at negotiating, scheduling and producing everything from the smallest dance to the biggest night club show, he was the perfect choice to run Dallas. So Bassett opened the Texas market and our newest employee, Tom Hulett, inherited many of his former responsibilities in the Northwest. To give Tom a vested interest in our success, Terry and I offered him shares in Pat O'Day & Associates. Linda Ott, Willy Leopold and Dan Fiala—all previously mentioned—filled out our Seattle office staff.

Terry opened our first Dallas office at the Cabana Hotel on the Stemmons Freeway not far from downtown. Built with money from Doris Day and the Teamsters Union, the Cabana was a slick, new, attractive financial flop, and management was delighted to permanently rent us two adjoining suites at very low prices. That gave us nice digs, perfect for creating good first impressions. Later, as business boomed, we moved into the equally-desirable 21 Turtle Creek complex, which remained our home for nearly a decade. The name Pat O'Day *&* Associates, which had worked so well in Seattle, meant nothing in Dallas. So, we called our new Dallas arm *Concerts West*, and, within one year, embraced that name for our entire operation.

Cry Like a Baby
The Box Tops, 1968

SOON WE WERE PARADING A VARIETY OF ROCK ACTS across the South. Our first tour, by bus, included Paul Revere *&* the Raiders, The Box Tops, The Five Americans and Merrilee Rush. Tom Hulett flew down to help Terry on the bus tour, and one of his duties was taking care of concert proceeds. Most of that was cash and, by the time they reached Lubbock, Tom had nearly $50,000 stuffed into his briefcase. After that night's concert, he decided to go out to dinner. Not wanting to carry that much cash with him, he carefully stowed it between the mattress and box spring in his hotel room. Dinner ran late, and Tom had little sleep before boarding the bus for El Paso at 6:00 A.M. He immediately fell asleep and didn't wake up until noon. When he awoke, he reached for his briefcase, opened it and finally remembered the money. "Oh shit!"

Leaving Terry to run the show, Tom jumped off the bus at the next town, rented a car and raced across Texas back to Lubbock. Along the way, he had ample time to contemplate the money's fate. He feared calling the motel and placing his trust in the hands of someone he didn't know on the other end of the line. Cash is cash, and once it's gone, it's seldom recovered. Fifty grand was a small fortune in 1967, and losing that much money would be a major setback for our company. Most of that money was due to be paid to the performers at the tour's end. Tom called me in Seattle, explained his predicament and agreed with me on a plan.

When Hulett reached the hotel, he would go straight to the room, knock on the door and, if someone answered, tell them he was a cop and needed to inspect their room. If the room was locked and unoccupied, he would go to the manager and have them accompany him to the room. Either way, he would quickly learn whether a Lubbock hotel maid was now $50,000 richer and on her way out of town.

When Tom arrived around 6:00 P.M, the winter sun had set, and lights shining through the curtains indicated the room was occupied. Time for Plan A. He walked up and banged on the door.

"I'm a cop!" he announced as he barged in, walked up to the bed and yanked back the mattress. Spread across the box springs were beautiful packages of $100 bills. Saying nothing, he opened his briefcase, shoved the money inside and headed for the door.

"We appreciate your cooperation in this matter," he said to the man and his scantily-clad companion as he disappeared into the parking lot.

For weeks to come, we speculated on the reactions in that room after Tom left. We assumed that the amount of money Tom grabbed that night grew with each retelling of the story. In no time, it no doubt amounted to millions. If that couple reads this story, they'll at last know the truth.

Let's Work Together
Canned Heat, 1970

OUR MOVE INTO TEXAS CAUGHT THE ATTENTION of Ron Terry, a brilliant young agent at Creative Management, New York's largest talent agency. [You first met Terry back when I told of my fight with Phil Basile over the rights to Jimi Hendrix.] Ron was handling all of the company's cutting-edge acts and viewed the concert business, as did I, as behind the times and unprepared to effectively handle all the new rock performers wanting to go on the road. When Ron flew down to Dallas to negotiate some dates for the Supremes on behalf of Creative Management, his bigger goal was to spend a weekend brainstorming with Terry and me.

After my show on KJR ended that Friday at 6:00 P.M., I ran to the airport without telling anyone I was leaving, having learned long before that deejays, like mice, will play if they know the cat's away. The next day, Ron, Terry and I sat around the Cabana's pool exchanging ideas and bonding. The extent of our plans surprised and pleased Terry. No other concert company was then thinking of tackling the entire nation. Ron revealed that the day was fast approaching when the stifling corporate mentality at Creative Management would become more than he could bear. By dinner time all was decided: Ron Terry liked us, we liked him and we all three thought alike. So, why not work together? It was as simple as that. We concluded our arrangements for a Supremes tour knowing that Ron Terry would soon join Concerts West.

I had learned to compartmentalize my thinking. On Saturday, in Dallas, using one compartment, I dreamed of a nationwide concert company; on Monday, in Seattle, using other compartments, I digested a report at an 8:00 A.M. sales meeting about how many cars a dealer sold over the weekend due to our advertising, met with deejays and record promoters for hours, lunched with an advertiser, did my three hour radio show and returned home in the evening to see my kids. It amazes me what people can accomplish, without stress, if they like what they're doing.

It didn't take long for Ron Terry to prove his sincere interest in working with us. Contrary to his employer's interests, but in Jimi Hendrix's best interests, he put Concerts West together with Jimi to handle his tours. Normally, Jimi would have been piecemealed out to a long list of local promoters in exchange for pledges to hire the agency's lesser acts, acts with minimal chances of making a profit for anyone other than Creative Management and themselves. Instead, Jimi Hendrix went with us. Soon after that, together with New York attorney Steve Weise, Ron brought us together with another guitarist, Jimmy Page, someone I had known from his Yardbirds days, and three other musicians: Robert Plant, John Paul Jones and John Bonham. Led Zeppelin! They, too, signed on with us. If Ron Terry ever decides to claim responsibility for the success of Concerts West, he won't get an argument from me. We might have done fine without him but, looking back, I'm glad we didn't have to try!

Won't Get Fooled Again
The Who, 1972

THERE WAS GOOD NEWS AND BAD NEWS as we progressed into 1968. Although some of our shows—like Herman's Hermits, The Who, The Monkees and The Osmond Brothers—did well in the Northwest, Top 40-type acts lost money on week nights and didn't fare much better on weekends. Music tastes were changing, and so was our audience. There was a funny and kind of sinister side to our Seattle operation that was buffering us from losses during the transition. Seattle, like Berkeley, had become a green house where the protest and counter culture movement was rapidly growing.

The counter culture movement in Seattle hated me and my radio station, and their reasons were understandable. We were seemingly oblivious to their frantic attempts to move the populace left! My conclusions from the outset had been that the movement was small, its impact would appear greater than its radical footprint and the overwhelming majority of our audience had not changed. As such, I resisted the pleas of some of my air staff and the protests from the counter culture newspapers, etc., and held to a straight-down-the-middle course.

Typical of the times was when the Beatles' *White Album* was released, a couple of my deejays wanted to play the album from cover to cover, non stop, on their shows. They felt the album was an ultimate statement of some kind and were furious when I refused to consider it. My pointing out that we were a service of hit music, not a meditation or contemplation refuge, didn't budge them from their point of view, and, before long, it was best for all parties that they depart KJR. There was an FM station in Seattle, KOL-FM, where my friend Pat McDonald, music critic from the *Seattle Times*, and others were playing, exclusively, the albums and music of the new movement. The fact that they couldn't rise beyond a two percent share of the audience should have offered satisfactory proof of the futilities in appeasing that portion of the populace. Oh yes, KJR was playing everything from County Joe and The Fish and Moby Grape, to early Cream and, of course, Dylan, but I refused to allow our proven method of playing only the broadly-accepted hits to be detoured. Above all, I wouldn't allow our deejays to venture into political dialog of any sort!

At Pat O'Day & Associates, knowing that this new movement, although fractional in numbers, was a major force in concert attendance, we went in both directions. A new entertainment venue was packing them in! Eagles Auditorium in downtown Seattle had become what Bill Graham's Fillmore Auditorium was to San Francisco. These were the meccas of the new music movement and so, with a gentleman named Boyd Graphmire, who was much loved in the "hip community," as our front man, we remained silent partners and the financing behind "Eagles." It had to be kept a secret in that the stalwarts of the counter culture scene, who mainly hung out near the University of Washington campus and around the offices of the *Helix*, which was the big underground newspaper of the time, would have had nervous breakdowns had they known then that I was the actual promoter of the Eagles Auditorium shows which they so fervently and helplessly loved. They later became furious when we came out of the musical closet, so to speak, and presented "The Gold Creek Park Love-in" at a resort in Duvall, east of Seattle. This giant outdoor festival sold out, with Jim Morrison and the Doors, the Byrds, Country Joe and others appearing. Immediately "Pat O'Day is a Shuck!" bumper stickers appeared around town as they contended that music should be "free for the people!" This was, of course, ludicrous, as all the acts, including those they worshipped with such devotion, wanted big money to come and perform. Such were the dichotomies of the time!

We took a serious hit when we booked a tour with The Who and Canned Heat across Canada. It was in February and coincided with a two-week-long blizzard that simply paralyzed the Northern Hemisphere. I found myself at the bank re-financing my home to make up the shortfall caused by several thousand folks that wouldn't risk their lives to come out in the blizzards to buy tickets and see our shows. My friend Jim Clapp was still offering me funding for the tours, but that money was guaranteed by me personally and had to be repaid. Also, with all our Texas activities, we were going beyond his area of comfort. Neither Terry Bassett nor Tom Hulett had any personal resources, and I was getting nervous. Such financial pressures on me would continue until Les Smith and Danny Kaye entered the picture as described in earlier chapters.

Rhinestone Cowboy
Glenn Campbell, 1975

RECOVERY FROM THE WINTER DISASTER in which we also had shows cancelled in Oklahoma and northern Texas was made possible by successes with Jimi Hendrix, Donovan, Jefferson Airplane, and an old friend, Glenn Campbell. Glen was road-managed by Roger Adams from the Jerry Perenchio Talent Agency in Los Angeles, and Roger liked the way we did business. Glenn I had known well since he was with the Champs, then again when he took Brian Wilson's place on tour with the Beach Boys. But Glenn had now become a giant star in his own right with a highly-rated weekly network television show. Glenn, along with his show sidekick, the talented country singer Jerry Reed, would bring their entire TV cast on the road and oh, could they sell tickets. For a moment, may I sidetrack to tell you an incredible story of an "after the show party" during a Glenn Campbell tour?

For the most part, the Campbell tours were handled by Terry and myself, putting a real strain on me because Glenn wanted more than weekends. This tour cost me my vacation time at the radio station in 1968, but the big picture had to be kept in focus. (I made up for it later!) So I take you to a Wednesday night in Denver, Colorado. The house was sold out, and I was thrilled to be able to host my cousin, Bruce Hubby from Colorado Springs, and his wife. I took them to dinner before the show, then put them in front row seats next to a friend of Campbell's who Glenn had told me deserved special attention. That friend was the sheriff of Alamosa County, Colorado, whom Glenn had met while he and John Wayne were there on location filming their movie *True Grit*. The good sheriff had attended a pre-show cocktail reception for Glenn where he became noticeably drunk! Other than standing for extended periods of time shouting for Glenn to introduce him to the crowd—which Glenn already had done—it appeared no great harm would come from his inebriated state. The operative word in this paragraph is *appeared*!

Following the show, we all retired to the Cherry Creek Inn for another party. The entire cast was in the large suite we had arranged along with local deejays, writers, Glenn Groupies, and the sheriff, who was accompanied by his wife and brother. All was going well, although it was later pointed out that the sheriff was again consuming large quantities of alcohol.

Glenn was in the middle of entertaining everyone with a story of a golf match he had with Dean Martin when it happened. The sheriff lunged at Glenn, falling to the floor, getting up and trying again. He was shouting and sobbing, "Glenn, you son-of-a-bitch, why didn't you tell me you were a golfer? Golf is a fag game. All golfers are fags, and that means you're a fag! I invited you into my house, I let you ride my horse and all the time you're a God-damned golfing fag!"

At this point, he went for his gun that was revealed in a shoulder holster as he ripped open his coat. His brother saved the day by giving him a rabbit chop across the neck that left the sheriff momentarily stunned and on the floor. His wife relieved him of his pistol, and the brother applied a full Nelson hold to his neck as he arose—but before he could fully recover from the rabbit chop! This didn't prevent him from screaming continued obscenities at Glenn as he struggled to gain his freedom and attack again. He was finally drug out of the suite, with help from several in attendance, and taken to his own room, which, by the way, had been paid for by Glenn. Glenn was ashen and badly shaken by the incident. It had been a great show, a great night, a great party to that point, and he was exhausted and disappointed. Within minutes he excused himself and went to his room, leaving us to evaluate the incident. It was Jerry Reed who made the point that this was the first time he had ever heard the game of golf associated with sexual preferences. Jerry said he had heard such things about male figure skaters and ballet dancers, but never golfers. We speculated that the sheriff must know something that we didn't. After all, he was a big sheriff and must know what he's babbling about. Jerry offered that maybe golf, like men's figure skating, had become an activity heavily populated by gays. We had fun, going down the list and discussing the possible sexual inclinations of Jack Nicklaus, Arnold Palmer, Gary Player and others. Soon the sheriff's wife returned to the suite to announce her husband was asleep and apologize for his outburst. She said he was taking a medication that didn't interact well with alcohol. I told her that she should immediately get him to his doctor for a new prescription before he shot every golfer in the state of Colorado. She didn't think that was very funny, but Jerry did!

Communication Breakdown

Led Zeppelin, 1968

OUR COMPANY SOON GREW TO BECOME the largest concert presentation firm the world had known. All of my and Terry's relationships of previous years came into play and, with Ron Terry, Tom Hulett, my merger of Concerts West with Kaye-Smith Enterprises that coming Fall, we were off and running. With headquarters in Bellevue, Washington, we also had offices in Dallas, Chicago and Atlanta. Hendrix, Zeppelin, Three Dog Night, Steppenwolf, Elvis Presley, Chicago, Elton John, Creedence Clearwater, The Moody Blues, Grand Funk Railroad, Cat Stevens, The Doobie Brothers, Bread, The Beach Boys, Bachman-Turner Overdrive, Bob Dylan, Bad Company. The Eagles, Linda Ronstadt, The Rolling Stones, Neil Diamond, John Denver, Paul McCartney and Wings, and Frank Sinatra were among the performers we handled either in large part or totally. By 1976 we were presenting over 600 shows per year in the US and Canada. We had branched out into the Orient and were running tours from Tokyo to Australia. We were handling the closed circuit telecasts in every city in the US of the Ali fights, such as the Thrilla in Manila against Joe Frazier, the Rumble in the Jungle from Zaire against George Foreman, and all the other great Ali fights.

This may be a good place to salute and thank the employees who were so instrumental in our success. In Seattle, Linda Ott and then Janice Merrill, administrative assistants. Down in Dallas, these duties were handled for years by one Gloria McCall. Later, with the operation now located across Lake Washington in Bellevue, one Carolyn Deaver moved north from our Portland radio offices to administratively run things.

And, oh, did we have manpower! In Dallas, Charles Stone (Elvis coordinator), Carl Dooley, Jay Hagerman and, of course, Terry Bassett. Hagerman eventually moved up to run the Chicago office. Dick Curtis returned to the company and opened our Atlanta base. Meanwhile, the crew trained in Seattle became essential to our running hundreds of shows a year. Willie Leopold, Dan Fiala, Mike Crowley, Joe Crowley, Paul Gongaware, and Craig Chatain were just some of those who allowed us to operate in almost any city in the world. Mike Crowley on a given night might be in Melbourne, Australia with Creedence Clearwater while Terry Bassett would be in Los Angeles with the Eagles and Dick Curtis in New York with Bob Dylan.

Unbelievably, that is how it was! We were a promotion machine without equal, and it was our people, our vision, our efficiency, our home office support with accountants like Bill McKenzie and Irv Karl and their staffs that made it all work. Lester Smith's business instincts were also critical to our success, to say nothing of the company's bank roll! Little old Pat O'Day & Associates had graduated into the planet's biggest and most efficient promotion firm in history. However, a cancer was growing within our company, and it was painful.

Tom Hulett, and Terry Bassett as well, had become absolute giants in the entertainment industry. Terry remained the same guy in personality and integrity that had joined me many years before; Tom Hulett did not. To Tom's everlasting credit, he was responsible for bringing Creedence Clearwater Revival, The Moody Blues and, in part, Elvis, into our fold.

Another gentleman played a large role in gaining us Elvis and Frank Sinatra, John Denver and Neil Diamond. He is the dynamic, famous producer of many great films such as the new *Oceans Eleven*, and, in the past, *Nashville*. He was the personal manager of the Four Seasons when I first met him, and he was another of the catalysts that created the magic that was Concerts West. He is the famous producer, manager and entrepreneur, Jerry Weintraub.

Jerry, through no fault of his own, after 1973, was the best thing and the worst thing that happened to Concerts West. The best because of the above. The worst because Tom Hulett decided he wanted to be Jerry Weintraub. Without Jerry requesting it, Tom became Jerry's disciple. Tom grew desperate in his rush to achieve Jerry's kind of power, charisma and show biz image. The problem was, Tom Hulett wasn't Jerry Weintraub, he was Tom Hulett, the guy from Seattle who was counting cars in used car lots for the bank when we hired him. He couldn't stand it, and he couldn't stand Terry and me because we taught him his concert skills and we knew from whence he came. He just couldn't live with that. None of us begrudged Tom any of his successes, or his demands which ranged from Rolls Royce company cars to expense accounts that exceeded the salary of most executives. We were nothing but pleased by the growth he had experienced, by his personal and professional successes. Tom's flanks were always protected by loyal partners. In his frantic attempts to become someone he wasn't, loyalty, friendship, and honesty were the first victims.

Tom had a short time earlier told us all that if we talked with Colonel Parker, we were to tell him Terry Bassett wasn't with Concerts West any more, and that Hulett had fired him. According to Tom, Terry had done something that displeased the Colonel and this was the only answer. I told Tom that to say such a thing about our partner was a stupid, shitty trick and wouldn't work, and that the Colonel was smarter than that, and that he knew that Terry was an owner, and that what Tom was doing should never have been said!

This was all typical Hulett at this point. I had been on the road with BTO the previous week, and our paths crossed in Charleston, West Virginia. Elvis had played Charleston that evening and I had BTO in the same auditorium the next night. We had agreed to meet in the bar to visit. When I entered, Tom was sitting with Colonel Parker at the bar and, after the Colonel greeted me, I sat down next to Tom, who whispered to me, "God, Pat, don't say anything! Why don't I call you in your room? We'll meet later."

Not overly surprised, in that Hulett was seemingly always weird of late, I finished my drink, said good night and went to my room to await a call that never came. I tried to reach Tom at 8:00 A.M. and was told he had already checked out! Can you imagine, friends and partners, on the road, in West Virginia, and he does this? I talked to him on the phone a couple of days later and asked for an explanation, but Tom said it was too complicated and he would tell me about it later. I imagine Tom had probably told the Colonel he had fired me as well! It was becoming clear that Tom was attempting to separate himself from his company, which was impossible. He wasn't Concerts West. He was the lucky recipient and user of the cumulative strengths of Concerts West. It was our massive staff, organization, accounting offices, banking power, his partners, Les Smith and Danny Kaye that made his success possible.

A meeting was held in our Bellevue offices with Les Smith, Bill McKenzie (who had brilliantly served our concert company as comptroller), Terry, Tom and me. We had a big problem in Tennessee. That state's Attorney General, along with their Department of Revenue, had uncovered a scam where tickets for the front four rows of some Elvis Presley concerts were forged and sold without the state receiving their admission taxes. The amount of money involved for the State of Tennessee was not great, but the gross amount of money that was being siphoned off somewhere else was substantial.

We didn't know what the story was, but the State of Tennessee was threatening to go public, and we had to find out whether it was true or not. Given that Tom ran the Presley tours, we figured he must know. He certainly did. The highlight of the meeting followed Bill McKenzie's report on his conversations with the Tennessee AG. Les Smith asked Tom Hulett what he knew.

Tom went into orbit. He jumped up and started screaming about how the whole thing was unfair.

There is no appreciation for what I do! It's easy for you, Pat, and you, Terry, because you don't have to sit in Vegas at the roulette table with the God-damned Colonel [Tom Parker] night after night and lose thousands of dollars. Here I am, risking my family's welfare to keep the Colonel happy so we can run Elvis forever, while you have your cushy lives and then you drag me in here and give me this shit! Besides, it was the Colonel's idea, and I had no choice but to go along with it. So the Colonel takes half, and I use my half to pay off the gambling tabs I run up to keep the Colonel happy. So what do you want me to do, get out my checkbook and give you all some more money?

There was a long pause. What was there to say? Someone changed the subject, but whatever the new topic, no one was listening or much cared at that moment. The meeting soon broke up, and Tom stopped by my office. I said, "God, Tom, I salute you. That was really creative!

"Screw you!" Tom responded as he stormed out, slamming the door.

At that moment, I knew that I was going to depart my company as soon as possible in that other things were changing as well. Les Smith, my mentor, father figure, friend and trusted partner had become totally absorbed in his and Danny Kaye's purchase of Seattle's new major league baseball expansion team that was to be called the Mariners. Les was to be managing partner, and was constantly on the phone with Bowie Kuhn or Walter O'Malley's son or some other baseball big-wig. It was rapidly changing him, as he felt the pressure of entering into a business he had never experienced. Also, there was the added pressure of protecting his and Danny's investment, which was also major league.

Another typical and silly indication of our problems came one day in 1976 with a call from Hulett demanding I have a talk with Les. Although he had been misquoted, a story about Les, Danny and the new team had appeared in *Sports Illustrated* that week in which Les was quoted as saying that he had created Concerts West. Hulett was telling me "The entire entertainment industry believes Weintraub and I started this company. Colonel Parker believes it, Frank Sinatra believes it, and bullshit like this from Les could ruin everything!"

I called Terry Bassett to pass along the conversation because it was so funny and so sick. Terry and I laughed as only we could, remembering those heady-but-scary days of 1967 when, without help from anyone, he and I alone, with some assistance from Ron Terry, had created the concept, the name, the initial image, the financing, the dream, risking our fortunes and futures. Neither of us gave a damn who got the credit.

Meanwhile, the Lester Smith I had known for years was no longer in his office, big cigar lit, puffing away as we kicked around ideas. I don't think even he was acquainted with the new Les Smith, and I couldn't somehow arrange an introduction for myself. All of that was many years ago. Les and Danny eventually sold the team after getting it off to a successful start. Danny Kaye, whom I counted as a good friend, and who certainly was Les Smith's closest friend, passed away some time later, as the world lost one of its most compassionate and entertaining citizens.

I see Les from time to time, and my wife Stephanie, daughter Kelsey and I had Christmas Eve dinner with Les and his wonderful wife Bernice on Maui two years ago. I am happy to report the original Les Smith has returned. We never discuss those tense years, because they are history. Somewhat painful, maybe for both of us, they are better just summarized and then left alone.

It wasn't too long after Hulett's "I steal to entertain the Colonel" speech that I began to look around for a radio station to buy. I had left KJR at the end of 1974 feeling I had been there 15 years and wanting to drive down a different street to work. I left the station in fine shape, with a rating share of 13.2 percent of all radio listening in western Washington while the second place station had but 7 percent. Also, our FM station, KISW, was rapidly ascending, and the two had become the most profitable stations in the market by far. I was feeling that radio itch again, and suffering inside over the corruption I saw in what had once been a gloriously honest and respected company. My relationship with Hulett, the man I had hired, trained, supported and always befriended, was basically over. We did have dinner a few times, and conducted business as usual, but it was very tense and remained so.

In a further demonstration of the deterioration of my relationship with Hulett, Bill Doner called to tell of a conversation he'd had with Tom. Doner, shortly after our great times together in Mexico, became Vice President of Caesar's Palace in Las Vegas in charge of all entertainment. He decided to bring the Beach Boys to Caesar's to play nightly in the big room, and Tom Hulett was at that time handling the Boys. It was a phenomenal success, due to the Beach Boys themselves, but also due to some extra planning by Doner.

Nightly, when the Beach Boys would do their hit, *Be True to Your School*, the UNLV cheerleaders, in their red and white outfits, would suddenly run out on stage. One of them would pretend they just noticed that famous UNLV basketball coach at that time, Jerry Tarkanian ("Tark the Shark"), who would be sitting at a table near the front. They would interrupt the song and shout to Mike Love of the Beach Boys, "There's Jerry Tarkanian!" and Mike would say, "Jerry, Jerry Tarkanian is here! Stand up, Jerry!" whereupon the Tark would stand and wave his famous white towel in the air.

The crowd would go nuts, and the Beach Boys would jump back in with the line "Rah, rah, rah, sis boom bah." It was fabulous theater, and every show sold out. Following the last show, Doner invited Peter Golden from the William Morris Agency, Tom Hulett and a couple of others into his big office for drinks.

The conversation had just begun when Bill, wanting to congratulate Tom, said to everyone, "Is this Hulett amazing? Here you are, Tom, running the act that sells out Caesar's! You've done a hell of a job! You've come a long way since you started working for Pat!"

"Pat who?" Hulett asked.

"Pat O'Day!" Doner replied.

Enraged, Hulett shouted, "That's all bullshit! I've never worked for Pat in my life!"

Doner, never at a loss for words, said, "Tom, what's happened to your memory? I was with Pat the day he hired you. He gave you me as an account when I would buy booth space from you for Pat's Teenage Fairs. Tom, I'm sorry, but Pat started you."

Tom jumped up, replied, "This is all bullshit!" and walked out, leaving behind a puzzled group, including Doner.

I wasn't puzzled. Tom lusted for something that could never be, and the realities of life and the friendships it offers he chose to abandon. It wasn't long after that that I made my settlement with the partners, said good-bye to Concerts West and went out buying radio stations.

Within two years, Tom joined with Jerry Weintraub to buy out Les Smith's and Danny Kaye's portion of the company. Shortly after that, in a classic double cross, Tom threw Terry Bassett out of the company Terry and I had founded. My original dance business partner, Dick Curtis, had rejoined our company four years earlier. He was the one who had pleaded Tom's case to me when I hired him so many years before. Dick ran our Atlanta office before becoming Bob Dylan's concert manager, as well as manager of the Frank Sinatra tours. Dick was doing a marvelous job and was much loved by Dylan and Sinatra. Yet, after my departure, he was treated with such disrespect by Tom, now his boss, it caused him to resign those lofty positions and come work for me as general manager of the radio station I had purchased in Honolulu.

You wonder why I tell you all this, especially in light of Tom Hulett's death from cancer ten years ago. My answer is, it concludes my concert stories, and I can't leave you, the reader, wondering how all of that ended. It would be like writing the story of World War II and leaving out Hiroshima. I never disliked Tom, regardless of his actions. I guess inside, I understood and sympathized with him and his troubling battle with himself. After making millions of dollars, Tom was somehow broke when he died, as well as disillusioned.

On another front, Terry Bassett, with his super-human concert and entertainment business acumen, recovered quickly from his Concerts West ejection and continues as a major power today. Over the years he has handled the exhibitions of Warren Miller's ski films, the Eagles, bought and very successfully sold radio stations and become a wealthy, happy man.

After Danny Kaye's death, Les Smith continued moving forward with their enterprises. They sold the Mariners long ago, and Les their radio stations since. At the age of nearly 80, Les reinvented himself and became a powerhouse in the printing business. His son Alex Smith runs the new company and Les, still puffing on his cigars, visits the office daily when he's in town. Privately, he enjoys life with Bernice in Hawaii and at their lake front home in Bellevue.

You Gotta Be a Football Hero
Al Lewis, Buddy Fields & Al Sherman, 1933

SEATTLE HAD LONG SOUGHT A FRANCHISE in the National Football League, but it wasn't until the voters agreed to the construction of the Kingdome (which since has become obsolete and been demolished) that this community was moved onto the league's front burner for expansion. Immediately, two distinctly different groups stepped forward with proposals seeking the league's blessing and award of an expansion franchise. One group, eventually successful, was led by Seattle's Nordstrom family of department store fame. The Nordstroms teamed with other deep-pocketed, highly-respected citizens — people like Herman Sarkowsky, developer, Howard S. Wright, developer, Monte Bean, Chairman of the Board of the Pay'n'Save drug store chain, and Walter Schoenfield, co-founder of Britannia Sportswear.

Then, there was this second group. To say "the second group was puzzling" is a healthy understatement. It all started when a certain Wayne Fields, a wealthy friend of President Nixon's, arrived in town and recruited a reigning Seattle hero. He was the former University of Washington All-American from the early '50s, ex-San Francisco Forty-Niner Hall-of-Fame running back, Hugh McElhenny. Hugh had once been dubbed "The King" of runners, and it's accurate to state that Hugh is a Seattle icon.

Fields, who gave no real satisfactory answers as to how he became so deeply involved in football, wanted our "Hurryin' Hugh" (another nickname from football running days) on his executive team. After all, who better to have in the executive chambers of an NFL team than a revered, Hall-of-Fame player like Hugh McElhenny?

What was clearly strange was whom Fields selected as his team's secretary/treasurer. That individual would be one Edward Nixon. Edward was the brother of President Nixon and lived ten miles north of Seattle in Lynnwood. This brother is not to be confused with Donald Nixon, another brother of the President who ran a hamburger stand — later foreclosed on by lender Howard Hughes — in Whittier, California.

At the time, I guess most assumed he was hired as some kind of favor to the President, in that Edward Nixon had no previous connection with football, professional sports, or any sport for that matter. Possibly, it was reasoned by skeptics like myself, the President had, in the past, done Wayne Fields a favor of such magnitude, only the appointment of his much-less-than-famous brother Edward to this position was appropriate. There was also the possibility that Edward's presence, what with him being the President's brother and all, would catch the fancy of Pete Roselle, then Commissioner, and other NFL owners who would eventually vote on which group would receive the coveted Seattle franchise.

This is a good point in the story to establish that Hugh McElhenny is a most lovable individual. Never did his great fame of the '50s dilute the man's humility, honesty, and gentle spirit. He had not left football a rich man. Some errant investments in Bay Area super markets had taken a great deal of his money, and football players in those years, simply were not rewarded as they are today. By necessity, Hugh was now an advertising sales executive with a Seattle outdoor advertising firm. Loved by all, trusted implicitly, he appeared awkward when one evening the media attended a big press reception in the lobby of the Olympic (now *Fairmont* Olympic) Hotel.

It was the big announcement by former-Governor Fields that when their group was awarded the franchise — which he assured all would be the case — the team would be called The Seattle Kings, in honor of Hugh "The King" McElhenny. Fields neglected to comment on the interesting and obvious implications of the new chosen name in that Seattle is in King County and the new domed stadium had already been named the Kingdome.

To indicate that Hugh was the sole reason for the team's name was less than believable and totally unfair to Hugh. Ending the evening, Fields answered the question as to why there was a gold four-door Cadillac Seville parked in the center of the hotel's lobby. He brought Hugh forward again to the stage and, with great pomp, handed him the keys to the car, shouting, "A token of our respect, King. This is yours! A brand new Cadillac!" (It was sort of like a moment on *The Price*

Is Right! where they say, "Here is your brrrrand neeeeww carrrrr!") Hugh seemed embarrassed.

After the press deal ended, I sat with Hugh and some friends in the bar, where he told us he was uncomfortable in that he'd already had the car for a couple of months and didn't seem happy about the whole thing. Soon thereafter, a giant football—a big, round, brown, replica football, twenty feet high with the words "The Kings"—appeared atop a warehouse on Seattle's First Avenue across from where construction was taking place on the Kingdome. Further to the east, much bigger things were happening in the other Washington due to a thing called Watergate.

I needn't take space in this book to remind readers of the national convulsion Watergate caused. It was right at the height of denials, subpoenas, tape recordings, indictments, midnight massacres, resignations, and an administration struggling for survival that the King's secretary/treasurer, Edward Nixon, made his first pronouncement. He stated to a reporter that the Kings were beginning negotiations for space in the vicinity of the new Kingdome as a site for President Nixon's Presidential Library! Now, this was big news! Very, very, big news and it didn't make much sense. President Nixon was from California, born and raised in Whittier. He spent all his time outside of Washington, DC in New York or in San Clemente, California, on the beach where he created his West Coast White House. What in the hell would he be doing building his Presidential Library in the less-than-attractive industrial area that then surrounded the new Kingdome? And in, of all places, Seattle, Washington? Are you kidding?

They were saying the same thing at the White House, where no sooner had the story broke in Seattle, than denials came pouring from the nation's capitol. The White House said the story was ridiculous, that the Seattle reporters simply must have misunderstood the President's brother. It was called irresponsible reporting, a big misunderstanding. It might be said that the White House "protested too loud." Well, the Seattle media hadn't misunderstood Edward Nixon, but the story really had nowhere else to go. Edward clammed up and hid from the press! The White House denials were emphatic, and Seattle news reporters were left to assume that the President's brother must have ingested some bad grapes that day. Soon, the whole affair was forgotten. But not by me!

As I spent hours traveling on planes flying to different cities with various rock groups, I often entertained myself by contemplating things such as this. I knew something was going on that didn't meet the eye, but couldn't figure out exactly what. Then, I caught a little story some time later in the *Washington Post*. The story read that while investigating reclusive and mysterious industrial magnate Howard Hughes' illegal gifts to various individuals in government, one former Hughes aid from his Summa Corporation had stated that Hughes had given millions in cash to a certain Charles "Bebe" Rebozo. Rebozo was Nixon's close friend from Miami, Florida.

The report stated that the amount of money in question was about 10 million dollars. The money, according to the Hughes source, was being held by Rebozo as he and Nixon, after Nixon left office, were going to buy a professional football team with the money. The same story included Rebozo's heated denial, saying the money was a political contribution without explaining how or why it found its way into his safe. There were many reports such as this one appearing in those days. As a result, many pearls of information were lost in the tide of excess information. Thus, nothing more was heard on the matter. There was so much cannon fodder for the press in those days, you can't really fault them for not chasing every little angle.

Nothing more has been heard about Rebozo and the Nixon/Howard Hughes money. Nothing more until recently, that is! We also haven't heard much in recent years about President Nixon's daughters, Julie and Tricia. Julie, you will recall, married David Eisenhower, grandson of President Dwight D. Eisenhower. Tricia, (Patricia) married and became Tricia Cox, and neither sister made much news until early 2002, when a major-league squabble developed. It was all about a major windfall of money from the will of one now-deceased Bebe Rebozo to the Nixon Library in an amount of around 28 million dollars. The Nixon girls were fighting each other in California courts as to how the money was to be handled. Wow! Twenty-eight mill from good old Bebe!

Given what we know of Nixon's various dealings, I think purchasing some stock in the "Howard Hughes/Bebe Rebozo/Richard Nixon football scheme story is probably a good buy. I wouldn't sell that short. We also know that, after leaving office in disgrace, Nixon not only couldn't comfortably receive the money, he didn't need it. He was well taken care of between his retirement package and his publishing royalties. Also, having been driven, as he said in his own words, "from the highest mountain to the lowest valley," there wasn't much chance of him risking further reputation annihilation by touching that loot.

I speculate that Wayne Fields was the front man for Nixon, who figured he could use his position as President to pressure football into awarding the expansion franchise to Fields, and that he could assume his ownership position upon leaving office. It was scheduled to begin operating in 1976, which would be right at the end of his term. After all, he had likely speculated, why wouldn't they? He was good friend of Pete Roselle, the commissioner of the NFL. After the two triumphant terms he assumed he would gloriously complete, they would be begging him to take that Seattle team!

The thing that probably threw the Washington, DC press core quickly off track and off the story was that Nixon was a big Washington Redskins fan. They may have speculated, or even asked Jack Kent Cooke, Washington Redskins owner, whether he had any plans to include Nixon in ownership, which I imagine Cooke would have denied, thus ending the story. They probably overlooked things and didn't put two and three together. Or maybe they were simply unaware of the bizarre, strange goings-on with Wayne Fields, Edward Nixon and the Kings out in sleepy little Seattle. Seattle was, after all, the last place a DC writer was going to go looking for new Watergate and Nixon stories.

So, as I revise this book, I can speculate that maybe mine will be the first story to reach print on this subject, depending on how fast my co-writer, Jim Ojala, works, or, better said, how difficult my writing has made life for him. But, more important, I also speculate that there was once a time, long before his death, that a conversation between the powerful Greek, Bebe Rebozo, and Richard M. Nixon, who remained very close friends until the end, may have gone something like this:

"Well Dick, I'm still sitting on that original ten mil that Hughes gave you for the football team. What in the hell do you want me to do with it? With interest, it's now a big wad and growing."

Nixon probably thought about it for a minute, then said something like,

Well, just hang onto it for now. My wife Pat will never need it. Both Julie and Tricia married money and they won't need it! Besides, it would probably be complicated getting it to them. Not just complicated, but also dangerous. That's for sure. And how would we explain it? We never could, and we can be sure of that! So, Bebe, let's be perfectly clear. Why don't you just hang onto it? Keep it in a good interest-bearing account and put in your will that, when you pass on, it's a gift from your estate to my library? And maybe the library will really need it. You know, Bebe, I have to build the library with my own money and donations I receive. Those Democrats, you know how much they hate me. They hate my guts, and they might try and find a way to stop funds for on-going support. Those bastards would do that, you know. Yes, that's a good plan, and no one will ever figure it out! Good old Howard Hughes! God, I'm glad neither of us will go like he did, laying there in Acapulco, hair down to his waist, no one around but a bunch of Mexicans! Besides, hell, Bebe, I never wanted to live in Seattle in the first place! God, remember Edward getting screwed up and telling the press up there I was going to put my library in Seattle? And remember Haldeman and Ehrlichman going crazy, screaming "shut him up!" Remember that, Bebe? It's probably better for all concerned that whole thing didn't work, that's for sure! And you know, Bebe, I think I'm still going to have a great legacy!

Hit the Road, Jack

Ray Charles, 1961

I FELT THAT THIS BOOK OF MY CRAZY LIFE would be incomplete if I didn't tell you that during the busy, exciting, fun-filled years this story encompasses, I gradually began using too much alcohol. Yes, I was a good drinker. Having the proverbial "wooden leg," I could consume Jack Daniels with the pros. I am told I was a virtual three ring circus when sufficiently moistened. I have accomplished amazing feats, ranging from conducting business, to doing my daily radio show, to making television appearances, all after having several cocktails, and all without it being detected.

It was a friend named Dan Sandal, a Seattle restaurant owner, who pointed out to me that in one afternoon in a long business meeting I had consumed an entire fifth of liquor. I had driven home—likely flawlessly, in that, over the years, I never fell down, vomited, never had hangovers or got into fights, and would usually just get funnier! Dan correctly figured I was endangering my health. He gathered some of my friends for support and suggested I get assistance and quit. Which I did!

I will be forever grateful to Dan and the Schick Shadel Recovery Hospital in Seattle who continue to provide a service that separates one from any drinking and drug addictions in less than two weeks. My enthusiasm over their treatment, which has an 80 percent success rate, has caused me to become part of the hospital ownership. At present, I proudly do radio commercials for the hospital, telling others of the simplicity and finality of their treatment. I never was much of a "do-gooder," but Schick Shadel and its staff have a story I just can't resist sharing. Their treatment eliminates the years of guilt, anxiety and craving. It's true what I say in the commercials. You leave there, not to attend meetings the rest of your life as a "recovering alcoholic," but rather, free of such burdens as you are truly an "ex-alcoholic!" I know, as I have now been totally sober—and happier—for 18 years.

In retrospect, I think of alcohol as a pleasant-but-very-dangerous drug for most young adults. It makes us courageous, sociable, able to overcome complexes, immaturity, and, in a perfect world, we would all have slowed down our drinking by the time we were 30. Then, we should quit before we become 40 and enter into old drunkhood. Unhappily, through no fault of our own, many of us are genetically susceptible to alcohol addiction and, once we start, we just can't turn it all off by ourselves. There's such a fine line between the happy young drinker and the "old drunk." Thanks to Dan Sandal and Schick Shadel Hospital, my problem was fixed, apparently before I totally crossed over that line.

Back in the USSR
The Beatles, 1968

IF YOU HAVE A CHANCE TO JOIN the ever-growing number of people visiting little Friday Harbor on San Juan Island in Washington State, I hope you will stop by my real estate office (John L. Scott). This island has become recognized as the Martha's Vineyard of the Seattle area. It's totally crime free and sort of a Mayberry, surrounded by beautiful blue waters that come alive with salmon, seals, whales and boaters. Located just north of Seattle, it can be reached by car ferry, boat or airplanes which fly here nearly every hour. I'm always in the office, so be sure to stop by and say hello and please, bring this book along for me to personally sign for you.

Life is wonderful on this island with my wife Stephanie and my darling daughter Kelsey, who turns thirteen as this book goes to press. She is now my big promotion, and I find it exciting coaching her girls basketball team and Little League fast pitch team. Also, there is the nightly fun of helping her with homework and generally being part of her life.

Stephanie is the leading land use attorney in our county, which works well with my real estate efforts, and we have now been married 22 years. There are occasional visits from my sons, Jerry, a jeweler, Jeff, who owns a large leasing operation and Garry, who is a full time free spirit. Then there are my grandchildren, Jacquie, a student at Washington State, and Jessie and Colby, who are still little guys.

I am constantly asked if I miss life in the fast lane, the life of radio and concerts. My full answer to that question is so long and complicated, I would never bore anyone with it. But surely, I miss radio. However, it has changed so dramatically, and the de-emphasis of artistic contribution is so great, the radio I miss no longer exists. As to the world of rock-'n'-roll, it is in many ways a dangerous business psychologically. To have been there, lived there and departed from there without noticeable scars leaves one inclined to leave well enough alone.

One last story. I was seven years old and flying model airplanes with the next door neighbor on December 7, 1941 when someone rushed out to announce that the Japanese had attacked Pearl Harbor. In 1945, I was at my grandfather's house in Brunswick, Nebraska when the little town's only fire truck led the celebration of victory with its siren screaming and its hose firing water high into the air over Main Street. Then followed 45 years of tension as Joseph Stalin threw countries into bondage and threatened the world with a dumb, elitist-concocted concept of society called communism. During this time, Russia created the Iron Curtain, and I wasn't alone in my belief that I would never personally see Eastern Europe, let alone Russia. Those places may as well have been on the planet Mars, so separated was the "Free World" from the Communist Bloc countries. The world seemed larger in those years, as jet travel had yet to appear and thoughts of visiting places like the Soviet Union, even without the barriers, were dreams not allowed to cross a rational kid's mind.

I write this to help you understand the emotion, the inability to comprehend that I felt in May 1993, as I stood on the very cobblestones where the Russian Revolution started in 1917 listening to myself on the radio. Several months earlier, a Seattle businessman, Clay Loges, had approached me to help him get his new rock-'n'-roll radio station in St. Petersburg, Russia off the ground.

After the collapse of Communism, the Russians entered into numerous joint ventures with American business in an attempt to bring the post-Soviet economy back to life. Loges was in the cellular telephone business in Moscow and had acquired a radio station in St. Petersburg. I was there training the newly-recruited deejays on the fundamentals of entertaining radio. Broadcasting, under Communism, had meant dreary, state-run programs that centered on lectures and indoctrination. Music radio like what we are accustomed to was foreign to them. Working with an interpreter, although some of the recruits spoke a little English, I had the honor of guiding them through the first few grades of Pat O'Day's Radio School. I carefully explained the basics and the importance of giving the time, temperature, weather and traffic information. How to effectively deliver commercials, how to pitch one's voice when introducing different types of music. I taught them how to script and produce their shows, making them tight and exciting for maximum appeal. I explained the importance of humor on the radio. All those things that you hear daily on the radio in our country were a brand new art form to them. In fact, the art form has been around in our country only since about 1955.

How exciting, having this chance to share what we in American radio have learned with the excited youth of a country we so recently had been calling The Evil Empire! On my last day of training the staff, they asked me to go on the air personally and give a demonstration of my air work. At first I deferred, but they pointed out that there were so many English-speaking people in St. Petersburg that having a genuine American disc jockey on the air for a few hours would create quite a sensation. Leaving nothing to chance, I recorded the three hour show, which would be aired on my last Sunday afternoon in the city.

I had set aside that particular afternoon to travel around that historic and stunning town to shoot some video for my wife and daughter to enjoy upon my return home. I was being driven around to all the photogenic and historic sites by Evgenei Nikitin, an old commie bureaucrat turned radio entrepreneur. One of our stops was at the Winter Palace (the Hermitage), home of the Czars, where some of the first shots of the October Revolution were fired. While standing there with my video camera rolling, the car's window was down and on Evgenei's blaring car radio I heard this all-too-familiar voice echoing across that historic courtyard saying,

> Don't you just love it! The voice of John Fogerty. They call the group Creedence Clearwater Revival, and the song's called *Bad Moon Rising*. It's three twenty-five P.M. in St. Petersburg. My name is Pat O'Day, proud and pleased to be playing great music for you this Sunday afternoon here on Radio Adin. Now, the great Peter Cetera. The group is Chicago. The song's called *If You Leave Me Now*.

I couldn't emotionally handle it! As we continued driving around seeing the sights and listening to my show, tears were running down my cheeks. All I could think was, *How can any one person be so fortunate?*

So fortunate to experience, participate, see, feel and thrill to all that life has so generously heaped on my plate. The kid from Norfolk, Nebraska somehow climbed to the very top of the ladder. He landed smack in the middle of history's biggest revolution in music and media. And now, here he was, talking to and playing his music for millions of people in, of all places in the world, St. Petersburg, Russia. The tears that wouldn't stop were saying, "Thank you, God! Thank you, radio! Thank you rock-'n'-roll! Thank you, thank you, thank you for allowing me to be Pat O'Day, truly one of the luckiest people on earth!"